TWENTIETH-CENTURY FRENCH LITERATURE

TWENTIETH-CENTURY FRENCH LITERATURE

Germaine Brée
Translated by Louise Guiney

The University of Chicago Press
Chicago and London

Germaine Brée, the *doyenne* of French letters in America, was born in
France and has lived in the United States since 1931. She has taught
at Bryn Mawr, New York University, the University of Wisconsin, and
Wake Forest University; is a past president of the Modern Language
Association; and is the author of numerous books, including *Albert
Camus* (1968), *Camus and Sartre* (1972), and *Women Writers in France*
(1973).

The University of Chicago Press, Chicago 60637
The University of Chicago Press, Ltd., London

Originally published in Paris as the sixteenth volume in the series
Littérature française under the title *Le XXe Siècle II: 1920–1970,*
© Librairie Arthaud, Paris, 1978.

Library of Congress Cataloging in Publication Data

Brée, Germaine.
    Twentieth-century French literature, 1920–1970.

    Translation of: Le XXe siècle. Volume 2 / Pierre-
Olivier Walzer, Germaine Brée.
    Bibliography: p.
    Includes index.
    1. French literature—20th century—History and
criticism.   I. Walzer, Pierre Olivier. XXe siècle.
English.   Volume 2.   II. Title.   III. Title: 20th-
century French literature, 1920–1970.
PQ305.B64   1983   840'.9'0091   82-15980
ISBN 0-226-07195-2

Contents

Contents

Preface to the English Edition

Written in the midseventies, this volume is the last in a new, sixteen-volume history of French literature, under the general editorship of Professor Claude Pichois of the University of Paris. The purpose of the series was to place the French literary enterprise within a broader historic and cultural frame. The preceding volume, by Professor P. O. Walzer of Bern University, covered the period 1896–1920, thus determining my point of departure. Nineteen-seventy, at the time my book was written, was, of necessity, a somewhat problematic cutting-off point. Cultural climates change fast in our times. Yet today, ten years later, it still seems that the years 1970–80 did herald a turning point in contemporary French history. The "quiet revolution" of the socialist comeback in 1981 seems to signal the end of the post–World War II "Gaullist" era. It is accompanied by a reaction to the theoretical dogmatisms that had flourished in France since the sixties. A new school of historians and sociologists has moved away from the rhetorical patterns of structuralism and semiotics, and the theoretical viability of Lacanian orthodoxy is under fire.

The "experimental novelists" of the sixties are being superseded by novelists whose fictional worlds have opened out on the broad vistas of the imaginary (Le Clézio, Michel Tournier, etc.). Their writing is freer in structure, making use of the dynamic, associative flow of language. Barely under way in 1970, the debate on the problematic of *l'écriture féminine* and the vigorous impact of feminine and "feminist" writing, theory, and criticism dominated the 1970–80 decade, a vigorous offshoot of the revolutionary mood of 1968. It seems now to be merging into the literary and ideological mainstream.

I have not, therefore, attempted to rewrite this book, which, despite its inevitable limitation and subjectivity, will at least reflect as objective a point of view on a vast and

turbulent period as I could master in the seventies. I am particularly in-
debted to my many colleagues and to my graduate students at New York
University and Wisconsin whose critical insights and erudition helped me in
a task that often seemed to me well-nigh impossible.

February 1982

Introduction

The task assumed by the present volume is a difficult one: to present a critical and historical study of French literature during fifty years of the twentieth century. How can we gain the necessary distance in relation to something we have lived through day-to-day ourselves? In this rich harvest of events and works, how can we discern the significant features of an extremely complex cultural life? Not that we lack for documents. If anything, we have too many. Since the year 1920, our chronological point of departure, "French self-scrutiny," as described by Jules Romains in 1954, has been pursued relentlessly and with increasing intensity on every level. Essays, accounts, memoirs—or, in the case of Malraux, antimemoirs—autobiographies, interviews, surveys, reports and journals pile high and ever higher. There is hardly a French writer of any stature whose work does not include, in one form or another, an element of personal testimony. Until the great collective research required for complete analysis of all this documentation has been accomplished, our knowledge of it will perforce be incomplete.

We have also, especially since midcentury, witnessed what can only be described as an explosion in the production of scholarly studies, historical and sociological as well as critical. Along with an abundance of fact, they also offer us an abundance of attitudes toward an era characterized by abrupt change, strong contrasts, and profound reversals in the life of a nation that went from poverty to prosperity, from war to peace, and from the Third to the Fifth Republic during a period of worldwide upheaval. We have experienced this upheaval in person, along with our entire generation born before the "Great" War and marked by the twenty years that were dramatic ones for us, 1929–49. No matter how hard we may try to be objective, our viewpoint will always contain a strong note of subjectivity.

Sociologists have taught us not to trust our own impressions when we try to understand our own time, because they will be riddled with myths of which we are not even aware. It is thus no easy task to identify the principle trends of an era that is still obscure to us, because still so much a part of us.

Is it even possible to see the period 1920–70 as a sort of entity, and can the terminal date of 1970, in particular, be justified? Although any chronological division will of course be arbitrary, 1920 can be considered a point of departure. In 1920, France had emerged victorious from World War I, but the nation's substance had been deeply afflicted, and the period of reconstruction it faced was an uneasy one. While France was apparently yearning above all to renew its ties with the past, a new world was in the process of emerging.

In 1920 the League of Nations took up its home in Geneva, and on November 1 the first plenary session was held, but without United States president Woodrow Wilson. Hopes and fears were already strongly intermingled.

At the Congrès de Tours a minority group of communists from the Confédération Générale du Travail founded the Third International and assumed direction of Jaurès's newspaper *L'Humanité*. Among "men of good will" there were only a few intellectuals who at that time expressed any curiosity regarding "that great light in the East"—dawn for some, for others conflagration—the Russian Revolution. But it was then that the Russian enigma, which was to haunt French thought and the French imagination in one form or another ceaselessly from then on, first made its appearance.

Other signs of the times were less obvious. While the Vatican was canonizing Joan of Arc and France honoring her dead at the tomb of the unknown soldier, the first manifestations of Italian fascism were occurring; also occurring in the year 1920 were the first Nazi meetings at the Hofbrauhaus in Munich, which resulted in creation of the "German National Socialist Workers' Party." In France the euphoria of victory was succeeded by the dual problem of how to face the consequences of the past and the possibilities of the future.

For most average French people of the time, however, the important thing was the present. A movement of collective release had begun before the war had ended with the production of *Parade*—an avant-garde ballet uniting the names of Diaghilev, Picasso, and Satie, all of whom were already known, and that of a virtual unknown, Jean Cocteau—and of Apollinaire's farce *Les Mamelles de Tirésias*. One entire segment of the Parisian social and artistic world had decided to renew its ties with the great pre–World War I current of aesthetic innovation. Despite the heavy losses suffered during the war—in which approximately two thousand writers lost their lives—literary and artistic circles formed again after the war around the same personalities as before: Barrès, France, Loti, on one side; Gide and the *NRF* on the other. Some of the great names were missing, notably, although not widely known, those of Péguy and Apollinaire. In 1920 at the Palais des Fêtes, dada, which had left Zurich, launched its first challenge to the Parisian public, but André Breton meanwhile was engaged in polite negotiations with the *Nouvelle revue française,* which had resumed publication the year before, and the young Radiguet had no trouble mixing with Max Jacob, Jean Cocteau, and André Breton. The resumption of literary and artistic life took place amid a certain amount of chaos, but according to the old rules. The change was in the feverish atmosphere. Politically and socially the nation was dreaming of security, but art and literature seemed determined to pursue all the revolutionary adventures begun before the war. It is perhaps only now that we can begin to see more clearly, beneath this superficial continuity, the "novelty" characteristic of the era, and the line severing it from the past.

After 1965 a new phase appeared to be developing in the evolution of French society and French attitudes, with the political events of 1968 constituting its most dramatic manifestation. Spengler's *Decline of the West* was published in 1919. Fifty years later—and this was symptomatic of the times—Western civilization and the place occupied in it by France was being examined in a completely different way by sociological studies of more modest scope. We are referring to studies such as Michel Crozier's *La Société bloquée* (1970), or Pierre Sorlin's *La Société française contemporaine 1914–1968* (1971). These writers were not particularly interested in "the decline of the West." In the year 1970 they were less concerned with the problems of a civilization in decline than with the problems of taking part in a new one. And the background for their thinking was no longer the same, either. Spengler's great speculative and prophetic synthesis was replaced by rigorous, methodical research and the objective observation of facts. This is the predominant tendency in every field as we near the end of the century, and contrasts strikingly with the romanticism and neo-idealism of the twenties.

Our knowledge of how our society works has increased considerably since 1920. This new awareness is one of the most fundamental characteristics of the period. As the sociologists have shown, however, it is still far from complete. We are reluctant to form the kinds of judgments that have been repeatedly proven false over the years by events. The fate suffered by Spengler's predictions, and by those of the various interpreters of Marxism-Leninism, encourages prudence. "It is hard for us to understand the time we live in as it is to recognize as ours that strange, just-recorded voice the record is playing back to us," as Morand pointed out in *L'Heure qu'il est.*

However, one thing does seem clear: increasingly, since the end of World War I, France has been undergoing a profound transformation, to which its institutions have had difficulty adapting and whose outward signs in terms of technological progress and daily life, are easier to grasp than their effect on the attitudes of the French people. If it is true, as Valéry believed, that the

1919 peace treaty inaugurated the era of the "completed world," with more and more conformity in its styles of life, nonetheless a country with a culture as old as France's experienced some difficulty "entering the twentieth century." Valéry had sensed that on the deepest level this meant, for France, a cultural crisis or, as he would put it, "a spiritual crisis"; it involved problems specific to France, and this was understood by the young Drieu La Rochelle when he emerged from the trenches and in four brief essays "took the new measure of France" (1922) and expressed his anguish at the loss of prestige that Europe, and particularly France, were suffering in the modern world.

It is on this level that the recent substitution of a theory of transition for the Spenglerian theory of the death of civilizations—specifically Western civilization—debated throughout this half-century appears significant. The fear of the future, evidenced in Valéry's celebrated words, "We civilizations know now that we are mortal," has been succeeded by a fear, evident down to the vocabulary of everyday life, of being unable to become part of the modern world fast enough. Crisis, anxiety, change—these are the bywords of our time.

In 1970, it seemed, the French were trying to define themselves in terms of cultural change, but a cultural change going far beyond the borders of France and whose origins were elsewhere, mainly in the United States. In France, the terms "culture" and "being well read," particularly in French literature, were long synonymous. When de Gaulle created a Ministry of Cultural Affairs in 1959, the term "cultural" was used to designate a fairly vast area of intellectual and artistic activity: science, technology, philosophy, and sociology, as well as art and literature. It is thus not surprising that the crisis in culture led to a crisis in literature, nor that the very concept of literature should have been one of the most constantly debated questions of the era.

In 1920, literature in France enjoyed great prestige, which its brilliance seemed to justify. Literary works took their place within the huge fresco of the history of French literature, the French patrimony, where they continued, or gave new life to, a long tradition. The French, almost to a man, readers and nonreaders alike, thought of literature as the most outstanding manifestation of the "Higher French values." The dadaists were the first to attack this edifice openly; the students of 1968 appeared to want to finish it off for good. As the half-century ran its course, historical events, socioeconomic problems, and technological progress seem successively to have relegated literature to the background of French intellectual concerns, threatening it with loss of its privileged status. There was no group of writers in 1970 with the influence and prestige of the generation—controversial as it may have been—that took over in 1920: Claudel, Gide, Proust, and Valéry, to cite only its most eminent members. Yet around 1970 a number of studies came out—*La Littérature en France depuis 1945* (Bersani, Autrand, Lecarme, and Vercier 1970) being one good example—that attempted to identify the new directions a literature in gestation was taking. Academia was not particularly quick to show interest in this literature-in-progress. The first teaching and research center devoted to contemporary literature was founded at the Faculté des Lettres of the University of Strasbourg in 1959, and it was not until 1970 that a society for the study of the twentieth century was established—its first *cahier* appeared only in 1973. But outside the university the need to place current literature and to define it in relation to the past recalled the twenties, when a succession of "panoramas," anthologies, and *Histoires de la littérature française* were published. Corresponding to Bédier and Hazard's 1922 *Histoire de la littérature française*, which had taken up where Gustave Lanson (first edition, 1894) left off, were the 1958 *Histoire des littératures*, in the *Encyclopédie de la Pléiade*, volume 3 of which presented an *Histoire des littératures françaises, connexes et marginales*, a new concept; and the 1968 *Littérature française* by Adam, Lerminier, and Morot-Sir. A many-sided work of revision, criticism, research, and partial interpretation resulted in a new "overview" seen from a new perspective. The university opened its doors to the literature of 1920–65 and also looked with a new eye on the vigorous development of francophone literature outside strictly French boundaries. The disintegration of the national and geographical boundaries that had contained the phenomenon of French literature accentuated the disintegration of French cultural structures, one of the distinctive marks of this period.

The half-century from 1920 to 1970 does appear, therefore, from the viewpoint of today, to have its own distinctive physiognomy. It was a period dominated by the fear and the experience of war—international or colonial—and obsessed by the idea of revolution, a revolution that finally came in a form totally different from the one that had been both longed for and feared; it was a period that, in its violence, appears to be moving away from us today. But in what direction? Our terminal date of 1970 can tell us scarcely anything about the future. It is difficult to make selections among the many works that have come to our attention and among the many familiar names that belong to men and women we have known in person. In fifty or a hundred years, which of these names and works will seem to be the most significant? A historian is not a prophet. Furthermore, today there is no longer any accepted aesthetic criterion by which we can judge and classify.

We have therefore decided to follow as far as possible the general organization of the series Littérature Française (published by Arthaud), of which the French-language edition of this volume was a part, that is (with the exception of the final section), a study of "great writers" and their works. Within the limits set for us, we had half a dozen writers at most to choose from. No consensus is yet possible as to who these should be. Our solution was to take key figures and works and use them to illustrate the dominant trends illuminating the changing attitudes of the era as well as its continuity.

Within the 1920–70 time span we have identified three distinct periods:

From 1920 to 1936, when the postwar period became the interwar period and when, pivoting around the economic depression of 1929–33, the "Roaring Twenties" were replaced by a profound anxiety that pervaded intellectual life. Until 1936, Paris remained at the center of literary activity. The major literary figures of the time—Claudel, Gide, and Valéry—assured the continuity of a great tradition whose value was almost never in dispute. It was a period rich in trends of various kinds, but united by a common culture.

From 1936 to 1952, when, starting with the Spanish civil war and the brief triumph of the Front Populaire, and ending with the Korean war and a subsequent diminishing of the obsession with war, intellectual life in France took place in an atmosphere of apocalypse and was dominated by concern for the destiny of mankind in general, and the French in particular, and also by concern for what appeared to be the collapse of an entire civilization. During this period French writers were profoundly affected by historical events they tried to understand and, through political involvement, to influence. In due course, the literary world also suffered from the historical backlash. Greatly diminished by the many losses suffered in the war, it never regained either the vitality or the richness of the interwar years.

After 1952, despite the problems involved in decolonization and various national and international political crises, new directions in literature, already discernible in 1944, grew more distinct with the conclusion of the Algerian war. At first the French people sought to relate themselves on every level to the two great power blocs—the United States and Russia—facing each other in the cold war, but this obsession evolved imperceptibly as the threatening aspect of the era faded. A new generation of writers then attempted to divorce French literature and French philosophy from structures that were considered outmoded. In 1970, in contrast to the enthusiasm and effervescence of the twenties, a certain disarray reigned in the world of literature.

One major theme runs through all three of these periods, though orchestrated in various keys: the theme of the modern world. The frequently reiterated themes of war and revolution—technological as well as social— linked to those of violence, adventure, action, absurdity, and history are all modulations of it. Political and social crisis, the conflict of ideologies, were but the superficial manifestations of a transformation through which in the space of fifty years, over the course of three constitutional reforms, a major disaster, and a spectacular economic recovery, France evolved from the Third to the Fifth Republic, and from the concept of French Empire to that of the "hexagon" and a nation gradually becoming integrated into a federated Europe. In France, as elsewhere during this period, there was sharp conflict between the established routine and the spirit of reform; between national interest and international structures; between the need for rational organization of the nation's activities and the tradition of individualism it has always been proud of. On the whole, however, France managed, despite certain setbacks, to maintain a climate of intellectual freedom throughout the entire half-century. This fostered an intellectual life of great richness and diversity, despite the anxieties, the excesses, and the denial of the past. The resulting state of mind led some to voice suspicions as to the function of a literature "guilty" of complicity with an outmoded middle-class world. The halo of prestige that had surrounded literature was tarnished. The question "What is literature?" became "Why literature?" and then "Is literature possible?" It seemed at times that the very concept of literature was disappearing. Yet the era is singularly rich in works which, because of their diversity and their novelty, are often difficult to deal with. A period of decadence, some would say; of great vitality, others believe; in any case a period of saturation as far as literary criticism is concerned.

In the course of these years observers have frequently had the impression that an era was coming to an end—in 1929; in 1934–35; in 1940 and again in 1945, notably with the dropping of the atomic bomb on Hiroshima; finally, in 1968. It was certainly extremely difficult for a literary historian to present in this context the intellectual odyssey of at least three generations of writers, most of them born before World War I, and at the same time adequately to describe the cultural history of such an eventful period. The enterprise itself would be considered futile by those in France who refuse to "place" a literary work in relation to its historic and social "extratext." This viewpoint belongs to one of the currents of thought stemming from the research, hypotheses, and methodology connected to linguistics and semiology. But it does not seem to us to be the only useful one. As the American linguist Peter Caws has said, "language has nothing to say, either about itself, or about anything else. Individuals use it in order to say things, but it is they, not the language, who are the source for what is said, even if—which is true—they have been strongly influenced by it. This is because the source of the influence goes back to other users of the language." From this point of view, the "extratext" again becomes the context for literature, a context indispensable for understanding a literary work in all of its complexity. The period we are about to address was a dense one in which the most diverse and most contradictory currents intersected with one another, creating numerous shifts in emphasis and point of view. This volume does not propose, nor should it, to decree, but merely to describe, and to raise questions to which the future will no doubt bring the answers.

In our view, the *literary movement* as a whole is part of a social and historical process reaching beyond the confines of the aesthetic. Even at the very beginning of the century, writers and artists demonstrated their conviction that a new age was coming that would require a new kind of art. The transformation undergone by avant-garde art and literature was accomplished much more swiftly, in fact, than that of a society whose energies were completely mobilized by two wars. This process of transformation, which affected the entire Western world, was known as "modernism." In 1920, dada broke with "futurism" by questioning the cult of the machine and the entire cultural tradition. The first decade of the "modernist" period, which included surrealism, was rich in ideas, in theories, and in works, particularly poetic ones. Breton and Cocteau were its spokesmen. During its second decade, the need felt for novelty became social, a spirit of political controversy characterized literature, and modernism calmed down, its gratuity and outrageousness replaced by a social concern favorable to fiction. In about 1950, the modernist spirit began to change and to retreat before the new critical and scientific spirit; we then enter a "postmodernist" period, which after 1970 appeared to be directed toward a new but as yet imprecise aesthetic.

The most that a volume as brief as ours can do is to present a sketch combining the sociological, scientific, and technological events on which literary attitudes depend. Modernism seems to us to define the intellectual climate of France after World War I; by the half-century mark it had received a strong boost from World War II. Writers and artists recognized then that they were no longer announcing the coming of a new world, they were already living in it. The facts have, on the whole, been well established, but where they stand in relation to each other, less so. We hope the present volume will be an aid to a better understanding of the era's contradictory trends, disconcerting aspects, and apparent incoherence. Evaluation will perhaps be easier a few years from now. Here we cannot give in-depth studies of many specific works. There is an abundance of critical studies devoted to them and supplementing our own work, the purpose of which is to provide the clearest and fairest possible overview of this half-century of literature.

One

The Background:
Historical,
Political, Social

The Political Climate, 1920–36

"The victory celebration was to be first and foremost a memorial celebration for the Dead. Everyone knew this, had thought about it and agreed" (Jules Romains). By 1920, when France installed the Tomb of the Unknown Soldier beneath the Arc de Triomphe in honor of her war dead, the heady unity of the victory parade was only a memory. On January 11, the already controversial Treaty of Versailles went into effect. The moment of respite between war and peace had been brief. During the next ten years, "sensual and intellectual Paris," oblivious to "danger, dreaming only of pleasure," tried to make that moment last. The Roaring Twenties, the Years of Illusion, the Phony Peace, the decade ending in the Wall Street Crash of 1929 and followed by virtually worldwide economic depression was for many simply the time when "happy days" came back again. The trace it left in the memories of Parisian high society was a brilliant one. Cosmopolitan and superficially prosperous Paris during those years played as never before her role as capital of the Western world.

In 1932, Julien Green referred in his journal to "the end of a happy era" and expressed amazement at the "carefree unconcern" that had reigned in his life. Claude Mauriac, younger by a generation, felt the same nostalgia: "I preserve to this day a nostalgia for those wonderful years, although I did not experience them directly and merely observed the participants from afar." This "postwar Sunday" had its apotheosis in 1925 with the Exposition des Arts Décoratifs, Paris's celebration of her new, updated modernity. The exhibition becomes symbolic in retrospect. To people such as Raymond Queneau, however, it was the surrealist movement that left them a precious memory of "having been young once." The first surrealist exhibition, an inconspicuous fringe event in relation to the Paris of official festivals, also took place in 1925 and proclaimed one group's determination to break with the Art Deco style and the "beautiful symphony" of the postwar years. It was also about 1925 that certain trends began to be discernible through the tumult of years that foreshadowed the future and were already marked by the Riffian war.

This festival atmosphere continued into the thirties and shed its final glow on the Exposition Coloniale, which, with few exceptions, enchanted a whole new generation—an example being the young Brasillach in *Notre avant-guerre*. To the Western world of 1931, submerged in social unrest, unemployment, and crisis, this exhibition presented a contrasting image of imperial France: rich, powerful, and uniting under her banner a disparate band of subservient peoples in Africa, Indo-China, and Oceania.

The gulf between this near-mythical France and the true position of the French people at the conclusion of World War I was great, but we should not be overcritical of the era's carefree spirit. After the nightmare of the trenches and the misery of wartime deprivations, the French understandably thirsted for pleasure. London, New York, and Berlin also, each in its own way, showed symptoms of the same fever; but it was a fever that could not obliterate the fear that helped to feed it.

After the war, intellectuals in France debated the big questions: "intellectual crisis" "the future of Europe," or of the West for that matter; the destiny of France, of Germany; the nature of the modern world. For Valéry's generation, however, speculation and discussion usually took place on a purely intellectual level. Generally speaking, the writers of the twenties were not particularly interested in politics.

Social unrest was a fact, of course, as were vague aspirations toward social reform, especially among the young, regardless of class. This was borne out by the strikes and protest marches of 1919. But suppression was swift, and when the dadaists launched their challenge to society in 1920–22, they reached only a small audience of the intellectuals and the middle class. They had no effect on politics whatsoever. Feelings that were deep but unfocused—hope for a better world, hatred of warfare—were satisfied by the promises implicit in President Wilson's Fourteen Points, and by the creation of the League of Nations. In 1920 a superficially united France turned her back on the upheavals of 1919 and restored to political power the democratic, liberal, parliamentary prewar government which in the eyes of most had been responsible for winning the war. Ten more years were to pass before this regime was called into question.

In the disorder of the postwar period the French government faced serious problems, some of them unprecedented and many not susceptible to short-term solution. In an unstable postwar world full of new, little-understood forces, reconstruction of the country on a vast scale had to be undertaken and social reforms instituted that had been repeatedly postponed by the vacillations of the government before the war. The country's future in the arena of foreign affairs also had to be provided for, but there was a dearth of fresh political and social concepts that could have given new political impetus to the country. When fresh concepts did appear, first on the left and later on the right, they were aimed at destroying the regime, not at improving its effectiveness. In 1924 a new factor on the political scene slowly began to erode the system. This was the presence of a monolithic, more or less numerous group of communist deputies hostile to the regime and often subjected to harassment. They divided the Left and diminished its effectiveness.

The ministerial instability of this period, particularly between the years 1930 and 1935, has become legendary. It was more apparent than real, however. Taken as a whole, the years 1920–36 witnessed a fairly consistent alternation between governments of the Left and Right: 1920–24, Bloc National; 1924–26, Cartel des Gauches; 1928–30, Union Nationale; 1936, Front Populaire. Furthermore, until the acute governmental crisis of the thirties, the French economy seemed to run fairly smoothly and even to be improving. A trend toward increased prosperity between 1924 and 1930 spread to the lower-middle and working classes, giving people an impression of being better off.

France's reconstruction was carried out under the leadership of the great prewar political figures, Poincaré on the right, and Herriot and Briand on the left. These men seemed the perfect embodiment of the French public's "split personality" described by François Goguel as perpetually oscillating between "craving for order" and "craving for change."

In his first successful novel, *Bella,* written in 1926, Jean Giraudoux attempted to illustrate this political situation through the confrontation of two families, one named Rebendart, the other Dubardeau. It was no secret that Giraudoux had based his characters on two contemporary figures closely identified with the destinies of the country: Poincaré, and Berthelot of the Quai d'Orsay; and that he had also, working under Berthelot's direction, taken sides. The "Poincaré side" was represented by the Rebendarts—shrewd lawyers and politicians who were devious but upright; narrow-minded teetotalers whose sole interests were legacies and financial settlements. The Dubardeau family, on the other hand, was depicted as cultivated and broad-minded; its men generous statesmen and cosmopolitan visionaries dreaming of France's role in the new Europe. In this book Giraudoux subjected the rhetoric of both Right and Left to gentle satire.

Meanwhile, the newspaper *L'Action française* was striking up the old Maurras themes—xenophobia, anti-Semitism, anti-Protestantism, nationalism—orchestrated by Léon Daudet and reinjecting into political debate the appeals to violence once associated with the Dreyfus case. Eloquent, irresponsible, lacking all sense of current problems and with scant regard for truth, Daudet attacked what he called "today's liberalism" on all fronts, political, social, cultural. In works such as *Le Stupide du XIXe*

Siècle, exposé des insanités meurtrières qui se sont abattues sur la France depuis cent trente ans (1922), he returned to vilification of a political regime with its roots in the Revolution and continued the indictment of the romantic movement begun by Maurras and his followers before the war. Repeatedly and indiscriminately, Daudet directed ad hominem attacks against "Bergson, the little fancy-pants Jew," "Jewish banks," "Jewish journalism," Kant and Schopenhauer, Protestantism, Judaism, and "vulgar republican intellectuals." For Daudet, "France" did not mean contemporary France but France "when she was great," a utopian France long past—or present in spirit among a citizenry deluded by its leaders but whose true aspirations the group at *L'Action française* stood ready to represent.

At the opposite extreme, self-designated heirs to the radical, Jacobinical tradition reviled by Daudet, were the communists, who identified France's cause with that of Soviet Russia. The communists were antimilitarist and anticolonialist. They viewed French culture as a bourgeois prerogative, a political tool used to mystify and exploit the proletariat for profit. Thus a culture which had sought to be humanist, liberalizing, and universal was seriously questioned on both the extreme Right and the extreme Left. The myth of "two Frances," revolutionary and reactionary, cast a long shadow over the country's future, sowing irreconcilable differences among all who dreamed of a classless "new order." It also created a mystique among middle-class youth of "the people" (on the right) and "the proletariat" (on the left), neither of which concept was likely to facilitate fruitful consensus.

On the right, there were new factors to contend with. The fate of the French franc was subject to the economic interdependence of the Western nations so catastrophically illustrated by the 1929 Wall Street Crash; and Russia's absence was felt in a system of alliances barely being kept in balance by the "Petite Entente." On the left, Briand's policies were based on faith in the League of Nations, an organization with no means of effective action at its disposal. Neither monetary stability nor the strict application of the Treaty of Versailles—exemplified by the occupation of the Ruhr in 1923—any more than the Locarno Agreements of 1925, German membership in the League of Nations, or the Kellogg-Briand Pact, could resolve France's problems in the current international situation. In addition, although the French economy, despite bouts of speculation and recurring fincancial crises, had managed to recover fairly swiftly after World War I, that recovery came to a halt in 1929. The great social reforms cautiously initiated in 1924 under the Cartel des Gauches also slowed to a standstill for lack of funds. It is perhaps understandable that toward the end of the decade the French, stalemated on every front, often for reasons beyond their control, experienced a painful sense of powerlessness and "absurdity" and retreated behind their Maginot Line.

When the 1929 crisis swept from New York to London, carrying away with it the Weimar Republic, it affected France more slowly and less dramatically, allowing an illusion of prosperity to persist. But the world order established under the Treaty of Versailles was gone forever. France was defenseless in the face of German rearmament and, until 1936, vacillated between fear of war and fear of Germany, fear of financial instability, and need for the vast program of social reforms required to put the country back on its feet economically. With Nazism on the rise, from 1930 onward France stopped moving forward, apprehension increased, and public opinion became politicized in opposition to the government. There was talk of revolution. However, although right-wing groups such as the Camelots du Roi, Croix de Feu, and Jeunesses Patriotes were vocal, they were a minority composed primarily of young people from the middle class and viewed by the masses with distrust. The spectacular, fascistic 1934 riots did more to shake imaginations than to shake the government, weak as it was. The great mobilization of antifascist intellectuals, mainly writers, sponsored by Romain Rolland, Gide, Malraux, and others did have an effect on domestic politics, but it also blinded the country somewhat to the external realities of the situation. It was in this pre–World War II period that literature from extreme Right to extreme Left assumed the task of dealing with politics. A moment of great ferment was at hand.

Writers and Politics: The Politicization of Culture

The problem of the writer's social and political responsibilities first became an issue in intellectual circles during the twenties, in profound response to the two great events of the time, the First World War and the October Revolution. At its first congress in 1923, the PEN Club discussed the intellectual's role in revolutionary conflict and responsibility for creation of a "new world." In France the decade was to witness a proliferation of "groups" that engaged in interminable discussions addressing the same question. The years 1927 to 1929 were marked for a portion of the younger generation, whether on the surrealist or the intellectual side, by despair in the face of Poincaré's France. In 1927, Nizan and Aragon joined the Communist Party, and in 1928 Henri Lefebvre followed. The atmosphere of futility and disarray inhabited by a confused generation who felt themselves adrift in a rudderless world was recreated ten years later by Nizan in his novel *La Conspiration*.

The *équipes sociales* (social action teams) organized by Robert Garric to carry on the work of the popular universities and composed mostly of students were also inspired by this social awareness. Emmanuel Mounier, a young Catholic who could not accept the alliance between the Church and the rich and who founded Esprit, a political action and study group, felt it as well.

On the fringes of *L'Action française* there was another rightist group, just as brilliant, just as disturbed, and just as biased toward fascist social action:

Drieu La Rochelle, Jean-Pierre Maxence, Thierry Maulnier, Maurice Bardèche, and later, Robert Brasillach.

In response to the fascist leagues, the leftist "groups" expanded during the thirties and, with Russia serving as their axis, became internationalized. There was the Union des Ecrivains Révolutionnaires in 1931 and in 1932 the Association des Ecrivains et Artistes Révolutionnaires with a membership of about five thousand writers, artists, and intellectuals under the leadership of Aragon, Nizan, and Malraux. A delegation of French writers attended the Soviet Writers Congress in Moscow in 1934 and the International Congress of Writers in Defense of Culture in 1935. Speaking on behalf of Stalin at the 1934 Moscow Congress was Zhdanov, who formulated the doctrine of "social realism." This was the official party line for literature and defined the writer's role in relation to the regime. As an "engineer of hearts and minds," the writer was charged with producing an accessible, true-to-life literature, but one which also would guide and enlighten the reader according to the dialectical precepts of official Marxism on his history and his obligations. This was the beginning of Marxist aesthetics and Marxist criticism. Whereas in capitalist France the "bourgeois writer" and "bourgeois literature" reflected a political bias, "leftist" literature's duty was to be militant, to reflect "critical realism" and enlighten the middle class by exposing the mythic quality of bourgeois representations of reality.

Throughout this period, manifestos, position papers, and political-cultural essays proliferated, in themselves constituting a separate literary genre, a sort of high-class parajournalism. Every French political "family" had its own spokesman; to name a few: Daniel Halévy, André Gide, Emmanuel Berl, Henri Massis, André Breton, Jean Guéhenno, André Malraux, Drieu La Rochelle, Henri de Montherlant, Emmanuel Mounier, and, with *La Condition ouvrière,* Simone Weil. A minor genre which has so far received little attention from scholars, this type of essay probably attained its apogee after 1945 in Camus's *Actuelles,* Sartre's political series entitled *Situations,* and Mauriac's *Bloc-Notes.* Thriving in the shadow of the more conventional literary trends, it was favorably received by an informed public who saw reflected in it their own foremost political and social concerns which, in 1929–30, had begun to eclipse the literary and aesthetic preoccupations of both writers and artists.

The myth of salvation through revolution was reinforced by widespread enthusiasm for utopian Russia and the optimism it engendered in leftist circles, whether intellectual, middle-, or working-class. A flood of fledgling reviews appeared, representing the various groups seeking to establish a new revolutionary order "beyond civilization's breaking point." *Réaction, La Revue française,* and *L'Ordre nouveau,* to name just a few, advocated commitment to and the guiding principles for a renaissance that would save the country. This ferment was polarized and politicized by the great fascist-communist political confrontations that preceded the Second World War.

We can judge the persuasiveness of these myths by the extent of Gide's enthusiasm for the "new revolutionary gospel" and by the reprobation expressed in leftist circles in response to the slight reservations he included in his brief but perceptive account of his trip to Russia, *Retour de l'U.R.S.S.* (1936). But considering the ineffectiveness of these debates, we can understand Montherlant's bitterness in *Service inutile,* his 1935 denunciation of mediocre "petit bourgeois-ism" selfishly absorbed in its own narrow existence, lulled by its own illusions and oblivious to the dangers threatening the country. André Chamson, a politically active socialist, also recorded, in *La Galère* (1939), the dereliction and irresponsibility which over the years had set the country on its rudderless course. And yet haughty and skeptical Montherlant himself lived, unaware of it, in the very state of self-absorption he denounced; and Chamson's vision, out of tune with the times, seemed to confine itself to the France of the Jacobins.

Politically, France managed to keep anxiety at bay amid the prevailing confusion by clinging to the great myths that reflected her aspirations. These myths were codified in ideologies with political intent but with repercussions that were felt in the domain of literature. Ironically, when the Front Populaire and its platform of social action was finally elected by landslide in 1936, France's powerlessness was being tragically underscored by Hitler's occupation of the Rhineland and the outbreak of the Spanish civil war.

France's obssession with security and her reliance on myths were probably her only safe refuge from hard facts, in spite of all her intellectual activity. Confronted with the threat of political chaos, the French sensibility evidenced an underlay of stoic fatalism. Renoir's film *La Grande Illusion* was produced in 1936–37 when war was already a reality in both China and Spain and the French themselves stood on the threshold of a life with no horizon save that of war. And yet it profoundly expressed what most of the French seemed to feel: the futility of war.

2

A Nation
Disunited, 1936–52

For the French, the year 1936 marked the beginnng of a
quarter-century that was to be one of the darkest, most
controversial, and most troubled periods of their history,
one from which they did not emerge unscathed. This
period, dominated as it was by a war of apocalyptic dimensions, may well have seemed as insane to the French as
the devastating frescoes drawn out of it by Céline in *Les
Beaux Draps* (1941), *Féerie pour une autre fois* (1952–56),
and *D'un château l'autre* (1957). Dispersed and isolated
from one another, differing violently among themselves,
they nonetheless lived through it in a spirit of collective
participation in the common drama. It was this spirit that
gave underlying coherence to years whose seasons were
crisis, catastrophe, and violent and conflicting emotions.
This was a time when France, sealed off from the rest of the
world, concentrated on crucial questions of national self-
interest and above all, on whether or not the country
would survive.

French intellectuals, as spokesmen for the nation's hopes
and failures, evasions and dissensions, had a major role to
play. Political leaders became writers, like General de
Gaulle with his *Mémoires,* and writers like Malraux became politicians or else, like Mauriac, Bernanos, Sartre,
and Camus, passionately committed political commentators. For these writers, the collective destiny of the
French people and that of humanity as a whole were one,
and they responded to the events around them by placing
literature at the service of their country. The period was a
costly one in terms of human life, illusions, and material
loss. Worse still, as the Resistance fighter Jean Cassou was
to write from his prison cell, the French people were
stricken not only in their national pride but in their moral
unity. The predominant literary trend of those years,
somewhat vaguely called "existentialist" or, to use Sartre's

term, *engagé* (committed), sought to express this moral unity and sense of human community. This is what gave it its prestige. Many Frenchmen believed that only through the renewal of revolution could moral and political unity be achieved in postwar France. But of the two conflicting revolutions, one begun in 1940 and the other in 1944, neither was to prove successful.

However, even before the conclusion of World War II, preparations were already being made by various groups of experts in London, in Washington, and in wartorn, occupied, economically drained France itself for the reconstruction of the country. The task was facilitated by France's state of dilapidation at the end of the war. With the first Monnet Plan (1946–52), the era of economic planning began. Its first effects were felt in the fifties, when a steadily increasing birth rate was providing an additional symptom of renewed vigor. In 1952, three events in three different areas demonstrated the extent to which progress had been made: Paris became, not without reluctance, the world headquarters for NATO; the huge Donzère-Mondragon hydroelectric dam was inaugurated, as was Le Corbusier's "Cité Radieuse" in Marseille. That same year, Camus published *L'Homme révolté,* in which he renounced the attitudes and obssessions of the forties, causing violent dissension on the left and his eventual break with Sartre. This incident was revealing. It showed that the group of men once united by national calamity was now in the process of disintegration. Clearly, the day of the writer as moral and political conscience of the nation, filling the void left by the collapse of its institutions, was drawing to a close. The day of the technocrat was dawning. For literature, a long and painful readjustment lay ahead.

Although 1952 marked an economic turning point, it may seem an arbitrary date to choose in terms of politics. In the area of literature, however, there was a distinct change of climate. It was characterized not so much by generational conflict, as in 1968, as by the emergence of a new attitude, a revolt against the moral and political didacticism and *engagement* of the preceding years. The period between World War I and World War II had been an extremely rich and diverse one, intellectually; after 1936, the nation's tragic dilemma cast certain trends into relief at the expense of others. The tendencies which had remained latent or marginal during the forties began to reassert themselves at the half-century mark with the entrance onto the scene of the "New Wave" generation. This transformation occurred in three distinct stages.

1936–40: Reprieve

The Spanish civil war broke out in July 1936. Before it was brought to an end in 1938 by the victory of General Franco, Austria, soon to be annexed by the Reich, was already being invaded by Nazi troops. Czechoslovakia's turn came the same year and with it the crisis culminating in the Munich

Agreements. On September 1, 1939, the Wehrmacht invaded Poland. The Second World War had begun.

The French were in some confusion as they watched these events, which were punctuated by Nazi parades and the ravings of Hitler. In the wake of the social reforms passed by the Front Populaire, most of them just lived from day to day, as though under a "suspended sentence." This atmosphere of relative calm was accurately captured by Sartre in the first two volumes of his unfinished novel *Les Chemins de la liberté*. Among army units that had been mobilized but remained inactive on the front month after month, this somnolence continued right up through the Phony War, a strange atmosphere recreated by Julien Gracq in his novel *Un balcon en forêt*. Thousands of French men and women identified with the popular "Tout va très bien, Madame la marquise" (Everything's just fine, Madame la marquise), in which singers Pills and Tabet listed the symbolic, comic, and macabre stages in the destruction of a château. But the general feeling of futility was perhaps best expressed on the screen by Jean Renoir in *La Règle du jeu*, a much-misunderstood film when first released, based on an ambiguous, tragicomic scenario dealing with country "gentry." Heading the best-seller list in France in 1939 was Margaret Mitchell's *Gone with the Wind*, the historical romance of the American Civil War that describes the destruction of plantation life in the South and is told from the southern point of view. For the French, this was escape reading with a vengeance, historically and geographically.

On the other hand, however, ideological conflict and inflammatory journalism were on the rise. The Spanish civil war appeared to intellectuals as primarily an ideological confrontation between two political systems, democracy and fascism, with the future of the world at stake. The war drew intellectuals from many different countries to serve in its ranks as volunteers, the most famous from France being André Malraux. It was not long, however, before the ideological demarcation lines began to blur. For example, Bernanos started out as a *L'Action française* man and wound up writing *Les Grands Cimetières sous la lune*, a pamphlet denouncing *franquista* brutality. Claudel meanwhile was deploring the fate of Catholic martyrs victimized by Spanish government troops. As Gide had done on his return from Russia in 1936, Malraux, a leftist, also discreetly expressed certain reservations concerning the politics of Stalin's communism in his novel *L'Espoir* (1938), an epic, lyric documentary based on his own experiences in Spain. Céline fired off three virulent pamphlets in a row, *Mea Culpa* (1936), *Bagatelles pour un massacre* (1937), and *L'Ecole des cadavres* (1938), all of them anticommunist, anticapitalist, and anti-Semitic. Militant communists on the left like Paul Nizan, who could not in good conscience condone either the Stalin trials of old Bolsheviks, in which Zinoniev and Bukharin were condemned to death, or the German-Soviet pact of nonaggression, faced hostility from their erstwhile comrades—Aragon, for example—who had remained orthodox.

France's frontiers were being overrun by refugees from Hitler's terror and the Spanish civil war, her fundamental antimilitarism reinforced by a skeptical xenophobia that fed on the theme "France betrayed": sold out by bankers and politicians to the "Anglo-Saxon capitalist conspiracy," to financiers, to Jews, or to international communism. Nevertheless, in September 1939, Frenchmen from right to left responded with resignation to the military draft. They obeyed the draft call unenthusiastically, but they obeyed, and for eight months they remained at the front while the rest of the country lived through the suspense and anxiety of the Phony War.

On May 10, 1940, the devastating German offensive in Belgium and the Low Countries brought an end to this atmosphere of unreality. The next six weeks have become legendary, their every detail recorded in our literature: the hundreds of planes covering a German armored advance that could not be checked by the handful of French pilots whose futile gallantry has been described by Saint-Exupéry in *Pilote de guerre;* the surrounding of the French army; the British and French retreat to Dunkirk; the two million men taken prisoner of war; the waves of refugees and soldiers fleeing southward; the total confusion of government officials and civil servants as they fled toward Bordeaux only to be overtaken by the enemy advance; Italy's declaration of war; the German army's June 17 march through Paris, which had been declared an open city and lay silent and deserted. In a famous poem entitled "Richard II Quarante," the poet Louis Aragon expressed the disorientation the French were experiencing: "My country is like a river boat / Abandoned by the pilot." Their shame, anger, and hatred aroused by this humiliation exploded in Céline's violent attacks against army and government in *Les Beaux Draps* (1941) and, two years later, in Lucien Rebatet's *Les Décombres* (1943).

Historians are still trying to analyze this "strange defeat." Marc Bloch, later a victim of the Gestapo, was one of the first. In 1940 he wrote: "What we have just lost is that beloved small town we all have inside us, a town where buses dawdle, bureaucrats doze, and the days drag by, . . . where the life of the barracks cafés is easygoing, . . . a town of small trades, petty politicking, library shelves bereft of books, . . . suspicious of anything that might disturb its comfort" *(L'Etrange Défaite).* There began a time of general soul-searching that has been recorded in numerous volumes of memoirs. Often, as in the case of soldier Jean-Paul Sartre, this soul-searching was accompanied by guilt feelings, with the result that the French tended either to abdicate all responsibility in favor of a leader or to make unforeseen personal decisions themselves. There was nothing comfortable about those years. They provided some of the French, among whom writers and academics (both students and teachers) ranked high, an opportunity to prove themselves in action and to make up in part for the void left by the collapse of 1940.

1940–44: The Great Torment

Four years later, on August 19, 1944, Paris began to rise up against the occupiers. General Leclerc, leading his French troops and followed by the allied battalions, marched into a delirious, insurgent capital. On August 25, following some preliminary negotiations, Paris welcomed General de Gaulle as leader of the provisional government. Four years of enemy occupation had created in France the unique circumstances of a drama that touched every conscience and that altered the country's political and intellectual configuration, its sensibility and even its social structures. Although a film such as Marcel Ophüls's *Le Chagrin et la Pitié,* made retrospectively, was partially successful in recreating the atmosphere of the time, it is to history and to literature that we must turn if we are fully to grasp its complexities and confusion.

As a consequence of their defeat, the French had lived for four years in isolation. Now they were suddenly expected to take part in the allied victory as members of the "Big Four." An image of "France triumphant" was pieced together from the 1918 model and the 1940 "France humiliated" image, accepted at home and abroad during the Occupation, was exorcised. However, the France triumphant cliché was only a superficial answer to the country's real problems.

In the latter part of 1940, islands of resistance had formed inside France, in addition to Gaullism, around various individuals working either with the Gaullist or with British secret service, or independently. When Germany invaded Russia, the tough, efficient, disciplined, anti-Vichy, anti-Gaullist militants of the Communist Party emerged from isolation and joined the fight. Under the guise of unity, the communist leadership attempted to dominate the Resistance movement, and to pave the way for the revolution most anti-Vichy intellectuals were hoping for. Each succeeding year saw the struggle against the occupying forces intensify. Transmitting information, fighting repression with aggression, the Resistance networks sometimes found themselves pitted against a militia composed of their own compatriots, in a conflict of mutual hatred in which no quarter was asked or given. The constant danger, the activity of double agents, the fear of denunciation and betrayal, and, above all, the fear of torture created an atmosphere of high tragedy. But with the thrill of action, the duplicity and codes, disguises and secret messages, parachute drops and sabotage, the Resistance fighters led a life of cloak-and-dagger adventure. Friendships were strong and went deep. Dramas were heartrending: the word "Resistance" often meant death under torture. In his book *Drôle de jeu* (1945) Roger Vailland has described the chaos and the disorientation, but the accounts of other participants make fiction pale in comparison. As a result, the novel suffered. Deep ties bound the members of the Resistance to one another, uniting them against the common danger and in shared love for their country. This extraordinary way of life provided the context for a literature and a philosophy that sought to define the human condition in terms of its two extremes: the cowardice and brutality of man; and his selflessness and heroism. The idea that each individual is responsible for choosing his own destiny was one whose time had come.

The French had been widely dispersed. Prisoners of war went to Germany where they were followed by deportees and forced laborers sent to replace German factory workers drafted into the army. There was a large French population residing in North Africa, most of them loyal to Marshal Pétain. The Gaullists had established themselves in London. Refugees went to various places, mostly to New York but also to Brazil and Mexico. France itself, isolated from the rest of the world, was divided into occupied and southern zones, later to be reunified by the Germans at the time of the American landing in North Africa. The choice between collaboration or resistance, between Vichy and de Gaulle—and the ultimate consequences these choices implied—were matters of endless debate. This debate was pursued in relation to a multitude of individual viewpoints and loyalties, prejudices and bias too subtle and diverse to be accommodated by the oversimplified "collaboration/resistance" option. When it came to staking their future, the French had a wide gamut to choose from, ranging from total identification with the destinies of Germany, to total identification with those of Russia or Britain. Yet most of those who chose to act, rather than simply to wait out the duration, did so in the name of an idealism that was both nationalistic and humane. This idealism also swelled the ranks of the Resistance movement with men and women who were revolted by Nazi brutality or disgusted by the behavior of the Vichy government in abandoning to Hitler's forces a Jewish population ill defended by their French hosts and compatriots.

Representatives from the various Resistance networks, including about two dozen writers, met in Paris at the Conseil National de la Résistance to draw up plans for a postwar France that would achieve moral and political renewal through socialist structures. They believed they were preparing the transition "from Resistance to Revolution," but this motto concealed a multitude of differences. There was general agreement on one point, however— the respect felt by all for Russia, a country whose wartime ordeals and hard-won victory had enhanced her image and, along with it, that of the Communist Party and its more militant members as well. Unity of the Left seemed at last to be a reality. Unfortunately, the deeds and the spirit of the Resistance, which had united its members across lines of class and belief, were transformed following the Liberation into a politically useful but dubious myth. This fact cannot, however, destroy the reality of their existence, nor the heroism of those acts.

In 1944, France returned to the world of political realities. Mystique was replaced by politics. In the very euphoria of victory the brutal reprisals took place that served as a prelude to the harsh and often arbitrary purge that followed. That these reprisals were political in nature soon became obvious, even to certain members of the Resistance itself such as the writers Paulhan, Mauriac, and, later, Camus, who were disgusted by it. The politicians of the Third Republic had been liquidated in 1940, and now the Communist Party set about liquidating in its turn. Ideologically, it was the beginning of a reign of terror. However, thanks to the military situation at the time, to the policies of the British and American allies and to the opposition of the Gaullists, revolution was averted. France's crisis led, not to a new unity, but to a new political confrontation, this time between Gaullists and communists. French intellectuals, many of whom had belonged to the Resistance, were profoundly affected by the new realities.

1945–52: Return to Normality

Aragon, while he was in the underground, wrote a poem entitled "La Rose et le Réséda," really a call to unity in which he celebrated the courage of two young Frenchmen, one a Christian, the other a communist, who were united in a common struggle. But by 1945 the Communist party was again reasserting its independence, and it swiftly evolved from a progovernment to an opposition party. The revolutionary dreams of the Resistance were shattered by the dilemma of the post-Resistance split in the Left and, consequently, of the new relationship between the leftist intellectuals and the party. The rivalry between the USSR and the United States, and the threat of a conflict against which the newly created United Nations Organization seemed but a feeble defense, increased the disarray among French intellectuals. On the domestic front, order was restored to the country by General de Gaulle and a provisional Assembly composed of Gaullists and members of the Resistance.

It was with the inauguration of UNESCO in Paris toward the end of 1946 that the schism among intellectuals came out into the open. Three Frenchmen from the worlds both of letters and of the Resistance took the floor to deliver a series of lectures on the future of culture in the postwar world. They were André Malraux, Louis Aragon, and Jean-Paul Sartre. Aragon violently attacked Malraux for his advocacy of an "Atlantic civilization" with its decided bias in favor of the Western democracies. Aragon defended the thesis of a universal "French" humanism with a tradition stretching, according to him, from the revolution of 1789 to the revolution of 1917, uniting proletarian cultures that had sprung from each revolution. Sartre meanwhile proposed a revolutionary humanism to be defined by a new breed of socially aware intellectuals, tirelessly dedicated to elucidating the significance of historical configurations and their inevitable relations to the evolution of human history. For Sartre, the liberation of mankind lay through non-Stalinist Marxist dialectics. With little regard for the realities of economics, intellectuals were again playing the old game of ideologies, this time in an economic context that was changing. In 1953, with the creation of the first great European economic organization, the Coal and Steel Community, a new era dawned.

3

A New Country?
1952–70

The Era of Paradox

Life in Europe was dominated from 1914 until 1952 by political events of great impact. By 1952, however, events of individual significance for a specific country, such as the Algerian war for France, were overshadowed by the general transformation affecting European society as a whole. Compared to the France of 1940, the France of 1960 was really a "new" country. By 1970, she had gained a place among the fully-fledged technologically advanced nations. Economic prosperity seemed assured for some time to come. Unfortunately, this prosperity, and the international economic system on which it depended, were both undermined in 1974 by the politics of the Arab nations controlling that essential source of energy, oil. As inflation began to threaten her improved standard of living, France—along with the other great industrial nations—saw a new era of scarcity looming ahead: would the material means be available to maintain her consumer society?

Seen from the outside, France appeared to hover on the brink of disaster until the year 1962, when the Algerian war was finally brought to an end. Paradoxically, however, it was during this time that she was quietly continuing old reforms, or initiating new ones, that were effectively transforming outmoded structures. In this new intellectual climate, first priority went to the social and natural sciences and to systems analysis. As a result, the prestige of literature and writers suffered. Sociology, psychoanalysis, anthropology, and linguistics introduced concepts, problems, and problem-solving methods that seemed better adapted than literary and philosophical debate to the needs of society in a complex world. *Pourquoi des philosophes?* (1957) asked Jean-François Revel in a slight, satirical work attacking the limited horizons of French intellectuals and

their lack of practical knowledge. The executives responsible for modernizing the country's demographic and economic structures did not rely on the
intellectual community for inspiration. A whole group of young writers,
taking their name, Les Hussards, from the title of a novel written by one of
their number, Roger Nimier's *Le Hussard bleu,* defined themselves as anti-
intellectual and anti-"academic."

The spread of new, future-oriented business methods involving such
things as collective bargaining, high technology, and government subsidy
began to obliterate old patterns. People at every level of society were made
aware of their own position relative to the rest of the country and to future
expectations, by new methods of social research, including opinion polls,
surveys, and computerized statistics. The rapid development of the mass
media and of television in particular also played an important role during
this period. In 1953 there were only 53 thousand television sets in all of
France, compared to 15 million in 1972. Even the literary world became an
object of sociological scrutiny. Seen from this unaccustomed perspective it
was learned, for example, that 54 percent of all French people over fifteen
years of age never purchased a book; and that the French, on the average,
read considerably less than their British or American counterparts, whom
they had traditionally thought of as relatively uncultivated. The French
literary world, a fairly closed one, again concentrated in Paris, began to be
aware of its own isolation and its illusions in presuming to serve as mirror,
voice, conscience, or guide for the country. So marginal had the literary
establishment become in relation to the vital forces moving the country, that
it was taken completely by surprise when radical students overturned the
university system during the uprisings of May 1968.

Between Past and Future: Gradual Depoliticization

At times the country seemed on the edge of civil war. Absorbed in dealing
with the hardships of the post–World War II period, it was only somewhat
belatedly that the French realized they had been waging a disastrous colonial war in Indochina ever since 1946. The 1954 defeat at Dien Bien Phu
alerted public opinion and brought the war to an end, but on November 1
of the same year, in Algeria, the uprising took place that transformed that
country's state of latent revolt into a full-scale war for national liberation.
By 1956 the terrorism, torture, guerilla brutality, and spread of clandestine
violence to mainland France, especially Paris, had had a galvanizing effect
on French public opinion. The day of the great revolution seemed to be at
hand. Radical indignation was matched by the outrage of army and colonists who believed themselves betrayed by civilians. While all this was
going on, General de Gaulle repaired certain weaknesses of the regime
through constitutional reform, and the Fourth Republic was replaced by the
Fifth. It took four years to settle the Algerian question; but, when the

changeover came, it was accomplished without a revolution and without damage to France's democratic foundations.

The bitterness of this moral and political conflict once again brought together a majority of left-wing writers, notably Sartre and Simone de Beauvoir—this time in their common hatred for colonialism. Although this bitterness was amply reported in the French press, particularly in the occasionally censored periodicals of the Left, it is in novels that we find reflected the complexity of the events arising from the two colonial wars and of the feelings and impulses aroused by them. In *Les Chevaux du soleil* (1968–70), for example, Jules Roy, an Algerian-born Frenchman and a supporter of Algerian independence, retraces the French invasion of Algeria step by step. His format is a huge historical novel in which he attempts to clarify the true attitudes and feelings of colonialists whose affective ties with the Algerian soil ran deep, but who were mistreated and misunderstood by the mainland French public. Mass market novels such as Jean Hougron's six-volume *La Nuit indochinoise* (1950–58), which included, among others, *Tu récolteras la tempête* and *Mort en fraude,* and Jean Lartéguy's very popular *Les Centurions* (1960), recreated a highly romantic, exotic scene alien to French reality. They describe a life-and-death struggle played according to rules that had less to do with political conviction than with the craving for violence that had also characterized the wartime French underground. The ultimate futility of this kind of romanticized clandestine action was ironically portrayed in Pierre Gascar's *Les Moutons de feu* (1963). The main characters in this novel are two young Parisians, Alain, who specializes in planting plastic explosives, and his enemy Dandrieu, a leftist militant. Both are equally ineffective and both wind up in prison, victims of their respective activist illusions. The Algerian war was not brought to an end by the activity of militants, either on the Right or on the Left, but by long, patient negotiations and the determination of General de Gaulle. When it ended, the political mobilization of intellectuals as mentors and standard-bearers in the cause of redemptive revolution also ended. Sartre, who eventually went on to become the mascot of the post-1968 student Maoists, was the only intellectual who never abandoned this role.

Toward a "New" Country

In the meantime, other, less spectacular developments went largely unnoticed. The economic planning begun during the Fourth Republic bore fruit and was extended during the Fifth. The violent upheavals of the Algerian war had obscured the success of a French decolonization policy under which, by 1960, and with the exception of Algeria, all the African territories had been granted independence. Nevertheless, this success was real. A bold monetary reform, also carried out in 1960, introduced the new franc and promised a more stable currency for the French.

International cooperation also progressed steadily from year to year, its effects felt on every level of French society. New frames of reference were needed to accommodate both the concept of a united Europe and the strong resurgence of nationalism born of wartime defeat. Scientific research, in particular, was redefined in terms of the major European and international organizations. Research both pure and applied was carried out by teams of scientists working at centers like Sarclay, under the auspices of organizations such as the Centre National de la Recherche Scientifique (created in 1936) or the more specialized Commissariat de l'Energie Atomique (established after World War II). In astrophysics, biochemistry, and electronics, French scientists once again occupied a respected place in the international scientific community.

The impact of these fresh initiatives was felt on the national level. First of all, the Common Market began to work. Then the customs barriers between member countries gradually began to fall, and, finally, all constraints on individual movement were eliminated. Passports were no longer required. Scientific and industrial planning transformed daily life, at first slowly and then more rapidly. The vigor of French technological innovation was confirmed, in the automotive industry by production of the Citroën 2C.V. (1945), the D.S. (1955), and the Dauphine (1956); in aviation by the Caravelle (1959); and in communications by the SECAM color television process. Achievements of a more controversial nature were the development of nuclear and hydrogen bombs and the satellite launchings, overshadowing the practical applications of nuclear energy and the continuing search for alternate forms of the energy essential to the modern way of life.

There were reforms in the area of public welfare, some of which, relayed through the Vichy government, were a legacy from the Front Populaire. The metamorphosis of society was at its most dramatic in the rapidly growing cities. Slowly but surely, Paris was undergoing modernization and redevelopment. Nowhere was the changing shape of the country more obvious than in the greater Paris region. A number of factors combined to give Paris an image of growth: the gradual rise of skyscraper developments at La Défense and Maine-Montparnasse; construction of low-cost housing (HLM, or Habitations à loyer modéré) at Sarcelles and elsewhere; the creation of Parly II and other similar new communities on the outskirts of the city; suburban modernization aimed at the reduction of urban overcrowding; the program for cleaning public monuments in central Paris; the law requiring sandblasting of old buildings; the renovation of older sections of the city, such as the Marais; and, finally, appearing in the city for the first time, supermarkets, drugstores, and a proliferation of "snack bars" alongside the existing cafés.

The transformation taking place in the provinces was more uneven but just as pronounced. There was development of the Grenoble, the Marseille-Aix and the Lyon-Saint-Etienne regions, and even the southwest began to awaken from its long somnolence. Cities like Grenoble turned into regional capitals. The old contrasts between life in the provinces and life in Paris were not as sharp as they once had been. Automobile, air, and modernized rail travel changed the old relations of the provinces to Paris. Now, interchange between city and country, country and city, was constant. Farm workers migrated in increasing numbers to the urban centers, while members of the prosperous middle class fanned out into the countryside, converting old farmhouses into vacation homes. A growing movement of "vacationeers" carried a mixed bag of people to the ski slopes in winter and the beaches in summer. The younger generation began to exhibit a uniformity which tended to blur class distinctions, the result of wider availability of activities once the sole preserve of the leisured classes (such as skiing, swimming, camping, and travel), of improved standards of public hygiene, and of the rapid dissemination of clothing styles through television and magazines. Personal income was rising. With a few important exceptions, France was living the good life. Between 1950 and 1954 there was a 49 percent per capita increase in consumption. Car ownership per French household, a mere 10 percent in 1950, had increased to 56 percent by 1969. Clearly, French society was undergoing a process of social homogenization that exerted a gradual impact on the class structure but a far more intensely felt generational impact.

The French people began to feel the pressure. They were torn between desire for a better standard of living, ruthless economic competition, the accelerated pace of life, a technology and communications explosion and conflicts between the old and new, between foreign and domestic policy, between economic necessity and the old political reflexes. Attitudes toward the new world in the process of creation contained a note of anxiety, tinged with regret for the relative peacefulness of the old ways.

Revolt was smoldering, and in 1968, following a police raid into the grounds of the Sorbonne, it broke out. The student uprising which then occurred in Paris spread in attenuated form to the provincial universities, and then back again to the Parisian lycées. Violence on the part of both rioters and authorities was kept under control, however, and in an atmosphere of festive disorder Paris seemed for a brief moment to be reliving the heady days of 1789. Students camped out round the clock in the Sorbonne and the Odéon Theater, both of which they occupied. They organized marathon political debates in which leftists of every stripe confronted one another, and they negotiated with the civil and university authorities who had been caught napping. The initial generosity of the students' spirit, their demands for freedom from constraint, and their dream of solidarity with the working classes were highly appealing. In the minds of those who were there, the legend of 1968 lives on. It provided the driving force behind the Maoist political movement and nurtures the latent discontent still prevalent in some university circles.

It is difficult to evaluate an event that was preceded by similar outbreaks in Japan, Germany, and the United States and was extensively reported and documented at the time. The movement definitely influenced the reorganization of the French university system, already under way, and resulted in greater democratization on every level. Politically, it seems to have marked the end of the postwar period and hastened the departure of General de Gaulle, although his government remained in power. Young student protesters from the middle class had shaken the conscience of the establishment, perhaps paving the way for profound changes in the country's social and cultural foundations. But the *Revolution* they dreamed of never came to pass.

Two

The Social Climate

Introduction

The social climate in France was profoundly affected by the political and historical events of this first half-century. The middle class, holding in its grasp the reins of power and responsible for the country's fate, lived in a state of increasing unease. It is with this class, as Sartre clearly perceived, that the writer's destiny is intertwined, whether he himself comes from the upper-, lower-, or middle-middle class. The moment he achieves success and enters the category "man of letters," he also assumes a specific rank in the social hierarchy. This rank was a privileged one in the period between the two World Wars. France respected her writers. In a highly secularized society the writer, untainted by political power, represented moral authority and saw himself as the conscience of the nation. Between the writer and the social class to which he belonged—his readers—there thus existed a relationship of complicity. Even the surrealists, who rebelled against the social and political mores of their time, were assimilated by the system through practice of the literature they were denouncing. Breton was associated with Paul Valéry and Valery Larbaud as an editor of *Commerce;* Gallimard published Eluard. When the Marxists claimed that French literary culture was linked to the tastes and avocations of a specific social class, they were right. As this social climate began to change, slowly at first and then more rapidly, repercussions were felt in the world of literature, forcing it to adjust to a different social context.

With Malraux, Sartre, and Camus, the era of the writer as "spiritual guide" came to an end. Our emphasis in the present work on social change is a reflection of the effect this change had on writers who found themselves—perhaps only temporarily—outside the mainstream of a society avid for life, information, technology, and new life styles. When this happened, the literary world reacted by turning in on itself, absorbed in a life of cliques and coteries.

4

Old Quarrels and New Alliances, 1920–36

French society as a whole changed very little, if at all, between the two world wars, at least until 1936. The loss of manpower suffered during the First World War had a more insidious effect on the fabric of society than the material damage. Although this may not have been obvious, for a country with France's low birthrate it was crucial. The male population between the ages of twenty and thirty in France in 1914 was approximately three million; 27 percent of these men never returned from the war. Of this 27 percent, many would have provided the country with an intellectual dynamism it badly needed: "Half of the teachers who were drafted and a third of the lawyers, plus eight hundred students from the Ecole Polytechnique and two thousand writers and journalists were killed." The France of 1920 had lost almost a million and a half men; more than a million of those who did return were permanently disabled.

Exhausted by an experience for which they had been unprepared, the men who came back from the war were often ill-equipped for recovering their equilibrium in a world that had learned how to get along without them. Many opted for the narrow life of the government pensioner. Emmanuel Bove, himself a veteran, described this phenomenon in his book *Mes amis,* in which his disabled antihero lives from day to day and from café to café. For some, however, this aimlessness was only temporary and eventually led to some kind of commitment: "I spend hours pacing around the table in my hotel room; I wander aimlessly in Paris, I spend whole evenings by myself on a bench in the Place du Châtelet; I am prey to a sort of day-to-day fatalism" (André Breton, *Entretiens*). The extraordinary popularity of novels such as *Le Diable au corps* by the young Radiguet or the French Canadian story *Maria Chapdelaine,* of Sacha Guitry and of silent film stars, was proof that people were putting private joys and sorrows ahead of everything else. The era was characterized by a vague romanticism that throve on people's absorption in themselves and indifference to others.

As one war veteran, Jean Norton Cru, demonstrated, the countless stories about the war perpetuated not the truth but a series of heroic myths manufactured on the home front. These myths were attacked by the philosopher Alain in *Mars ou la guerre jugée* (1921) and ferociously caricatured ten years later by Céline, in the person of his antihero Bardamu in *Voyage au bout de la nuit*. In *La Comédie de Charleroi*, Drieu simultaneously denounced both myth and reality. A nostalgia for genuine heroism led some young veterans to adopt attitudes that could be considered antisocial: Montherlant, for example, was "in love with the front," with "the great community" he had found there. He dreamed of escape from participation in the "burdens" of peacetime life; of belonging to a "male holy order, a sacred realm of the strong" (*Le Songe*, 1922). Other members of this generation returned to civilian life as revolutionaries, radicalized by a strong "sense of the futility of so much human sacrifice" and by a determination to "settle accounts back home with a bunch of 'never-say-die' civilians whose patriotism had gone hand in hand with unscrupulous profiteering and a vast disruption of family life." When censorship was lifted, these young men were revolted to discover "the true extent of the wartime ravages" and of the "mindless propaganda" that had accompanied it (Breton, *Entretiens*). After the war was over there were some, like Giono, who blamed "machine-age society" for the sufferings of the *grand troupeau*—the human flock gone astray. Barbusse, Guéhenno, and others blamed the disaster on bourgeois, capitalistic society. They put their faith in international socialism, and they worked at popularizing it through periodicals like *Clarté* and *Europe* existing on the fringes of small, militant Marxist cells affiliated with a sparsely supported Russian bolshevism. Still others shared the attitude of Drieu, who, while waiting to find a happy medium between Moscow and Washington that would serve him as an aid in "restoring France to herself," collected signs of his country's "decadence" in a series of bitter vignettes: bar scenes featuring the aimless and the frivolous, drug addicts, ne'er-do-wells, and young war veterans obsessed with making money. There was doubtless some truth and also some injustice in this young, middle-class Parisian's harsh diagnosis of his compatriots: "When the French people emerged from this war they were sick, with all the manias and failings that go with being sick. Obscurely sensing their inability to view their own malady clearly . . . they have resigned themselves to half-measures and prefer to look no further than the ends of their noses."

The psychological aftereffects of the war, though hard to evaluate, left a distinct mark on the era. In many cases there was a widening of the generation gap, expressed by Raymond Radiguet in his own peculiar way through his hero and alter ego in *Le Diable au corps* who complains of his parents' withdrawal when confronted with the adolescent he is. Communication between the generation that "lived through the war" and the first peacetime generation was poor, no doubt because, after four years of abnormality, the former found themselves ill at ease in a peaceful world.

The postwar Parisian society denounced by Drieu was described in another novel published at the same time, Victor Margueritte's notorious best-seller La Garçonne (1922). Anatole France said of this novel that it gave a true picture of "a society whose like had never before been known in France—a society created by the war." Margueritte's target was the sophisticated, political world of upper-middle-class business, and the hordes of newly rich and newly uprooted that were drawn to it. It was against this background that the adventures of his heroine Monique Lerbier took place. Superficially, the novel's theme was a timely one—the emancipation of women. Monique turns down a "sensible" marriage and decides to become an interior decorator. The novel's real theme, however, is its description of the depravity and cynicism rampant in a business-oriented society where the only important thing is money. Here we have a traditional Balzacian theme in a new social climate. Monique's odyssey first leads her far from the respect for appearances required of well-brought-up, wealthy middle-class women and into open homo- and heterosexual love affairs, a frenetic life of receptions, dinner parties, cocktail parties, night clubs, and bars until, finally, her journey ends with the discovery of a love both noble and moral. In a riot of jazz, tango, sex, race, morals, drugs, and radically new styles— short hair for women, tailored suits, and lamé shifts—a new Parisian "high society" was indeed abandoning itself to new ways. The behavior of "emancipated womanhood" was only one aspect of what was happening.

Back to Tradition

The notoriety of La Garçonne, and its success (750,000 copies sold in just a few months), were symptomatic. The French public was enthralled by descriptions of behavior it disapproved of—behavior actually engaged in by only a relatively small group of highly visible sophisticates. Other social strata remained strongly attached to tradition and were only very gradually affected to any significant degree by the new liberated life styles. On the other hand, at every level of society the celebration of traditional values— real or imaginary—was a literary theme common to a large majority of novels: the aristocratic values of Alphonse de Chateaubriant; the solid family virtues of Jean Schlumberger's middle-class protagonists; the patient industry and endurance of the lower-middle-class characters filling the pages of Duhamel; and the proud independence of Jean Giono's peasant poets— all carry the same message. Many of the French saw a cure for their social ills in a return to the traditions of the past that would exclude the "modern world."

In 1923 and 1924 Loti, France, and Barrès, the literary masters of the Belle Epoque, died. With the exception of the more eclectic Proust, the men of the succeeding generation—Claudel, Gide, and Valéry—were originally influenced by their contact with Mallarmé. In 1925 the eminence of this group was formally recognized by Valéry's election to the French Academy. For these men, the literary enterprise was the exercise of an art beyond the reach of political events and isolated from day-to-day reality. Because this attitude corresponded to a latent need on the part of the French public for stability and continuity, they fell easily into place as the literary masters of the interwar years.

Under the influence of men like Jacques Maritain and Gabriel Marcel, the Catholic renewal among intellectuals initiated at the beginning of the century was continued. Both Maritain and Marcel came to Catholicism as converts, the former before the war, the latter in 1929. However, the Catholic constituency was sorely tried by two events disturbing to men of good conscience: Pope Pius XI's condemnation of L'Action française, and the Spanish civil war. The violence of the polemics that resulted among the faithful deeply stirred consciences and fueled an entire school of literature. With the work of Claudel in the forefront, Catholic novels by François Mauriac, Julien Green, and, later, Bernanos and the Catholic poetry of Pierre Jean Jouve bore witness to the vigor and independence of Catholic thought on both right and left. Frequently, however, Catholic intellectuals kept their distance from the "self-righteous" faithful, whom they considered conformist and reactionary. For these conservative Catholics, tirelessly condemned by Georges Bernanos, social reform usually meant communism and the anti-Christ.

Many literary works reflected the influence of Catholic education on the moral and artistic sensibilities of a generation conditioned by parochial schooling, even in the case of individuals who later detached themselves from Christian teachings. The Church controlled a number of newspapers (La Vie catholique) and magazines (Revue critique des idées et des livres, Revue universelle, Etudes) and used them for the dissemination of critical opinion which much of their readership accepted. As Drieu noted in 1942, summing up "twenty years of the real Paris": "The Catholics had a tremendous resource, the powerful framework provided by their theological view of man, and a psychological system still unexhausted because enriched by experience much of which has been secular. Furthermore, they had the provinces, confused, overburdened, but, unlike Paris, still kicking" (Preface to Gilles). One of the most illuminating Catholic novels is Lucien Rebatet's Les Deux Etendards (1952). The story concerns two young men of Catholic background from Lyon. Rebatet follows their feelings of inner conflict and anguish when they come into contact with the intellectual currents of the interwar period.

The esoteric investigations of a Georges Bataille or a novelist-essayist such as Raymond Abellio (*La Structure absolue,* 1952) may plausibly be assumed to have their source in the vague yearning for a spiritual and mystical "beyond" inherited by a secularized world from Christianity. It also seems to us that the need felt by writers to be missionaries—even when their mission was the preparation of revolution by "desanctifying literature"— was really just Christian messianism in another form. In any case, it is clear that the ideological conflicts, politics, and literary themes of this period often were connected at a deeper level to the latent presence of the "theological view of man" referred to by Drieu, even though its precise influence remains difficult to determine.

Parisian Society and the Modern Avant-Garde

At the time of the First World War a social "set" emerged in Paris, the sophisticated, ill-defined "Tout-Paris." Differing markedly from society as described by Marcel Proust, it was the group Margueritte attempted to portray in *La Garçonne.* Serving as hotbed and nerve center for literary and artistic fashions, it marketed these fashions much as the Parisian couturiers marketed fashions in dress. In the years following the war this group, itself in a state of constant flux, saw its numbers grow as a result of easy money made in currency speculation, wartime profiteering, and reconstruction swindles. International political upheaval brought to Paris a mixed population from very different backgrounds: allied commissions and military personnel; refugees from Russia and Central Europe; shady businessmen and adventurers. Paris, more tolerant than in the past, became cosmopolitan and liberal, a shifting milieu of constant intrigue where anyone with a little luck could make it. It was an era punctuated by bankruptcy (Madame Hanau) and gigantic financial swindles (the Oustric case in 1929; the Stavisky case in 1933) which demonstrated the extent to which a web of conspiracy radiating from Paris reached financial and political power centers throughout the country, encompassing the police, the courts, and the press.

In this "republic of equals," money was the key for opening the doors of a Tout-Paris that preferred cabarets to drawing rooms, night club entertainment to traditional social ceremony, dancing and cocktails to tea, and bridge to conversation. To a memoirist like Maurice Sachs, writing retrospectively, these scenes were representative of "a generalized disorder of all values, ... an obvious moral corruption, an extraordinary lack of greatness, ... a nation that from top to bottom of the social ladder seeks only pleasure" (*Au temps du bœuf sur le toit*). In some exasperation, Sachs also identified as one of "the major historical events of postwar French society" the fact that "everyone was tacitly granted the possibility of breaching society's bastions with only the most cursory letters of credit." Sachs's point of view was valid, but for one particular segment of society only.

In the country as a whole, social structures had actually hardly changed at all. Life was as austere as ever; and for the lower-middle class, the workers, and the peasants it was often very hard indeed. There was a wider gap than ever before between the Paris-based image of French life as luxurious, stylish, fashionable, and intellectual and the real moral standards persisting in a society that was still traditional and highly structured. The polarization on which the novels of Mauriac were based—"austere and immutable provinces versus brilliant, tempting Paris"—reflected this. Outside of sophisticated Paris the class hierarchy remained virtually unchanged, as did modes of access to employment and certain types of careers. An elite minority of "intellectuals" was channeled into the professions by way of the university system, the Ecole Normale or the prestige professional schools *(grandes écoles)*. Things were different in postwar Paris, where literary or artistic notoriety could open doors even when money was lacking. More than ever before, people could "make it" through writing. "Paris became the haunt of the literary . . . and speculation had sharpened appetites. People put their money on writers, painters, and musicians. But they still referred to Art. There were conferences, there were performances, there were meetings, and with each passing month there was the birth of a new magazine" (Philippe Soupault, *Le Bon Apôtre*). For a time, any door would open if you were young, and the young who knocked came from the bourgeoisie, determined to be different from their parents and filled with the spirit of defiance. "The great enemy was the public. We had to get at people any way we could; . . . we had to be outrageous, . . . to shock. . . . Why not admit it? We were madly in love with being shocking. It's what kept us going. We wanted to be outrageous, and we were outrageous."

It was in this context that the "avant-garde," the literary and artistic successor to the old, prewar "Bohemia," fused with the hundred or so personalities making up the Tout-Paris, and the various coteries and cliques gravitating around them. Money, talent, daring and success counted for as much as family connections. Although by 1925 the Tout-Paris had become less exclusive and was beginning to relinquish its role as promoter of the true avant-garde, it continued to serve as an incubator for literary and artistic activities of a semicultural, semisocial nature. Around these events it fostered a sort of "snobbism" of taste, wealth, fashion, and novelty, a "Parisianism" that had a profound effect on literature and art. The result was an in-group snobbery and aestheticism of the privileged few that turned art into decoration, creativity into play, and often confused merit with notoriety. This typically Parisian elite recreated its own closed circle everywhere it went: in 1924–25, for example, it popularized the Côte d'Azur at the expense of Deauville, and transformed it into a summer holiday extension of Paris. This group also dominated the juries that awarded literary prizes.

Riding high on cubism, futurism, *l'Esprit nouveau,* the Ballets Russes, and Stravinsky, Paris—in the words of Jean Cocteau, the man who served as her impressario—amused herself with "the mad prodigality of a city of genius," embracing a group of painters, composers, and writers who prolonged, heightened, and extended the daring of the prewar years. Drawing inspiration from each other, combining different media, throwing themselves into a search for new forms, new artistic languages, composers, painters, writers, young film makers, couturiers, and men of the theater came together during those years at the sumptuous *soirées de Paris* given by patrons of the arts such as the Comte de Beaumont or the couturier Paul Poiret (who called one of his parties, aptly, "la Soirée des Nouveaux Riches"); in the salons of the Vicomte and Vicomtesse Charles de Noailles, Princesse Blanche de Polignac and Princesse Marie Murat; at the Ballets Suédois or with Diaghilev's circle; in night clubs and in cabarets such as the famous Bœuf sur le Toit sponsored by Jean Cocteau. A "modern life style" had come into being which marked an entire era.

The Ballets Russes, and to an even greater extent the Ballets Suédois, important both artistically and socially, were at the center of this vortex. Within five years, Rolf de Maré and the Ballets Suédois created twenty-four ballets, including the landmark *Les Mariés de la Tour Eiffel* (Cocteau, 1921) and *La Création du Monde* (Milhaud, 1923), bringing together every name and every style currently in fashion. Scores were by Satie and Les Six, the avant-garde *nouveaux/jeunes* group that included Milhaud and Honegger, with a little Cole Porter on the side. Librettos were by Cendrars, Cocteau, and Claudel; scenery was by Léger, Picabia, and Picasso. There was an effort to integrate and unite all the arts and all styles through ballet, "words and music, . . . poetry, dance, acrobatics, drama, satire." In 1924, the production of *Entr'acte* by the young René Clair introduced the *divertissement cinématographique*. Innovation in other areas flowed from the aesthetic laboratory of the ballet. In 1924 Léger created a furor with his *Ballet mécanique* combining music, film, and a mechanical set complete with airplane propeller.

The Exposition des Arts Décoratifs was a triumph for the "1925 style" and its cubist affiliations: the stars of the show were the reinforced concrete block and the architectural concepts of Le Corbusier. "Modern" furniture, still somewhat overdecorated, perhaps, made its appearance, emphasizing the importance of the functional, the metallic, and the straight-lined. Stage sets and lighting, advertising posters, and women's clothes became stylized. The "Chanel look"—short hair, boyish figure, cloche hats, tailored suits, and short hemlines—replaced Poiret's luxurious oriental fabrics, turbans, and long, hobbling skirts.

Literary life, concentrated in Paris around a few "young" publishing houses led by Grasset and Gallimard, also underwent a transformation. Although the publication of purely literary works was still the personal responsibility of individuals, backed by reading committees of recognized writers whose first priority was the literary quality of a manuscript, literature was nonetheless becoming increasingly commercialized. Promotion of Radiguet's short novel *Le Diable au corps* (1923) was typical. Earlier still, for the publication of *La Garçonne* in 1922, Flammarion had launched what amounted to a publicity campaign; Grasset did something similar for the Canadian novel *Maria Chapdelaine*. Both books became best-sellers. But with *Le Diable au corps,* Grasset turned the publication of a book into a literary "happening." Every possible publicity device was used: posters, photos, interviews, prizes, and even films. The publicity referred to Radiguet's youth, his good looks, and the lucrative contract he had signed. The importance of the author as a unique, extraordinary phenomenon was stressed rather than the quality of the book. This approach scandalized the French critical establishment, whose members were outraged by the new-fangled idea of selling books like patent medicines.

But the race was on. Hyperbole and shock value became regular features of bookselling, a trade that until then had been relatively low-keyed. Starting in the 1920s, serious publishing houses were no longer able to estimate in advance the potential public for a book either in the provinces or in Paris. Until then, a "literary" novel by an author like Henri de Régnier, published by Mercure de France, could usually count on an average sale of 2,500. Now, especially in the case of novels, which had gained wide popularity among a public avid for something to read, the era of the blockbuster edition was on—and the era of uncertainty. Publishers printed editions of 100,000, but sales fluctuated unpredictably. Readers chasing after the "latest thing" were not the same animal as the stolid provincial bourgeois who had long since given up trying to keep in step with Paris. Literary quality became confused with successful marketing, which placed value on novelty and surprise. Literature was no longer conceived of as it had been by Gide, Valéry, Claudel, and Proust—the great interwar generation. For these men, literature was the highest activity of which the human spirit is capable. It was also a means for attaining social rank; it was art, of course, but business too. The line between "serious literature" and consumer literature was wavering.

In the chaotic Paris of the 1920s, the relatively homogenous bourgeois culture based on a common reading experience came to an end. Now there were new, nonliterary tastes shared, on different levels, by both the masses and the avant-garde: silent movie stars, vamps, and Charlie Chaplin; the circus; Josephine Baker and jazz; the art of Mistinguett and Maurice Chevalier. Chanel pioneered the democratization of feminine fashion. Advertising widened the circle of people for whom a writer could be just as much a celebrity as Charlie Chaplin. Here was counterculture in the making, years before the term was coined, and, for this counterculture, "literature" declined in value.

The Purist Reaction: Denying the Present

The group around André Breton, which had evolved from a literary clique influenced by Apollinaire and Reverdy, to dadaism, and, finally, to surrealism, aimed their "will to destroy" as much toward the Parisian conspiracy of art, entertainment, money, fashion, celebrity-mongering, and publicity-seeking as toward the social and literary establishment. From January to April 1920, and again in 1921, the dadaists staged a number of demonstrations and protests designed to provoke and shock Paris. The most successful of these events was the mock trial of Barrès (1921), because it touched one of the high pontiffs of the literary establishment. Three years later, when Anatole France died, the surrealists committed a second offense, circulating an inflamatory pamphlet entitled *Un cadavre,* which attacked the concept of the writer-as-object-of-sacred-veneration, and the self-righteousness of official rhetoric.

The last of the surrealist outbreaks occurred in 1925 during a literary banquet in honor of the poet Saint-Pol Roux. This time there were signs that the group was changing its aim. The Riffian war had made them politically aware. Marxism was beginning obscurely to trouble the bourgeois French conscience. Although in the beginning the surrealists' quest for a new language and their attempts to combine the plastic arts with the written word had given them an affinity with Cocteau's "modernist" aesthetic, now their targets were completely different. They wanted not just to transform art but to transform society. This perhaps explains why a movement which long remained inaccessible to the majority of French people did eventually exercise a broad influence. In any case, by the end of the decade aesthetic games and aesthetic scandals were displaced by political demonstrations and financial scandals. The last of the 1920s-style avant-garde outrages had only a limited impact. When two experimental, violently antisocial films were shown, *Un chien andalou* (1928) and *L'Age d'or* (1930) by Bunuel and Dali (both virtually unknown at the time), they provoked a police reaction, but not an aesthetic one. With the worsening of the political situation, the "modernism" of the twenties faded and a taste for the serious began to develop. "When Hegel and Marx can replace Rimbaud and Lautréamont as objects of veneration for the students in our elite schools," wrote Sachs of those years, "a historic change has taken place." In fact, as early as 1924 André Breton had already felt an urge simultaneously to "transform life," in the manner of Rimbaud, and to help "change the world" in the manner of Marx. However, it was not until the 1930s that this concern for history began to predominate.

A Vast Social Reckoning: The Novel between the Wars

The "novels of the individual" that proliferated during the twenties began to yield to novels describing the evolution of whole social classes: the upper-middle class, in Martin du Gard's *Les Thibault;* the lower-middle class, in Duhamel's *La Chronique des Pasquier;* Aragon's epic cycle *Le Monde réel* describing the attack of an upwardly mobile working class on decadent, capitalist society; and, finally, the ordeals suffered by an entire country entering the modern age as described by Romains in *Les Hommes de bonne volunté.* Traditional in form, these works reached a wide middle-class audience. Generally speaking, they offered a rather serene, detached image of social evolution. Yet, the impact of world events in the late thirties profoundly affected the way both Jules Romains and Martin du Gard looked at the world, introducing into the final volume of their series a note of pessimism that had not been present in the earlier ones. The anguished work of Drieu La Rochelle, little known at the time, had been characterized by this same pessimism relative to French society in general. From *Etat-civil,* written in 1921, through *Gilles,* 1939, Drieu La Rochelle prosecuted a middle class in the midst of decadence. In these novels, the individual drama coincides with the degeneration of an entire group. The problem of social class was thus usually equated with the relation of the traditional middle class to the world of large-scale modern capitalism. Social protest made its appearance mainly among a small though growing group of young intellectuals from the lower middle class who were relatively independent economically. It was this group that succumbed to the temptation of revolution through political commitment to one or the other of the two great ideologies of the time, Marxism or fascism.

In this interwar period, the novel reigned supreme; the theater may have dominated the artistic scene, but that was essentially a Parisian phenomenon. In the background was the novel, offering, in the tradition of Balzac, a vast panorama of French society ranging from the Parisian outlaws depicted by a Carco and peasants from every corner of the nation, to the great, landed, semiaristocratic, clannish, exclusive families that occupied the center of the stage in novels like Jean Schlumberger's *Saint-Saturnin* (1931) and Jacques de Lacretelle's *Les Hauts-Ponts* (1932–35). The most important of these novels were inspired by a keen sense of social transformation and a new awareness of the relations between individual behavior and social structures. In general, the novelists of the 1885 generation concentrated on their own past. The image of society and its evolution they presented was based on a more or less consciously accepted system of values. In the novels of the "1910 generation"—Duhamel, Romains—social climbing was the predominant theme. Georges Duhamel, in *La Chronique des Pasquier,* traces the career of a family whose pre–World War I origins were lower-middle-class, as its members rise to professional status in the arts and sciences against the background of a democratic, fundamentally humanistic society providing the necessary preconditions for the formation of a new elite. Jules Romains, adopting a Jaurès-style socialism, undertook in 1933 to describe the transformation of the collective imperatives governing manners and morals with their greater freedom and diversity, the modern social structures appearing between 1908 and 1933, and the new social types created as a result. Roger Martin du Gard was less optimistic. In *Les Thibault* he described the extinction, during the period just before the First World War, of a certain type of prominent Catholic bourgeois, the evolution of their progeny in scientific or literary careers beyond the pale of Catholicism, the demoralizing effect of this revolt against family and social constraint; and the destructive aftermath of the 1914–18 war, which almost no one in the family survives. In *L'Ame enchantée* (1922–33) Romain Rolland takes a woman, Annette Rivière, as his protagonist, breaking with the traditional social viewpoint of the novelists just discussed to excoriate bourgeois society for the inhumanity and selfishness that transform his heroine into a militant revolutionary and a Marxist. With this book the social fresco turned political. The new men of the 1920s generation— Aragon, Drieu La Rochelle, Paul Nizan—were even tougher on the middle class, and their list of bourgeois crimes was a long one: marriages made for money; women who were bigoted or mercenary; sparsely populated, disunited families carefully sheltering from reality the few children they did produce; bourgeois children overprotected to the point of helplessness, able to dream but never to act; "dreamworld bourgeoisie," perpetuating itself, coasting on its illusions, paying lip service to traditional virtues and high ideals while actually sunk in greed, dancing to the tune of the rich and powerful. These intellectuals believed the only salvation for the "disaffected bourgeoisie" lay in the path they themselves had followed: revolution through political commitment. It was political commitment—fascist according to Drieu, Marxist for Nizan and Aragon—that would wrest the bourgeoisie from its isolation by imposing upon it the model of a "new man" integrated into a utopian "new society."

The Marxist point of view was popularized by Emmanuel Berl in three successive works—*Mort de la pensée bourgeoise* (1927), *Mort de la morale bourgeoise* (1929), and *Le Bourgeois et l'amour* (1931)—and forcefully restated by Paul Nizan in *Les Chiens de garde* (1932). Here the problem of literature and social class is presented from a fresh perspective, one destined to predominate throughout the rest of the century. Berl, himself a member of the upper-middle class, wrote, "I believe that most of the ideas nourishing our literature are nothing but bourgeois rationalization. I further believe that as modern capitalism and communism dismantle the bourgeoisie, the power of these ideas will diminish proportionately." Two main themes dominated Berl's thinking: the decadence of the bourgeoisie, a privileged class incapable of finding a place for itself in the modern world; and, in terms of literature, the question of how to justify a culture that was the pride of this decadent social class. For Berl, most of this culture is simply the proving ground for the self-justifying myths of an exclusive social class. Jean Guéhenno, a man of the people, in *Caliban parle* (1929) describes the dilemma of an intellectual from a lower-class background who finds himself dedicated to a culture that separates him from his own class. Guéhenno voices alarm at the growing gulf between the masses and the bourgeoisie. In a judgment that is even harsher, Nizan accuses intellectuals of being the "watchdogs of the oppressors." The word "bourgeois" was beginning to take on vague connotations of "plutocrat" or "non-Marxist," and to designate an attitude rather than a social classification. At the same time "proletariat" was being substituted for "people," and this placed the working class in opposition as much to the peasantry and lower-middle-class merchants as to the capitalists and bourgeois industrialists. In their study groups, or "sections," an elite group of militant workers began to acquire the rudiments of a culture that had nothing to do with the classically oriented "general culture" dispensed in lycées.

Berl, Nizan, and Guéhenno were all making the same point: there was going to be a confrontation in France between two separate cultures, one descended by divine right on the middle class and expressed through the institutions of learning; the other slowly evolving among the workers and technicians of the modern world. All three authors accused the school system of being the source of the evil. This indictment of the educational system, begun earlier by Péguy, bore a relation to the condemnation of literary authority initiated by the *Premier Manifeste du Surréalisme*. It was subsequently to be increasingly linked with political criticism of the establishment.

According to Berl, the myth of womanhood and particularly of "maidenhood," central silhouette in the work of Giraudoux, which incarnated the bourgeois fantasy, constituted one of the most tenacious of all the bourgeois myths he attacked. The moral weaknesses and emotional conformism of the young, middle-class male formed the theme of another whole segment of literature that portrayed bourgeois youth as spoiled babies, a "hag-ridden," "weaker sex." Meanwhile, in contrast to this view, a new representation of womanhood reflecting social change was beginning somewhat timidly to appear. Margueritte's feminist novels, Gide's trilogy (*L'Ecole des femmes*, 1929; *Robert*, 1930; *Geneviève*, 1936), and Romain Rolland's *L'Ame enchantée* all describe middle-class women who demand their right to exist outside of marriage and who assert themselves by working for a living. The role of these heroines was to forecast social transformations still to come. In real life, French women were less active politically than the suffragettes in England, the United States, and Scandinavia: they were not allowed to vote, and when they married they were subject to a Napoleonic marital law that reduced their status to that of minors. To Berl, middle-class marriage was "just a financial agreement under another name."

Nevertheless, middle-class French women were beginning to achieve emancipation socially. In her *Mémoires*, Simone de Beauvoir gave us one example of how passionately a new generation of young women students devoted themselves to preparing for the unrestricted exercise of a profession. This determination to be independent was also demonstrated in the person of Simone Weil. Sexual taboos were slowly beginning to give way.

Flirting was replaced by the camaraderie described by Simone de Beauvoir, and parental surveillance of young women—parents' right to know every detail of every activity—diminished. Social taboos were more tenacious. The myth of the secretary who marries the boss, or of the poor boy who wins the heart and hand of an heiress, though dear to the then highly popular American film, had currency only in dime novels. The bourgeois themes of love, adultery, domestic drama and the "eternal triangle" nourished the brilliant and sophisticated plays of Sacha Guitry and were also the favorite themes of the *théâtre du Boulevard*. But in the serious novel these themes began to fade in importance and others to exercise an equal claim on the imagination: travel, sport, aviation, politics, war, revolution. There was a change of scene for literature as well as for society, both of which were coming out of the bedroom. Although the base for literature was still the bourgeois world, the question of a *worker's literature* now arose.

The problem of the working-class writer first made its appearance in about 1920. It was then that Henry Poulaille sought to gather other working-class writers like himself, from Paris and the provinces, around a review which would provide a forum unconstrained by the standards of the bourgeois literary "clan." In 1932, Poulaille's group launched the *Manifeste de l'Ecole prolétarienne,* endorsed by a half-dozen or so good novelists such as Charles Plisnier, Edouard Peisson, Tristan Rémy, Eugène Dabit, and others. The group also organized the first Exposition Prolétarienne. Poulaille used three criteria to define the proletarian writer: (1) he must be born into the proletariat; (2) he must be self-educated; and (3) he must be currently employed either as a blue- or white-collar worker or as a school-teacher. In other words, he must be someone who has remained close, not necessarily to the "working class" as described by Marx, but to "the people." He must be someone unaffected by the alienation denounced by Guéhenno. There was an important distinction, for the Proletarian School, between themselves and the *groupe populiste* formed in 1928–29 by Léon Lemonnier in reaction to "fashionable" literature. The latter group advocated a return to the realistic tradition portraying the "common man" as in Léon Frapié's *La Maternelle* (1904), or in the works of Charles-Louis Philippe. "We called ourselves populists," wrote Lemonnier, "because we believed the common man offered a rich, virtually untapped source of novelistic material." Poulaille and his group, on the other hand, wanted a literature rooted in the occupations, preoccupations, and avocations of the common man. In reality, writers like Eugène Dabit, Louis Guilloux, Jean Guéhenno, and André Chamson—men of the people who started out as populists—were fairly quickly assimilated by the "clan" of the literary intelligensia. But in 1928–29, Poulaille's group interacted frequently with Lemonnier's.

In a series of reviews including *Nouvel Age* (January–December 1931), *Le Prolétariat* (1933–34), and *A contre-courant* (1935–36), Poulaille published a wide variety of authors: Maiakovsky, Victor Serge, Upton Sinclair, Pio Baroja, Pasternak, and Zweig, cheek by jowl with Cendrars, Giono, Malraux, Ramuz, and Vildrac. In addition, writers affiliated with the group produced a number of novels, most of them autobiographical, following in the tradition of Marguerite Audoux, Charles-Louis Philippe, and Lucien Jean, and giving a striking picture of working-class life and its hardships. Pierre Hamp drew a sort of profile of "man's suffering through the sweat of his brow" in his descriptions of the trades by which the working man earns his living. In *Le Pain quotidien* (1930), *Les Damnés de la terre* (1935), *Le Pain du soldat* (1937), and *Les Rescapés* (1938), Poulaille described the life of a working-class family—his own—through the year 1920. Earlier than that, the working-class presence in literature had already declared itself with some force through Louis Guilloux's *La Maison du peuple* (1927), Tristan Rémy's *Porte Clignancourt* (1928), and Dabit's *Hôtel du Nord* (1929).

When the worker-writers group published their manifesto in 1932, it was a declaration against what they regarded as the negative orientation of the Russian Communist Party. The Kharkov conference of 1930, which brought to an end the great Russian literary effervescence of the twenties, had decreed literary expression to be the domain solely of intellectuals; once again the workers were consigned to their trades. Poulaille's group was not recognized by the conference as the literary pioneers of France; this recognition went to the militant bourgeois writers like Aragon. At the first congress of Soviet writers in 1934, the French Communist Party sent a group of bourgeois intellectuals to represent them: Jean-Richard Bloch, Louis Aragon, André Malraux, and Paul Nizan.

In fact, however, the contribution of the worker and populist groups was closer to that of establishment writers such as Duhamel, who created Salavin, than to that of someone like Aragon, whose image of the working-class world was highly idealized. The worker-writers and Duhamel painted the same picture of working-class conditions: constant uncertainty; fear of being laid off; fear of reprisals during strikes; the brutalizing process of physical labor; crowded living space with no toilet facilities; dark, foul-smelling corridors. Lives without hope and yet lives in which a sense of mutual loyalty, love for craft, and a certain contempt for money prevailed.

In the final analysis it was a physician, Céline, in *Voyage au bout de la nuit* (1932) and *Mort à crédit* (1936), who most forcefully denounced the misery of working-class Paris: shoddy construction in working-class suburbs where buildings started to fall apart even before they were occupied; overcrowding under hazardous health conditions; disease, alcoholism, ignorance, brutality, and filth; a great city growing haphazardly, abandoned to the real estate speculator and victimized by entrepreneurial greed. Jules Romains on the other hand, with an optimism shared by former worker Pierre Hamp, described in *Les Hommes de bonne volonté* the liberating effect of automation on the worker and the accompanying improvement in working conditions;

but neither had a profound vision of social change, any more than a communist like Aragon did. They saw increased freedom in improved living conditions and a bourgeois social structure made more flexible by upward mobility—a material well-being accessible to all. In this regard they were not so far from the ideas of the Front Populaire. André Malraux, for his part, located the great dynamic, significant, collective social movements of the period outside of France in China, Germany, and Spain.

Poulaille's initiative remained marginal, as did traditional regional literature with its fidelity to outmoded models. It was in Paris, the world of publishers and literary reviews, that reputations were made; a homogeneous environment, despite its political and social differences, that by and large addressed its appeal to the same fairly restricted public of the "cultivated" middle class and the "intelligentsia." For sociopolitical opinion the urban lower class and the increasingly large working class put their faith in mass circulation journalism. The younger generation, as a rule more interested in boxing and soccer than in politics, also developed an interest, through magazines, in cars and in the fledgling sport of aviation. Culturally, what people liked was film—films by René Clair, films starring Charlie Chaplin (especially *Modern Times*)—and popular songs by Maurice Chevalier and by Pills and Tabet: semipoetic, semisentimental, and sometimes slightly satirical.

In the provinces, the lower classes and peasantry were more isolated, remaining attached to traditional ways already abandoned to some extent by the younger generation. This no doubt explains that image of "peasant" France maintaining "French values" so dear to the mythmakers of the Right; and also the utopian denial of the modern world fueling the imagination of a Jean Giono or the hatred of a Céline. Meanwhile, Bernanos, exasperated by Catholic apathy in the face of social ills, angrily denounced "the pusillanimity of the self-righteous" and their spiritual indifference—all in the name of a Christian idealism that was quasi-medieval and extremely militant (1931).

Seen in terms of economics, the literature of the period was affected by the same factors as any other form of production: the inflation of the twenties was followed by the ever-worsening recession of the thirties. There was a decrease in demand and publishers brought out fewer titles in smaller editions. Literary trends reflected the general mood of the times as perceived in intellectual circles: the sophistication and brilliance, the aestheticism and outrage of the twenties subsided before the more philosophical sociopolitical concerns of the thirties. Although it did not predominate, the voice of a new breed of intellectual belonging to the people, whether in Paris or in the provinces, was heard. This voice challenged the "modernist" aestheticism of a Cocteau, as well as the investigations of a Proust or a Gide, with a taste for traditional, popular, humanitarian realism. But the most significant sociocultural event of the thirties was the adherence of an increasing number of intellectuals to the aesthetic doctrine of social realism formulated by Zdanov, based on the precepts of Lenin. Writers were transformed into political militants responsible to the party leadership for the sociopolitical tenor of what they wrote. It was thus that political orthodoxy entered the domain of literature.

5

A Social Mutation, 1936–70

The upheavals of the war years hardly affected the class structure of French society; the workers were still a class apart. But the bourgeoisie was shaken. The 1940 defeat, followed by two failed "revolutions," discredited the pre-war administration, whose members were dismissed almost to a man. "The former administration stands condemned in its entirety . . . In August 1940, not a single dignitary from the old government would have been safe in the streets," wrote André Géraud under the pseudonym "Pertinax" at the time of the 1940 debacle. The Vichy government was taken care of by the postwar purges. The bourgeoisie stood accused as the class of this governing elite. Its members were rebuked by Marc Bloch for having paralyzed France by remaining a "closed caste"; Pertinax accused them of having "dug France's grave" through lethargy and lack of patriotic spirit. But the new "pure, hard" France envisioned by the Resistance was compromised by the purges and political maneuverings at the time of the Liberation and afterward. It was nevertheless the upper layers of the bourgeoisie, the young businessmen, managers, and graduates of the Ecole Polytechnique, that provided the new personnel for the "plan" and got the country moving again economically. The France of 1945, unlike the France of 1920, was not governed by a gerontocracy. But tensions between the old structures and the new persisted.

The end of the war resulted in changes whose repercussions were felt by every social class in France, within the family initially and then as a gap, rather than a complete break, between the generations. Not until about 1950, however, did basic structural changes begin to be evident—stemming frequently from the country's wartime situation—heads of family away from home, material want, the creation of a new moneyed class through black marketeering, uncertainty concerning the future.

France, until 1945 a country with a low birthrate, after 1945 experienced a spurt in population growth due to legislation for the protection of the family: family allowances, social security, subsidies, credit. In 1963 France had a population of forty-seven million; in 1970 this had increased to more than fifty million. The first postwar "teen generation," born just after the war and maturing in or around 1965, made a decided impact on the country. Young, middle-class lycée and university students, especially in Paris, insistently demanded a new independence. But changes that were perhaps even more profound affected the workers and the peasants, still the two most distinct castes in terms of the country as a whole. In certain areas of activity, specifically the nascent agribusiness complexes, a new factor was the tendency of these two groups whose respective outlooks had once been antagonistic, to draw closer together. Agricultural workers were decreasing in number and so were industrial workers, although the latter still accounted for about one-third of the total population. New methods of so-called "postindustrial" business organization led to the development of two new social categories with much in common: technocrats and managers. Technology, besides transforming the conditions of everyday life, seemed at last capable of guaranteeing the worker first-class citizenship in a society that for so long had been marked "no entry."

The Peasants

The peasant class was disappearing. Stimulated by legislative measures and the demands of the Common Market, the trend away from one-family subsistence farming and toward large-scale land exploitation accelerated. The farm population decreased in numbers and changed in character. The peasants were better informed, joined collective associations, acquired modern machinery, and became farmers. Rural electrification in some areas meant modern conveniences for the farm: running water, refrigerators, bathrooms, radio, and television. Only a few isolated farms remained. Cars, radio, and television lessened the isolation of a rural population beginning to speak out and make known its aspirations: better education; an easier life; a larger and more direct share in decisions affecting its life.

The Workers

"I owe my birth to the Family Allowance," says the heroine of Christiane Rochefort's somewhat ironic novel *Les Petits Enfants du siècle* (1961). Her story of a working-class childhood illustrated the rapidity with which the long overdue transformations in working-class living conditions were effected. Moving from a "filthy room with the cold water tap on the landing" in Paris's thirteenth arrondissement to a "Residential Park for Large Families," where she occupies an apartment with inside bath, washing machine, three rooms, and a kitchen-living-room that she qualifies as "OK,"

Josyan at first, nevertheless, leads the hopeless life of the working-class ghetto, even there. But little by little things begin to open up: first there is a motor scooter, making other neighborhoods accessible; then a "magical 2 C.V." (a small, two-horsepower Renault) bought "secondhand and on credit"; and then the revelation of Sarcelles: "It was beautiful. Green, white. Neat . . . They did everything to make it nice; they asked: what do we have to do to make it nice? and then they did it . . . I stopped on the bridge one more time when I was leaving, I turned toward the Town . . . I couldn't get enough of it . . . Was it ever beautiful! I couldn't get enough." And then it's marriage with a young man of the new breed, an assembly-line worker who makes television sets, the "coming things"; a subsidy for the baby on the way, credit for buying furniture, the problem of where to live: "I told him about Sarcelles." This young working-class couple typifies the life style of a "new working class," better assimilated into the fabric of society, planning for the future, less political, with tastes, clothes, and leisure activities more consistent with those of the middle class. Instead of the old craftsmen, a new working-class aristocracy was appearing: these were the workers skilled in a technological specialty, and they were still in short supply in France, although demand for their services was increasing in new fields like electronics. In these areas, work methods were changing, and the relation between management and labor was changing along with them. There was a tendency for labor-management cooperation to replace the old adversary relation between worker and boss. A few isolated experiments in management by the work force introduced workers to the responsibilities of administration. As a result of general prosperity, French workers also benefited from social legislation and paid vacations (so hard won in 1936, going from two, to three, and then to four weeks), setting them apart from a new proletariat of immigrant workers with tenuous status. French workers were casting off the exterior signs of their class, such as the characteristic blue coverall or *bleu,* but they remained self-consciously outside of middle-class society. They were freer in gesture and language than their middle-class counterparts; they lived in the present, caught up in technological innovation, fascinated by the tremendous developments in space exploration, for example, or in electronics; in other words, they had more in common with the technocrats and cared little for the traditional forms of bourgeois culture.

The Old and the New Bourgeoisie

The middle class, under a continuous hail of attacks, grew in wealth and in numbers. It was this class that absorbed young people migrating from the country and found new employment for the small shopkeepers slowly but inexorably being displaced by modern marketing methods. The upper-middle class, securely anchored in its elite traditions and privileges, changed very little. The Association of Young Executives (Association de Jeunes Patrons), drawing its inspiration from new methods introduced by techno-crats and middle-management civil servants, frequently railed against the old ways and old hierarchies, but with scant success. Middle management *(les cadres),* whose numbers were on the increase, played a dynamic role in the transformation of bourgeois life. Practical rather than theoretical, open to change and comparatively relaxed, they were distinguished by their in-creased freedom from the old middle-class environment. In particular, the obsession with accumulating and preserving wealth, with husbanding and transmitting a material legacy, was in their case superseded by a taste for living life as fully and luxuriously as possible on salaries and credit. It was these young executives who, along with the workers, felt most at ease in the consumer society. They were the target for Georges Perec's novel *Les Choses* in much the same way as the working-class world had served as the object for Christiane Rochefort's irony.

Two New Forces: Women and "Youth"

In the absence of men, *women* had been forced to handle the problems of day-to-day existence during the Second World War as they had been during the First. In the Second World War they also participated actively in the Resistance, sometimes, like Marie-Madeleine Fourcade of the "Noah's Ark" network, as leaders. They were exposed to the same risks as the men were: deportation and torture. A woman like Simone Weil became exemplary through the intensity of her spiritual quest and the passion with which she lived to the death the drama of her time. In 1945, French women belatedly won the right to vote, and in 1946, thirty-nine women were seated in the National Assembly. Thus began an emancipation movement that developed only gradually. In 1949, anticipating by fifteen years a trend that was to become worldwide, Simone de Beauvoir in *Le Deuxième Sexe* examined the problem of woman in the context of a cultural mystification maintaining the myth of feminine inferiority for the benefit of men. The transformation of women's roles, symptomatic of profound social metamorphosis, though latent as yet, was on the way.

Youth, more than any other group in society on any level whatsoever, was affected by the events of the war and the Occupation. The scrupulous, lower-middle-class men and women of the materially deprived wartime cities of France had gone cold and hungry, and their children had suffered the consequences. The black market, a source of profit for the peasantry, had intensified class differences; but all young people were affected by the anguish, fear, and uncertainty surrounding them.

The brutal and contradictory reversal of learned values, due in 1940 to defeat and then to the tragic paradoxes of the Occupation and subsequent Liberation, were profoundly disconcerting. Also, slight differences in age changed the context for a given experience and prepared the ground for a swift metamorphosis in people's attitudes. To have been fifteen to twenty years of age in 1940 was to have successively experienced the most tragic events of the era and to have been tempted by the widest number of options. To have been less than fifteen years of age in 1940 was to have relapsed at age twenty from the heroic to the prosaic, often with the vague feeling of having missed out on a great destiny. Those who were young at the time of the 1940 defeat had turned toward their elders for moral guidance, but the generation of the Liberation turned away. Many were primarily aware of being the "children of Hiroshima." Hence their self-absorption, their "gang psychology," their predilection for violence cum melancholy and their haste to get on with real life. Hence also their manifest or implied scrutiny of the past, the sign of a progressively widening rift between the generations whose cultural repercussions are difficult to assess. The Saint-Germain-des-Prés phenomenon, lasting from 1944 to 1947, was symptomatic of the state of mind shared by the young bourgeoisie. Flocking to the Café de Flore and the Café des Deux-Magots, nerve centers from 1942 onward of the occupied-zone literary and *anticollabo* Tout-Paris, how delighted they were, in the midst of their confusion, to run into Jean-Paul Sartre, Simone de Beauvoir, occasionally Camus and Mouloudji, or Jacques Prévert and Raymond Queneau.

It was surely Boris Vian—brilliant trumpet player, passionate jazz lover, admirer of Duke Ellington and Louis Armstrong, amateur of bizarre automobiles, destined for premature death from cardiac failure—who best typified this generation and its alienation from its elders. Engineer, journalist, cabaret singer, playwright, novelist, as gifted as the young Cocteau of the twenties had been, Vian was moved by a destructive, macabre, and at the same time witty imagination, which he used against the "existentialist" pomposity currently in vogue. In *L'Equarissage pour tous,* the first of his three plays, he stripped warfare of its heroic aura, dismissing as unproved the case for both sides. The same casual contempt was evident in his provocatively entitled spoof *J'irai cracher sur vos tombes,* a parody in the style of the then popular American detective story which Vian passed off as a translation. The novel caused a sensation and became a best-seller. He composed five novels, from *Vercoquin et le Plancton* (1946) to *L'Arrache-cœur* (1953), that were symptomatic not so much of a sensibility in revolt as of one that was out of step with the tragic, metaphysical attitudes of the day; they were little read at the time. Twenty years later, Vian's novels were more in tune with a generation turning its back on the past.

Between 1944 and 1947, two cabarets, Le Tabou and La Rose Rouge, symbolized by Juliette Greco framed in her long, black hair and singing songs by Jacques Prévert (whose 1944 collection *Paroles* was a best-seller) to music by Joseph Cosma, seemed emblematic of an alliance between the group of "Resistance" writers that came out of the war and a new generation seeking more popular forms of expression. Semiliterary, semipopular songs by Prévert or making up Agnès Capri's repertory, styles of dress and casual boy-girl friendships seemed to indicate not so much a total break with the old middle-class tastes and values, as an evolution. The "golden age" didn't last long. Twenty years later, in his preface to a new edition of Nizan's *Aden-Arabia*, Jean-Paul Sartre criticized this generation of young people for having, in his words, turned themselves into living "corpses." But Sartre did not fully comprehend either them or the time they lived in. It was these young people who launched the existentialist vogue that made the name Jean-Paul Sartre famous in the first place, "under a misapprehension," write Guillaume Hanoteau, historian of the "golden age" of Saint-Germain-des-Prés, and certainly despite Sartre himself. And yet it was to this group that, for one thing, Paris owed the spirit of renewal informing the next decade of theatrical activity and the "new wave" cinema. For another, it was Saint-Germain-des-Prés that enabled Paris, from 1944 to 1947, to regain for a while her preeminent rank as intellectual and artistic capital of the West.

What Sarcelles had meant to Christiane Rochefort's young working-class woman was represented for the generation of the sixties by the "pretty pictures" of slick magazines, television, and advertising. This was the emancipated generation, enjoying more freedom than ever before in an urban setting. Films like *Les Tricheurs, Les 400 Coups,* and *La Chinoise* created a legend around a generation exposed to magazines such as *Paris-Match* that featured "brilliant young millionaires"—Françoise Sagan, Vadim, Brigitte Bardot—attaining stardom. From England, from the United States, came teenage styles that were tried out and taken over. In France as elsewhere, clothes, hairstyles, phonograph records, transistor radios, relations between the sexes—everything was meat for advertising, which was replacing the authority of the family. Teenagers had their own staging areas—Saint-Tropez, for example; their own radio programs; their favorite pop stars; their own jargon; and their drugs. They also had a new code of sexual behavior. The new conflict between generations did not, however, break out in the context of the family, as it had in the past and as it was still pictured in novels such as Hervé Bazin's *Vipère au poing* and *La Tête contre les murs.* It broke out in the universities, polarizing a generalized discontent which in 1968 shook the entire country badly, especially the intellectual community. In this new climate the need for less centralization and greater accessibility to cultural activities prompted various attempts at cultural decentralization: summer festivals in provincial capitals, the creation of provincial *maisons de culture* and art centers, with the implication that perhaps there would now be a new, freer, less academic conception of the function of culture in French daily life. Its fullest expression was to be found in Paris's Centre Beaubourg.

Institutions: The Church

Following the Spanish civil war, Catholic opinion in France split in two: the majority supported General Franco, considered to be the defender of Christianity against communism; the minority, which included Maritain and Bernanos, denounced *franquista* brutality and repression. Although a certain segment of the Catholic Right had been discredited once and for all by its participation in the Vichy government, those who had been led by feelings of patriotism into the ranks of the Resistance were many in number. The Church's response to the misery of the lower classes had been to encourage the social action movement initiated by Marc Sangnier. Catholicism was no longer, in the eyes of the people, the religion of the plutocrats.

Emmanuel Mounier and the review *Esprit*, little interested in theoretical debate, gained the adherence of young Catholics who demanded that the Church become more aware of its responsibilities in regard to the working class. They conceived of Christianity in terms of human community and protection of the individual. Their concern had much in common with that of priests who were worried about the "de-Christianization" of modern society. The social action movement was given additional impetus by the spectacle of wartime misery and the feelings of outrage it aroused in Christian consciences. The formation in 1940 of a group of worker-priests whose mission was to discharge their ministry while living as their fellow factory workers did was significant: its effect was to loosen the tie between Catholicism and the conservative middle class. Two Catholic asociations, the JAC (Jeunesse Agricole Chrétienne) and the JOC (Jeunesse Ouvrière Chrétienne), broke with the establishment and participated vigorously in the fight against the injustices of the sociopolitical system. In 1959 the Church put an end to the worker-priest movement, but this move did not lessen appreciably the doubts felt by young priests as to their proper role. A new breed of priest was beginning to make an appearance, exemplified by the hero of Béatrice Beck's *Léon Morin, prêtre*, a "far out" priest who did not equate sexuality with sin. A new religious viewpoint was on the way.

Toward the end of the fifties, another split became apparent in political and religious attitudes. A nascent and growing quest for spirituality was discernible, drawing its inspiration either from the religions of India or from the ideas of Father Teilhard de Chardin.

It was about 1950 that Pierre Teilhard de Chardin's ideas began to gain a hearing, especially with the posthumous publication of his most important work, *Le Phénomène humain,* in 1955. A paleontologist and geologist working for many years in China, Teilhard de Chardin had conceived a cosmic philosophy of evolution capable, he believed, of reconciling modern science with Christianity, and thereby of opening up a great future to mankind. Controversial though it was, Teilhard de Chardin's vision moved many young Christians with its breadth and optimism.

Vatican II, the council that met in Rome from 1962 to 1965, was obliged to take both of these trends into account. The extent of the council's accomplishment can be measured less by such basically conservative liturgical reforms as the substitution of French for Latin or the partial liberalization of the rules governing the conduct of the priesthood, and more by its ecumenical spirit—its rappochement with the churches of other Christian denominations. According to Jean-Marie Domenach, who succeeded Mounier at *Esprit,* the French Catholic Church in 1939 saw itself as a fortress to be defended against the double threat of secularization and communism. But after Vatican II the Church evolved—not without difficulty—toward a "new Christianity" open over a broader front to the modern world.

Reaching beyond the borders of France, the trend in religious attitudes seemed to reflect a vague anti-intellectualism and the kinds of affective needs associated with romanticism, but a romanticism denying its own antecedents.

Education

The action of Michel Butor's 1962 novel *Degrés* was set in the third-year class of a fictionalized Parisian lycée, the Lycée Taine. It was a challenge to the entire system of secondary education. Socially the preserve of the middle class, the Lycée Taine had no children of the working class among its students. Teaching methods—oral quizzes, memorization based on out-of-date textbooks, essays, compositions—perpetuated a régime of boredom, "a purgatory of platitude." Overcompartmentalization of subject matter drowned students under "an enormous mass of fact" that was without meaning and without purpose. There was no dialogue between teachers and students, the students' only motivation for working was fear of failure in the baccalaureate exam. Butor's diagnosis was harsh, but it was at least partly fair: society was changing, and intellectual horizons were changing with it; the educational system, however, was still subsisting on the myth of a general culture that supposedly represented the norm but actually could not.

Butor's voice was neither the first nor the only one raised in favor of educational reform. Such eminent thinkers as Lévi-Strauss (in *Tristes Tropiques*) and Jean-Paul Sartre repeatedly denounced the failures of the system in the course of recounting their own intellectual development. The democratization of education had already been discussed as far back as the twenties. Yet the fundamental principle of an educational system designed for the formation of an elite class and based on the study of French, Latin, and mathematics had not been called into question. Until 1939, more than 60 percent of all lycée students specialized in the classics. Textual analysis (*explication de texte*) combining language and literature was the keystone of secondary education. A feeling for literature was valued above all else. Education at the university level, accessible only to a small minority, emphasized teaching skills over research. Here, too, specialists in literature enjoyed the greatest prestige. Writers and their readers both, therefore, shared the same "universe of discourse" just as they did the same social sector and the same culture. It was this culture's role that was the problem, a highly controversial one. Was education transmitting a rich moral and aesthetic heritage to future generations? Or was it nothing but an outmoded instrument for maintaining without change a social system, a conditioning process disguised as an ethic?

The proliferation from 1945 onward of projects for educational reform was an indication of the problem's urgency. Fundamental reforms were proposed on all sides: complete democratization of education, decompartmentalization of subject matter; reorganization of schools as "total environments" with a basis in real life. At the university level, general education began to be superseded by scientific research training.

And yet, in his 1957 *Panorama des idées contemporaines,* Gaëtan Picon could still point to the archaic nature of the vast educational edifice: "The culture ... dispensed is still that of the old world. The new world makes only a timid appearance, in footnotes, in the small print of appendixes, in the optional courses offered outside the official program. [Students] ... learn their history from books glorifying the white race, heir to Greco-Roman humanism, civilizer of the barbarian peoples ... fine flower of universal democracy."

The old structures were dismantled after 1959 by thoroughgoing reforms. Abolishing compartmentalization, broadening access to higher education as well as course options at the lycée level and baccalaureate examination subjects, instituting technological specialties—these reforms completely overturned the traditional framework of primary and secondary education. The universities' turn came with the legislation of 1968: the number of French universities was increased; the divisions between disciplines and the five traditional faculties were done away with; team research was organized under the UER (Unités d'Enseignement et de Recherche); fresh priorities were set for new subjects—social science, linguistics and, in the natural sciences, technology—all of which tended to diminish the status and prestige of literature. These transformations coincided with an explosion in the school-age population resulting in increased enrollments and creating a degree of social and psychological tension that affected the entire country.

The 1968 uprisings originated in the universities of Paris, spread out to the provinces and into the lycées, and hastened the disintegration of the old system. This about-face took place in the midst of confusion. The ultimate goal—the dissemination of culture to every segment of society, increasing its effectiveness through modernization—was sometimes lost sight of in the confusion of the moment. But, although at times the object of bitter dispute, fundamental reforms were effected: an attempt was made to replace the ex cathedra lecture by independent research and two-way communication between student and professor; to replace the authoritarian discipline of the teacher by freedom of discussion and an appeal to students' own sense of responsibility; and to do away with strict selection procedures benefiting an elite minority, in favor of the intellectual development of the greatest possible number. Linguistics, sociology, and psychology were added to the basic disciplines of French and mathematics. Pilot programs were developed in "experimental schools" and "progressive universities." Regionalism replaced the centralization of the old system, a basic reform whose application was somewhat complicated by the addition of regional languages such as Basque and Breton to the study of French. An unexpected factor came into play: the politicization of various student and teacher groups, leftists of every persuasion, or orthodox Marxists whose major concern was to dismantle the cultural "superstructure" of the "bourgeois" elite. The transformation of the educational system, required by the demands of a society caught up in a process of accelerated modernization, could not help but have a profound effect on literary tastes and habits. The status of literature as the primary tool of culture was lost. Furthermore, the crisis in education was closely connected to the crisis in language.

The French Language: Evolution or Decay?

The viability of the French language had already been questioned following the First World War. At that point, however, the problem was seen primarily in terms of the role of French as a universal language, the expression of a great culture, and the vehicle for international exchange. The preeminence of French on this level was threatened by competition from English.

Internationally, the French language underwent an eclipse in 1945. Not without difficulty was French accepted as one of the four official languages of the United Nations. But by 1960 the international position of French had begun to improve. Decolonization gave fresh impetus to new nations adopting French as their official language. There was a simultaneous spread of French to other countries as the language of culture and international exchange. In 1962 the review *Vie et Langage* estimated the number of Francophones, or French speakers, to be 120 million worldwide; in the same year *Esprit* devoted its November issue to the future of the French language. By its very nature, however, this new status was enjoyed by a language no longer coinciding with the political unity of French nationhood—with France. In the Maghreb, as in Black Africa, the urge to promote a native cultural patrimony affected the dissemination of French. In the early 1950s, novelists from the Maghreb began to form a distinct school of their own, and when the first festival of Black African art was held in Dakar in 1966 there was doubt expressed as to the meaning of the traditional term "French literature." It was thus during the sixties that the concept of a Francophone community developed. The French language slipped from the grasp of an educational system concerned with transmitting it in its official acceptable form. As the French language spread, it also changed.

This change affected the language within France itself. During the fifties there was a real battle on the subject of the language's deterioration. Factors such as the massive introduction of foreign vocabulary, especially American, and imported idioms; the decline in spelling; grammatical weaknesses and errors of usage; and the fad for technical jargon—all were denounced in the attack on "Babelese" and "Frenglish." Radio, television, mass circulation journalism, and advertising employed a linguistic shorthand designed for the rapid communication of the greatest possible amount of currently relevant information. This required new words and a simplified syntax; also an accelerated evolution in the language, considered by some to be inevitable. In 1968, the Conseil International de la Langue Française and, in 1961, the AUPELF (Association des Universités Partiellement ou Entièrement de Langue Française), composed of forty-six Francophone universities, both seemed to express a desire at least to slow down the fragmentation of the language. For writers, the linguistic evolution created a serious problem, that of elite versus popular culture. In French cultural circles, "language" for three centuries had meant the language of literature. Among the cultivated, the distance between the written and the spoken language had been relatively slight. Now this distance was growing. Rare were the writers such as Raymond Queneau or Le Clézio who, in the tradition of Céline, could draw their material primarily from a vast reservoir of spoken language, creating a particular brand of literary language equidistant from both popular speech and the "cultivated" language of their readers. Writers, their language in the process of mutation, grappled with the problem of choosing the proper voice.

6
Literary Life

From 1920 on, the development of literary life revolved less and less around salons and cafés, more and more around major publishing houses, the literary reviews and series financed by them, and the increasingly numerous, decreasingly influential literary prizes that were given out every year. Actual literary life bore no resemblance to the ordered sequences presented by studies of literary history. It was enlivened by innumerable debates, investigations, and polemics, and by the publication of quantities of works destined for oblivion. Recent sociological studies show that 80 percent of all literary publications disappear within a year, and 99 percent within twenty years. But while even knowledge—invariably incomplete—of the relationship between literary production, best-sellerdom, and fashion may be important, the fact remains that works destined to occupy a place among the great masterpieces of all time are not subject to the laws of marketing; this kind of staying power is drawn from other sources. It is therefore difficult, when dealing with a recent historical period, to see one's way clear through an area which is all the more thorny in that the media instantly reflect every twitch in the political and economic fortunes of the country.

Publishing Houses between the Wars, 1920–36

Of the hundreds of extremely diversified French publishing houses, several dozen shared the literary sector among them. Most of the others—Calmann-Lévy, Armand Colin, Fasquelle, Flammarion, Garnier, Larousse, Albin Michel, Nathan—devoted a part of their huge production to literature, combining reprints of well-known works and "list" authors with the riskier publication of new works. They were the somewhat belated followers of literary trends. Other publishing houses specialized: for example,

Bloud et Gay in Catholic works; Editions Socialistes (after 1930) in Marxist works. Addressed to a limited public and ultimately intended as collectors' items were the privately printed editions of poets—the surrealists in particular—by poets: thus the G.L.M. Editions (Guy-Lévis Mano), justly renowned during the thirties.

Two publishing houses, and in terms of the literary movement two of the most representative, were founded before 1914 and shared the interwar market in young writers—especially novelists; both exercised considerable influence on literary tastes and reputations. Book lover and shrewd promoter Bernard Grasset, aiming for literary quality, but also for a larger reading public, launched almost every "comer" within a period of ten years. Some of his front-runners were Giraudoux, the four famous M's—Mauriac, Maurois, Montherlant, and Morand—Cocteau and Malraux when they were just starting out, and also Radiguet. Gallimard, an offshoot of the *Nouvelle revue française (NRF)*, less daring, more austere, made its name a hallmark for excellence, often by picking up an author already discovered and published by Grasset (as with Proust) or by some other prospector after the author's value had become established, and also by giving space to poets. Beside these two, but less powerful than they, houses such as Kra or Denoël catered to the more revolutionary trends—surrealist in the case of Kra or, as in the case of Denoël with *Voyage au bout de la nuit,* totally out of the ordinary. Among the titles published by other houses such as Stock or Plon were novels in translation.

In order to stay afloat, publishers were constantly looking for gimmicks. The literary explosion brought with it a profusion of collected editions of all kinds; "notebooks" *(cahiers),* which appeared periodically anywhere from once a month to three times a year; and "notes" and "papers" under the general editorship of eminent personalities and directed toward various segments of the reading public. Every publishing house had its own series. At Grasset, Les Cahiers verts, edited by Halévy, were an attempt at continuing Péguy's *Cahiers* and contained essays (or essay-novels) like Malraux's *La Tentation de l'Occident;* while Les Ecrits, edited by Jean Guéhenno, launched socially significant novels and research. Kra published a series of "panoramas" covering contemporary foreign literature of various kinds. Under the direction of Maritain and Massis, Le Roseau d'Or at Plon published primarily Catholic writers. Some of these publications reflected deep-seated antagonisms, as in the case of the two great rival groups, the Catholic Roseau d'Or and the liberal, Protestant *Nouvelle revue française.* All were more or less affected by the depression of the thirties.

Two initiatives taken by Gallimard in the thirties are worthy of note. One, the Bibliothèque de la Pléiade, through its format and its discreet but uniformly distinctive presentation of a body of work usually reserved for the critical edition, made accessible in compact form, first the great classic French literary texts of all time, and then the "modern classics." This was a continuation of the Editions de la Pléiade created by Jacques Schiffrin, who in 1930 had launched a "hardback series" and inaugurated it with the collected works of Baudelaire edited by Y.-C. Le Dantec.

The Pléiade editions subsequently also accepted foreign "classics" in translation. Another series inaugurated in 1930 was the Bibliothèque des Idées, which presented in relatively low-priced editions such works as Spengler's *The Decline of the West* and even doctoral theses formerly accessible only to specialists. The dividing line between academic erudition and a love of letters was beginning to blur. There were strong repercussions in the field of literary criticism, which until this time had been led by a brilliant group of Parisian men of letters. Henceforward, this breed of literary critic was doomed to extinction; on the other hand, especially after the hiatus created by World War II, academic scholars participated increasingly and uninterruptedly in the presentation of literary texts and the dissemination of critical methods.

One theme predominated in this chaotic picture; a fundamental agreement on literary values and on their precedence over questions of fashion and sales. There was a sense of cultural community, of respect for the literary hierarchies, and a broad acceptance of literature from foreign countries. Examples of the latter were two neighboring bookstores on the Rue de l'Odéon, Adrienne Monnier's Les Amis du Livre and Sylvia Beach's Shakespeare and Company: both served as meeting places for literary personalities—French, European (particularly British), and American; old and young mingled, argued, browsed, and purchased the latest books, some of which, like James Joyce's *Ulysses,* were not only sold by the two stores but published by them as well.

The Heyday of the Periodical

As in the past, literary columns in the large dailies, signed with respected names—Paul Souday in *Le Temps,* Henri Régnier in *Le Figaro,* André Salmon in *L'Intransigeant*—informed a fairly clear-cut public on topics of current literary interest. But the prestige of the daily column was on the decline. The literary weekly, on the other hand, in the period between World War I and World War II, flourished and then foundered, but provided a transition between the two eras. The literary weekly was based on the proposition that modern journalistic techniques could be placed at the service of literature, thus bridging the gap between great literature and a broad public. In 1922, Roger Martin du Gard launched *Les Nouvelles littéraires,* a "literary, artistic, and scientific" weekly in which literature predominated. The format of the literary weekly differed from that of the literary review; the former's headlines were larger, and more space was devoted to current events and documentary features. The weeklies published short new works and brief articles informing readers on events of literary interest: award presentations and the commemorative centenaries and semicentenaries that were celebrated as a ritual.

The literary weeklies also contained news articles and, starting in 1924 under the heading "An Hour with . . .," Frédéric Lefèvre's famous "Entretiens" with prominent writers. The "literary lion" had been born, and information about him began to replace articles of literary criticism. *Les Nouvelles littéraires* spawned imitators. Swiftly becoming political , it was nonetheless on novelists—Pierre Benoît, Mauriac, Vicky Baum, Bromfield, Faulkner, Hemingway—that all of these weeklies ultimately depended for success.

At the height of their popularity, the circulation of literary weeklies fluctuated between 150,000 and 300,000, proof that a public eager for fresh information concerning cultural events existed. With the exception of the *Figaro littéraire* and the *Nouvelles littéraires*, however, none survived the Second World War. Although foreshadowing new directions in literary journalism, the literary weeklies, regardless of their individual political bias, stood squarely in the groove of established literature, as the names appearing in them most frequently indicate: Edmond Jaloux, André Billy, Albert Thibaudet, Benjamin Crémieux, René Lalou, Ramon Fernandez, Robert Kemp—men of letters all, and arbiters of taste.

Periodicals and Groups

Periodicals were many and various. The *Nouvelle revue française,* whose prestige increased right up until 1939 (when it had a circulation of twenty thousand) was the one that, through its political orientation and the writings it presented, best defended and best represented the predominant spirit of the time. After World War II the *NRF* reaffirmed its purely literary principles of selection, which were exempt from "political, utilitarian, or theoretical" influence, and steadfastly maintained its place in the center of the literary movement, forming rather than informing its readers. Dedicated to the "belles-lettrist" conception of literature and to high culture, the *NRF* lost its preeminent position following the political hiatus of 1936.

Given the perspective of time we can see that it was in reviews such as *Le Minotaure* that the new, if as yet unsure, literary trends first came to light. There they sustained a current of thought that undermined more definitively than surrealism had done the idea of "great literature" and "high culture" on which, basically, literary life rested. When the literary world, under pressure of events, began drifting toward politics, the editors of *Le Minotaure* were engaged in a stimulating investigation into the psychological sources of expression through form, especially plastic form, drawing on Freud and surrealism, ethnology, and the history of art. In the thirteen issues put out by *Le Minotaure* there appear, next to the name of Breton, those of Jacques Lacan, Michel Leiris, Georges Bataille, Pierre Klossowski, and

Roger Caillois. The work undertaken by this group burst through the boundaries of traditional frames of reference, both literary and critical.

The word "review" implies a coterie, or a "group." The number of intellectually active, antagonistic, disputatious, controversial literary groups was large, and each one had its own characteristic bias. The NRF group, headed by André Gide, distinctive for its austerity and its "Protestant" brand of liberalism, earned the antagonism of the dogmatic and conservative rightist Catholic group whose spokesman was the critic Henri Massis. More ephemeral and with links to prewar literary and artistic Bohemia was the somewhat frivolous literary circle that gravitated around the strange personality of the poet Max Jacob; Jean Cocteau, meanwhile, freely circulated among all the groups, from the Boeuf sur le Toit, to Jacques Maritain's Thomist salon, to the NRF.

Aloof and distant, the personality of Romain Rolland dominated the group of "committed" leftists whose outstanding member was Henri Barbusse and whose major outlets were the reviews Clarté and Europe. The discreet Brambilla Club gathered, around critic Edmond Jaloux, writers such as Paul Morand and Jean Giraudoux who shared a taste for romanticism.

But it was the young surrealist platoon, drawn up behind their leader André Breton, that introduced a new phenomenon into the literary scene: this was the "collective," a sort of commune whose principle weapon was intransigence, whose members were united by shared dogma and imposed discipline, and whose controversial and disputatious development had repercussions that were felt on virtually every level of French literature. It is worth noting, however, that groups whose sole concern during the thirties was literature, tended to lose ground in favor of groups with a literary and political bias, such as Action Française and the Front Populaire.

The Literary World and the War: 1936–52

The series of political events that occurred between 1936 and 1952 badly shook the intellectual conscience of the French. Both the bombing of Guernica, its horror immortalized in Picasso's painting, and the bombing of Hiroshima, whose psychic resonances Resnais attempted to capture on film, also had an impact on literature. The anguish caused by the global dimension of these events lent a note of similarity to literary works of divergent origins. There was a split in the literary world; literary personalities began to make their political affinities known. Criteria of a purely literary nature, which until then had prevailed despite political differences, were discredited.

During the years of the Occupation, two opposing literary worlds coexisted, each increasingly closed to the other. To their honor, many intellectuals succeeded through their writings and their actions in maintaining a climate of critical independence that opposed facile submission. To their dishonor, many intellectuals—occasionally although rarely the same ones—placed their prestige at the service of hatreds that were murderous. The reprisals that followed the real or imagined betrayals of the "collaborators" maintained around all intellectuals a pervasive aura of discredit. In 1940 an entire segment of contemporary French literature—the works of Proust, Gide, the surrealists—had been accused of undermining the moral fiber of the nation and facilitating defeat. Actively, in occupied France, less actively, in the unoccupied zone under the Vichy government, writers and literary works were prosecuted for reasons—race, politics—that were not literary. In 1944 the same thing happened all over again, but the criteria were reversed. It was thus in terms of a political context that writers identified their friends and their foes, and that reassessments of literary value were made and then promptly opposed.

Gradually, between 1948 when Mauriac called for reconciliation and 1951 when Jean Paulhan attacked the excesses of the postwar purge in his *Lettre aux dirigeants de la Résistance,* the inquisitorial climate changed. The unity of the "Republic of Letters" was regained only with difficulty. But there had been no *literary break,* properly speaking, with the past. The predominant attitude in books and articles written at this time was of a strengthened feeling among French intellectuals concerning the continuity of French culture and its humanistic, universal, exemplary values. Two factors characterized French literary life under the Occupation: decentralization and the vigor with which writers struggled against the problems that beset them in order to preserve France as a "great intellectual nation."

Decentralization: 1940–45

First the mobilization and then, to an even greater extent, the exodus and the Occupation dislocated the French literary world, scattering French writers to the four corners of the globe. Many went into exile in Switzerland, London, the United States, Mexico, Brazil, or Argentina; many into German camps as prisoners of war or deportees; later, writers who had collaborated with the Germans emigrated in the wake of the retreating German army. Some went to North Africa, mainly to Algiers, or fought with the Free French under de Gaulle. In France, Paris was at first deserted and then again became a pole of attraction drawing, on the one hand, a group of writers openly collaborating with the Germans or remaining neutral and, on the other, the group that played the double game of clandestine activity and that in 1943 formed the Conseil National des Ecrivains. The Parisian cultural sector continued to be brilliantly active under the patronage of the German fraternization policy: there were endless concerts and lectures; the theater, though subject to censorship, the opera, and film were the last refuge in France of some semblance of life. Fashionable theater was dominated by the popular Sacha Guitry during the years between 1940 and 1945, and a rich crop of brilliant plays was produced besides: Jean-Louis Barrault's production of *Le Soulier de satin* (1943), the première of *La Reine morte* (1942), *Les Mouches* (1943), *Huis clos* (1944), and Anouilh's *Antigone* (1944). After the Liberation of Paris, *Le Malentendu* (1944) followed by *Caligula* (1945) and Genet's *Les Bonnes* (1947) heralded a new wave of playwrights; and, dazzled by Giraudoux's posthumous play *La Folle de Chaillot* (1945), Paris was also reminded of the former generation's merits.

In the unoccupied zone (or *nono* as it was called), which at least until November 1942 was less subject to Nazi surveillance, definite literary "regions" formed: on the Mediterranean coast, with active centers at places like Aix, Marseille, and Villeneuve-lès-Avignon; at Lyon, which became the capital of intellectual Resistance in the South, as it was of the whole Resistance movement in the South. After 1945, Paris skimmed off the cream from these groups, though certain centers persisted—at Saint-Paul-de-Vence, for example, and at Lyon—for several more years.

The Literary Resurgence in France and Abroad

After the shock of defeat and an instant of hesitation, writers almost everywhere began to react. Censorship and anti-Jewish decrees eliminated an entire segment of literature from the official circuit. Although the Germans did not oppose the dissemination of Irish literature—authorizing Roger Blin's productions of Synge, for example—Jewish writers (Kafka, Freud, and Marx) were banished along with the Anglo-Americans, as noted by Pierre de Lescure in the Editions de Minuit manifesto (1942): "No more Meredith, Thomas Hardy, Katherine Mansfield, Virginia Woolf, Henry James, Faulkner, and all the others we love. Don't put any more Shakespeare, Milton, Keats, or Shelley in your bookstore windows, no more English poets or novelists of any era, so decrees the Syndicat des Libraires, under orders from Propaganda." In Paris, writers who were not pro-German remained silent, leaving the floor open to those who were collaborationist. In the unoccupied zone the official Vichy line—return to the classical tradition—discredited Jewish writers, "leftist" writers, or those who, like Gide, were considered "decadent." It was this official policy of the collaborationists, their newspapers, and their magazines that impelled the intellectuals to speak out. Starting a review, as René Tavernier did in Lyon with *Confluences* (thirty-four issues from 1941 through August 1944), devoted to publication of French literary texts of the highest quality, was the same thing as defending the integrity and dignity of French thought. In Algiers, Max-Pol Fouchet published *Fontaine* to fill the gap left by the *Nouvelle revue française* when it went over to the collaborationist side under its new editor Drieu La Rochelle. Later, again in Algiers, came *L'Arche* and *La Nef*. Suspicion was less easily aroused by poets, who were quick to organize. In Villeneuve-lès-Avignon, Pierre Seghers launched *Poésie*

40; Jean Lescure published *Messages,* and Nöel Arnoud *La Main à plume* editions. This literature, by its very existence, testified to freedom of thought, passing from intellectual Resistance to Resistance, period. In 1942 Pierre de Lescure and Vercors (Jean Bruller) founded the Editions de Minuit, which published texts that were openly resistant; and in Paris, at the end of the year, *Lettres françaises* brought the majority of Resistance writers together under one masthead.

Survival was fairly difficult for these publications, even though they suffered less harassment than the political broadsides and military liaison papers such as *Libération* and *Combat,* to which the same writers sometimes contributed. The scarcity of paper, censorship, seizure by the police of whole issues, distribution and communication problems, the danger of recognition despite pseudonyms, and the risk of deportation all demanded from these "Resistance writers" an extraordinary expenditure of energy. Many led a double life: fighting for the underground, like Malraux, Chamson, or Char; writing for the underground, like Paulhan, Camus, Aragon, or Roger Vailland; and, like deported poet Robert Desnos, sometimes dying for the underground. Under conditions such as these, every word counted.

Literary networks sprang up almost everywhere around literary personalities—sometimes foreign ones—and around reviews. In London *La France libre,* edited by Raymond Aron, took political questions as its primary concern; in Switzerland *Les Cahiers du Rhône,* edited by Albert Béguin and H. Hauser, was steadfastly literary, as was *Lettres françaises,* edited in Argentina by Roger Caillois. New York was the refuge for Jules Romains, André Maurois, Maritain, Julien Green, Saint-Exupéry, and, somewhat later, André Breton. One publishing house—Les Editions de la Maison Française—and one school, the Ecole Libre des Hautes Etudes, where scholars such as Focillon, Gustave Cohen, and Lévi-Strauss taught, kept French intellectual life going in New York. The distribution of French books was handled by Canada. Bernanos launched his appeals to the French conscience, which he eloquently defended, from Brazil. Contact with metropolitan France was established clandestinely, with publications circulating, for example, from Paris to London and then being parachuted back into France like weapons—which happened to Eluard's poem "Une seule pensée" ("Liberté"). From the literary point of view, this was no time to innovate or destroy. The values and historical continuity of a culture represented and safeguarded by its writers had to be maintained.

The Purge

When it came, the literary purge, even today a matter of controversy, was harsh: many writers were sentenced to death (Brasillach the most notorious), to jail, or to public ignomy. Those guilty, or under suspicion, of collaborating now fled from France in their turn: Drieu La Rochelle took his own life; Céline went to prison in Denmark. During the months of September and October 1945, the Comité National des Ecrivains placed a ban on the works of about one hundred writers, among them Giono, Montherlant, and Morand. Now it was their books' turn to disappear from bookstore windows. Also falling under the ban were reviews and newspapers that had either collaborated or remained neutral, and these disappeared from view as well; allocation of scarce paper reserves passed into the control of the Resistance. A vacuum of sorts developed in the world of literature. The "new" writers coming out of the Resistance were determined to give literature a new identity. This is the context in which Sartre raised the question of politically *committed* (engagé) literature, and undertook the task of redefining the position and responsibilities of the writer.

A Reordering of Values

Between 1945 and 1952 an imperceptible reordering of values occurred. The great generation of writers born around 1870 was shrinking: Paul Valéry died in 1945, André Gide in 1951, the same year as Alain. The two last great representatives of that generation, Colette and Paul Claudel, followed in 1954 and 1955 respectively. Jean Giraudoux and Antoine de Saint-Exupéry both died in 1944. An ailing Bernanos abandoned the novel, as Duhamel and Mauriac had done, in favor of the political essay. Martin du Gard had fallen silent; Breton, back from America, did not regain his old authority; Jules Romains even less so. Brasillach and Drieu La Rochelle were out of the picture for good; Montherlant and Giono for the time being. The gap was filled by Aragon and Eluard, André Malraux, Sartre and Camus, who dominated the literary, and what appeared to be the political, scene. In the relative vacuum of the immediate postwar period, three new periodicals were launched: *Les Temps modernes,* edited by Sartre and his group; the *Table ronde,* under the direction of François Mauriac; and *Critique,* edited by Georges Bataille. These periodicals, of differing tendencies, were an indication either of new directions in critical thought and literary perspective or, as in Bataille's case, of the frank expression of a small coterie's ideas, ideas that had been in the process of development ever since the twenties and that were opposed to existentialist thought. These differences were a sign that the unity *Les Lettres françaises* had hoped to create was at an end.

A Temporary Disruption: Publishing from 1936 to 1952

Literary life was dominated by the Second World War, which also conditioned its attitudes. When defeat had become a certainty, the overriding literary criteria became patriotism and concern for the nation's traditions; the avant-garde subsided, disappeared, or went underground. Attempts to recreate literary life in France were sporadic until 1944. To fill the gap caused by the hardships that the great Parisian publishers experienced (scarce paper supplies, censorship), French publishing houses were established abroad: Editions de la Maison Française in Canada and New York; Editions Fontaine in Algiers. The most active center of French publishing during the war was located in Switzerland with the Editions de la Baconnière, Ides et Calendes, and Egloff (LUF). After the Liberation, when Paris once again became the center of literary publishing, the divisions among publishing houses had changed.

Gallimard, most of whose influential authors had been connected with the Resistance, survived the vicissitudes of the war years and published "new" writers like Sartre and Camus along with the old; other houses, like Grasset and Denoël, compromised by their political affiliations, were managed temporarily after 1944 by judicial administrators. In this partial vacuum new publishing companies made their appearance, some of them a product of the Resistance. Forced into a confrontation with the problems of the postwar period, they had to create individual images. Four were successful in doing so: three—Seghers, Les Editions de Minuit, and Julliard—by becoming highly specialized; and the fourth, Les Editions du Seuil, by choosing the opposite course and becoming known for determined diversification. With his review *Poésie* (1940–44), Pierre Seghers had created a communications center at Villeneuve-lès-Avignon for poets living in the unoccupied zone. When the war was over, he added to it the Poètes d'Aujourd'hui, a relatively inexpensive pocketbook series in a modern format combining more or less reliable basic information with a critical text and a selection of poems. The initial volumes in the series were devoted to the Resistance poets—Eluard, Aragon—and to Max Jacob, a victim of the Occupation; but starting with volume four, Seghers showed great eclecticism. The success of this formula encouraged Seghers to publish "collections" of other kinds, but his name was always primarily associated with his efforts to popularize the work of poets.

Les Editions de Minuit, founded in 1942 and famous as an underground publisher, fell upon hard times when the Liberation came; but after publication of Samuel Beckett's *Molloy* (1951), and powered by the energy of editor Jérôme Lindon, it got its second wind with the acquisition of virtually exclusive access to a group of contemporary unknowns, the *nouvelle vague* novelists of the fifties. Julliard, whose standards were less stringent than Gallimard's, opened its doors to young novelists of the immediate postwar period such as Françoise Sagan. But Editions du Seuil, propelled by a group of *nouveaux critiques* (including Claude-Edmonde Magny and Jean-Pierre Richard), was the publishing house that between 1945 and 1947 got off the mark the fastest. First by launching its Pierres Vives series and then its Esprit series, and by reviving Albert Béguin's Cahiers du

Rhône under the direction of Dominique Rolin and novelist Jean Cayrol, Editions du Seuil transformed the topical series—literature, music, travel, Third World—into the tool of an enterprise embodying the fresh intellectual trends of the postwar period. It was Editions du Seuil, for example, that published the early works of what later became the *Tel Quel* group.

Among the weeklies, only *Les Lettres françaises,* originally a journal for Resistance writers founded in 1942 by Jean Paulhan and Jacques Decour, was appreciably long-lived (1947–72). In nineteen issues published clandestinely during the war, it brought together a vast array of names: Mauriac, Valéry, Duhamel, Camus, Eluard, Leiris, Sartre, Vercors, Benda, Martin du Gard, Malraux. Its editorials, reviews, and poems were patriotic. Its literary criticism showed little concern for other criteria. Falling under communist editorship in 1946, *Les Lettres françaises* perfectly exemplified the problem of the relation between literature and politics. Until 1953, when Louis Aragon took over as editor, the literary criticism in *Les Lettres françaises,* faithful to the hardening party line and the Jdanov directives, was totally partisan and depressingly mediocre.

Politically anti-German, but also literary in the tradition of the *NRF,* reviews such as *Confluences, Fontaine,* and *L'Arche* did not survive, and neither did several other new literary reviews, among them the excellent quarterly *Cahiers des saisons* or the more luxurious *Cahiers de la Pléiade* (1946–52), devoted to the work of young writers. Three periodicals attempted to fill the void left by the temporary suspension of the *NRF,* which reappeared in 1953 under the title *Nouvelle nouvelle revue française,* before reverting in 1959 to its original title. Under the influence of Mauriac, the *Table ronde* (1948–69) tried to confine itself to the publication of literary criticism and new works; but it was not able to maintain standards and before it eventually disappeared it resorted to putting out special numbers and publishing articles on social problems. The concern for pure literature almost completely disappeared from *Les Temps modernes* and *Critique,* the two most representative reviews of the period. Concentrating its efforts on the relation between literature and collective social reality, *Les Temps modernes* attempted, during the early years of its existence, to provide moral and political direction to a younger generation badly shaken by the war. *Critique* tended toward the esoteric—with Bataille leading it on an exploration into the psychological roots of art and the relation between art and religion. Both periodicals protested against the narrow categories in which literature had been enclosed, extending the concept of literature to forms of expression from which it had previously been excluded. Aesthetic criteria had no place in their analyses, which were based on new ways of looking at writing.

Political events had a decisive impact on the interrelations making up the literary world. At the same time, the giants of the prewar period were disappearing. The small coterie, bound together by politics and past friendship, like Sartre's group, or the larger but less tolerant communist group, dominated the literary life of the era.

But the beginnings of a more normal literary life were there. Reviews that had been suppressed under the Occupation reappeared under slightly different titles: *La Revue (des Deux Mondes)*. In 1950 the atmosphere began to change. Two works, Raymond Dumay's *Mort de la littérature* and Julien Gracq's *La Littérature à l'estomac* denounced the inflation of literary reputations and the mediocrity of a literature that had become totally "existentialized." In December 1948, a group of young communist intellectuals launched a new review, *La Nouvelle critique,* whose attitudes—concern for accurate information, and particularly for theoretical experimentation— were harbingers of the intellectual trends to come. Literary criticism occupied relatively little space in this journal, compared to film, theater, and the other arts. Political commentary predominated. But the rigor of *La Nouvelle critique*'s analyses undermined *Les Lettres françaises,* which suffered in comparison. New avenues of literary criticism had been opened up that embodied a new concept: using the periodical as a tool for collective research and a systematic theoretics. In April 1949 the short-lived journal *Empédocle* (edited by Jean Vagne with Albert Béguin, Albert Camus, and René Char) attempted to return to the concept of a literary review devoted primarily to new works. Book, art, and film notes, plus a column entitled "Aujourd'hui," represented only about one-fifth of the total. And at Saint-Paul-de-Vence in 1951, in protest against political literature and reaffirmation of the need for renewal, the review *Roman* (edited by Pierre de Lescure and Célia Bertin) made a demand for the autonomy of literature. A turning point was soon to appear; after 1952, a newly centralized literary life began to pick up speed.

New Directions: 1952–70

Publishing changed radically in order to adapt to a new public and to the methods and techniques of *marketing,* a word imported from the United States along with the thing itself. Publishing was affected by two crucial factors. Systematic studies of the book market based on surveys, statistics, and computer data (like the one undertaken at Bordeaux by a research team headed by Robert Escarpit) cast a new light on all aspects of bookselling. They showed, first, that mass production had created a crisis in the book trade. Joining the ranks of traditional literary themes was the book as an object of mass consumption. There was a tendency in the sixties for publishing houses to merge and to become internationalized. Three groups predominated: the Hachette group absorbed Grasset, Fayard, and Stock, and controlled 70 percent of trade publishing. The Presses de la Cité absorbed Plon and Julliard. Hachette's erstwhile partner Gallimard, finding itself once more at liberty, bought out Le Mercure and took over Denoël (which had itself taken over J.-J. Pauvert). An enterprise like Editions Bordas typified the new directions in publishing during the sixties, with its vigorous expansion into every sector of the industry, an expansion that could conceivably have been jeopardized by the crisis of 1973–74.

Second, and as a result of the above, the pocket-sized paperback *(livre de poche)* created a real revolution after 1952, eventually saturating the market. The formula had already been tried in France back in the twenties, by Fayard with its Livre de Demain series, by Flammarion, and by Armand Colin, but pocketbooks didn't really get off the ground until the appearance of the two great pocket series Le Livre de Poche and J'ai Lu (Librairie Générale Française), followed by the Union Générale d'Edition series 10/18 (Presses de la Cité). By 1970, more than thirty publishing houses were putting out one or several familiar paperback series. Aimed primarily at the student market, collections of literary and critical texts in pocket format, and even pocket-sized reviews, became commonplace: Les Ecrivains de Toujours (Seuil); pocket poets, and along with them pocket plays, films, and dictionaries (Seghers); Idées (Gallimard); and at Presses Universitaires de France, the vast, encyclopedic series Que Sais-je? and the Twentieth Century Classics. These critical anthologies were often edited by academic scholars and included preface, notes, and bibliography. With few exceptions— Editions Sociales, which was Marxist, being one—the choice of texts and the image this choice conferred on the series as a whole was determined solely on the basis of commercial considerations. Personal antagonisms and preferences were being replaced by market competition. Even bookstores began to look different, modernizing their appearance to conform with the changed appearance of books that had been transformed by new techniques of printing and illustrating: bright colors, bold typefaces. Books broke into the drugstore and supermarket chains. Conventional bookstores, especially in the provinces, had trouble surviving.

The one certain beneficiary of this explosion would seem to be popular familiarity with literature. Paperbacks inform and instruct, but without the didactic tone and tedium of the abridged text or "selected pieces" found in schoolbooks. Apart from required readings for school, however, the public tended to prefer nonliterary lines such as Planète, Petite Planète, or Poche Noire. This put new literary works trying to find a public at a disadvantage. In order to be published in a paperback line with a first printing of tens of thousands of copies, a book had to have some chance of surviving and continuing to attract a public that sometimes, as in the case of Boris Vian, for example, was slow to materialize. Publishing a book by a young unknown became a risky venture, a matter of prestige, a luxury rather than the publisher's primary function. As a result, paperback publishers tended to specialize. For a dozen years or so Les Editions de Minuit provided a home for the strongest literary group of the period, the "new novelists": Beckett,

Nathalie Sarraute, Robbe-Grillet, Claude Simon. Les Editions de Minuit assumed the role of talent scout and promoter once filled by Grasset and Gallimard in its early days. Ten years later, Maspéro had become the main publisher for the unorthodox political Left, Pauvert for the erotic and the esoteric. After 1960 a strong center of French publishing developed in Montreal—Editions Parti-pris, Editions du Jour, Presses de l'Université de Montréal; followed by Editions Naaman (Quebec and Ottawa), and Editions de l'Université Laval (Quebec). Others began to appear in Africa (Yaoundé), following in the footsteps of Présence Africaine and specializing in the publication of Francophone literature produced outside the "hexagon."

The development of *periodicals* seems to have been effected by three factors: the proliferation of books; the increase in scholarly works dealing with modern literature; and the international component in their subscription lists. The financial underpinning for reviews was provided by university library subscriptions, most of them American and sometimes accounting for up to 50 percent of the total number of copies printed. As a result, the character of the literary review changed. Reviews gradually accumulating on library shelves became reference books, documents rather than mediums of exchange, their original contributors reaching only a limited immediate public. Circulation was therefore somewhat byzantine.

Despite various attempts *(Carrefour, Gazette des lettres, Figaro littéraire, Arts,* later *Arts-Spectacles),* the literary weekly disappeared. General-interest weeklies, notably *L'Express* and the *Nouvel observateur,* assumed the role of intermediary in relaying current news quickly to the public. In general, commercial magazines of all kinds, from luxurious *Réalités* to *Paris-Match,* did much the same thing. When the literary review survived, it still did not thrive.

When the *Nouvelle (nouvelle) revue française* reappeared on January 1, 1953, its masthead bore the names of a recognized, long-established crew: Saint-John Perse, André Malraux, Léon-Paul Fargue, Henry de Montherlant, Jean Schlumberger, Maurice Blanchot, Jules Supervielle. The intention was to continue doing what the *NRF* had always done: present the best current literary texts available. The magazine lived partly off its past reputation and partly off the literary flair of its editor, Jean Paulhan. But the "young review" characteristic of the prewar literary scene found it difficult to gain a foothold. It was not enough to be, like the *Parisienne* (1953, edited by François Michel), launched by a brilliant group of young novelists including—besides Nimier—Antoine Blondin, Jacques Laurent, Félicien Marceau, and Michel Déon. The *Parisienne,* despite the briefness of its life, marked the reappearance on the literary scene of a depoliticized Right angered by existentialist pontification and advocating a return to the spirit of the twenties, to Paul Morand and Jean Giraudoux. This was perceived as an obvious sign that the literary hegemony of the Resistance writers was at an end. Nevertheless, the *Parisienne* still shared the fate of journals like *Fontaine, Mercure de France, Cahiers du Sud, Revue de Paris, Lettres françaises*. Apart from the *Nouvelle (nouvelle) revue française*, almost no journal survived unless, like *Esprit*, it had social significance or carried articles of general interest. New, more specialized journals were taking the place of the old.

For a few years, *Tel Quel* made common cause with the *Nouvelle critique* group, moving toward linguistic and semiological research, and loudly expressing a determination to demystify the concept of great literature by demonstrating that a literary text is a "formalizable" linguistic object located at the intersection of sociology, psychoanalysis, and the erotic. *Tel Quel*'s technical vocabulary was tuned in accordance with a supposedly scientific concept of criticism. Its peremptory tone and the assertiveness of its missionary fervor made *Tel Quel* an irritating but dynamic review, one that was determined not to become entrenched in rigid positions. On the masthead appeared the inevitable constellation of fashionable intellectual leaders: Bataille, Barthes, Foucault, Lacan, Derrida; and also their acknowledged precursors: Artaud, Ponge, and, in the beginning, the *nouveaux romanciers,* along with prominent linguists Roman Jakobson and Noam Chomsky. *Tel Quel* published the most revolutionary and the most controversial experimental and critical texts being written at the time. Reaching a circulation of six thousand by 1970, this journal made the public familiar with the names of Jean-Pierre Faye, Guyotat, Kristeva, Pleynet, Ricardou, Denis and Maurice Roche, and Sollers. The *Tel Quel* group also edited a series published under the same name at Editions du Seuil.

There is a vast field to be studied concerning the effect of these periodicals outside of France, particularly in the United States, where contemporary literature has been a subject of scholarship for half a century. For a few years past France has been experiencing the same attraction toward the contemporary as America. There has been a proliferation of publications in periodical format—*Cahiers, Carnets,* and *Archives*—on contemporary writers, most of them published annually and devoted either to a single author or theme. Increasingly, they have been made up of scholarly articles addressed to the specialist rather than, as in the past, to the cultivated amateur (see Minard, *Revue des Lettres modernes*). This semiacademic formula was repeated by *Cahiers de l'Herne* (1961; founded by Dominique de Roux), each issue of which is devoted to a single literary personality who is famous but controversial (Céline, Ezra Pound), famous but not widely known (Samuel Beckett, René-Guy Cadou, Borgès, René Char); or to an entire group like the *Grand Jeu*. The pages of *Cahiers de l'Herne* are filled with unpublished work, memoirs, articles, critical essays of various kinds, and documents, both biographical and bibliographical, creating a somewhat disparate whole addressed, under a familiar format, to laymen as well as specialists. Similarly, for theater and cinema, were the periodicals such as

Cahiers Madeleine Renaud–Jean-Louis Barrault and *Cahiers du cinéma* (1950) and for television, *Les Cahiers littéraires de l'O.R.T.F.*

Here was a heterogeneous offering out of which the public had to make a choice. Journals able to survive without subsidy from official sources or publishing houses were rare. Under the circumstances, extinction threatened the purely literary review.

Fragmented and dispersed worldwide, the readership for the French literary review had changed, becoming almost wholly academic in composition. It was a readership of specialists, not cultivated laymen, and they apparently preferred the theoretical and critical journal to the periodic offerings of often ill-matched and incomplete literary texts presented by the traditional literary review.

Replacing the Pontigny "Rencontres" that before and just after the 1914 war had brought groups of book lovers and intellectuals together, there were now a plethora of *colloques,* the most famous being the Colloques du Centre International de Cerisy-la-Salle and its publications, which are transcriptions of the debates. These colloquia have made it possible to follow current ideological disputes and intellectual trends through panel discussions dealing with criticism, literature in the classroom, narrative, paraliterature, etc. The colloquium, in one form or another, and not the salon, the review, or the literary coterie, had apparently preempted the central position in literary life, leaving scant room for the expression of personal taste, for the reverie or emotional reactions reading inspires. This reflected the new trend toward theoretical research and collective effort. Instead of the old "schools" and avant-garde groups, new "collectives" or "research teams" were being set up on the scientific model.

Despite frequent criticism, literary prizes constantly increased in number. More than four thousand prizes of all kinds are awarded annually in the French-speaking world. There are also international prizes like the Nobel Prize—which does carry great weight—and the Lenin Prize. On the level of the Nobel Prize, the Lenin Prize, and the Grand Prix du Roman we can also mention the Grand Prix National des Lettres (1951) and the Grand Prix National du Théâtre (1969), both awarded by the Académie Française. All are given in recognition of an established body of work, and the first two, particularly the Nobel, draw winners to the attention of the international reading public. (French authors awarded the Nobel Prize since 1945 are Gide, Mauriac, Camus, poet Saint-John Perse, Sartre—who refused to accept it—and Samuel Beckett. The Lenin Prize was awarded to Aragon.) But in France the biggest waves of the annual prize-giving season are created by the four big awards for new novels: the Goncourt, the Fémina, the Renaudot, and the Interallié. For the winners and their publishers these prizes guarantee an astronomical rise in sale and hence considerable economic gain. There are, in addition, the Prix Médicis, the Prix des Critiques, the Prix Fénélon, and the more recent Prix International de Littérature, all awarded for new work and all conferring a certain amount of prestige; this is true also of the Prix Apollinaire, the Prix Max Jacob, and the Grand Prix de la Ville de Paris, all awarded for poetry.

Prize-winning works, although perforce uneven, are rarely totally devoid of interest, and the novelist of merit who has never won a prize is the exception. Despite the blaze of publicity surrounding the awards, which obviously throws literary values and reputations into some confusion, they are judged by established writers and discriminating critics and perform a useful initial sorting-out for the general reader, who would otherwise be buried under a mountain of books. It also confers a sort of glamor every year on the literary enterprise.

Literature and the Intellectual

The term "intellectual" was coined at the time of the Dreyfus Case, insidiously invaded the whole era, and made the labels "man of letters" or "cultivated man" obsolete. By the thirties the prestige of the writer was beginning to merge with that of the leftist or rightist "intellectual." Debate on the intellectual's role coalesced around Marxism and carried overtones of the political critique. Ideologues, whether Jean-Paul Sartre (in *Qu'est-ce que la littérature?* 1946) or communist Jean Kanapa (in a series of articles written between 1950 and 1957, published under the title *Situation de l'intellectuel,* 1957), all saw the intellectual's role as restricted to its immediate effectiveness, ideally a revelation of society's inner workings. From this point of view, writers found themselves in a subordinate position relative to social scientists, and they began to lose their autonomy on their own ground.

In an attempt to define the meaning of the term "intellectual" exactly, Raymond Aron in *L'Opium des intellectuels* (1955) noted the diversity of the activities covered by it, writing being only one among many. The society that emerged from the Second World War witnessed an increase in the number of intellectuals working in the fields of science or technology. One sector of this activity—communications technology—had a major impact on the cultural sector. The man of letters became an "expert," slowly but surely adulterating the literary world; "literature" was becoming intermingled with advertising, public relations, and communications. Radio, television, paperback, magazine, and specialized periodical publishing offered the literary man or woman (and women were numerous in the field) alternate ways of earning a living, integrating them more than they had been in the past into society as a whole.

Following the hiatus created by World War II there was a constant increase in the production of literature, especially novels—although less, proportionately, than of nonfiction books of all kinds. The Parisian literary world, reconstituted, grew. Competition waxed keen, with the inflation of literary production and of literary reputations resulting in more cliques and more flash-in-the-pan celebrities than ever before. This essentially Parisian world was more bourgeois than the sophisticated, Bohemian literary world of the twenties. The 1960 census showed that, out of 170 authors polled, 154 lived in Paris and, with the exception of a dozen or so, all were following careers connected with publishing, journalism, or university teaching. "Our literature," noted François Nourrissier in 1960, "is Parisian, it is bourgeois . . . and it has almost as many college professors in it as men of letters. We have a Paris-based literature of the leisured class, left to the mercy of professional book- and idea-mongers . . . The French writer by definition is an upholder of the established order."[1] This situation was not appreciably altered by the 1968 political upheaval, even though a small group of leftist writers did take advantage of it to form a "Writers' Union," occupy the headquarters of the Société des Gens de Lettres, and, inspired by the example of the USSR, to suggest the title "intellectual worker" for writers. In 1976 the Syndicat des Ecrivains de Langue Française (SELF) was founded, with novelist Marie Cardinal elected as its first president. Outside of this limited context, however, the prestige of writers depended less on the books they wrote than on the image they projected through the communications media.

Perhaps more than any other group belonging to the intelligentsia, writers were feeling the effects of the social changes going on around them. During the thirty-year period between 1920 and 1950, the prestige of the French writer, both at home and abroad, had been higher than at any other time in the country's history. Even today there is still a certain prestige associated with being a writer. But no single writer—perhaps due to the fragmentation of the public since 1950—has been able to gain the universal acclaim once enjoyed by Sartre, Simone de Beauvoir, and Camus. A writer favorably received by *one* more or less large segment of the public will be ignored or reviled by others. Journalism and television increasingly lure writers to Paris and to a world which, while ostensibly serving a large audience of television viewers, actually operates under fairly tight political control. In any case, no matter what writers do, they are always profoundly connected to the "bourgeois" society that, regular as clockwork, they denounce—which perhaps explains their ambivalence toward their craft.

[1]*Ecrivains d'aujourd'hui (1940–1960)* (Paris: Grasset, 1960), p. 43.

Three
Intellectual Trends

Introduction

In 1922 the *Revue hebdomadaire* conducted a survey on "today's literary masters." Fifty-eight young writers were asked two questions: "To which literary masters do you owe the most, and why?" and, "What influences do you believe will determine the future direction of literature, or, more specifically, will traditional forms die out, or will they be revived?" Fifty years later, these questions would not have seemed worth asking.

The *Revue hebdomadaire* was traditionalist and undoubtedly chose its respondents advisedly; nevertheless, their answers reveal what people were thinking at the conclusion of the First World War. With few exceptions—Aragon, Soupault, Drieu La Rochelle, André Maurois, Gabriel Marcel, Jacques de Lacretelle—there was virtually complete unanimity. Cited as masters were Barrès, Bourget, and Maurras. Only occasionally did another name join the list: Stendhal, Flaubert, Mallarmé, Péguy, France, Alain, Claudel, Gide, Proust. As for the future: a return to tradition and neoclassical equilibrium, and continuing development of the novel. Standing almost alone were Aragon and Soupault, with their vision of a break from traditional forms and an eruption into literary discourse of the language of poetry. Only rarely was mention made of any writer who was not French: Nietzsche once or twice, Dostoevski, or Tolstoy. Gabriel Marcel, however, in his answers to the questions, unveiled a perspective that was totally different. His preferences ran the gamut from Dostoevski to Nietzsche, to the German romantics, neo-Hegelianism, Strindberg, and Chekhov, Synge, and Tagore, to musicians—but to only a single Frenchman, Bergson—to everything that might "implant anxiety" and be capable of "communicating emotions susceptible of extension into thought." An anxiety Drieu translated by demonstrating the contradictions between "the conservationist doctrine of books" and the adventure of history, afraid himself of being "ill prepared through insufficient practical experience in science."

Cursory as it was, this survey gave a fairly accurate profile of a generation stranded intellectually by the nationalistic reaction accompanying the war. But what statistics cannot show are the contradictory impulses indicative of other needs: the need for an opening to the outside world; the need, and the search in all the arts, for a new language, and the need in philosophy for new ways of thinking; the need to recognize the importance of science. These were the three main trends that did exert an influence on the future of the French literary enterprise.

We should note, however, that not once but twice—during the Occupation and again in the sixties—when later generations were also seeking coherent forms for their philosophy, they also turned to masters who were French: phenomenology and existentialism came from Husserl, to be sure, but reinterpreted by Sartre and Merleau-Ponty or, in Christian form, by Gabriel Marcel; Marx, yes, but by way of Sartre, first, and then through Althusser; Hegel, through Koyré, then Kojève; Jung through Bachelard. France discovered anthropology through Lévi-Strauss, sociology through Roland Barthes, and, belatedly, Freud, reinterpreted by Lacan. Forty years after the fact, France also discovered the source of linguistic theory in Saussure's *Cours*, occasionally in the work of Wittgenstein or that of the Viennese Linguistic Circle. Unlike the language of paraliterature and pure science, the language of the social sciences and philosophy seemed impossible to assimilate without the prior mediation of a French guide. The bitterest intellectual conflicts of this half-century were waged on the battlefield of philosophy. The conjectures of the young ideologues of the fifties were based on Saussure, Marx, and Freud, occasionally on Hegel, later Nietzsche. They were looking for new philosophical forms to answer new intellectual needs.

After 1950 an important new scientific development was added to the quest. In the words of Leprince-Ringuet, the invention of the transistor (1946) "started a mutation in civilization." The transistor led in turn to the development of cybernetics, a science of information making it possible to formulate a physical theory of language and brain function. The transistor was followed by electronic computers and, with them, the entire problematic of communication, coded "messages," the relations between man and language considered as a conditional system. Broadly speaking, we can divide the major trends affecting literature into chronological trends, each predominating in its turn, and all closely interconnected:

The twenties were characterized by the search for new art forms, and by the eruption of these new forms onto the cultural scene.

During the forties an anti-Cartesian, anti-Kantian dialectic developed that was inherent in the philosophies of history and existentialism subsequently polarized around Marxism.

At midcentury, with the development of cybernetics, came the problematic of structure; and the synchronic relations addressed by structuralism cast doubts on the diachronic mode of thought inherent in Marxism.

In the area of letters the eclectic, willfully modernist élan of the twenties receded before a literature of metaphysical dimensions aiming to be all-encompassing. At the half-century mark there was a new movement toward formal research, but this time pursued with greater method, and by a more restricted group. Its ultimate goal was the development of theoretical linguistic and literary "models," and in this it sought to be scientific, experimental, and fully "modern" in a sense that, because of the disregard for the aesthetic, made it very different from the "modernism" of the twenties. The effect of scientific modernism on criticism was more obvious than it was on literature properly speaking. But, taking all of the above trends together, we can see the emergence—gradually at first and then, after 1950, at an accelerating pace—of basic questions concerning the very foundations of thought itself. These questions had an impact on the concepts of consciousness, language, and "self" that led to a critical examination of what "I" really means, and decisively influenced the very idea of literature. The old themes inherited from the romantics—identity, sincerity, the importance of the individual personality and destiny—suffered a loss of prestige.

7
Opening to the Outside World

"Worldwide" Literary Internationalism

So great has been the transformation in the cultural environment that the phrase "outside world" is disputable. Before World War I there had already existed an artistic cosmopolitanism and a social cosmopolitanism that occasionally—as in the case of the Ballets Russes—joined forces. Members of the literary establishment congratulated themselves on belonging to a universal "republic of letters," a society of the cultivated (that is, of the initiates to Western culture) and a meeting ground for the great minds of the past. Pre–World War I Paris was one of two centers where artists from all over the world were inventing new modes of expression. And Paris lived in ignorance of the other, which was Berlin. As a result, the artistic renaissance of the period appeared to be a French phenomenon, all the more so as its spokesmen were French poets—Max Jacob, André Salmon, Philippe Soupault, and, above all, Guillaume Apollinaire. The French were able to nurse a feeling of being in the avant-garde of modern culture, owing to the balance they maintained between "innovation and tradition," in the words of Apollinaire. In the area of literature, salons presided over by such people as the keenly Anglophile Jacques-Emile Blanche and Americans Nathalie Clifford Barney (Remy de Gourmont's "Amazon"), Edith Wharton, and Gertrude Stein—to name only a few—made Paris a cosmopolitan capital par excellence. The same held true for French men of letters, some of whom, like the highly cultivated, well-traveled Valery Larbaud, served as intermediaries between France and the other literary centers of Europe. Writers like Gide, Charles Du Bos, Edmond Jaloux, and René Lalou encouraged literary exchange and saw to it that foreign works were published in literary reviews. Until the First World War, however, these exchanges had remained sporadic and subject to the whims of personal tastes or connections, the hazards of chance readings or translations. Writers past and present were indiscriminately absorbed into the French context. Gide translated Blake, Conrad, and Tagore almost simultaneously, for example, interpreting all of them from the point of view of a French man of letters. For these "literary tourists" the work of foreign writers was a sort of annex to the vast domain of French literature.

After World War I, things changed. Edmond Jaloux was to describe much later the immense yearning for new horizons characteristic of the twenties: "Journals were founded whose outlook was less limited than ever before; publishers welcomed newcomers. The *NRF*, Bernard Grasset, Daniel Halévy, and I bent our efforts toward familiarizing the public with writers from abroad; we witnessed the birth of Rainer Maria Rilke and Hugo von Hofmannsthal, James Joyce and Virginia Woolf, Anton Chekhov and D. H. Lawrence . . . We rescued Jean-Paul Richter, Novalis, George Moore, and Turgenev from oblivion" (*Essences*, 1952). Translations of literary works from all over the world were published with an increasing frequency that remained undiminished by—and perhaps was even stimulated by—the Occupation. In November 1920, *Europe nouvelle* conducted a survey on "the reciprocal influence of French and foreign literature." In 1927 *Cahiers du Sud* voiced considerable editorial concern for "the importance of foreign literature." In 1947 *L'Age nouveau* inaugurated a new column, "Literary Interpenetration"; and one year later there was a reference in *Cahiers de la Pléiade* to "universal literature."

Four factors played an important role in this spread of foreign literature in France: the presence in increasing numbers of people capable of acting as intermediaries—selecting and translating foreign books and then reviewing them for the literary magazines; the growth of a reading public that was becoming more and more curious about the events taking place beyond their borders; greater cultural and academic cross-fertilization and the addition of courses in comparative literature to university curricula; and, lastly, the rapid development after 1950 of an international book market. It is virtually impossible to evaluate the exact nature of these exchanges and the extent of their influence. All we can have is a rough idea. One thing, however, is clear: the literary game in France will never again be played as it was before World War I. As Julien Gracq has noted, "the frame of reference for today's French writer is a vast contemporary literary environment and not a literary past, French or otherwise" (*Préférences*, 1961).

In 1922 the *Revue de Genève* stated as its mission "recreating a European spirit" by reestablishing dialogue between writers, and especially between French and German writers. Two groups in France responded to this initiative: the *NRF* and Gide, eager to work toward a "demobilization of minds"; and Romain Rolland and the *Clarté* group. Ties were renewed. Ernst Robert Curtius, a German intellectual highly knowledgeable in the area of French literature, opened a dialogue with the *NRF,* which had also found a remarkable interpreter of German culture in the person of Bernard Groethuysen. In 1923 Heinrich Mann, a pro-French pacifist, appeared at the Pontigny debates. Two young French experts in German literature, Félix Bertaux and Geneviève Maury, contributed significantly to the renewal of contacts with Germany. At the same time the dadaists and surrealists were, of course, international and violently antipatriotic. The need for broader horizons was making itself felt on every front. It was time for a Gide, not a Maurras. This receptivity had spread half a century later, in literature and in art, to include the whole world.

The arrival on the French literary scene of certain foreign works can be located approximately; the passing fad distinguished from the lasting presence assimilated into the literary configuration of the period; or some literary influences identified. But the field is vast and uniquely complex. If we confine ourselves to the novel, we might say, for example, that between 1922 and 1970 in France, the only non-French writers who attained the status of acknowledged classics on a par with Balzac, Stendhal, or Flaubert, were Poe, Dostoevski, and Tolstoy. Of these, Dostoevski enjoyed a kind of cult status that, under the influence of the Russian émigrés, gave way around 1922 to a less disproportionate appreciation. With a few exceptions—such as Nathalie Sarraute and Albert Camus—the generation of Mauriac, Green, Bernanos, Duhamel was the last to be haunted by Dostoevski in his role as the originator of a new psychology. Roger Martin du Gard, a member of this same generation, still turned to Tolstoy as a model, but otherwise it had been twenty years since Tolstoy's work had served as a source of inspiration and innovation for young novelists. What attracted the *Clarté* and *Europe* writers to Tolstoy was his "message": his pacifism and his conception of the social function of art, a theme reiterated by Marxism and in the work of Sartre. Conversely, James Joyce's *Ulysses* (1922), published in translation in 1929, and *Finnegans Wake* (1939), although not widely read, were seminal. Because of their technical virtuosity they exercised a determining—perhaps even an excessive—influence on the post-1950 development of the French novel. The two works offered young novelists primarily a new technique, stream of consciousness; but also a whole new problematic of style. American novelist William Faulkner, himself a Joyce reader, joined him in the French literary pantheon during the thirties.

One of the beacons for two generations of French writers was Kafka, at first apparently as little read as Joyce. Of the three German authors introduced to the *NRF* by Groethuysen around 1925–26—Kafka, Broch, and Musil—only Kafka "made it," but, according to perceptive critic Marthe Robert, he made it for the wrong reasons. First he was "surrealized" by André Breton. The first Kafka translation, dating from 1928, was *La Métamorphose,* published by Gallimard, but in 1930 *Le Procès* came out in *Bifur.* Thus did Kafka come to represent the fantastic, modern style: black humor, hallucination, a penchant for sadism. Kafka's works were banned during the Occupation, but they circulated clandestinely in English translation, turning Kafka into a sort of spearhead for existentialism, the man who, according to Sartre, opened the way to Kierkegaard and Hegel; or the herald of the absurd; or, in Blanchot's view, the incarnation of how vain it is to write when faced with nothingness. Now, however, with the 1966 publication of the complete works and a thorough reinterpretation of each one, sound knowledge appears to be replacing the Kafka myth, much as it did in the case of Dostoevski back in 1922. Compared with the key figures of Joyce, Faulkner, Kafka, Pirandello, and Brecht—all more or less contemporary—Melville is a special case. Although originally translated in 1937, it was not until after 1941, when Gallimard published *Moby Dick*, translated by Lucien Jacques, Joan Smith, and Jean Giono, that this work, then more than a century old, acquired overwhelming novelty for a few select French readers, among them Albert Camus; the only other novel of Melville's to do the same was *Billy Budd*.

Other foreign influences on French literature are more difficult to evaluate. What real importance should we attribute to the mania for the Orient, especially China, professed by the surrealists? It seems merely to have been the obverse of their revolt against Western values, and the success of a book like Morand's *Bouddha vivant* (1927) primarily a symptom of the general yearning for exoticism characteristic of the period following World War I. Somewhat later, however, the Orient, its civilization and its art, was to exercise an attraction on certain intellectuals that went considerably deeper; an attraction powerful enough to send the young Malraux off in pursuit of a dream Orient that bore little similarity to the realities of the revolutionary Orient he found when he got there. There were several major works in the post–World War I period that did reflect an Oriental influence, but either it was not immediately perceived by the contemporary public, as in Claudel's case, or, as in the case of Victor Ségalen and Saint-John Perse, the works themselves were not at first widely read. Because of the interest aroused in pacifist circles by Gandhi's doctrine of passive resistance, India enjoyed a certain vogue, the responsibility for which lay largely with Romain Rolland. His studies of India were an answer to a generalized feeling of need for mysticism devoid of dogma, another symptom being the success in certain Parisian social circles of Russian "guru" Gurdjieff—whose most famous disciple was Katherine Mansfield—and his teachings. Because he had won the Nobel Prize (1913) and because, in the same year, one of his collections of stories, *L'Offrande lyrique,* was translated by Gide, Rabindranath Tagore achieved a prestige in France almost equal to Gandhi's, which helped to give India an idyllic and pastoral Golden Age image. The Orient in general appeared to be simply an extension of the prevailing romanticism that was drawn primarily from European sources.

With the help of his centenary and his Francophilia, Goethe enjoyed a certain vogue in the interwar period, but his works were revered rather than read. This was not the case for the German romantics—Jean-Paul Richter, Hoffman, Arnim, Kleist, Hölderlin, and Novalis—whose works were consistent with a sensibility best expressed by surrealism's combination of poetry and dream. They were also well received elsewhere. Both in connection with the *Revue européenne* and thanks to the predilections of the Brambilla Club (Edmond Jaloux, André Béguin, Jean Cassou, poet Jean de Boschère, and, briefly, Jean Giraudoux and Paul Morand) the German romantics found publishers in France. Their use of dream and the fantastic, their tendency toward the metaphysical and recourse to the imaginary, sustained an inner landscape reflected to varying degrees in the work of writers as diverse as Giraudoux, Julien Gracq, René Char, Henri Bosco, and Henri Thomas. The pathways linking these interconnections have been traced in Albert Béguin's milestone critical work, *L'Ame romantique et le rêve* (1937).

Probably in antithesis to this neoromanticism, a latent, eroded Nietzscheanism colored the way people looked at things and was concentrated in a few clichés: the death of God; the myth of the superman; an exaltation of virility and action; contempt for Christian virtues. It was Nietzsche who provided Montherlant, as much as Malraux, and the young Sartre, as much as the young Camus, with their basic nihilistic anguish and a lyrically charged rhetorical model.

Different circumstances at different moments crowned one literary domain with success rather than another, or gained acceptance for certain kinds of work at the expense of others. The twenties enthusiastically adopted the young English novelists and the *Cahiers de Malte Laurids Brigge*. These books were consistent with the cult of the intimate and sincere then prevailing; but the enthusiasm for Aldous Huxley's *Point Counterpoint*, published in France in translation in 1929, was infinitely greater. Thomas Mann's success dates from the 1931 translation of *The Magic Mountain*, its hermetic world and ideological discussions giving a foretaste of later preoccupations.

China found great favor with intellectuals after 1950. But despite the attraction exerted by non-Western philosophy in some circles, and the participation of some intellectuals in Ashram meditation meetings, the influence exercised on the cultural world in France by the East was evidently still not profound.

There were many books that achieved commercial success and yet had no apparent significance from the standpoint of literary history—Musil's *Man without Qualities* earned a belated welcome; the Italian novelists were mid-century successes, as were Russians Pasternak and Solzhenitsyn; so was Malcolm Lowry's *Under the Volcano*. Also worth noting is French indifference to some writers: Fitzgerald, Gertrude Stein, in part D. H. Lawrence. And also the resurrections, as happened in 1970 with Virginia Woolf. What role, if any, has the support of eminent French writers played in the reception of particular foreign works? The first edition of the French translation of Virginia Woolf's *Mrs. Dalloway,* in 1925, had a preface by André Maurois; the preface to Katherine Mansfield's *La Garden Party et autres histoires* (1924) was by Edmond Jaloux. How much did the French translation of *Lady Chatterley's Lover*—at a time when D. H. Lawrence was virtually unknown in France—owe to Malraux's preface, and how much to scandal? And in 1933, did Faulkner owe the meteoric rise in his reputation to the preface by Malraux for *Sanctuaire (Sanctuary)* and, in 1934, to the one by Larbaud for *Tandis que j'agonise (As I Lay Dying)?*

In the literary domain, however, the determining nature of some encounters is well established: Giono with the *Odyssey;* Butor with Joyce; Sartre with Dos Passos; Camus with Melville; Claude Simon with Faulkner; Nathalie Sarraute with Virginia Woolf. But, generally speaking, the decisive factor has usually been the climate of the French literary milieu at the time and the constraining influence of tradition. Foreign literature is "important"; it is read; but only rarely has it been creative or arrived on the scene at just the right psychological moment to fuel fresh departures, solve problems, tilt the balance in favor of a particular literary tendency, or indicate new avenues to be explored. Joyce was influential, true; but Proust more so. So were the Russian formalists, but in the wake of Mallarmé. And, behind the problematics of narrative and viewpoint, stood the rarely cited investigations of Gide.

It is therefore easy to understand the intensity that in France surrounds discussions on the future of literature and the bitterness with which a constraining literary past is attacked. Today, the widening gulf between French writers and their public is no doubt due to an exaggerated faith in the technical experiments these concerns engendered.

For the average reader, foreign literature usually simply communicates the joys of the unaccustomed. Professional writers, on the other hand, frequently attempt to assimilate and force it to serve their own purposes. Works are intellectualized, and the abstract model derived from this process absorbed into the French context of the moment. For example, Joyce's and Faulkner's technique of mixing narrative time sequence was adopted by Claude Simon and applied even more systematically. Another writer might take a foreign work and extract from it the single theme consistent with his own sensibility. Malraux interpreted *Lady Chatterley's Lover* as an example of erotology in the Georges Bataille mode; and in *Sanctuary* he saw a violent, fatalistic world akin to his own. Sartre, for whom Faulkner's various characters all bore the single mask of an "Aztec idol," shared this view. Melville's *Moby Dick* provided Camus with a model for the symbolic and metaphysical composition emblematic of human revolt against cosmic injustice which was later to form the basic theme of *La Peste.* Here we have an explanation for the "sea change" some works suffered in France, notably those of Dostoevski and Kafka; and we can also see why Virginia Woolf

drew a few young novelists of the thirties down a narrative path that didn't
lead anywhere until after 1970. And why certain aspects of Samuel Beckett's
work—for example, his sense of humor—escaped his French critics entirely.

In France, the non-native literary work tended to assume the characteristics of a symbol or sign to be fitted into the contemporary system of
signifiers. This explains the fate of efforts such as Cendrar's first *Anthologie
nègre* (1921), which was before its time, and the limited audience for Far
Eastern literature even when presented by someone with the stature of a
René Etiemble. Obviously, as Cocteau once pointed out, there is not so
much a style of the time as an ineffable "aroma" congenial to some works
and not to others. Themes and theories travel by means of a kind of osmosis,
and it takes time before the significant configurations of a given period can
be discerned. But the French sensibility has certainly been colored during the
twentieth century by the waves of immigrants that have succeeded each
other throughout: Russians fleeing the October Revolution; Germans—
primarily Jewish—fleeing Hitler; Russians and East Europeans fleeing Stalin; Spaniards fleeing Franco. Many writers of foreign origin did integrate
themselves successfully into the French context. The worldwide prestige of
French language and literature, French culture's long internationalist tradition, and its concerned awareness of broadly humanistic values with social
as well as literary implications guaranteed an audience for all of them. These
expatriates had a considerable contribution to make. Adamov, Cioran,
Ionesco, Kessel, Roblès, Schéhadé, Tzara, Troyat, Sarraute, Wiesel. Along
with them, the "Francophones"—Belgians, Canadians, and Swiss; North
Africans; West Indians, Black Africans, Madagascans, and Indochinese—
each developed a style of their own. French literature in the twentieth century has reflected a geographical and historical relativism of unprecedented
proportions.

Francophone Literature

Before 1960 the heading "Francophone Literature" would have been
inconceivable. Any book of recognized literary merit written in French prior
to that time was simply assimilated into the mainstream of French literature:
J.-J. Rousseau, French writer, born in Geneva. It was only in the post-1945
context of decolonization that the rise of nationalism all over the world
revealed the problem of literatures written in French but struggling to free
themselves of French culture and the French literary tradition. It took
twenty more years for these literatures to become fully self-aware and to
understand some of their own problems. Accompanying this new maturity
was a lively critical sense that in just a few years evolved the first criteria for
recognizing and evaluating a whole category of works designated as
"French-language," or "Francophone"—a term used to distinguish them
from the literature of metropolitan France. Publishing houses—Présence

Africaine was one of the first—and university centers sponsored publication of theses, bibliographies, sociological and critical studies, anthologies; the new category was further legitimized in university curricula and through establishment of special university chairs. Pioneering efforts on the part of French Canadian universities were responsible for uniting all the different factions under the auspices of the Centre d'Etudes des Littératures d'Expression Française (CELEF) at the University of Sherbrooke, and, in Montreal, of the Association des Universités Partiellement ou Entièrement de Langue Française (AUPELF), the two organizations providing an umbrella for French language universities located all over the world that would not be affected by the hegemony of the metropolitan French.

The term "Francophone" is fairly self-explanatory: it refers to the literature of any one of a number of diverse countries containing within its borders a cultural group that is French-speaking. In Europe this includes the Belgian Walloons and the French Swiss; in North America, the French Canadians—particularly in Quebec; in Africa, the inhabitants of the Maghreb (Algeria, Morocco, Tunisia) and those of "Black Africa," whose literature is frequently compared to that of the West Indies and the Indian Ocean. But this is not as simple as it might seem, first, because each of these divisions presents significant individual differences, both from the sociocultural point of view, and in relation to France; second, because no satisfactory method of classification has ever replaced the linguistic. In what category, for example, ought we to assign poet Henri Michaux, novelist François Mallet-Joris, or playwright Jean Vauthier? All three are Belgian, but all are more French than they are Belgian when compared with playwrights Crommelynck and Ghelderode—who were born Flemish but write in French. A Swiss, Alfred Berchtold, in his study *La Suisse romande au cap du XXe siècle,* brings to his readers' attention many French Swiss writers, musicians, and philosophers, only a few of whom ever gained an audience beyond the borders of their own country. Is it only by accident that writers like Ramuz, Jacottet, and Robert Pinget are considered as belonging to France—the latter two, in fact, even more than the first? Many writers in many areas of literature and criticism should be classified as Francophone rather than as French. But this raises problems of ethnology, sociology, psychology, and history. The question is, Can systematic linguistic analysis, alone, settle the matter satisfactorily? In addition to thematic differences, are there also *linguistic* differences indicating cultural affiliations? Perhaps, as Serge Brindeau has suggested, in the preface to his anthology *La Poésie contemporaine française depuis 1945,* "the nearest country to us . . . and most dear" will always be our language.

Three main groups of Francophone writers may, however, be usefully distinguished.

Belgian and Swiss writers share a long European cultural tradition and have many links with France, but they come from small countries, of which one is bilingual (Belgium: French and Flemish) and one quadrilingual (Switzerland: French, Swiss-German, Italian, Romansh). Their problem is how to reach beyond the limited public at home, and the danger they face is the same faced by regional writers everywhere.

French Canada has the largest Francophone population of any country outside of France. Six million French Canadians, out of a continent containing 250 million English speakers, define themselves by the language they speak, but also by the cultural realities of their situation. Their struggle is twofold: against assimilation by the numerically stronger English-speaking population in Canada, and against assimilation by the culturally stronger metropolitan French. French Canadians also have to fight for intellectual freedom within the tradition of their own provincial and religious restrictions (*automatistes'* manifesto, 1948). For French Canadians, the linguistic question is crucial: should they obey the lexical and grammatical strictures of French, or should they incorporate Canadian usages into what they write? Here again we see the problem of audience and of literary standards. Should French Canadian literature be judged according to traditional French criteria? As literature, it is less than a century old and did not really come of age until the generation of 1945.

In the vast, extremely diverse domain that includes the African nations (Maghreb and Black Africa), the West Indies, and the Indian Ocean, French is the literary language of a small group of "developed" writers who, although they may have been educated in French lycées, still belong to non-European cultural traditions that are not French and are essentially oral. In the Maghreb, the initial manifestation of this phenomenon occurred in Algeria with the "Ecole d'Alger," which for a few brief years was defined by reference to the Mediterranean culture of which it was a part and within which the poet Jean Amrouche and the novelist Mouloud Feraoun forged links of friendship with French Algerians like Fabriel Audisio, Emmanuel Roblès, and Albert Camus.

It was in France, during the thirties, that the Black African movement coalesced among the young black intellectuals who were studying there and who gravitated around little magazines like the *Revue du Monde noir, Légitime Défense,* and the *Journal de l'étudiant noir,* in whose pages future leaders Léopold Sédar Senghor, Aimé Césaire, and Léon Damas, as well as lesser lights such as Birago Diop, developed the concept of "negritude" defined by Aimé Césaire in a basic text, *Cahier d'un retour au pays natal.* This concept, which other black writers were later to attack, defined the African personality in relation to an ancestral cultural tradition and allowed for a faint glimmer of hope that, once regained, this original culture would assimilate the French culture that had been artificially grafted onto it, thus creating a genuine humanism.

The fact remains that Francophone literature in both Black and Arab Africa has no past. Bursting on the scene during the pivotal years between

1930 and 1950, it is a function of the national liberation movement in the French colonies. The French-speaking writers of Africa, whether from the Maghreb or Black Africa, used a language that was not their own and a mode of expression—writing—dramatically separating them from their own traditions. The problem of distribution for these works is therefore almost impossible to solve. Their readership, apart from a small group of intellectuals, is either French or else composed of scholars. They have even, on occasion, exerted an indirect influence on metropolitan French literature. For the West Indies the problem was not quite the same, because there the French language is much more deeply rooted.

In Canada, awareness of an independent, *Québécois* literary personality coalesced between 1930 and 1945, reinforced by Canada's position during World War II. At that time Montreal and Quebec assumed a crucial role in the publication and distribution of French books, carrying on for France after the defeat. It was in this way that French Canadian publications first made their appearance on the market. Canada's independence in relation to French patronage became evident during the "purge" following the Liberation. The Canadian publishing houses refused to obey directives issuing from the Counseil National des Ecrivains (1946–47).

By contrast, African writers—Arab or Black—found themselves over the course of a quarter-century in a rapidly changing situation involving adjustments in relative position that were sometimes painful for France, and sometimes for their own countries; the problem of cultural identity was a hard one to solve. All of Albert Memmi's works were attempts to elucidate this question, as were Frantz Fanon's more violent essays, *Peau noire, masques blancs* (1952), and *Les Damnés de la terre* (1961); and Sartre's more controversial preface to Léopold Sédar Senghor's *Anthologie de la nouvelle poésie nègre et malgache* (1948).

All of this literature can, however, be objectively defined, leaving aside the question of literary *merit,* according to criteria proposed for Canadian literature by David M. Hayne of the University of Toronto.[1]

According to Hayne, Francophone or French-language literatures are "relatively narrow," of fairly recent development, modern, generally published in small editions, and they are written in French, a language with a centuries-old literary tradition. The relation of Francophone literature to the French literary tradition is therefore that of minor literature to a major language. The problem for this literature is how to find its own direction within this dualism. Francophone literature is affected by politics, which in turn can have repercussions tending to sterilize the language. Under the circumstances, French Canadian literature seems to have a brighter future than Arab or Black African Francophone literature. In both cases, however, we are dealing with writers seeking their own identity under trying political

[1]Conference, 20 April 1964; see *Littérature canadienne française* (Montreal, 1969).

and social conditions, and also, in the words of another Canadian, G.-André Vachon,[2] with the problem of "inventing a tradition" or transposing one from oral to written form. These are emerging literatures. For all, the problems of audience, sales, ultimate goals, and future potential do occasionally overlap with the concerns of the metropolitan French writer. On one point, however, they differ: attentiveness to *content*. The content of most Francophone works has an obvious sociological aspect: love of the soil; violent revolt against traditions, or nostalgia for them; the search for equilibrium between the native and the colonial cultures or, in countries whose independence has been achieved, between the old ways and the new urban society.

Some of these writers have achieved positions of eminence in France. Aimé Césaire, poet and playwright, and Edouard Glissant, poet and novelist, both from Martinique; poet Léopold Sédar Senghor, president of Senegal, and Birago Diop, also from Senegal; and, to return to the Canadians, poets Saint-Denys Garneau and Anne Hébert, and novelist Marie-Claire Blais. And lastly, fully integrated members of the Parisian literary world: Tunisian novelist and essayist Albert Memmi, Algerian novelist Mohammed Dib, Moroccan novelist Driss Chraibi, Algerian poet Kateb Yacine, and, from Martinique, Frantz Fanon, interpreter of colonized Africa's anguish and aspirations. Within the scope of the present work we cannot, unfortunately, examine further the vast area of this vigorous literature, an entity under continual critical reevaluation.[3]

[2] Ibid.
[3] See Bibliography for further information.

8

From
Avant-Garde to Technology:
The Media

Art, Literature, and the Development of New Methods of Expression

In 1920 a newspaperman gave the name "Groupe des Six" to the young composers—Auric, Durey, Honegger, Milhaud, Poulenc, and Germaine Taillefer—who under Satie's direction and Cocteau's auspices were then making their Parisian debut. An exhibition of *jeunes peintres français* the same year indicated that Cubism was losing its hegemony. An avant-garde of young writers working on the magazine *Littérature* demonstrated increasing impatience with recognized literary masters. There was a new avant-garde on the way in, and its members—painters, writers, and composers—were collaborating more closely with one another than in the past. This collaboration grew during the twenties and then dwindled; yet it remained one of the fundamental characteristics of an era when all kinds of artists were expressing themselves through all kinds of media: Jean Cocteau, a writer, was also a film maker and designer; Jean Arp, a painter and sculptor, was also a poet; Henri Michaux, a poet, was also a painter. Picasso, a painter, went from one plastic art to another with extreme virtuosity; so did Dubuffet. Some artistic encounters have since become famous: Paul Eluard and Max Ernst; Breton and, for a time, Dali; Jean Paulhan and Braque; Sartre with Calder's mobiles and Giacometti's sculptures; and for the development of Claude Simon's style, painting played a major role as both visual and technical stimulus (composition by juxtaposition; symmetry, repetition, motifs). The confluence of cultural currents was obvious, with the years 1920–29 and 1946–55 the pivotal ones for literature as well as for all the other arts; an analogous trend during the 1960–70 decade led to the emergence of scientific laboratory research carried out by "collectives"; the visual art and algorithmic music research collectives corresponded to literary groups like *Change* and *Tel Quel.*

It has been said that art after 1920 was dominated by four great personalities: first, Diaghilev, who died in 1929; then Picasso, Stravinsky, and Schönberg. For the pre–World War I period the names that come to mind are the two poets Mallarmé and Apollinaire. Literature, however, though sharing with the other arts after 1920 the two characteristic exigencies of the era—a desire to break with the past, and a continuous quest for new modes of expression—nevertheless lagged behind in achieving them. A generation of literary greats—Proust, Claudel, Gide, Valéry—dominated the century until 1950. The immediate repercussions of the dadaist revolt were felt primarily in the plastic arts. The surrealist doctrine had of course been articulated almost exclusively by writers—André Breton, Paul Eluard, Robert Desnos, Benjamin Péret—but, as earlier with futurism, it was the painters, inspired by this doctrine, who were the first to gain the attention of the international public.

At the 1954 Venice Biennale, surrealism received a sort of consecration: the painting prize went to Max Ernst, the sculpture prize to Hans Arp, the prize for graphics to Miró. Simultaneously, and this was also true of literature, a new generation was on the way up: Mathieu, de Staël, Fautrier, Dubuffet, Hartung, Wols, Soulages; in sculpture, Schöffer and César. A new tendency, the search for structure, was everywhere in evidence: Nicolas Schöffer's cybernetic structures; Boulez's serial music; "mass" reproductions based on one original; prefabricated "living units." The surrealist denial of form became for some artists a search for form. We can nevertheless assert, without undue oversimplification, that the principal trends in twentieth-century art all had their roots in the great 1917–25 upheaval.

The search for a new aesthetic is not necessarily revolutionary in itself. What is revolutionary is the speed with which the pre–World War I spirit of adventure evolved into a confrontation with, and a radical break from, the past. "For the man seeking what he has never seen there are no models," said Eluard; and, we might add, for the one seeking what he has never heard. In the visual arts, as Malraux was to underline, the artist has seen everything there is to see, thanks to the modern museum and the camera. In music, Schönberg was also impelled to seek an entirely new and different idiom by his conviction that the conventional tradition had nothing more to give.

To depart radically from the more or less consciously accepted principles that govern an art form does not present the painter or composer with the same problems it does the writer. A newly created artistic or musical idiom is immediately perceptible. It is an inherent quality of the created object: we *see* a Picasso canvas or a sculpture by César; we *hear* an étude by Pierre Boulez. Reading is an infinitely more complex intellectual act, and the writer's "medium"—language—is one that has many more demands of its own to make. It is therefore hardly surprising that music and the plastic arts, in their determination to become completely transformed, progressed with an alacrity that at first shocked and then fascinated a public which gradually began to grow tolerant and involved. This public witnessed the evolution of jazz from music hall entertainment to the status of an independent art; and it also witnessed the swift metamorphosis of the surrealist "objects," which had originally been considered as beneath contempt, into objets d'art acquiring high market value. The distinguishing marks of modern art were more clearly indicated in music and the plastic arts than they were in literature.

Painting and the Concept of the Avant-Garde

Up to the sixties, painting was the most dynamic and the most lavish of all the arts. Deploying its products in Paris, New York, London, and South America, it spawned during the lifetime of its "masters"—Picasso, Matisse, Braque, and Léger—artistic trends and schools of great diversity and in great numbers.

Three principal but divergent trends, all with roots in the pre–World War I period, developed during the twenties. They were:

Constructivism, its headquarters the Bauhaus in Munich and its adherents painters Kandinsky, Klee, Mondrian, Fernand Léger; sculptors Lipschitz, Brancusi, and Germaine Richier; architect Le Corbusier.

Expressionism, based in Berlin where during the twenties it provided the inspiration for artists of the Montparnasse group such as Modigliani and Soutine.

Surrealism, with its much closer ties to the Parisian literary world.

The essence of constructivism made it the equivalent in the plastic arts of Schönberg's musical aesthetic. In the new era of science it set out to obliterate the past and rationally, objectively, and rigorously to construct a modern art based on three fundamentals: volume, surface, function. Constructivism had certain affinities with the work of Gide and Valéry. It gave birth to Mondrian's abstractions, one of the forms assumed by nonfigurative art. The highly subjective expressionists represented the other extreme, attempting to project onto canvas the emotions—wonder, anguish, horror—inspired by the spectacle of the world. This kind of dynamic lyricism involved a distortion of forms leading ultimately to their disappearance and the creation of a formless, nonfigurative art. From the canvases of the surrealists sprang a host of motifs that were unexpected and extraordinarily rich: objectified worlds of subjectivity that destroyed reality and replaced it with the fantastic. Such works included paintings by Max Ernst, Chirico, Tanguy, Man Ray, Salvador Dali, Hans Arp, Miró, and Masson; also the creations of sculptor and painter Giacometti.

An artist working within any of these three movements was required to forge his own individual idiom. The avant-garde concept decreeing that the individual language of a creative artist breaking away from academic tradition becomes the artistic style of the future held sway until 1950. But this concept of the avant-garde rests on the supposition that art is like an organism that develops according to laws that govern its direction and logical continuity. When the flood of invention we have been describing began to recede toward 1960–65, revealing the tremendous diversity of the works that had been produced and the way in which conflicting trends had coexisted, the whole notion of the avant-garde began to disappear and, with it, the sense of art being "directed" along a temporal, linear progression. The avant-garde faded, and its place was taken by the experimental collective, the very word "experimental" emphasizing the shift in viewpoint that had taken place.

A certain amount of philosophical reflection was therefore stimulated during this period, not by literature, but, unsurprisingly, by art. As early as 1925 the question of the "dehumanization of art" was raised in reference to nonfigurative art by Ortega y Gasset. In 1929 Elie Faure published his thoughts concerning "the spirit of form," followed in 1936 by Henri Focillon's work on the "life of form." The core of the Proustian enterprise contained the issue of the meaning of art, and at midcentury it inspired Malraux's great meditative works: *Le Musée imaginaire* (1947); *La Monnaie de l'absolu* (1950); *Les Voix du silence* (1951); *Le Musée imaginaire de la sculpture mondiale* (1952–55); *La Métamorphose des Dieux* (1957). As Paulhan, referring to nonformal art, has suggested, artists used to start with a meaning and would then try to find the signs by which it could be communicated; artists today create signs, hoping they will find meaning. But when a writer asks, "What is literature?" the context in which he does so is a vast and a disturbing one.

Art, Literature, and Technology

Starting in the twenties, a few, as yet rare, composers attempted to introduce new elements into the musical system. Satie integrated the sound of a typewriter and an airplane motor into *Parade,* anticipating *musique concrète.* Edgar Varèse used the newly invented acoustical recording machines as musical instruments: by increasing or decreasing the number of revolutions per minute when playing a record he could obtain a decomposition of sound producing new sonic material; and by playing the record backward he could reverse the order of the musical structures transcribed on it so that, to the listener, they "progressed by retrogression," as it were. These early experiments ultimately led to the post-1950 laboratory research through which the new materials now used in electronic music were developed. They have also survived in the research of the algorithmic musicians, whose computer-programed compositions eliminate the instrumentalist along with the old musical notation.

Also a result of radio, the transistor, records, and tape was the increasing number of people living against a background of music; jazz, pop, classical, and modern music formed the backdrop to everyday life. This was something new. A new generation of young people, whether they really listened or merely heard, was learning how to manipulate the new machines and understood what the research was all about; often they were more receptive to it than were the experienced critics.

The new materials available to the plastic arts, and the new methods they made possible, would take too long to enumerate; to name just a few: painting straight from the tube with acrylics; painting on photography paper; for sculptors, synthetics, welded scrap, compressed cars; a whole new gamut of synthetics available for the use of architects.

Museums were transformed into machines for seeing and teaching, often on a lavish scale. Technology also provided the means for artists to exceed limitations formerly inherent in certain art forms: Vasarely's kinetic paintings made the static mobile; Schoffer's sculptures in colored light were weightless. A piece of recording tape could project a mobile, rhythmic, continuously changing picture onto a screen. Artists became engineers. Of the two basic questions the public instinctively asks when confronted with a work of art—What does it mean? and How was it made?—the second was now the more important. Conventional aesthetic opinion, long since abandoned by art historians, became a matter of personal taste or passing fad. The prevailing concept of art as action and manipulation of raw material also fostered a democratization of art. In any case, it explains the general renaissance in Western society of minor arts such as ceramics, weaving, and tapestry. And it was the guiding spirit for experiments—spontaneous or systematic—impelling the artistic media toward new methods of expression: collages; frottages; papiers collés; three-dimensional relief on two-dimensional canvases; writing on paintings; painted geometrical forms; machines and abstract "automata." Although there were some artists—a Mathieu or a Michaux—who saw their canvases as "scriptures," an antithetical group introduced objects from the everyday world into the museum setting, either integrated into paintings, or as is: raw art, or pop.

Writers moved by the same determination to break with the past and become innovators often wrote pieces that were attempts either at analysis or at synthesis of what contemporary artists were trying to do (André Breton, *Le Surréalisme et la Peinture,* 1925; Jean Cassou, *Situation de l'art moderne,* 1950; Jean Paulhan, *L'Art informel,* 1962). They themselves did not enjoy the same opportunities for transforming their "material" nor, insofar as they could transform it, for communicating the result directly to

the public, especially to the international public that guaranteed the popularity of modern art. The obstacle in their way was language. The communications media (radio and television, advertising, newspapers, and magazines) manipulate words, it is true, with an effect on the masses that is
undeniable, and even frightening. But this power is inseparable from transmission of a message, i.e., an immediately graspable syntax and semantic.

It is different for the creative writer, who must employ structures of
greater complexity. When he attempts to revolutionize his "raw material"
by introducing new elements into his text—extracts quoted from newspapers, for example, or from advertisements or radio broadcasts—using the
technique of collage, in fact, he interrupts his narrative line and undermines
the syntax. He destroys the code that makes language the art of communication. In the plastic arts the artist produces objects—paintings,
sculptures—which remain visual, or in the case of music, auditory. When a
writer experiments with words, he does things like dissociating sound from
sense. This shatters the alliance between word and meaning that provides a
literary text's immediate readability. When Isidor Isou, in 1946, decided to
separate words into phonemes and only use their sounds, he created a kind
of onomatopoeic vocal chant, not a "literary" text. The impulse on the part
of some writers to break with the linear constraints imposed by writing and,
through typographical manipulation—unorthodox spacing and print—to
create new expressive possibilities, goes back to Mallarmé. Mallarmé's
Coup de dés was an attempt to produce writing with spatial dimensions. In
Calligrammes, Apollinaire combined writing with drawing; and Picabia
made a page into a visual ensemble, only one element of which was the
word. At this point, the word stops being literature and becomes painting.
In the sixties this tendency was pushed to its logical extreme with Pierre
Garnier's concrete and spatial poetry: the page becomes the locus for the
elaboration of a strange calligraphy, a sort of imitation musical score whose
sole referent is itself; a visual object, not a literary one.

The technology-based experimentation underlying some of Michel
Butor's works is of a more complicated kind. In *Mobile,* a sort of poetic
representation of the multidimensional reality making up the United States,
Butor tries to create a new, structurally oriented linguistic medium comparable to serial music: lists of place names are arranged in a spatial framework; various other categories of series—recurrent objects, elements in the
landscape—introduce thematic materials that are repeated, varied,
alternated; vertical and horizontal groupings on the page emphasize different levels of existence and the latent conflicts between them. In *6,810,000
litres d'eau par seconde,* Butor attempts to represent Niagara Falls verbally,
through creation of a sort of polyphonic score whose sonic effects can be
modified by manipulating earphones. The text is on film, with a soundtrack,
and has been projected in the new amphitheater at Grenoble, which is
equipped with individual earphones for the audience. The work is designed

so that the various thematic voices can be separated sonically, with the listener "distancing" them from one another as he likes. This is less a literary text than an operatic score. And what are we to say about Butor's 1971 *Dialogue avec trente-trois variations de Ludwig van Beethoven sur une valse de Diabelli?*

Even the book itself has become an object to be manipulated. Saporta's *Composition no. 1* presents the reader with 150 pages of narration, unbound, unpaginated, each page complete in itself, and the whole resembling a deck of cards with its infinite possibilities. Queneau bound together twelve sonnets constructed according to the same rhyme scheme and then cut them up, line by line, thus obtaining "a hundred thousand million" (10^{14}) possible sonnets. This kind of fooling, along with other, more complicated attempts to break with established conventions, can be entertaining for a public of initiates, but it can never touch the wider public the way the visual arts can. These are esoteric texts, unreadable for the average reader. Perhaps the reason Canadian professor Marshall McLuhan's spiritual followers were able to accept with such unseemly haste the idea that "print culture is dead" is that books have a built-in resistance to the metamorphoses foisted on them through gratuitous analogy with transformations in the audiovisual arts.

In 1920, writers were at the forefront of the avant-garde. Two fairly fluid, mutually receptive groups were riding the crest of the postwar wave: the Groupe des Six with Jean Cocteau as its spokesman; and the dadaists. Artists from both camps collaborated on the few dadaist films that were produced, and it was here that between 1924 and 1926 the aesthetic/anti-aesthetic trends of modern art briefly converged; cinema, according to André Breton, seemed at the time to be "the only absolutely modern mystery." Dadaist films like René Clair's *Entr'acte* or Léger's *Ballet mécanique* were exuberantly experimental, poking fun at "great art." They played with a machine—the camera—and with the laws of optics, destroying the conventional visual organization of space. Using montage, and casting logic to the winds, they blended images, distances, perspectives, forms, and movements. By doing so they created deformations, juxtapositions, and rhythmic changes, producing a "narrative" whose elements, although taken from the concrete world, were no longer in any way mimetic.

The cinematic continuum of the dadaist films, their space and time, denied serial causality; they displaced temporal continuity, and then transformed temporal discontinuity into another continuity, freshly perceived. These films obliterated the lines of demarcation between the human, the mechanical, and the object, forcing on the spectator a constantly fluctuating succession of images that emitted a finely nuanced humor. Humor, in fact, was inherent in a broad range of modern art forms—from Duchamp's *Ready-mades* to Niki de Saint-Phalle's *Nanas;* in Michaux, Queneau, and Prévert, or, again, in Dubuffet's *Cycle de l'Hourloupe.*

The objectification the camera allows enabled these early films to make fun of the aura of solemnity associated with art. Playing with words, with images, they indulged in mystification and were determined to demystify. For one brief moment dadaist films gave free rein to invention, and then concerns with narrative and message again took over the medium. During the same period, the same gratuitous quality was shared by Max Ernst's frottages, the pranks of the surrealists, and the inventions of a Picabia or a Duchamp; young composers, meanwhile, foreshadowed by Cocteau and his light 1919 work *Le Coq et l'Arlequin*, were drawing their inspiration from the music of fairground, circus, music hall, and café concert. Cocteau re-created the same motifs and the same novel techniques in *Les Mariés de la Tour Eiffel*. But writers after 1924–25 became obssessed with a concern for coherence, and the experiments of film makers and surrealists alike took a new turn; Cocteau, meanwhile, going in rather swift succession from cinema to plays, to poetry and then to criticism, tried to establish the conditions for a "modern" aesthetic.

New Experiments in Theory and New Structures

The need for renewal also appeared in a completely different, less spectacular form: the theoretical. What the surrealists did certainly called into question the foundations of aesthetics, but surrealist theorizing was based on psychology, and surrealist methods offered no new system of expression reflecting the specific imperatives of language. What Breton was interested in uncovering were the laws governing the mind and how it works. Things were different, however, in the field of music. Composer Arnold Schönberg, working in pre-1914 Vienna, had constructed a new system for music based on the twelve tone chromatic scale. It involved a total transformation of the established structural principles governing key, rhythm, melody, and harmony. Schönberg's system employed instead a strictly regulated structure based on the permutation of tone rows. This dodecaphonic system, the guiding principle of serial music, remained unfamiliar in France until after 1945. It was only then that, fifty years after its inception, it received a warm welcome from young composers like Pierre Boulez. The Vienna group, which in addition to Schönberg included Webern and Alban Berg, was working on ideas similar in some ways to the aesthetic preoccupations underlying some of the literary debates taking place in the twenties, preoccupations that in fact were a legacy from Mallarmé. The concept of "pure poetry" was debated in somewhat hazy terms; also the notion of the "pure novel," which Gide had made pivotal to *Les Faux-Monnayeurs*, and reflections regarding "pure cinema." But no new literary theory emerged from all this. Not until midcentury was reached and the question of renewing literary forms was broached once again, did the need for a systematic theory analogous to the one that had produced dodecaphonic music become obvious. At that time a new generation of writers again took up the question of language per se, and how it could be disentangled from the various "languages" of the other arts. Serving as the point of departure for this new venture was the science of linguistics and the work of the Russian formalists. The dadaists had worked in a context of random improvisation, but this "scientific" school used formal theory as the basis for arriving at the text-as-an-object. For both dadaists and formalists, however, the created text represents only one moment in the course of a dialectical process with primarily social goals: to attack society by undermining confidence in the language. The creation of a literary text is not in itself the ultimate goal. But in both cases, the text always eludes the dialectic. Once printed, a text becomes retrievable and therefore, whether we like it or not, transformed into literature; literature of a more or less marginal kind, perhaps, "avant-garde" as it once was, "experimental" today, but literature nevertheless.

Literature and Film: A Borderline Case

"When I see a film like the one we just saw, a kind of magic transports me onto the screen . . . and I begin to feel like one of the heroes in the story." Thus speaks one of the characters in Raymond Queneau's *Loin de Rueil* (1945), as he leaves the theater after seeing a film set in the mythical American *Farouest* (Far West).

Queneau is one of many French writers to have reflected at length on this newcomer to the arts; others are Jean Cocteau (*Entretiens autour du cinématographe,* 1951), Nicole Verdrès (*Images du cinéma français,* 1945), and André Malraux (*Esquisse d'une psychologie du cinéma,* 1946); these have been joined by film makers themselves, and by sociologists (Edgar Morin, *Le Cinéma ou l'homme imaginaire,* 1956). Its structures have been analyzed by Christian Metz in *Communications* and in *Poétique.* Films have had an obvious effect on literature, but one that is difficult to evaluate precisely.

Queneau believed film was essentially a popular art form, a "dream factory" offering the masses a chance to escape from everyday life into the wonders of a "story." Malraux wrote that "film is for the masses, and what the masses love is myths, good or bad." Thus film purveys popular myth on the same level as "photo-romance" magazines, themselves, in turn, off-shoots of popular "cine-romances." But a film maker can just as well purvey great heroic ideals as dreams and illusions. Again Malraux: "Myth begins with Fantômas and ends with Christ." Outside of the exuberant dadaist, then surrealist, avant-garde, film makers from the start had other ambitions. Pursuing their search for a new, "total" language, they made historical panoramas like Abel Gance's *Napoléon;* every imaginable kind of serial—vamp films, gangster films, westerns, films about nightlife in New York and Chicago; epics like Eisenstein's *Battleship Potemkin,* made in the twenties;

and, thirty years later, documentaries like Alain Resnais and Jean Cayrol's *Nuit et Brouillard* (1955), recreating the tragic spectacle of World War II concentration camps; horror films like *The Cabinet of Doctor Caligari* (1920) and *Nosferatu* (1921); comedies with Charlie Chaplin; farce with Laurel and Hardy, the Marx Brothers, or Buster Keaton, or, thirty years later, with Jacques Tati (*Les Vacances de M. Hulot*, 1953).

With the 1928–30 advent of sound, and then color, the potential born with film continued to be exploited. It was apparently clear from the outset that the importance of film did not lie in the *content* of what it projected, but in its *ability to project*. Following the dadaist initiative, it may have been the surrealists of the twenties who, with the last three great experimental films of the era—Luis Bunuel's *L'Age d'or,* Bunuel and Dali's *Un chien andalou,* and Jean Cocteau's *Le Sang d'un poète* (1928–30)—best perceived one of film's most distinctive features: its power to project onto a screen, in fully realized images similar to the ones we see around us in everyday life, subjective fantasies that normally remain hidden. The repressed impulses of the id, which according to Freud lie beneath the mask of civilized man—fantasy, escapism, and eroticism in all its guises—can, through film, take on shapes that are bizarre, or freakish, or horrifying; they, just as much as "the outer crust of reality," (René Clair) are film's chosen domain.

The camera, and the different ways in which film can be manipulated, as the surrealists saw, make it possible to convey an illusion of reality unrestricted by the logical sequence and coherence demanded by writing; on film, illusion maintains an appearance of objectivity and seems to have a life of its own. The development of film art has not occurred as the result of basic changes in what film can do, but in how it has been used. Technical improvements, commercialization, and the eventual universalization of its audience (a hit film today is seen by more than 700 million people) have created a film industry whose methods and aspirations were summarized as late as 1950 by the Hollywood image. The Hollywood system was most favorable to the big, romantic spectacle based on material borrowed from real life, from history, or from novels that had been more or less successfully adapted for the screen.

The impact of these screen adaptations on literature has been negligible; whether or not they recruited avid new readers for books like *Les Misérables* or *Le Rouge et le Noir* is still a moot question. The influence of film has been felt in ways that are more indirect, in areas that are difficult to analyze with precision; for techniques we associate with film, such as flashback, framing, speeding up or down, and tracking, were used by novelists before the advent of film. The one indisputable fact is that a great number of writers have been interested in film: writers who themselves were film makers, like Blaise Cendrars, Jean Cocteau, Jean Cayrol, Alain Robbe-Grillet, Marguerite Duras; writers who collaborated with film makers, like Robbe-Grillet. Jean Cayrol and Marguerite Duras originally worked with Alain Resnais, for example. Conversely, there have been many film makers who fell under the spell of a particular literary universe and felt impelled to recreate it on the screen. The writer more heavily committed than most to the dual pathway of film and novel, and one who himself has created filmlike novels, Alain Robbe-Grillet, believes there is no common denominator between the two modes of expression.

It was film's capacity for the imaginary that was most attractive to an initial generation of artists and writers; but the post-1950 novelists were attracted and intrigued primarily by the narrative techniques available to film. From the moment it first appeared, the impact of film on the public was indisputable: the young surrealists tirelessly attended film after film, enthralled by the vamps and by the fantasmagoria of adventures they later incorporated into their own mythology. *Les Mots* reminds us how Jean-Paul Sartre as a small boy approached with mingled terror and delight the fictional world of the filmed serial—*Fantômas,* for one—that for him replaced the real world outside. Ramuz described the confusion a little Swiss village in the Canton de Vaud was thrown into when the great legendary figures of the screen made their first appearance there; the hero of *Voyage au bout de la nuit* spends hours in New York movie houses, absorbed in the erotic fantasies inspired by movie stars. The spread of cinema's influence worldwide was momentarily arrested with the advent of sound, but the language barrier was overcome through dubbing. American films, Russian, English, Italian, and French films—more rarely Japanese, Indian, and Australian films—"good" or "bad," commercial, documentary, or experimental, all gave people "something to look at"; here, in fact, lay film's greatest strength. For millions of people the limits of the world and the possible were extended by the films they saw. Films presented alternate behavior models, value systems, and life styles. In fact, they invaded the area formerly considered the exclusive domain of, and justification for, literature.

Fully to grasp all the ways in which the two media—film and literature—interact in terms of theme, viewpoint, narrative style, and impact would take meticulous, difficult analysis. Was it really true, for example, as Claude-Edmonde Magny suggests in *L'Age du roman américain,* that American novels were responsible for the adoption of certain essentially cinematographic techniques by their French counterparts? Well before the American novels in question became popular in France, the influence of the scenarios Blaise Cendrars put together between 1921 and 1924, in the cinematographic style then current, is, for example, discernible in the pace and style informing a novel like *Moravagine* (1926) or a poetic autobiography like *Bourlinguer* (1948): the camera eye is evoked by rapid series of discontinuous images seen, in these writings, through the eye of memory; their abrupt tempo mimics that of the old silent films. But how much of this

reflects Cendrars the pre-cinema modernist, Cendrars the passenger on the
Trans-Siberian railway, is hard to say. Just as it is hard to determine exactly
how much "art film" framing was borrowed from the plastic arts.

It is probably on the theoretical and technical level that cinema art has contributed most to essential questions of literature, its aims, its methods, and
especially its basic form: the narrative line. The cinema in France has its own
National Research Center, its own magazines, film clubs, and film libraries;
keenly self-conscious in regard to its own brief history, it has lent itself from
midcentury onward to theoretical investigations of its function and micro-
scopic analyses of its techniques that have frequently been controversial.
Film makers like Fellini and Jean-Luc Godard have even gone so far as to
make film technique itself the subject of some of their films.

When we say "cinema" we refer to a series of images inscribed within a
strictly limited time frame—that of the full-length feature or the short subject. Sound, music, and words are subordinate to movement, primarily
serving to emphasize continuity. Even art films that project purely abstract
sequences of form and color show the latter in the process of changing and
moving. Thus a succession of images is transformed into a kind of story in
much the same way as the narrative line of a text transforms a series of
words into a story. Film can create any number of different backgrounds,
reflecting more accurately than a novel could the specific ambiance of an
era. No matter what the subject—even in a simple documentary showing
how a flower opens—the camera deprives objects of their reality, while at
the same time making them immediately perceptible. It therefore, as with
the other modern arts, undermines the validity of traditional mimetic
theory, but in a special way. The film maker starts by filming something
concrete. But through the use of tracking shots, framing, cutting, and
montage—in short, by manipulating the film and dislocating its focus—he
makes the concrete plastic. "Cinema," said Alain Resnais, "consists in manipulating reality through the manipulation of sounds and images." The
sleight of hand that lies behind all fictional narrative, from the most vulgar
to the most edifying, is exposed by what the film maker does. In a film, even
the most painstaking reproduction of everyday reality is just as obviously an
artificially confected illusion as the most outlandish montage; and the same
holds true for any narrative sequence, by nature always an abstraction in
relation to reality. The vocabulary of film is a sign image vocabulary that
demonstrates as it designates. From this bias it confronts all writers, not just
novelists, with the question of what specific conditions govern their own
sign-word universe, how they manipulate it, and how these conditions relate
to the reality it designates but does not demonstrate. More than any other
art form, perhaps, film raises questions regarding the specificity of what
critic Maurice Blanchot has called "literary space," a problem that from the
1950s on was to occupy an entire school of criticism.

Paraliterature

The development of the mass communication media opened up a whole new gamut of genres, languages, and modes of expression that multiplied the ways of looking at traditional literature. These developments came under the scrutiny of sociologists, linguists, and experts in computer science. The results of their investigations were published in specialized journals such as *Communications,* the organ of the Centre d'Etudes des Communications de Masse de l'Ecole Pratique des Hautes Etudes. Leaving aside advertising, the popular press, and, for the time being, radio and television, this paraliterature solely in book form presented problems of literary value or what linguists refer to as "literarity." Where does true literature begin, and where does it end? What were the reasons for the enormous success of the mysteries "Série noire" (under the editorship of Marcel Duhamel) launched in 1945? More than 500 million copies of the titles in this series were sold, 65 percent of them translations of works first published in the United States, and their readership was largely an intellectual one. And how can we explain the more recent popularity of spy stories? Or the success, starting in the fifties, enjoyed by American-style science fiction? What about comic strips, also, in their current form, of American origin? And what about that quintessence of pop culture, the photo-romance, originally conceived in Italy and currently selling at the rate of five million copies a month? Not to mention pop music, replicated ad infinitum on phonograph records, or—another example—the French television serial drama?

From category to subcategory, paraliterature extends continuously over an ever-widening, ever more diverse area. In our time it has become obvious that social interaction takes place within a universe of signs (words, initials, images, sounds) where both literature and paraliterature have their existence. Even Rimbaud had had an inkling that this was so, as did the surrealists. But for scholars and technicians it was unmapped territory. It turns out that the exact nature of the "literary act" is a hard thing to pin down. What is it, as Roman Jakobson has put it, that turns a verbal message into a work of art? Or, as Roland Barthes would say, what distinguishes a "person who writes" from a "writer"? Is it even possible to isolate, within the dimensions of language, a single discrete category of writings that could be called "literature"? There are no watertight divisions. Raymond Queneau's novel *Zazie dans le métro* ended up as a comic strip, and Simenon's detective stories have traveled in the opposite direction and become "literature." Boris Vian drew heavily on comic strip legend and Le Clézio employed the language of advertising; in one episode of *La Prise/Prose de Constantinople,* Ricardou borrows the theme of the intergalactic voyage dear to science fiction. Ionesco has acknowledged his debt to Groucho, Chico, and Harpo Marx, Artaud his to *Animal Crackers* and *Monkey Business,* and Beckett his to Buster Keaton, as Apollinaire, Desnos, or Queneau before them did theirs to Fantômas.

Paraliterature's immense reservoir of words and images has served as the object of numerous sociological and psychoanalytical studies into their cultural function and the reasons why they exert the attraction they do. Consisting of endlessly retold and infinitely renewable tales, paraliterature gives form to the basic myths, dreams, and desires of human beings who are always seeking ways to escape from the harsh realities of life. This is the language, according to ethnologists, that provides us with an anthropology of the unconscious and therefore constitutes the collective basis for the cultural life of the group. Paraliterary narrative is basically anonymous; its creators occupy the same position in relation to their public and their product as did the hirelings employed by Dumas and Willy to write for them. Four to five hundred mystery writers are published in the "Série noire," but only half a dozen or so are remembered by name, and we forget what was in their books the minute we put them down. This kind of text is easy to translate, is mass produced according to fairly complicated marketing criteria, and reaches a readership of millions. Does this universal verbiage, its substance superimposed on preexisting structures, have any cultural significance? If so, what is it? And who is doing the verbalizing? Whoever he is, his existence radically jeopardizes the concept of the writer as source and master of his own discourse.

Best-sellers

The twin phenomena of paraliterature and the best-seller are connected, but the latter is more complex. The best-seller is a special case, and its success with the public, which even advertising can never guarantee in advance, is unpredictable. We can see what three best-sellers like *Le Diable au corps* (1923), *Bonjour Tristesse* (1954), and Eric Segal's *Love Story* (French translation, 1970)—all three of which were also made into movies—have in common with the classic teenage romance, itself a variant on the Tristan and Iseut legend. Henri Carrière's fantastic success with *Papillon* reflected the book's kinship with the legend of the good-hearted convict à la Jean Valjean. The success of certain foreign novels—*Gone with the Wind,* in 1939; Canadian writer Mazo de la Roche's *Jalna* series during the Occupation; and *Jubilee,* the work of novelist Margaret Walker, who is more popular in France than in the U.S.A.—is apparently due to the romance of the exotic, which also accounts for the success of *Maria Chapdelaine* and the novels of Pierre Benoit.

Queneau's *Zazie dans le métro* (1959), and *Paroles* (1946), by Jacques Prévert, the only poet who ever achieved best sellerdom, were successful for a different reason: they belonged to a traditional popular literary vein, the oral narrative. Two prewar best-sellers, Marcel Aymé's *La Jument verte*

(1933) and Gabriel Chevallier's *Clochemerle* (1934), both humorous works directed at the average middle-class reader, also had their roots in the Gallic oral tradition. Romantic narrative, however, remained the quintessential best-seller form. This is what, in all of its different guises, an enormous mass of people chose to read, people who were as entranced by Maurice Dekobra as by Guy des Cars and in much the same way as blue- and white-collar workers were entranced by photo-romances. Escape and vicarious identification with a novel's hero continued to be the motors that made the romantic machine go round. We might well wonder, in fact, if it will not turn out to be the romantic narrative, in its various paraliterary guises, that will one day serve as the matrix for a renewal of literary language.

Close on the heels of the best-seller comes the "steady seller": Barbusse's *Le Feu;* Dorgelès's *Les Croix de bois;* novels by André Maurois, Jules Romains, Duhamel, and Françoise Sagan (after *Bonjour Tristesse*); and Maurice Druon's great historical fresco. Another example would be Henri Troyat's solidly successful novels—panoramic, multivolume social and historical works like the trilogy *Tant que la terre durera,* or the five-volume *La Lumière des justes,* a novel about Russia which enjoyed a large and faithful following. We could probably establish an "archaeology of taste" that would cast some light into the murky area of literary hierarchies, book sales, and the cases where sales and hierarchy coincide. These facts would point up the somewhat specious nature of the often repeated statement that the novel, with its plot and its characters, is dead. Best-sellers are not dead; their readers find in them the things contemporary literary novels no longer provide.

Referring generally to the mass media and their impact, Claude Lévi-Strauss has pronounced a basically optimistic diagnosis from the anthropologist's point of view: "It seems to me we tend to overemphasize the role of the [mass media] as the great levelers, forgetting the opportunity they provide to specific social or age groups for the rapid development of their own culture. In lieu of a traditional culture that filters down from generation to generation within the family circle, each new generation now finds at its immediate disposal—through newspapers, recordings, and television [and, we should add, films]—a profusion of disparate elements it can select and combine in original ways so as to distinguish itself from its predecessors." It could be that, in the last analysis, literary culture, heretofore the preserve of an elite, will open up to a larger public, one that is better prepared than in the past to grasp its essential qualities and that will experience no difficulty in outpacing literary constraints and conventions that have become outmoded. Literature in no matter what era will have meaning only insofar as it relates to the cultural climate of its time.

9

Trends in Thought

In *La Pensée française d'aujourd'hui* (1971), Edouard Morot-Sir suggests using the word "thought" to refer to the "cultural consciousness of a group," "ideology" to the ways in which "this 'thought' is put to use," and "philosophy" to "original modes" of thinking "terminating in some *logical conclusion*," i.e., either in Hegelian systematizations or Nietzschean "dispersions." This is the sense in which we use the word "thought" here. Michel Foucault, in *L'Archéologie du savoir* (1969), refers also to periods of cleavage—as between geological strata—when the bedrock of "thought" undergoes changes that introduce discontinuities into a cultural consciousness emerging through the successive accretion of "archaeological layers" rather than by continuous evolution. French thought, and perhaps all of Western thought, appears to be in the midst of one of these mutations now, its repercussions affecting "cultural groups" all over the world.

French thought has been affected at the deepest level, first, by historical events. But the long-term effect of scientific progress on culture is undeniable, both because of the visibility of technology applied to everyday life and, even more radically although less directly, because of its basic theoretical schemas. Modern technology may occasionally have provided the theme for a book, but modern scientific theory has confronted writers with fundamental questions concerning the nature of the world, of human life, and of language; concerning, in other words, the very nature of what he is doing. As was already the case in the nineteenth century with the theories of evolution and heredity, this disparate body of hard-to-grasp, frequently misunderstood, vulgarized scientific fact has created a number of misapprehensions. Inconceivable as the implications of these theories may have been for the uninitiated, they have nonetheless transformed the fundamental contemporary image of reality. People have been forced to think in ways they had not done in the past.

Scientific Research

"The age of beginnings is beginning again," said Malraux, writing around 1930 on the "human condition." Scientific discoveries made during the fifty-year period under discussion in the present book shook the foundations of Western thought. Impossible to summarize, their story has been characterized by a transformation in the scientific research paradigm, which now, instead of going from observation, through induction, to the formulation of a theoretical model, postulated a theoretical model first, and validated it afterward. Below is a brief list of the scientific developments that have had the greatest impact on contemporary thought:

1. From 1920 to 1940, the progress in modern physics due to new mathematical conceptions brought to bear on studies of how matter is formed; this led to the successful achievement of nuclear fission (1938), which was the first step toward mastery of nuclear energy. These developments also transformed man's conception of the cosmos.

2. The development of molecular biology.

3. Influenced by World War II, the post-1948 development of electronics, on which cybernetics, information theory, and computer science are based.

These revolutionary discoveries had an effect, although frequently a delayed one, on other areas of thought. Their influence was a reflection not only of the achievements of science but also of the immensity of the unknown that confronted scientists, who became askers of questions rather than providers of answers. Old assumptions were undermined, metaphysics affected, traditional beliefs put to the test, and mankind's ways of speaking about itself turned upside down. Literature, of course, was also directly affected.

The New Physics

In 1922, Einstein received the Nobel Prize. The award crowned a body of theoretical work, the fruit of a succession of investigations transforming the traditional Newtonian notions of time, space, energy, and mass. Einstein formulated a preliminary theory of relativity in 1905; in 1919 it was verified experimentally and rapidly followed by a general theory of relativity limiting the applicability of the Newtonian laws of gravity, whose universality had until then been taken for granted.

On the microphenomenal level, furthermore, quantum physics—the study of the constituent elements of matter (atoms) and light (photons)—revealed the existence of discontinuity and indetermination. Statistical probability derived from mathematics was put forth as a substitute for the strict causal determinism of traditional science. This novel concept, which many scientists including Einstein himself refused to accept, cast doubts on the axiom of the predictability of natural phenomena. What first struck the imaginations of the uninitiated about these theories was, besides their destruction of a familiar image of reality, the resonance of terms like "relativity," "fourth dimension," "discontinuity," "indetermination," and "uncertainty principle," all of which could frequently be found transposed into the nonscientific context of the everyday. More disconcerting still was the fact that Einstein had formulated his theory entirely on the basis of theoretical mathematical formulas, and not from direct observation and measurement of concrete phenomena: verification after the fact of formulation raised questions concerning the relation between the observable natural order and the abstract constructs of the mind. This initial empiric upheaval was followed by others in other sciences, and even in literary criticism.

Einsteinian physics no longer defined space in terms of only three variables (length, width, and height). A fourth had now been added: time. Einstein's physics replaced the three-dimensional universe proposed by classic geometry with a four-dimensional one. Some mathematicians, like Riemann, had also postulated that mathematics is by nature axiomatic, i.e., that it is basically logical and leads not to certainties but, through the rigorous application of logic and the principles of noncontradiction, to the consequences implicit in the original axiom it proposes. Euclidean axioms will thus generate Euclidean geometry; other axioms will generate other geometries. The conventional concept of a single temporal scale governing all cosmic phenomena gave way to the concept of different time scales for different phenomena. Observation of the galaxies from the perspective of earth, when the laws of light wave propagation were taken into consideration, thus implied observation of phenomena occurring prior to the temporal frame occupied by the observer. The difference would vary in proportion to the distance and had to be counted in light years. Any scientist who had once thought of himself as an observer existing independently of the phenomena being observed now had to recognize that he was working within a system, and that his observations were therefore relative. Differing according to the model used, the diversity discovered in the natural order raised a question: How much faith can we justifiably place in our representations of the world? A reinterpretation of the meaning of scientific "laws" was in order.

In combination with other branches of science—for example, chemistry—and as a result of technological progress, Einstein's theories became accessible to two fields of potential verification and spectacular research: astronomy and nuclear physics.

When technological progress after World War II made giant telescopes available to specialists, the cosmic importance of the basic theory of relativity became obvious even to the uninitiated. These telescopes made it possible to explore an astronomical realm only distantly related to the Newtonian universe. If, as has often been said, perhaps unnecessarily, twentieth-century man is still suffering from the satellite status imposed on him by Copernicus and the loss of his familiar place at the center of the cosmos, what can we say of the vast reaches of perpetually changing outer space described by new and contradictory cosmogonies? The study of how galaxies are formed, the discovery of novae and supernovae, interstellar matter, and incalculable numbers of planets, some perhaps inhabited or at least inhabitable, have disconcerted imaginations, exalted them or filled them with anguish, but, in either case, have stimulated considerable thought on the subject of the "human condition." It was cosmic anguish that inspired in André Malraux his eloquent, Pascal-like meditations, and cosmic anguish that provided some modern poets with a new system of imagery: in this system the earth is but the straightened home of man, turning as though lost inside a vast universe of fire and stone. Within this new cosmos, man's self-attributed importance appears derisory, and the anthropocentric universe of literature—for some thinkers, at any rate—seems to hark back to a system of representation belonging to the Dark Ages.

At the other end of the scale, powerful cyclotrons made investigations into the constitution of matter possible that ultimately resulted in the discovery of a *new energy source* with an apparently limitless potential for transforming the modalities of human existence. The Atomic Age was ushered in by an event striking a kind of terror into people all over the world: on August 6, 1945, the first atomic bomb was detonated over Hiroshima. From that moment on, nuclear energy's promise was eclipsed in the popular imagination by its power to destroy. Living under the shadow of thermonuclear warfare, threatened by the unresolved problems of radiation and pollution that go with this new energy source, the "children of Hiroshima" (Pierre Emmanuel) feel a menace weighing on their own future, and on the future of the planet.

Molecular Biology and the Genetic Code

"Funny life, the fishy life, finfunny, minminnow." Thus begins, in Queneau's novel *Saint Glin-Glin,* the monologue of a character thinking aloud before an aquarium's strange denizens. Descending the fish scale to the most primitive organisms, he wonders where the line separating conscious organisms from other forms of life falls. He states the question of biological evolution and the unity of all these bizarre creatures in reverse, and is unable to feel himself as representing its predestined end. What is life? And where does that complex organism called man belong in the evolutionary scheme of things, what is he? These are the great post-Darwinian questions in biology.

In 1970, two biologists, who five years previously had won the Nobel

Prize, published two essays: *Le Hasard et la Nécessité,* and *La Logique du vivant.* In them the two authors, Jacques Monod and Francis Jacob, discussed the implications of recent developments in the biological sciences. These new developments were the result of a discovery made in 1953 by two scientists, Watson and Crick, in the course of studying molecules at the ultramicroscopic level. What they discovered was the "double helix," or DNA (deoxyribonucleic acid). Their discovery cast new light on the function of the cell, that infinitely complex biological element central to a process shared by all living things and governing their reproduction. The research revealed that DNA, an element of the cellular nucleus, carries a code; that cellular activity is responsible for transmission of the code; and that the code exercises strict control over the organism's future development and reproduction. The DNA "double helix" carries all the information a living organism needs for its internal organization and future development. It therefore follows that a biological entity is primarily a physicochemical phenomenon, a system which can circumvent for a time the law of entropy, and which possesses its own system of cybernetic control, the genetic code. According to this school of biology, only *accidental* intervention, coming from either within or without, can introduce modifications into the characteristics of a given species, which would otherwise remain invariable. This implies, paradoxically, that the rigorous structural codes differentiating the various species from one another can only be modified through random occurrences. In this view, all living things, including man, are essentially the random outcome of a sort of "cosmic lottery" (Edgar Morin). According to Jacques Monod, human beings, like any other living organisms, can therefore no longer be thought of in terms of a force—God, élan vital, or history—endowing them with their place and their significance in a predictable and continuous evolutionary scheme. Evolution has no Prime Mover, no beginning, no end, no continuity. The biological organism we know as man is purely accidental.

"We can no longer think of life," wrote Michel Foucault (*Le Monde,* 15–16 November 1970), "as the great, continuous, voluntary creation of individuals; we must think of it as the calculable interplay between chance and reproduction." "Man," concluded Monod, "understands at last that he is alone in the indifferent vastness of a universe from which he emerged by chance. Neither his destiny nor his purpose are anywhere written." The biological science beginning to develop today opens onto austere perspectives, rejoining the "vision of the absurd" that Camus wrote about and Monod quoted. Some scientists, Monod and Jacob among them, have themselves been disturbed by the implications of their research, and have attempted—in the great tradition of Francis Bacon, Descartes, Pascal, Newton, Darwin, and Poincaré—to see the consequences of their research in human terms, and to rid their society of the obsolete theoretical mystifications under which it lives. The theories offered by these two scientists do, however, resolve a fundamental conflict: given the systematic nature of the laws of physics and chemistry, how can the emergence of living organisms be explained? The conventional belief that present phenomena are the result of linear, causal development—in other words, that every existing phenomenon has been *determined* by its diachronic history—is the exact opposite of the structural approach illustrated by the concept of the genetic code. This example is perhaps one of the most obvious instances of the many contradictions inherent in contemporary thought. In the area of biology, at least, it appears to have been resolved.

Information Theory

It was not until 1948 that the American scientist Claude E. Shannon formulated a "mathematical theory of communication." Another scientist, Norbert Wiener, published a book the same year entitled *Cybernetics,* which gave the young, vigorous new science its name. The word "cybernetic" derives from the Greek word for "steersman." It is used to designate "any theory dealing with communication and control in living organisms or machines." Information theory is a broader category, encompassing both cybernetics and its practical applications. The post–World War II development of electronics, a new tool based on electrical mechanics, gave the science of information just the boost it needed. In contrast to the general public's reaction to nuclear energy, the new developments in electronics were assimilated with ease into everyday life on a global scale: today, when we listen to the radio, look at television, use the telephone, or reserve an airplane ticket, we are using electronics. All around us, machines that have by now become familiar sights receive and emit signals of all kinds, transmitting messages, performing rapid and complex calculations, controlling other machines, and, without human intervention, even correcting their own errors. These machines carry out operations formerly assumed to be the prerogative of the human brain. Pascal once constructed a rudimentary calculating machine. But the huge electronic computers of today possess what are called, by analogy, "memories." They are machines that can record information and then preserve it for use in subsequent operations. These "memories," within the limitations of their programming, can provide answers in seconds to complex problems that would take a human brain untold hours of work to solve. How they do it is explained by a theory of communication whose jargon makes use of current terms such as message, information, and, of course, communication in ways that create a certain amount of confusion for the uninitiated—particularly since the most familiar medium of communication, language, is only one among many communication media dealt with by the theory in question. According to Shannon, the word "communication" refers to all those processes by which one mind is able to exert influence over another, a definition he himself considers incomplete, however, since in cases such as remote-controlled missiles the word "communication" is not applied to minds modifying other minds but to machines modifying the behavior of other machines. But words, the arts, indeed, all of human behavior fall in the field of information theory. And the theory is less concerned with the *content* of communication than with the *form*.

The science of information rests on a *physical* theory explaining the various means of expression used in the act of communication, i.e., methods of communication, and these include speech and writing. "Language" in this sense no longer carries with it the status of "logos." There exist two main areas of information theory research: the purely technical and—because the human brain and central nervous system in many ways constitute the "model" for all mechanisms of message reception, emission, and transmission—the biological. According to Shannon, problems of three types are involved in the communication process: (1) the degree of accuracy with which the symbols employed—writing, voice, two-dimensional image, mathematical sign—can be transmitted from sender to receiver (a technical problem); (2) the transition from transmission to interpretation, and how it is made (a semantic problem); and (3) message effectiveness, i.e., the reaction of the receptor and how it can be guaranteed and evaluated.

The communication process begins with a sender, who chooses, from an infinite number of possible messages, the message to be transmitted: the form this message takes can be a series of letters from the alphabet, musical notes, or blobs of color. The message is subsequently transformed, through the transmission agent, into a *signal* traveling along a conduit (electric wire, light ray, electrical signal) toward the receptor, which performs the operation of the sender in reverse. For a message to be transformed into a signal, it must be encoded. The problem is finding the most effective code. The word "information" in this context takes on a special meaning: it refers to the ratio between the sender's freedom of choice when encoding a message within a communication system, and the accuracy and effectiveness of the encoded message's transmission. This is a statistical problem, and therefore a mathematical one. A communications system must be able to transmit any message produced by the sender. Coding is based on the mathematical theory of probability: for example, when choosing any random group of letters from the alphabet, out of the twenty-six possibilities the first choice will be free, but, from the second choice on, freedom will decrease with each successive letter and, ultimately, word. The probability of a given symbol occurring is affected by what has gone before and can be reduced to a mathematical formula; this makes possible the creation of codes ensuring maximum transmissibility.

The practical applications of this science have long since become familiar. Now their implications in the field of literature are also gaining attention.

Information theory has transformed the way libraries are organized; it makes possible the rapid retrieval of bibliographical data and accurate day-to-day record keeping. Information theory also offers a tool for textual analysis whose full potential—and limitations—are still unclear. Even more important, perhaps, information theory has opened up new perspectives in language, and in the specific form of communication known as literature: a literary work, in terms of information theory, is primarily a problem of sign analysis.

Structurally, all human languages are actually code systems designed for "message" transmission; the sender's freedom-of-choice ratio in French is about 50 percent. It would therefore seem to follow that the potential area for verbal or written exchange is structured in advance; and that the system itself exerts a limiting influence on the number of new combinations transmissible within it. The impact of information theory on linguistic theory, and on the linguistic research of groups such as *Change* or *Tel Quel,* has been profound.

Cybernetics, particularly in conjunction with neurophysiology, has also raised questions as to the nature of thought itself. The fact is, the computer offers a mechanical "model" for both conscious and unconscious human thought processes, and it can already replace these processes in cases where maximum objectivity is required for simple decision making, even when there is an element of judgment involved. And yet judgment has always been thought of as a uniquely human quality. In the area of literature, however, we had already been made familiar with Paul Valéry's lengthy reflections on the operations he performed alone with his *Cahiers* in the early morning hours, choosing a random element—the first line of a poem with its inherent rules (rhythm, vocabulary, sound interplay)—and then going on almost mechanically (or was it not he, but the language itself going on?) to produce the entire linguistic system represented by a finished poem. Poet at work? Or language working through him? Some writers—Georges Bataille, for example—aspire to violate these limitations of the linguistic code in literature. After a thorough examination of the language of contemporary literary criticism in terms of its usefulness as a tool, many *nouveaux critiques* such as Roland Barthes have attempted to breathe new life into the "message" by renewing the linguistic code. And, as we shall see, the experiments made in a journal like *Communications,* what was done and how it was done, were influenced at least in part by information theory. Readers may sometimes have the impression that these experimental efforts were less scientific than was claimed, and that both research and discussion at times belie a bias that is willfully esoteric. Nevertheless, the questions raised by cybernetics have cast new light on how we see ourselves in relation to ourselves, and on what we as living organisms gifted with speech are really doing when we speak.

Linguistics

Modern linguistics has set itself the task of studying language as a system of signs—a semiology—and of describing it as accurately as possible without necessarily considering the meaning transmitted by it, or its previous history, so as to uncover the principles that underlie it on all levels: phonological, syntactical, semantic. In this the activity of the modern linguist is clearly differentiated from that of the philologist and his formerly historical, comparative domain. Fifty years separate Ferdinand de Saussure's *Cours de linguistique générale* (1916) from Emile Benveniste's *Problèmes de linguistique générale;* and research in linguistics during those fifty years took off in several directions. We will be taking a brief look at general linguistic theory here, because it is this that has had the most dramatic effect on literary theory and the vocabulary of literary criticism since 1960.[1]

Saussure's *Cours de linguistique générale* is a collection of posthumously published lecture notes. In them he proposes a problematics and a methodology of language that have been retrospectively linked with structural linguistics, which, strictly speaking, was developed concurrently but independently by a small group of scholars in Moscow and then in Prague, the so-called "formalists" Shlovsky, Eichenbaum, Propp, Jakobson, and Troubetskoy, among others, and later, during the fifties, by the American linguist Noam Chomsky. The work of Saussure and the formalists had no impact on France until Roman Jakobson and anthropologist Claude Lévi-Strauss met in the United States during the 1940s. Following the war, so-called "structural" linguistics was from the very beginning closely linked to anthropology, a state of affairs that occasionally gave rise to confusions in terminology.

Saussure's linguistics included a theory of the sign, which already had a long history behind it, and an original theory of language as system. Saussure introduced the concept of the linguistic sign as arbitrary, i.e., as not bearing any necessary relation to the objects to which it refers. From this it followed that the way in which words are arranged does not in any way depend on the way in which things are arranged—or on reality. According to Saussure, a sign contains two elements which, in Saussure's own image, are joined together like the two sides of a coin: there is the acoustic side, or signifier; and the conceptual side, or signified. Saussure made a further distinction between what he called *langue* and what he called *parole.* Following his hypothesis, *langue* refers to the synchronic system in which "everything depends on everything else," and *parole* refers to a segment of the system drawn on when individuals exercise the faculty of speech. This is a process of selection that takes place unconsciously, since individuals inter-

---

[1] The following explanation owes a great deal to five masterly pages by professor of philosophy Peter Caws, *Diacritics,* Summer 1973, 15–21.

nalize the linguistic code. *Langue* for Saussure is a collective phenomenon, and *parole* is the use made by individuals of the collectivity's linguistic code.

However, the relation between the concepts of sign and of system remained to be elucidated in order to obtain the concept of language as structure. This concept evolved gradually from phonology and then with Chomsky (who reiterated Saussure's concepts of *langue* and *parole*), from an examination of syntax as analyzed by Nicolas Ruwet in his *Introduction à la syntaxe généralisée*. Phonologists attempted to isolate the structure of every meaning-bearing sound in a given language; they attempted also to analyze the structure of every potential meaningful word sequence in the language. *Parole* for Chomsky was thus a "combinative," in the mathematical sense, involving both some constraint and some freedom of choice in the production of linguistic entities. At the phonemic level there is no freedom of choice; and for the creation of new words, very little. But when it comes to organizing words into sentences, freedom of choice increases somewhat, and when sentences are arranged in order to create new contexts and, thus, new messages, it increases even more. The constraints imposed by linguistic and phonological "rules" ensure the communicability of what is said or written; and when an individual explores the possibilities for fresh combinations, the linguistic system will also allow for what Chomsky calls the "creative" use of language.

The work of the Russian formalists was addressed solely to the language of literature and was therefore of greater relevance to literary theory and criticism than it was to linguistics itself. The formalists believed that every literary work and every literary genre constitutes a closed system whose linguistic structure must be studied independent of "message" or content. But of course, whether from the linguistic, or from what was later to become known as the "structuralist," point of view, shelving the semantic problem (that is, the relation between language and reality) was purely a matter of methodology, not a philosophical assertion that an unbridgeable rupture existed between language and reality, language and thought, or language and any other experience. To qualify a linguistic system as "synchronic," or existing totally in the "present," is to advance a hypothesis permitting the linguist to study how languages function, without having to deal with how they evolved historically. For example, when we say the structure of folk tales can be analyzed without taking into account the content of any one story, we do not deny that such content exists, we simply isolate the relational constants within the organizing system, or typogenerative "model."

Although some areas of linguistic study—phonology, for example—are indeed scientific, many have been the speculative forays based on metaphors borrowed from science that have not led to verifiable conclusions. This is an important fact to remember when dealing with the "models" for literary structuralism. These are hypothetical, descriptive, and analytical models that have served as tools for opening up new avenues, first, in the theory of

literature and, second, to a new rhetoric of discourse—if not quite yet to a
"science" of literature. A science of signs, or semiology, influenced by linguistics, has begun to emerge. With its first international congress in June 1974,
both its vigor and its uncertainties were emphasized. The eclecticism of the
viewpoints represented at the congress, while acting as a much needed corrective to the dogmatism of various French approaches, still served to demonstrate that semiology is far from its goal of becoming purely scientific.

This brief outline of the new scientific concepts based on complex mathematical formulas has been necessarily oversimplified. The important thing,
as the English philosopher Bertrand Russell once pointed out, is the intellectual demand they make on the individual. It will perhaps be another
two or three generations before certain mental habits and ways of looking at
things change. Our era has been characterized by an unprecedented and
apparently limitless increase in scientific knowledge; there is no way we can
foresee what that knowledge may include tomorrow. This process has affected the established representational systems which once gave some sense
of security to the life of the individual. One such system is nature and
natural law, or "reality." The ineluctable changes in mental attitude caused
by acceptance of current scientific theory have affected collective modes of
thought in France gradually and sporadically, for France is a country with
an ancient culture and generally slight inclination to embark on intellectual
ventures exceeding metaphysical constructs of a traditional, formal kind.
The same has held true for research into human nature and the relations
between individuals and society, which also evolved with, and was influenced by, scientific progress. As a result, with the exception of fairly
restricted groups of specialists, the inadequacy of the French intellectual
heritage became obvious only to the post-1950 generations. This explains
the latent revolt, the spirit of dissention, and the determination to find
something new that were characteristic of postwar academic and literary
circles; it also explains the fascination exerted on some members of these
circles by the language of mathematics and the theoretical processes of
science.

Human Behavior: New Perspectives

"Man," said Cocteau, "has not changed much since the days of Homer."
This classic cliché is one that the psychotechnicians of human behavior—
"behaviorists" in the United States, "Pavlovians" in the Soviet Union—do
not share.

Freud, on the other hand, did believe that human nature and the human
condition do not change; but he also believed that man, from time immemorial, has never understood them.

These two antagonistic approaches to psychological research were only
belatedly echoed in French middle-class circles satisfied with psychological

models that, with slight adjustments from the Age of Enlightenment but almost none at all from nineteenth-century Darwinism, were a legacy from the seventeenth century. These were the models that assumed the authority of textbook verities and continued to prevail in the theater, and in novels of moral analysis à la Paul Bourget. Behaviorists and psychoanalysts alike presented a challenge to one of the mainstays of the Christian, Cartesian, French intellectual heritage: respect in the individual conscience and a belief that every individual is endowed with the ability to order his own behavior according to the dictates of that conscience, source of all virtue and reason.

Psychotechnology

A psychotechnologist is someone who studies reflexes in living creatures—human and animal—and, under carefully controlled conditions, the ways in which both their physiological and their psychological responses can be automatically stimulated, and therefore controlled. On the basis of these observations, whole philosophies of education, ethics, politics, and even metaphysics can be, and have been, logically deduced. French writers remained comparatively untouched by this research, however, except perhaps for the occasional science fiction writer exploiting modern versions of the medieval "homunculus" in the form of man-monsters or robots built by mad scientists in their laboratories. Aldous Huxley, an Englishman with connections in the world of science, in 1932 published the best-selling *Brave New World,* virulently satirizing a fictitious society whose members are submitted to a mercilessly dehumanizing conditioning process conducted by a technocratic power structure and begun before they are even born. Solzhenitsyn's *Gulag Archipelago* (1974) confirmed the prophetic nature of Huxley's utopia. But it was probably not until midcentury, with the development of neurosurgery, biochemistry, and cybernetics, that people began to grasp the full extent of the widening chasm between established fact and current modes of psychological analysis. Psychological analysis, to the psychotechnician, is little more than empty chatter.

Psychoanalysis

It was Freud who, step by painful step, and against serious opposition, constructed a revolutionary theory of psychic function and a new therapy, *psychoanalysis,* whose influence was so profound its advent is considered by some to be the "single most important event" of our century. Whereas the behaviorists, or psychotechnicians, were interested in observable outward behavior and the laws that govern it, Freud turned his attention to the subjective, and often deeply hidden, processes that take place within the human psyche. The majority of Freud's works appeared in France, often years after the original publication, between the 1921 publication of Yves

Lelay's translation of *Psychoanalysis* and 1936, the publication date of *Five Lectures on Psycho-analysis,* translated by M. Bonaparte and R. Loewenstein. Thus *The Interpretation of Dreams,* for example, written in 1900, was not translated into French until 1925. Although cultivated circles in France remained indifferent to behaviorist psychology, their hostility to Freudianism surprised even Freud himself. Dr. Eugenia Sokolnicka, one of Freud's psychiatrist pupils and the model for Sophroniska in *Les Faux Monnayeurs,* attempted without success to enlighten the NRF group concerning the man Gide had referred to as "that imbecile of a genius." Only rarely, previous to 1914, did works appear in France that were inspired by Freud. After World War I the sole distributors of Freud's works were Charles Baudouin in Geneva and publishers in Belgium, where a 1924 issue of *Le Disque vert* had been devoted to him. A few psychiatrists—Drs. Allendy, Laforgue, and Marie Bonaparte—were familiar figures in certain exclusive intellectual circles, and they labored to make Freudian ideas known to the French. The Psychoanalytic Society of Paris was founded only in 1926, and it was not until 1953, on the occasion of Dr. Jacques Lacan's break with that society, that the French intelligentsia's indifference to Freud was transformed into a sort of infatuation. This delayed action craze was in fact triggered by a highly personal reinterpretation of Freud. Lacan had a new theory to propose regarding the function of the psyche. It was based on an analysis of language and was only secondarily concerned with Freud's stated goal of achieving a "concrete knowledge of man." The Lacan fad succeeded by 1960 in paving the way for widespread distribution of Freud's works, some of which were reprinted in paperback. From then on a continually increasing public responded to Freud's ideas, their substance, usefulness, and limitations, with continually increasing understanding.

Freud's therapeutic method has long since become familiar: the patient is asked to stretch out on a couch and is encouraged to speak freely, letting his thoughts wander; the psychoanalyst is present, but he is not visible and he does not obtrude. Freud gradually learned how to discern, in what his patients told him, associations that were disturbing, displacements of meaning, and superficially absurd lapsus linguae. The study of these phenomena eventually led him to formulate the hypothesis that unconscious processes of symbolization intervene in the representations of reality projected by the patient; that there apparently exists a kind of "censor" blocking the patient's conscious awareness of the psychic conflicts within him. Freud attributed this repression to the superego—an internalized paternal or divine authority figure reflecting social usage and punishing the guilty ego for transgressing an inviolable injunction or taboo. Freud connected this guilt complex with sexuality in the broad sense of "libido," that urgent yearning for pleasure, the most common form of which is sexual desire. Freud traced the ways in which this yearning is either satisfied or denied back to earliest infancy, and their initial occurrence in the family framework of mother, father, and child. Freud believed the conflict between superego and libido is the inevitable result of individual socialization, and that it results in psychological complexes, the most basic of which, according to Freud, is the Oedipus complex: the unconscious physical desire on the part of a male child for his mother, his rivalry with his father, and his subsequent feelings of guilt. Or, inversely and somewhat more complicatedly, in the case of a female child.

These ideas caused a furore at the turn of the century—proof, in Freud's opinion, of the power of his patients' self-inflicted censorship and the oblique nature of what they said to him, containing beneath the outward form an underlying message. Freud eventually began to connect this indirect language with the a-logical associations of dreams. He believed one of the ways repressed desire expresses itself is in the disguised, symbolic manifestations of the dream. It is the psychoanalyst's task to aid the patient in returning to the source of his emotional block, so that he will be able to elucidate its meaning for himself. It was not Freud's aim to judge the impulses causing the conflict but to free the patient from it by enabling him to gain insight into it; insight would then lead to normalization of the patient's behavior. Infantile behavior is determined by the *pleasure principle* and controlled by the libido, or need to satisfy desire; individual maturity is achieved when the limits and constraints of the *reality principle* are accepted. Conflicts between the pleasure principle and the reality principle are therefore a manifestation of the inevitable dualism of individual versus society. Although Freud believed conflictual patterns to be fundamentally invariable, he also believed that each individual relates to them and experiences them in his own way; each unconscious, we might say, formulates its own language. Freud's early friend and subsequent adversary C. G. Jung believed, on the other hand, that each individual unconscious is part of a collective unconscious specific to the human species and inscribed in its myths and legends. Although considered by the followers of Freud to be insufficiently scientific, Jung's theories were accepted more readily in France than Freud's; it was easier to relate them to French spiritualistic philosophical traditions. But Freud considered them pure mystification. Of the generation of novelists born in or around 1885, those who attempted to explore the troubled depths of the human psyche—Mauriac, Bernanos, Julien Green—all stood firmly within the Christian tradition, and their adhesion to the Christian dualities of body and soul, good and evil, sin and grace was incompatible with Freudian thought.

With the exception of a very few writers such as the poet-novelist Pierre Jean Jouve, this generation scarcely felt the influence of Freud at all.

The generation that came in with the new century proved more indulgent, although Malraux, as a man dedicated to heroic values of Nietzschean origin, condemned the fascination exerted on his contemporaries' imaginations by the "secrets" concealed in a subconscious he considered monstrous. He believed you cannot know man by scratching the surface of an individual, and that a man's "secrets" are less important than his actions: for

Malraux, a man is what he does. On this point he and the Marxists agreed. The surrealists—particularly Breton, who visited Freud in Vienna—were very warmly disposed toward Freud's ideas, but they were primarily seeking in them a kind of authentication of their own. Actually, on the relation between the subconscious and the surreal—the subconscious as the key to surreality, libido as the pathway to fantasy or to insight into how the mind really works—Freud had little to say.

There were some aspects of Freudian psychoanalysis, however— particularly analysis of the "complexes" and of the masks assumed by the passions—that penetrated novel writing to such a degree Emmanuel Berl felt called upon in 1930 (*Formes,* 5 April) to write denouncing the abuses of Freudianism. And yet it was only gradually, and after 1950, that Freudianism really began to make itself felt in France, in the novel especially. Perhaps James Joyce's *Ulysses,* the most Freudian novel of the time, was responsible for finally giving a generation of writers access to the Freudian vision.

Borne by a single voice, the "I" of a subject, novelistic worlds began to appear in which temporal planes exist vertically in relation to one another. Intersecting and blending together, these temporal planes presented the problem of the subject's myths, and his masks. Before, the Freudians had confined themselves to writing psychoanalytic literary biographies; now they were turning toward interpreting literary texts from the psychoanalytic point of view.

Freud believed artistic activity is analogous to dream activity, with the artist substituting for reality's inflexible world an imaginary world of his own. Authors who had once believed themselves masters of their work discovered, thanks to Freud, how elusive that work is, and how vulnerable their clearest intentions to various interpretations. Insofar as its basic premises were accepted by writers, the Freudian revolution changed the relation between author and text, and between author and critic. When literary criticism applies psychoanalytic methods of interpretation to language, its purpose is to illuminate the *obliqueness* of a literary narrative carrying a hidden meaning within it.

Psychology and Phenomenology

Chapter 2 of the last part of *L'Etre et le Néant* (1943), Jean-Paul Sartre's "essay on phenomenological ontology," is entitled "Existentialist Psychoanalysis." In a span of about ten years starting in 1943, this essay provided atmosphere, conflicts, and moral tone for an entire school of literature, and particularly for novels. But on a deeper level it was Husserl's *phenomenology* that served in France as the basis for the inquiries of Sartre and Maurice Merleau-Ponty, and that opened up new avenues in the theory of behavior. Starting in the thirties, phenomenology produced changes in the ways behavior is perceived and described. Sartrean psychoanalytic existentialism may have fed the literary endeavor of Sartre, Simone de Beauvoir, and the group that gravitated around *Les Temps modernes*—novelists, playwrights, and especially critics—but it was phenomenology that furnished the problematic for the *nouveaux écrivains* of the fifties. And this problematic transformed their conception of what a novel is.

The phenomenological problematic also served as the point of departure for a humanistic school of Catholic thought in the process of breaking away from the conventional intellectual patterns. Also connected in part to phenomenology were Emmanuel Mounier's "personalism," introduced in his *Traité du caractère* (1946), and the philosophy and plays of Gabriel Marcel. Existential psychology is both *method*—the phenomenological method—and metaphysics. But these two existential currents derive from two antagonistic intellectual sources: from philosophical idealism; and from the philosophical development known as existentialist, which from Hegel to Marx, from Kierkegaard to Nietzsche, flowed throughout the nineteenth century.

"Everything I know about the world, including what I have learned through science, I know from my own perspective, or from direct experience of the world without which the symbols of science would be meaningless," wrote Maurice Merleau-Ponty, explaining, in the *Phénoménologie de la perception* (1945), the philosophy of Husserl. This point of view had led Husserl to restate the problem of perception—and therefore of consciousness—in terms of a philosophical method: phenomenology. Phenomenology is the "attempt . . . to describe our experience directly, as it is, without regard for how it developed psychologically, or for the causal explanations scholars, historians, or sociologists might give for it." The aim of phenomenology is to strive systematically, as Descartes did, for "tabula rasa," and to thrust aside all of our accepted, "natural" reactions in order to reexamine the immediate impact of phenomena and the way perception "gives" them to us. In this sense consciousness becomes an "outlook" on the world.

Idealist philosophers divorce consciousness from the world and claim that our knowledge of the world can only be based on the images *(eidos)* we have of it. In the world/consciousness duality, the "real" world is suppressed. Positivist philosophers, on the other hand, see consciousness as a sort of observation post located outside reality. They believe consciousness can acquire objective knowledge about the world, but that it is not itself a part of that reality. For Husserl, the world and human consciousness of the world occur simultaneously. The world is experience, progressively revealing itself to the individual as his sphere of action. Perception of the world thus becomes a perspective on the world, an intentional and, therefore, a meaningful one. It is here that we come to a junction of epistemology and psychology.

Classic psychology posits *being* before all else, and all activity as a *consequence* of being. The empiricists and positivists define man in terms of *what he does*. Phenomenology, on the other hand, proposes equating the self with what the self perceives, that is, with how the self structures reality, and how this structure reveals reality to it. For writers, especially novelists, this was a revolutionary point of view. It transformed conventional conceptions of a "character" and his relation to his background. Traditional novelistic psychological analysis, objective descriptions of a locale, and the relation between individuals and their surroundings were all undermined. If an individual reveals himself by the way in which he structures perceived reality, both reality and the individual emerging from it become problematic.

Freudian psychology and phenomenology both addressed the question of how tenuous our representations of reality and the meaning we assign to them really are. Both disciplines blur the demarcation line between fiction and reality. Both question the heuristic value of traditional explanations for behavior, and advocate new ways of investigating and interpreting what we do; the Freudian patient's free, and superficially meaningless, associations gradually reveal the hidden nucleus controlling how they occur—through displacement, substitution, ellipsis. The structuring of reality, implicit in every human activity, became the locus of phenomenological exegesis.

But whereas the goal of Freudian psychoanalysis is to make an individual patient aware of a subjective process, phenomenology is directed toward the conceptual and social context that underlies individual perception of reality. Ultimately, phenomenology leads to an interrogation which is social and metaphysical.

10

Metaphysics,
Mythology,
and Humanism

"Today we no longer believe in the fixed, predetermined meanings presented to mankind by the divine order of ancient times, nor in the rationalistic order of the nineteenth century that replaced it; we put our faith in man: the forms created by man give meaning to the world" (*Pour un nouveau roman*, 1963). This statement by Alain Robbe-Grillet, though oversimplified, sums up the dominant intellectual trend of our time. The novels of Gide and Proust, Malraux's vision, Sartre's philosophy, and Bataille's experiments, despite their individual complexities, are all reflections of it. Lévi-Strauss in *Tristes Tropiques* echoes the rebellion of the young Nizan as well as the frustration of Sartre before an academic, idealist, rationalist, humanistic philosophy. Durkheim had already noted his contemporaries' penchant for presenting a specific intellectual style (clear, logical, Cartesian, French) as a model for all humanity. The confusion did not abate following World War I. There was a particular brand of narrow nationalism, widespread in intellectual circles, whose faith in the superiority of French culture was based on belief in the humanist ideal propagated by it, and its exclusive right to it.

Philosophical Conflict, Rational and Irrational, 1920–36

Catholic Philosophy

The year 1922 saw the publication of neo-Thomist Catholic philosopher Jacques Maritain's *L'Anti-moderne*. Maritain's doctrine was theocentric and rationalist, accepting both theological dogma and the hierarchy of values and authority it established. Maritain believed the purpose of philosophy is to justify this dogma rationally. Thomism posits a hierarchical organization of creation in which man, among all other earthly creatures, occupies the highest rank. Man is defined by a universal human "essence" of divine origin, which individuals endeavor to fulfill in the course of their existence. Maritain's *L'Anti-moderne* attacked Maurice Blondel's position, which was that God's presence can be discovered by the individual through voluntary commitment. In this view, the continuously renewed decision to live the Christian life liberates in the individual the spiritual energy that will open him to others, and to divine love. In his *Journal métaphysique* (1917), Gabriel Marcel, who was closer to Blondel and Kierkegaard than to Maritain, staked his claim to a territory of religious experience in which the divine mystery is approached through knowing and loving the individuals who embody it.

Deeply affected during the thirties by the spectacle of social injustice, Emmanuel Mounier identified the source of spiritual development—and hence of personality—with the participation in a Christian community actively concerned with current social problems. Simone Weil, on the other hand, who in the beginning had been close to Mounier, went off in a direction of her own, "Awaiting God" in an increasingly intense physical and intellectual ascesis pursued through social struggle on behalf of the proletariat and later against fascism. She experienced to the death in her own person the sufferings of invaded France. Despite Maritain's apparently dominant stature, the religious tenor of this period was actually determined by the forms of Christian philosophy that were not dogmatic. They reflected subjective experience and drew on the same sources as did existentialism; and, although refusing to consider man outside the metaphysical framework of Christianity, they did not, as "right-thinking" Catholicism did, rule out dialogue with communism.

In Search of Synthesis

Besides conventional Catholic literature, with its discreet, mildly moralizing spiritualism, literary works of a far more disturbing character were also being written that were based on the religious quest—books by Mauriac, Julien Green, and, most disturbing of all, Bernanos. The absence of, and the need for, religious certainties was perhaps also responsible for impelling minds like Georges Bataille's in their pursuit of the kinds of transcendence that in other civilizations have enabled human beings to burst through the boundaries of the human condition onto the level of the ecstatic, not through asceticism, but through practicing "excess"—eroticism, torture, debauchery—practices considered pathological in our own society. Death, in this perspective, is no longer seen as the prelude to some sort of eternity but becomes an obssessive limitation, a barrier which must be breached. This particular quest, almost by definition one that is impossible to communicate in the language of rationality, sustained a body of work that denounced or broke away from every literary convention.

"There is nothing," wrote Jules Romains in 1922, "to prevent the twentieth century from becoming a century of organization and of construction, as were, each in their own way, the thirteenth and the seventeenth." (*Ecrits du nord*, November 1922). However, no attempt at intellectual synthesis was successfully imposed. The era was marked by metaphysical doubt and the need to erect defenses against it. The main problem was how to achieve a radically new awareness of "human reality." During the twenties, it was surrealism that best embodied the determination to break completely with traditional thought, by means of a revolution that would "touch everything, everywhere, and be both unbelievably radical and utterly repressive."

Ideological antagonisms throve in the thirties on competition between conflicting intellectual systems. The need for certainties fostered a taste, heightened as the century progressed, for theorizing and jargonizing, for intellectual fads that caught on and burned out fast but left catchwords that seeped into the language.

Paradoxically, this urge for systematization resulted in a sort of anarchy; in this respect the 1970s resembled the 1920s, although each traveled a different route to reach similar destinations. In 1970, every synthesis immediately fell into place among individual or social "mythologies." *Anthropology*, that distinctively twentieth-century science, had in fact opened up new perspectives on the structures, religious or otherwise, through which societies ensure their continuity and transmit the collective experience from generation to generation. Explanatory systems that are rational in terms of the situation of the group and are consistent with the relationship network enabling the collectivity to exist seem from the outside to be so many "myths," or merely ways of describing reality as it appears through the grid of meanings and codes regulating the life of the group. Christianity, for example, will seem to someone outside the system of beliefs it advocates to be just another myth among many; and the same ultimately holds true for any system of representation of reality whatsoever. This explains why phenomenology, which is concerned with *present* structures of consciousness, was considered so important; and it also explains the importance of attempts to replace the traditional discipline of history of philosophy with either a dialectical or, to use Foucault's term, an "archaeological" reconstruction of the structures conditioning contemporary cultural consciousness.

"Between the Two Myths": From Essentialism to Existentialism

After the end of the 1914–18 war, it became clear that the vogue for Bergsonian philosophy had passed. Bergson had nevertheless had a formative influence on many intellectuals, some of whom, especially the literary critics (l'abbé Bremond, Du Bos, Thibaudet) were a kind of Bergson delegation, while others (Maritain, Benda) were harsh critics of their former master. A kind of intellectual vacuum began to form, and the polemics of the

immediate postwar period, in which the participants were drawn mainly
from the prewar generations, pitted traditional French liberalism against an
equally traditional dogmatism dedicated to maintaining an established
order that was considered immutable. Neither side questioned the primacy
of rationally based spiritual values and principles believed to be as indisputable as they were obvious, since, within the edifice of these discussions, spirit
and reason were one. It was to the defense of these principles that Benda, in
La Trahison des clercs (1927), dedicated the pure intellectual or "cleric,"
charged with weighing the events of his time, using implacable intellectual
rigor, against the standard of his principles. It was against this background
that a public controversy erupted after the war, in the form of the inquiry
launched in October 1922 by the *Revue de Genève* on: the future of Europe.

Already in 1919, Paul Valéry, in an article entitled *Sur la crise de l'esprit,*
had written as a European for whom Europe had until then been "the brain
atop a vast body" expressing concern for the "fragility of a civilization"
whose value he did not, however, question. Valéry deplored the priority this
civilization was apparently giving to the material over the spiritual. Gide
and the *NRF* group were meanwhile advocating "intellectual deregimenta-
tion" in order to free judgment from the political contingencies proposed by
Benda, and make it autonomous. It was in the name of this same spirit that
Romain Rolland fought for an internationalism enlightened enough to
understand the aspirations of the fledgling USSR; and that Massis opposed
him, evoking traditional classic, Christian French civilization as model for
universal humanism, that "priceless brain" atop the world Valéry had conceived of more broadly as European. The mind—which Valéry saw as being
crushed by the geographic, demographic, and technological mass world that
emerged after the war, Gide or Benda saw as the victim of its own unworthy
passions, Massis saw as inseparable from a superior national culture, or
Romain Rolland saw as inseparable from what is most noble in the
achievements of mankind—constituted for all of them, and indisputably, the
foundation stone for the universal civilizing values that bring humanism to
all men and for all time. None questioned the autonomy and primacy of his
own individual viewpoint and each, although antagonistic to the others, was
sustained by an idealism common to all.

It was in the next generation that doubts began to appear. In the preface
written in 1919 to a collection of essays entitled *Carnaval est mort,* Jean-
Richard Bloch had taken a stand against this conception of civilization,
reducing it to the status of an ideology entirely dependent on faith. "Man,
horrified by what he has wrought, has begun to reexamine that great ideology he had relied upon with such confidence, the ideology *civilization* . . . Carnival time is over [*Le carnaval est mort*], and that means, when a
system of belief no longer receives moral support, its ability to generate art is
ended as well." Bloch, who was a Marxist, sketched in the first outlines of a
new ideology and of a cultural criticism based on social factors.

Inquiries into the "spiritual crisis" and the "future of Europe" led to heated discussions on the question of what exactly civilization and culture—both ill-defined terms—really mean, and a growing awareness of how relative the two terms are. In 1920 René Grousset published his *L'Histoire de la philosophie orientale;* and in 1921 and 1924 René Guénon's *L'Introduction aux doctrines hindoues* and *L'Orient et l'Occident* came out. In 1923 Romain Rolland published his soon-to-become-famous book on Gandhi. In February/March 1925, *Les Cahiers du mois* published a series of articles "The Call of the Orient." Twenty-two writers took part in this debate, which with few exceptions—Lalou and Breton—turned out to be profoundly nationalistic. The participants, convinced of the superiority of the West, joined the "Party of Intelligence," led by Henri Massis, and were virtually unanimous in recommending support for "French" values based on the Greco-Roman and Christian traditions, to the exclusion of Oriental philosophical systems whose patently inferior pantheism might corrupt the critical rationalism on which French civilization is based. *L'Inde et le monde* (1926), by Sylvain Lévi, and *Défense de l'Occident* (1927), by Massis, both violently rejected any tolerance for Oriental philosophy, condemning the latter for being as "anti-West and antihumane" as bolshevism. These debates revealed the continuation into the postwar period of a narrow, closed, nationalistic spirit demonstrating little curiosity about other cultures or other ways of thinking. A small minority of thinkers, however, alerted by the awakening of the oriental nations, the prestige of Gandhi, and the development of oriental studies in France, did turn toward the East, hoping to find a more auspicious path toward spiritual renewal than the one offered by Marxism.

It was around the personality of Romain Rolland, a mediator if ever there was one, that these debates crystallized: intransigent nationalism was pitted against pacifism and Marxist internationalism; Christianity against communism; "French" culture against universal "human" culture; committed intellectuals against "ivory towerism." To the post–World War I bourgeois intellectual circles of Paris, in the throes of conventional reactionism, Rolland, a liberal and a tolerant, socialist supporter of Gandhi, began to look like a dangerous communist if not a traitor to his country.

In 1926 the problem of the crisis in civilization was presented in a new light in young André Malraux's *La Tentation de l'Occident.* Malraux, imagination fired by the mystery of human civilization, and filled with what he had learned from his stay in Indochina, presented the problem of intellectual crisis in a universal context: the meeting of two great modern civilizations, Chinese and Western, and the interaction between them. At this stage in his career, Malraux believed that if, in the general ferment of worldwide revolution, the profoundly held oriental conviction that human life counts for little in a cosmos of which it is an infinitely small manifestation—if this conviction should ally itself with the Westerner's thirst for power, and if the western belief in the creative potential of the individual should give way to oriental indifference, then both civilizations would founder: one into anarchy, the other into a kind of anthill existence. These were the terms in which Malraux, starting with publication of *La Tentation de l'Occident,* presented the themes of "the human condition" and "the future of humanity": in a new context, and with Nietzschean urgency. For Malraux's generation, the world's evil, irrationality, and violence loomed as the immediate conditions of personal experience, and not in terms of ideal "humanist" values. *La Tentation de l'Occident* was a chaotic work, symptomatic of this new intellectual climate. "Malraux is the new man," declared his friend Drieu La Rochelle, "and he has introduced the new man to us. Eternal man in one of his historical epochs. Man confronting his eternal problems: how to act, to love, to die" (*Nouvelle revue française,* 1 December 1930). It was on a basis of direct experience that this generation sought a coherent philosophy: it was thus that the *existential climate* came into being, a climate that produced surrealism as well as Gabriel Marcel's brand of subjective Christianity based on private experience; that also produced Mounier's social action Christianity and, finally, activist Marxism unburdened by exegesis or dialectics.

Alain: The Master Who Was Left Behind

In 1938, Célestin Bouglé, director of the Ecole Normale Supérieure, put together "a few remarks on the French conception of general culture" in which he defined that culture's purpose as follows: to provide every French person with the means of becoming an autonomous individual, his discernment conditioned by humanist culture and classical philosophy. "The thinking man of today," concluded Bouglé, "who owes his cultivation to his education in philosophy, has good reasons for wanting to uphold and defend against all comers a national culture which reserves the place of honor for a value he must prize above all others: intellectual freedom." This was the intellectual freedom prized by Alain.

A product of the idealist and reflexive philosophical tradition based on Kantianism and the Cartesian cogito, Alain in his *Propos* and his teaching applied to everyday life an intellectual method positing the conscious awareness of reality, rationally and freely arrived at, as the prolegomena to the "art of living" as a free man. This was an art that depended on self-control and the objective evaluation of each new situation. It was not to be an end in itself, however, merely the preliminary to action. "I do not," said Alain, "like painless thinking"; neither did he like "ideological tourists." Alain, like Benda or Maritain, rejected all appeals to the subconscious, the passions, the irrational; and like Bouglé he believed the mind is formed not by being brought into contact with abstract systems, which he despised, but with great writers. Because of Alain's probity, his suspicion of authoritarian pretensions ("A tyrant trying to be convincing is still a tyrant; a tyrant trying to make converts a tyrant still"), and his contempt for mystification of any kind, he enjoyed with observers as disparate as Simone Weil and Jean-Paul Sartre a prestige not accorded other philosophers. But his viewpoint, his methods, and his vocabulary belonged to an era that was past. Alain was a classic before he began.

The "Death of Man" and the Riddle of the Sphinx

Reference to the past is implicit in the classical conception that civilization is based on the transmission of culture from generation to generation. But the very idea of a historical past is problematical. According to Benedetto Croce, a historian and literary critic whose thinking after 1922 (the date when his *Breviario di estetica* appeared in French translation) takes up where Bergson left off, this historic past has no existence except as it is recreated by the mind, a recreation that is itself "continuously conditioned" by culture. Any representation of the past will therefore partake of the mythic in terms of the true facts. But for Croce the facts themselves are complex. They contain all aspects of civilization, particularly the artistic. The task of the art historian is thus not to discern the degree to which a work conforms to an aesthetic model, but its representational power, its grasp of the spiritual values by which a civilization is ordered.

Croce was heir to the intellectual legacy of his relatively little-known compatriot Vico and also, despite his avowed horror of systems, of Hegel. The problem identified by Croce was one of the most disconcerting of the period: if the culture of a specific group defines a member of that group only and gives form to his thoughts and his actions, art being one, then the classic conception of man basic to Western philosophy no longer represents more than a relative position within historical time. This was the thesis advanced by Spengler in *The Decline of the West*. In his view, cultures are closed, discontinuous, equivalent systems, sealed off from one another. Within the system, its participants do not question its validity and consider its structures as absolutes corresponding to reality itself.

From the outside, however, the same system will be seen as occupying a relative position in terms of temporal duration. The perspective changed. The anthropological view of human society, a twentieth-century phenomenon, came into play. Spengler believed it was time for the West to renouce its illusion that the configurations of its philosophy are definitive and permanent. They were already, in fact, according to him, in the process of disintegrating. The question insistently demanding an answer was a metaphysical one: what is the significance of human existence? A latent humanism, perceptible since the turn of the century, broke out. Casting aside the fallacy that return to a mythic past is possible, the young Malraux agonized over whether or not a whole cycle of civilization was coming to a close; and whether the Western concept of man was threatened with extinction. Malraux gave dramatic point to feelings that were fairly widespread among the intellectuals of his generation. These feelings of absurdity and meaninglessness were accompanied by criticism, criticism of the values mechanically advocated by society—the society of Gide's counterfeiters. The metaphysical question, when presented in these terms, could be answered only in the context of another question: does human history have meaning? Metaphysical anxiety changed its frame of reference.

The literature of the interwar period was charged with this metaphysical reverberation, though less dramatically than in the works of Malraux. Poets and novelists, whether their names were Proust or Bernanos, Giono or Julien Green, Saint-Jean Perse or Giraudoux, presented their readers with a universal view of the human adventure. Fictitious literary worlds that were hermetic, dissimilar, and often mutually exclusive replaced the shared world of an imperiled culture. Critics began referring to "vision" and "message." While writers became metaphysicians, specialists in aesthetics brooded over the nature of the creative act. It was a period infinitely rich in literary works, but ones that nevertheless failed to satisfy the demands and anxieties of young intellectuals such as Paul Nizan, Jean-Paul Sartre, Lévi-Strauss, or Albert Camus. This generation abandoned philosophical idealism in favor of other sources of inspiration: Hegel, Marx, Nietzsche, Husserl, Heidegger, and also, though less frequently, Kierkegaard, made their appearance almost simultaneously on the horizon. A new intellectual trend began to develop which was to become firmly implanted during the forties, and which gave philosophical structure and ideological direction to the existentialism prevailing at the time.

Philosophies of History and Dialectics, 1936–52

Hegel

It was to academia that Hegelian studies owed their resurgence during the thirties: to a course taught by Alexandre Koyré (1931–34), and to the scholarly work of Jean Hippolyte. But it was Alexandre Kojève, in a famous course entitled *Introduction à la lecture de Hegel*, given from 1934 to 1939 and published in 1947, who provided the authoritative interpretation of this philosophy. French Marxist criticism, which was just then getting its second wind, outside the constraints of the official party line, was strongly influenced by Kojève's reading of Hegel. Although philosophical debate after the Occupation coalesced around Marxist thought, it was the contact with Hegelian dialectics that transformed its style and, for a few years, its vocabulary. Extremely complex and considerably less systematic than suggested by explanations that of necessity must be oversimplified, the Hegelian dialectic distinguishes between two processes of reasoning: one, the logical, static thought that starts from strict definitions and procedes deductively, maintaining a rigorous respect for linear progression and the principle of noncontradiction; and the other, the dialectical process. Hegel believed the former—logical thought—suitable for dealing with daily life and limited situations, to be the basis for middle-class virtue. But he did not consider it remotely capable of elucidating the more complex realities involving progressions composed of reciprocal relations, conflicts, contradictions, the interaction of numerous heterogenous elements, or constructs in the process of continuous development. In one sense the Hegelian dialectic is a *technique*, similar to the Socratic dialectic, employed by mind in order to grasp this kind of movement. In another sense, however, it actually is the way in which reality develops. "The dialectic," said Hegel, "is the guiding principle of all movement and every activity found in reality . . . Everything around us can be treated as a manifestation of the dialectic." Everything, according to Hegel, implies its opposite; contradiction is the motive power of the world. All reality goes from momentary equilibrium to its opposite—a process generating severe conflict—and then to a state of synthesis more complex than the initial state, in which the contradictions of the second stage are assimilated and preserved. This third state serves as the point of departure for further development. Hegel uses Fichtean categories to designate these stages as thesis, antithesis, synthesis. The thought process follows the triadic rhythm of affirmation, negation or conflict, and reconciliation; thinking is a continuous process.

At a time when the idea of culture was broadening to encompass all the complex forces structuring society, the dialectic freed philosophical thinking from the constraints of Kantianism. It was belatedly seized upon by young philosophers such as Sartre: a new expository *style* developed which, in its dynamics and in terms of the surge of concrete examples it proposed, was not unlike interior monologue, though structured in a different way. Sartre made frequent use of it in his polemics, starting with *Qu'est-ce que la littérature?* The dialectic, for Hegel, is coordinate with a metaphysical conception of the spirit both complex and paradoxical. The spirit, in Hegel's system, is a universalizing activity. It is present in each individual, but it is also transindividual. In one continuous movement, it reveals the unity of the many and the universality of the particular. The spirit is materialized in the development of social and cultural institutions, and particularly in the political organization of states. The ever increasing materialization of the spirit is the goal of historical movement, historical movement being a teleological progression through which the universal spirit will become embodied in the terrestrial state. History is therefore the progressive realization and temporal projection of this universal Idea, which is dispersed among the consciousness of all mankind and which individuals will, from one dialectical stage to the next, impose upon themselves, thus becoming fully human.

The Hegelian dialectic is tautological, certainly; not a proof but a method, and a method that can be employed in other readings of history—the Marxist, for example. In any case, other interpretations of history exist (English historian Toynbee's; Father Teilhard de Chardin's biological approach) that see in human history, as Hegel did, a manifestation of humanity's progressive spiritualization.

Hegel's *Phenomenology of Mind* exercised a profound attraction on certain writers throughout this century—on Proust (at least insofar as it dealt with the role played by art), on Queneau, Bataille, Blanchot, Butor—and, most of all, on Derrida. André Breton has acknowledged its influence on him; it provided Sartre, during the thirties, with the outline for his theory of literature, and to a large extent with the basic terminology for his theory of ontology. But for a generation obsessed with history, it was Hegel's *Philosophy of History* that exerted the greater fascination. Its themes were assimilated, often from secondary sources. Hegel believed that history, through which the spirit becomes manifest, progresses in a single, linear movement. In this philosophers view, significant historical roles are played by only one state at a time, each, in accordance with the dialectical process, taking up where the last one left off. It was a fascinating exercise, for those who actually read Hegel in the original, to apply his method to interpreting or trying to understand historical events. In a more general way, for those who endured the 1940 defeat of France by Germany, the idea that meaning can be elucidated quasi-"scientifically" if History is interpreted dialectically added to Hegel's unshakable faith in the ultimate progression of the spirit through series of conflicts viewed as inevitable, and raised philosophy above the current political disarray that France was experiencing. History had become a subject of general concern. The classical man conceived by Kant assumed a new historical dimension, and new limitations. Phenomenology had raised the question of the self in terms not of a single concept of consciousness but of phenomenological categories of consciousness, and Hegel described a new relation between self and being.

In addition, Hegel placed art in an eminent position, next to religion and philosophy, all three forms of activity representing areas where the presence of the spirit, and its vision of the world, are revealed. Hegel's philosophy fitted in fairly well with current French conceptions of art as an autonomous activity, and of literature as the translation of a metaphysical world view. The great conjectures concerning the significance of artistic creation that characterized the period were made against the background of Hegelian philosophy. Artists were no longer considered the authors of their work and were transformed into vehicles for the materialization of the universal spirit's vision; this point of view had once been held by Proust and was to be held again by the *Tel Quel* group. Some of their writing, such as Philippe Sollers's *Drame* (1965), appear to be based on it.

The Marxist Dialectic

In 1920, French Marxism became confused with the official Communist Party line. Firsthand knowledge of Marx's writings, with few exceptions, was sketchy at the time and could be summed up in three or four slogans: the triumph of the proletariat; class struggle; the fight against fascism; an end to economic exploitation. Or else it was influenced by Leninist theories that defined the sociopolitical conditions for creating a revolutionary situation. Until 1940, Marxist thought was known to few people outside the Communist Party and generally only through "selected readings." The great movement of sympathy that swept a majority of leftist intellectuals toward communism at the time of Hitler's rise to power was political rather than philosophic. The prevailing aesthetic trends in France were also not particularly attuned to Zhdanov's cultural dogmatism, which was basically a reflection of Stalinist political policy. The fact that poets like Eluard and painters like Picasso rallied to the communist cause did not indicate any genuine comprehension of Marxist thought. Even Sartre himself discovered only belatedly—around 1950—that Marxism was his "horizon" and the intellectual horizon, or so he believed, of his generation.

Marxism Arrives, 1952–70

Marxist philosophy in France survived debate, research, exegesis, interpretation, events (i.e., the revolt of 1968), and confusions many and various; it grew in influence until eventually it did, in fact, profoundly affect every area of French culture and even modify the basic concept of what that culture is. In 1960 Marx's writings at last became available in scrupulously edited versions (the Pléiade edition being one). As sacred texts, they immediately became the object of exhaustive analyses such as those undertaken by the *Nouvelle critique* staff or by Louis Althusser, militant communists all; but there were also many specialists to elucidate their history and meaning.

Beginning in 1945 and continuing until 1970, Marxism was the pole around which discussions of the function of literature and the role of the writer coalesced; discussions, also, concerning how literature and literary criticism should be taught, and why. The impact of Marxism on the social and political consciousness of at least three successive generations reached far beyond the framework of the Communist Party. But Marxism's own limitations were revealed in the abstract and unyielding dogmatism of critics whose intellectual approach recalled scholasticism in the days of its decline.

Hegel remained faithful to the Western world's traditional, fundamentally Christian, concepts, and he accorded to the spiritual supremacy over the temporal: it is by its guiding philosophy, he believed, that a society defines itself. Marx and Engels reversed this hierarchy and demoted philosophy to a mere reflection of the collectivity's social and economic structures. It was thus that dialectical materialism and the materialistic vision of history were founded. Like the Hegelian dialectic, however, the Marxist dialectic is identified with the movement of history and also consists of the same triadic rhythm: thesis–antithesis–synthesis. But the underlying concept of Marxism is different: it is based on labor. According to the materialist dialectic, man's life is determined by the imperatives of subsistence; he makes his living by transforming his environment and by barter. It is these activities and relations that structure his thought, these that determine the ideological "superstructures" of any society. Human labor transforms the world and, consequently, the relations of men to the world and to each other and, therefore, the superstructures through which these relations are expressed.

The Marxist or Hegelian dialectic can therefore be applied to interpreting historical development, and to explaining it systematically. Multiplicity is reduced to unity through the incorporation of the negative, destructive phase a society must experience on its way from one state of social equilibrium to another, more complex one. But Marxist materialism had one great advantage over the Hegelian system: because it focused on labor, technology, and productivity, it seemed to offer a method for predicting future social developments. It held out to mankind the possibility of working with the tide of history, and for Marx there was no doubt as to which direction this tide was flowing: humanity was destined to free itself progressively from the natural constraints imposed by the struggle to survive. As the bourgeoisie had once succeeded feudalism, so in the course of the dialectical process, would the proletariat one day inevitably overthrow the bourgeoisie, establishing at last the classless society of a truly humanist culture.

Unfortunately, however, Marxist analysis also showed up the unreliable fragility of individual consciousness, each one perforce conditioned by its specific historical situation. Benda's "cleric," for example, that intellectual dedicated to the disinterested search for universal verities, suddenly stood revealed as victimized by, or guilty of, self-delusion. History destroys illusions. In *Les Mots,* Sartre used Marxist insights as the basis for a merciless self-critique.

Jean-Paul Sartre: Will to Synthesis

Jean-Paul Sartre from the outset left his own mark on every mode of expression he chose to employ: philosophical treatises and essays, literary criticism, fiction, drama, biography, autobiography, political essays, interviews. No other figure has inspired more commentary and debate than he, and none acquired an international reputation as vast as his, as swiftly as he did. As much through his ceaseless industry as through his political activism, violent language, outspokenness, and fierce independence, Sartre dominated the French intellectual scene for a good fifteen years. His philosophy served as a touchstone for other thinkers, who frequently disagreed with him: Raymond Aron, Albert Camus, Merleau-Ponty, Lévi-Strauss. Sartre, himself dogmatic, went to battle against the shortsighted dogmatism of orthodox Marxism. Step by step, molding his life according to the demands of his philosophy, he became, at almost seventy, the patron and occasional spokesman for the militant Maoist *groupuscules*. Sartre's influence was at its zenith, however, between the publication of *L'Etre et le Néant* in 1943, and *Critique de la raison dialectique* in 1960; it was during this period that the conflict between Marxism and what was known as "Sartrean existentialism" developed, a conflict that Sartre, as a good dialectician, attempted to resolve.

Existentialism has been described as a method for dealing with philosophical questions. It is an attempt to analyze the structures of human existence, and to give individuals a sense of the essential freedom inherent in material life. No contemporary thinker, however, not even Sartre himself, has ever claimed the title of existentialist philosopher. Sartre simply resigned himself to accepting it. This is how *L'Etre et le Néant* became, for many commentators, the "classic" existentialist work.

After 1943 it soon became obvious that for the generation of French men and women who reached maturity under the German Occupation, Sartre was the incontestable intellectual leader. His philosophy, in addition to its usefulness in terms of a then still unfamiliar methodology, seemed to offer every individual a chance for living life as a free man in a disoriented world. By relating to the edifice of his philosophical thought, first literary expression, and then political action, Sartre filled the vacuum left by the dissolution of traditional beliefs, a vacuum postwar nihilism had not been able to fill.

Sartre posited freedom as an absolute, a fundamental "given" of the human condition. The only limitation on this freedom, in Sartre's world, is the fact that we are not free to stop being free. It would be impossible in these pages to reconstitute the body of definitions—based on a terminology borrowed in part from Hegel—through which Sartre built up his ontology; nor to discuss whether or not it was sound. What did appear crucial to early readers, however, was the fact that Sartre did not admit the right of any preexisting moral or social structure to impose limits on that freedom. He believed human beings are free—but of course they live in a specific world, surrounded by other human beings. Freedom, therefore, consists in "electing to struggle in order to become free." Each human being's situation offers him a range of choices and a field of action in which, by making choices, he can realize his own essential freedom. It follows that every individual is responsible for what he becomes, and that human history is the sum of the choices individuals have made.

Sartre's ontology, largely conceived during the years of reflection that preceded the outbreak of World War II, was not concerned with action. Sartre limited himself to stating as axiomatic that "human reality is defined by its goals." Profoundly shaken, however, as he later stated repeatedly, at the spectacle of absolute evil represented by the massive resurgence of torture in the modern world, Sartre attacked the problem of action and the intellectual: how could philosophy be combined with action? Here is where he encountered Marx, whose works he had reread during the Occupation. In a series of articles, *Qu'est-ce que la littérature?* (1947), he returned to the points he had made in his 1945 manifesto inaugurating *Les Temps modernes* and expanded them. In terms of the literary enterprise, Sartre tried to reconcile man as decribed by his own ontology, and Marx's historical man.

In *Qu'est-ce que la littérature?* Sartre employed a Marxist-existentialist framework and a somewhat sketchy dialectic to outline a history of French literature, and the forms it had taken from age to age, as a function of the position of writers in the socioeconomic systems of their time. According to Sartre, changes in the socioeconomic position of the writer, because they define his public, will also define, from age to age, changes in the prevailing conceptions of literature. Sartre also attempted, in order to give firm direction to the contemporary trend of literature, to provide a coherent answer to three frequently debated questions: What is writing? Why do we write? and Who do we write for? This led him to the formulation of a fairly general theory of literature capable of satisfying both Sartre the philosopher of freedom, and Sartre the man discovering social evil for the first time. He defined the production of a book as a social act for which the author must assume responsibility: as with any Sartrean act, this act implies a free choice. But if the work is to have any worth, the author's point of view must also coincide with the movement of history. As Sartre saw it, the French writers of his own time occupied a moment in history when, in the struggle between the classes, the oppressed or proletariat class was demanding freedom and therefore becoming aware of it. In 1947 the average French writer was a member of the bourgeoisie, and the choice open to him was either to retreat into his class—that is, in Sartre's view, to a reiteration of forms that had stiffened with age—or to commit himself wholeheartedly to the social struggle by enlightening his middle-class readers as to the realities of their position in relation to the movement of history. This definition of literature as an act and a political commitment involved Sartre himself in paradoxes he could ultimately resolve only by progressively diminishing literature's piece of the pie. But he had incisively recast a question that had been smoldering ever since the pronouncements of Zhdanov: the *social function* of literature. The extent of Sartre's reputation and his impact was clearly the result of his being the sole contemporary philosopher attempting to reevaluate and solve, from a fresh viewpoint, the ancient problematic of freedom versus determinism that existentialism had resolved one way and Marxism another. By playing the role of dialectical devil's advocate, Sartre, in addition, took it upon himself both to rouse the bourgeois conscience and to incite a somnolent Marxist philosophy to reassume its creative role in the development of History.

Sartre's work was of the utmost importance, debatable and arbitrary as some of its constructs may have been, and riddled with an egocentricity that even he came to deplore. It was not greatly appreciated by orthodox Marxists. But Sartre's attempt to live life according to the dictates of the dialectic (to prove philosophy in action, rectifying theories so that, as Lenin advocated, they could be transformed into "praxis," never arresting the process by clinging to fixed positions) made him one of the most exemplary personalities of his time. By questioning the literary enterprise; by the successive and at times contradictory positions he formulated after 1945 on the subject of the function of literature; by the aesthetic principles he set forth in his first articles written in the thirties on the subject of the novel, even more than by his own literary works, Sartre provoked in literary circles an awareness and an uneasiness, a literary *fin d'époque* anxiety. But did this really amount to a rebirth?

Structuralism

The dialectic is not an ideology or a philosophy, and neither is structuralism. It is a scholarly tool for the study of phenomena in such diverse fields as anthropology, art, history, linguistics, mathematics, psychoanalysis, and sociology. Although the structuralist fad came after existentialism, the analytic principles proposed by structuralist methodology were already being used prior to 1914 by the anthropologist Marcel Mauss and by the emerging science of linguistics. This methodological trend was reinforced toward midcentury by cybernetics. In his 1972 preface to *Communications 18,* Edgar Morin underscored the opposition between the concept of structure (closed system) and the concept of history (dialectic), the two having already been identified by Morot-Sir as the poles of a cultural tension present in France ever since the moment when the 1940 defeat cast radical doubt on traditional philosophy.

As the vogue for structuralism grew, the obsession with history waned and the grandiose, utopian philosophical projections concerning the destiny of mankind and the "goal" of history began to lose their credibility. *Pourquoi des philosophes?* asked J.-F. Revel in 1957, later suggesting, in an ironic pamphlet entitled *La Fin de l'opposition* (1965), a "Glossary of Taboo Words." This list included all the words in the existentialist vocabulary: ambiguity, authenticity, modes of behavior, dialectic, existential, intentionality, etc.

In 1962, in the final chapter of *La Pensée sauvage,* the anthropologist Claude Lévi-Strauss took issue with Sartre and his conception of how society and culture are related. For the phenomenologist, the important thing is the object; whereas, as Lévi-Strauss pointed out, the important thing for the structuralist, and for the scientist too, is the relation between objects. An understanding of this relationship forms the basis for a hypothetical theory of the whole from which the investigator can then construct a model. The model, in turn, will reveal how otherwise apparently inexplicable elements function, by showing the ways in which they relate to the system as a whole. Structuralists therefore believe it possible to formulate a *science* of man that will relegate philosophical speculation once and for all to the past. According to Lévi-Strauss, there are a multitude of possible "permutations and combinations" on the level of social organization, only some of which will be realized in any one place and time; but they do not believe in the progressive linear development toward a single, ultimate model, as Sartre, following in the footsteps of Marx, had imagined.

During the sixties, the conjunction of Lacan's analyses of the structures of subconscious language, and Lévi-Strauss's on the function of the collective symbolic unconscious in the language of myth, plus the new theory and practice of linguistics, profoundly affected literary criticism. In combination, they sustained a vigorous and aggressive intellectual trend that broke up the old alliance between criticism and metaphysics. When literary "texts" began to be studied as "linguistic systems" or "word groups" susceptible to scientific analysis, they lost the privileged status they had so long enjoyed.

11

Literary Criticism

A Plurality of Languages

In an article entitled "Criticism and Invention," Michel Butor made the following observations: "Today, literary invention occurs within a context already saturated with literature. Every novel and poem, every new piece of writing is an incursion into this preexisting environment. We are all living inside an enormous library, we live out our lives in the presence of books . . . Why should anyone want to continue contributing new volumes to this huge mass, when only a tiny part of it can ever become familiar to each of us? But people do go on writing more and more, and more and more books are published" (*Critique,* December 1967).

Butor—a writer, critic, and teacher—here identifies one of the main problems faced by literary criticism today. The general catalogue of the Cercle de la Librairie enumerated seven thousand critical works, not including articles, published between 1956 and 1966, classifying them under four headings: literary history, literary theory, literary criticism, and miscellaneous writings on literature—an indication that no single heading can adequately cover the field.

Under the circumstances, it is not surprising that Baudelaire's "Of what use criticism?" was widely echoed. Responses to it ran the gamut from Remy de Gourmont's absolute negative, "There is no such thing as literary criticism and there can never be," to Paul Souday's lyrical affirmative, "Literature is the conscience of mankind; criticism is the conscience of literature. Is there anything greater than that?"

Literary History and the Triumph of the Critical Essay

The past may belong to scholars, but "newborn literature" and the art of "fresh, living" interpretations of the past belong to the critics. Academic scholarship, faithful to the principles established by Gustave Lanson (see Gustave Rudler, *Les Techniques de la critique littéraire et de l'histoire littéraire*, 1923), had been aimed primarily at compiling *histories* of—mainly French—literature based on compartmentalized study of a single author or milieu, a literary movement (Classicism, Romanticism), or one of the three main genres (theater, poetry, novel). These histories were objective and organized systematically into literary periods divided according to century. Criticism was supposedly scientific, in the sense understood by positivist historians. Organization within each individual literary period was based on the study of schools, genres, and great authors. Critical evaluation served to establish hierarchies that were dominated by masterpieces. Although these hierarchies were formulated with a semblance of strict impartiality, they in fact depended on aesthetic principles that were rarely stated but firmly rooted in classical tradition: clarity, coherence, respect for language and for both moral and literary conventions.

"Lansonism" came under fire (from Péguy) and was due for a fall. The aspect under attack was not the principles and methods of historical scholarship. Because literary history will always serve as the basis for literary criticism of any kind, they remained untouched. The problem was with the critical evaluations and their pertinence, the aptness of the concept of literature on which they were based. During the twenties the literary world demanded and achieved a radical revision of literary values that everything conspired to impose: the surrealist revolt; the "pure poetry" issue unleashed by Abbé Bremond; press attacks exposing the deficiencies of school curricula from which even Baudelaire was absent; and, last, the advent of a new group of literary masters influenced by symbolism and in particular by Mallarmé.

Two scholarly works, *De Baudelaire au surréalisme*, by Marcel Raymond (1933), and *L'Ame romantique et le rêve*, by Albert Béguin (1937), confirmed a reversal of literary values favoring the trend based on Gérard de Nerval and the German romantics that drew inspiration from dreams and the irrational. Seen under a different light, the literary field proved less amenable to the old categories and aesthetic criteria. In 1927–28, two works that were shocking for their time—Breton's *Nadja* and Bataille's *Histoire de l'œil*, along with the anonymous publication of *Le Con d'Irène* (Aragon)—exploded literary conventions and reaffirmed the ties linking eroticism, madness, and creative writing. Meanwhile, the literary historians—René Lalou, Henri Clouard, Christian Sénéchal, Albert Thibaudet—were attempting, on the basis of more or less arbitrary dates

(1900, 1870, 1789), to establish a topography of contemporary literature and some sense of where this literature was headed. All of them, however, thought in terms of continuity. Disregarding the radical break proclaimed by the surrealists, they set out, in the words of René Lalou, to "mark the paths of thought in a forest ever growing larger." They proposed new categories: Thibaudet's concepts of "literary affinities" related literature more directly to its cultural milieu, or the subjectivity of the writer; and the notion of literary "currents" or "climates," although vaguer than that of "schools," did orient inquiry toward definitions of literary "sensibilities" or "types" that were not limited by chronology. The Lansonian categories were gradually yielding to other organizing principles.

Albert Thibaudet, in his brief study *Physiologie de la critique* (1922), placed criticism as a genre among the literary *arts*. He identified three types of criticism: the ordinary, "oral" criticism of the man in the street; professional criticism; and—the best, in his opinion—the "creative" criticism of masters such as Valéry or Gide. In the period immediately following World War I these three types of criticism were more often than not inseparable from one another, Thibaudet being himself a perfect example.

In the dailies, the weeklies, and the reviews, lively critical dialogue was sustained by a solid group of writer-essayists: Edmond Jaloux, Jacques Rivière, Marcel Arland, Benjamin Crémieux, Henri Massis, Léon Pierre-Quint, and the more philosophically oriented Charles Du Bos and André Suarès. "Value creators," in the words of Rémy de Gourmont, they were eclectic, demonstrably unconcerned with methods or theories, and tended either to support or attack the four "masters"—Gide, Proust, Valéry, and Claudel. These critics broadened the perspectives on contemporary literature, underscoring its ties with the past, not only its originality; and, as in the case of Rivière, giving full consideration, if not full approval, even to the iconoclastic dadaist, a preemptive courtesy the dadaists did not particularly appreciate. Weaned on literature, educated in literary analysis, attuned to Parisian literary society, these men practiced *participatory criticism* based on a love of literature, distilling from works both past and present the "overall vision," the "message," the themes, and the intentions. Their preferred vehicles were the "literary" critical essay and essay collection, a dwindling tradition that was nevertheless maintained well into the fifties by Claude Roy, André Rousseaux (Grand Prix de la critique, 1933), Robert Kemp, and Robert Kanters. In general, this school of criticism gave first priority to the novel. For drama, there was Paul Léautaud, who wrote for the *Mercure de France* under the pseudonym Maurice Boissard, publishing acerbic if occasionally conventional commentary in either case vastly superior to the humorous but superficial criticism practiced by Jean-Jacques Gautier.

Trends in Criticism

Historically, this was a period primarily absorbed in the subjective modalities of the *creative act,* and so were its literary "masters." The dominant theme of Valéry's poems is the genesis of the literary work; into *A la Recherche du temps perdu* and *Les Faux-monnayeurs,* Proust and Gide, respectively, incorporated the story of how these works came into being and what ideas lay behind their structural organization. Claudel's *L'Art poétique* is a commentary on his own modes of creation and their relation to his overall conception of the universe. Generally speaking, these writers presented a *problematics* of writing as practiced by them, and not a critical theory as such. Gide's essays and prefaces for example, are full of critical insight touching on the nature of the bond between writer and work, morals and literature, society and the literary work conceived as a means of liberation and self-creation; he offers a kaleidoscope of viewpoints, not a system. The surrealists were trying to find a method with which they could explore every aspect of what they referred to as the spirit, and one on which a revolutionary life style could be based. Avowedly antiliterary, having turned their backs, as a matter of principle, on any writing that deliberately claimed the title of art, the surrealists had all the more reason to deny the validity of any pretension to critical objectivity and themselves practiced the criticism by fiat of the literary clique. They rejected venerated "masterpieces" and moved into advantageous positions on the literary board the formerly despised authors who were the only ones they were willing to acknowledge as their own precursors: Sade, Lautréamont, and Rimbaud.

"Criticism as a branch of science makes no sense," maintained Abbé Bremond, defender of the romantics. "There is no such thing as a science of the individual, and literary criticism deals only with individual men and individual works in terms of their individuality." Bremond believed that poetry, the essence of the literary enterprise, can only be grasped through a kind of interior meditation, analogous to praying, which escapes analysis.

Literary criticism was therefore based primarily on subjective reactions which, without benefit of any formal critical apparatus, delivered more or less profound insights into, and knowledge of, a more or less vast body of literature. This idiosyncratic criticism by guides and observers acted as a corrective to academic criticism, which was normative, didactic, and conceptualist. In it we see critical trends rather than critical theories. At its core was the concept of the classic-romantic dualism and an unshakable faith in literature's humanist vocation. The classicists among these critics were Thibaudet, Rivière, and Crémieux; the romanticists were Arland, Ramon Fernandez and Abbé Bremond.

The most erudite and prolific was Albert Thibaudet, and he was also the critic who most assiduously sought new directions for his craft. Literature for Thibaudet was above all a kind of barometer for measuring the collective sensibility impregnating every aspect of a given era. Through his study of individual literary works, the critic brings his own insights to this infrastructure, revealing from within the psychological profile of his time (*Trente Ans de vie française,* 1920–30; *Flaubert,* 1922).

Jacques Rivière explored the *psychological* climate of his time, diagnosing it in articles that became milestones ("Reconnaissance ·à Dada," 1920; "Crise du concept de littérature," 1924).

Benjamin Crémieux, more systematic than either, was an observer of the post–World War I European literary panorama who specialized in drama and novels (*L'Esprit européen dans la littérature d'après-guerre,* 1926); his aim was to analyze the mechanics of creation, the writer's creative "gift," the concept of the work and its execution. According to Crémieux, the critic's task is threefold: to understand, define, and identify. In his 1931 scrutiny of the French literary scene between 1918 and 1930 (*Inquiétude et reconstruction,* 1931), he discerned a change in the direction of literature and somewhat hesitantly predicted the emergence of a new classicism.

Crémieux's classicism made him a good foil for Marcel Arland who for over forty years maintained a connection with the *NRF.* Arland saw the work of art, which he considered "self-contained" and separate from its social context, as a means for understanding and dealing with the new humanism. As an informed reader of E. M. Forster's *Aspects of the Novel* (French translation, 1927), Arland addressed the architectural problems of the novel and how they reveal the novelist's unique "voice," his "substance" as distinct from his public personality. Arland's sensitivity to form heightened his awareness of the evolution of the genre toward the "poetic" and lyrical novel influenced by surrealism, and away from the analytical "intimate novel" dear to Rivière.

Ramón Fernandez, a Bergsonian philosopher familiar with Anglo-Saxon criticism—particularly that of I. A. Richards—addressed the problem of the relation in art between the work-as-an-object and the thought that informs it: "a work of art is the incarnation of a metaphysic," involving, in his view, a moral or a message the critic must identify. The preface to *Messages* (1926) describes this "philosophical criticism," defining as its goal: to locate the spiritual basis of the work, the writer's *attitude* rather than his ideas; to reconstruct the relation between the writer and his work; to throw light onto the ambiguous face of a subjective-objective book.

René Lalou was more methodical. Dissatisfied with the prevailing "doctrinal anarchy," he addressed the problem of whether or not criticism is necessary, affirming that it is. Although Lalou sided with those who denied scientific status to criticism, he nevertheless believed it should be methodical, with rigor all the more necessary because the critic of contemporary literature has his task complicated by lack of perspective, lack of documentation, and the pitfalls of publicity. Lalou also addressed a problem fundamental to criticism at any time: on what basis can the correctness of a critical judgment be guaranteed? "Metaphysical waffling" was Lalou's term for critical assessments based on nothing but a vague "act of faith in the universality of human intelligence." He believed the first principle of all criticism must be intellectual honesty; and that the function of criticism consists above all in understanding the literary work and in serving it with probity.

Sociocultural, psychological, philosophical, and stylistic criticism all existed side by side, with no effort made to formulate their implicit theoretical basis, or clearly to distinguish one from another.

The Pure Poetry Controversy

The somewhat sterile pure poetry controversy that kept Parisian literary circles in a turmoil for half a dozen years is a good illustration of the "Parisianism" characteristic of literary life at the time. A great deal of ink was spilled in the cause. The first shot was fired on October 24, 1925, the day Abbé Bremond, at a meeting of the five Academies, read a paper entitled "Pure Poetry" that was later published in *Le Temps,* where it drew an answering blast from Souday, to which Bremond responded, in turn, with two "Eclaircissements" in *Les Nouvelles Littéraires*. The dispute rebounded from there to the *Mercure de France* and then over to the *Revue de France*. The fight was on, and for five more years it generated a barrage of articles, more than two hundred in all. Actually, the "pure poetry" idea had been a common one among poets since the turn of the century, with each one attributing his own meaning to it. It had doubtless played a role in directing Gide toward the idea of the "pure novel." But Bremond and Souday both appealed primarily to Valéry in their efforts to justify their respective claims. Abbé Bremond, a scholar, historian, and man of taste who cared little for matters of form put himself in the position of the average reader and held that the pleasure dispensed by poetry is a "mystery." This pleasure, according to him, is somehow connected to an inexplicable inner experience analogous to mystical experience. Poetic response springs, therefore, from the presence in the poem of a spiritual current mysteriously transmitted by words in much the same way as an electric current is transmitted through the intermediary of wires, illuminating from one soul to another the presence of a divine force making possible the fusion of man with God, a process similar to prayer. Most characteristic of modern poetry, he believed, is this quest for pure poetry—a thesis he developed in *Prières et Poésie* (1926). No idea, however, could have been further from the genuine preoccupations of Valéry, an antimystical spirit if ever there was one. But from misunderstanding to misunderstanding, the expression "pure poetry"—acquiring a meaning completely opposite to the one advocated by Abbé Bremond— infected all the arts: What is the pure novel? pure cinema? pure drama? pure painting? Critical scrutiny of various expressive media had been set off that

increased and occasionally even inspired the experimental studies that ultimately led to the questions on "being and literature" (Barthes) of the sixties.

In Search of New Directions, 1936–52

"If we were to select the one aspect, among all literary judgments we have
seen, somewhat designed to surprise, it would be that critics seem oddly
unconcerned with justifying what they say, as if their statements were self-
evident and to be accurate needed only to be pronounced ... The least we
can say in such cases is that, of course, the Terrorist does not provide us
with proofs of what he says; but, what is more serious, he seems unaware
that he should do so." It was in 1941 that Jean Paulhan, in his essay *Les
Fleurs de Tarbes ou la Terreur dans les lettres*, made an initial approach to
criticism, a problem he returned to in his *Petite Préface à toute critique*
(1951). Former surrealist Paulhan's denunciation of "terrorism" was aimed
at the prejudices of the surrealists, but he was also attacking the fads and
fancies of journalists and academics, and hence a more generalized fault—
the extreme unreliability of all critical judgments. Paulhan wanted to "witness the birth of new critics" (*F. F. ou le Critique*, 1945) capable of developing a common critical vocabulary and a rigorous new rhetoric that could
be applied to contemporary literature and would be compatible with a new
concept of what a literary work is that contemporary literature was proposing. Paulhan believed this would provide the corrective for the confusion
and subjectivity being suffered by literature and literary criticism alike. The
same need was perceived by Roger Caillois (*Les Impostures de la poésie*,
1945; *Vocabulaire esthétique*, 1947; *Babel*, 1948). According to Caillois,
criticism should be essentially a descriptive stylistics; according to Paulhan,
a poetics. Since literature is above all a "language art," a poetics would offer
"criteria for judgment" on the basis of which more or less objective evaluations of a work's "degree of realization" could be made, this being the
quality that distinguishes literature from other types of writing. However,
although Paulhan and Caillois both approached criticism through an objective examination of language, neither had a theory to offer that would give
criticism the status of an autonomous discipline. A step in the right direction
was made by Jean Hytier, who at about that time formulated, in *Les Arts de
la littérature* (1945), a typology of literary genres.

Philosophers' Criticism

Philosophers and sometime literary critics Gaston Bachelard, Jean-Paul
Sartre, and Maurice Blanchot paved the way for the dawning of what
Georges Poulet called the "critical conscience." Casting conventional critical methods to one side, they approached the work of literature *from the
point of view of the reader,* in different ways, to be sure, but ones that were

each carefully explained. These men addressed the problem of the relation between the critic-reader and the text he interprets. The critic's initial option will appear in the form of a relativizing subjective factor. It is because of this factor that so much importance has been placed on the methodological assumptions and on "metacriticism," i.e., on examining the basic principles that define the critical viewpoint.

Bachelard

One sector of established criticism, thematics, was given new impetus by the publication between 1938 and 1948 of a series of works by Bachelard. These were: *La Psychanalyse du feu, L'Eau et les Rêves, L'Air et les Songes,* and *La Terre et les rêveries du repos.* The titles alone indicate the trend of Bachelard's inquiry, which was an exploration into the affective significance we attach to representations of the elements. Two subsequent works, *La Poétique de l'espace* (1957) and *La Poétique de la rêverie* (1961) clarified a philosophy developing inductively. A philosopher and physicist, a man in love with poetry, Bachelard contributed something new to criticism, which was the idea of the poetic image as a pivot for psychological analysis. Bachelard's early works dealt with the epistemological problems inherent in scientific knowledge. He explored the ways a scientific mind extracts concepts from the substrate of subconscious myth and error, *imaginary* but convincing structures that determine language and orient thought and behavior. This led logically to the study of the language of alchemy, the matrix from which science, through its demystification of it, was born.

In the light of Jungian psychology, the alchemists' "great reveries"—in particular those concerning the elements of water, fire, earth, and air—although they were devoid of objective scientific value, seemed to Bachelard to be rich in insights on the structures of the imaginary. A great reader of the surrealists, Bachelard discovered new images between the lines of their poetry that were different, he believed, from the "cultural web" of the collectivity. These configurations and their substantive elements do not, according to Bachelard, have any objective value; they are unreal. In order to explain how they develop, Bachelard had recourse to the Jungian hypothesis of a subconscious structure within the human psyche and manifest in the reiterated paradigm of the archetype. He then formulated an additional hypothesis of his own, which was the existence in man of a mode of consciousness differing both from the dream state, in which the subject loses his sense of identity, and the rational state in which an active consciousness separates subject from object. Bachelard called this third mode the state of reverie: a waking but relaxed state in which the contradiction between full consciousness and dream disappears; a state of mind expansion toward the world; a free, open movement centered on a substance or object—water, seashell, tree—whose image takes shape against a latent, internal architecture, an invisible substrate of dream, perhaps, or archetypes. Thus divorced from the web of contextual significance in which it occurs, the image no longer has its "source in the visible world" but becomes a "projection of that obscure soul" of which it is the thematic expression. Because it enables human beings to see themselves as free and creative while they are in the very act of creating, this submerged thematic is the origin, according to Bachelard, of what he calls "the creative image."

What Bachelard is presenting in his preface to *La Poétique de la rêverie* is, therefore, a phenomenology of the poetic persona, as distinct from the psychological. "Trying to locate an image's antecedents while inside the very existence of it is the mark, for a phenomenologist, of inveterate psychologism. Let us look, rather, at the poetic image as it is. The poetic consciousness is so completely absorbed by the image and its appearance on language at a higher than ordinary level, and the poetic consciousness speaks, with the poetic image, a language so new, that correlations between past and present can no longer usefully be considered. When we give examples of the kind of cleavages in meaning, sensation, and feeling we are describing, it becomes obvious that the poetic image falls under the sign of a new man. And this new man is a happy one."

Bachelard realized the concept represented a "crisis of methodology" for criticism but believed, nevertheless, that it "contributes a few methods, a few tools to the renewal of literary criticism." What he proposed was a method of reading: "To read and at the same time to empathize with the creative reverie"—a deep reading and an identification making it possible to distinguish the various levels and fissures in the fabric of the poetic discourse, and to differentiate the "cultural web" level of threadbare tropes from the "spontaneous response" level where new images are created. Bachelard suggests new ways of approaching the genesis of poetry critically, and of isolating certain linguistic features within the warp and woof of the text. Intuitive rather than systematic, he gives examples rather than presenting a systematic critical method in studies of Lautréamont and Huysmans; analyses of images drawn from surrealist poetry, especially Eluard's. He provides "readings," fragmentary interpretations of literary texts. But the nature of his inquiry is basically psychological; literature is the documentary evidence: "Only through reading can we come to know man, the marvel of reading by which he is judged."

Current thematics focused on themes that were developed in a text consciously and, in order to establish their significance, analyzed how they were articulated in the text as a whole. This kind of analysis lent itself to comparative studies, because it referred back to other uses of the same theme. Its contribution was to the history of ideas and of taste. The primary purpose of Bachelard's thematics, on the other hand, was to identify the configurations of subconscious images in the text, and to decipher their affective impact. Its ultimate aim was to articulate these images into underlying structures, or paradigms. This thematics was concerned not with the formal structures of the work but with exploring a psychological depth inaccessible through other methods and yet important to discover. A "new criticism" of literary thematics, inspired by Bachelard but more methodical than he, attracted a group of young academics who had fallen under his spell. The first two volumes of Georges Poulet's critical essays, *Etudes sur le temps humain* (1949) and *La Distance intérieure* (1952), were symptomatic of the new orientation in literary criticism that under the hands of Jean Starobinski, Jean-Pierre Richard, and—up to a point—Jean Rousset, was to dominate the field of academic criticism for at least ten years.

Jean-Paul Sartre as Literary Critic

Sartre's first critical essays came out in the *Nouvelle revue française* from 1936 to 1940, reviews of recently published novels by Faulkner, Dos Passos, Giraudoux, Mauriac, and Nizan. Sartre at the time employed a terminology that was post-Hegelian or Husserlian; his method was closely linked to theories about human reality and the "imaginary" structures of the work of art that he was currently formulating and later dealt with in his books *L'Imagination* and *L'Imaginaire,* and in *L'Etre et le Néant.* Theoretical schema and practical applications of it are closely intertwined in these essays. Sartre accepted these philosophical assumptions as irrefutable axioms conferring their authority on his criticism. The act of the critic, therefore, is an exemplary *demonstration.* Sartre performed it from his own vantage point as a reader, a perspective that was consciously, if not explicitly, determined. Each of Sartre's critical reviews reflects a theoretical bias allowing him to apply identical criteria of judgment to novels that were very different. Intrinsic to Sartre's ontology, these criteria were extrinsic to the literary works under review. What they lost in objectivity, they gained in consistency.

An explanation of Sartre's critical system in all of its complexity is not possible here, but we can sketch out a few of its main lines. Every technique, according to Sartre, implies a metaphysic. It is this metaphysic that the critic, through his examination of technique, must reveal; and it was upon this metaphysic that Sartre based his critical judgments, using his own metaphysic—which for a time he held to be irrefutable—as the measure.

Having stated the axiom that every individual be perceived as "freedom in context" and defined as "process becoming," Sartre condemned ipso facto all other representations of human reality as patently contaminated by "bad faith." Sartre took exception to the imaginary worlds of Faulkner and Mauriac, for example, insofar as they contained characters controlled either by fate or by divine plan; conversely, he considered Dos Passos a great novelist—until the time came when he began to disagree with this writer's politics.

In practice, Sartre's criticism was arbitrary and somewhat unconvincing;

beneath the mask of the critic, the iconoclast showed through. The value of his method lay elsewhere. Sartre dealt with the problem of the relationship between reader and text, reader and author, author and text. He tried to define exactly what the act of reading involves. A text is a collection of black marks on a white page. A book without a reader is a dead letter. The act of writing, therefore, is directed toward someone else's consciousness; it is an *appeal* to the reader. During this period (when *La Nausée* was published) Sartre believed that a novel is a strategy for escaping the contingencies of the real world through the creation of a coherent imaginary one, and that its unifying principle is to be found in the human yearning for transcendence. The reader's task is twofold: first, he must freely undertake to endow the imaginary world of the novel with his own temporality—the time he spends reading it—and then he must detach himself from this temporality, turn toward the world of the novel, and try to discover the nature of the "strategy" it entails. This is when the critical process begins, with an elucidation from the heterogeneous elements of the novel—descriptions, characterizations, plot, interrelations of characters, dialogue—the *intentionality* conferring significance on them. That is, the critic identifies the ontological premises of the author, believed by Sartre to be inherent in the novel's overall organization. The reader then must weigh these premises against his own vision of the world. For Sartre, therefore, a literary work is neither an end in itself nor an aesthetic object. It is a privileged "medium" of communication between two individual consciousnesses occupying two different "contexts" relative to the world of everyday reality. Sartre states as axiomatic the *intentionality* of the relation between the consciousness responsible for creating the text and the language in which it is created. He held also axiomatic that the referent for this language is the world of reality. The questions Sartre raised regarding the specific language and modalities of the written text are questions of broad human significance.

Sartre later enlarged his initial schema of "context" circumscribing "strategy" (the strategy of writing being one) to include other factors of increasing complexity: concrete economic and social structures, the concept of class, and the utopian, teleological myth of history identified with Marxist analysis; the structures of the subconscious that for so long had gone unacknowledged; and the belatedly recognized involuntary structures of language. But Sartre's basic method remained unchanged, and he used it in his *Baudelaire*, his *Saint Genet*, and his (unfinished) work on Flaubert, *L'Idiot de la famille*, casting the classic, academic "life and work" into a new form. Sartre believed "the work" should be analyzed in the context of "the life" for its concealed psychological meaning. His critical method was ideologic, reassimilating the literary text into the context of a multistructured cultural, economic, social, and psychological reality.

The virtue of Sartre's approach to criticism was that it radically undermined the conventional attitudes of academics and of the literate public in regard to the literary enterprise, and to literature considered as a sort of sacred patrimony or, to use Sartre's own words, "a public monument." Pointing out the social determinants of the literary phenomenon was a worthwhile thing to do. But using a rhetorical device to reduce literature to a socially significant fact in the Marxist sense—as revised by Sartre—proved foolhardy. There can be no question that the demystification process begun by Sartre sowed, in turn, its own share of myth and confusion. However, the great critical debates on literary dogma and critical theory associated with the sixties all began with Sartre's *Qu'est-ce que la littérature?*

Maurice Blanchot

Maurice Blanchot's infrequent reviews, published in the *Nouvelle revue française* and *Critique,* were eventually collected in book form, the first three volumes—*Faux Pas, Lautréamont et Sade,* and *La Part du feu*—appearing between 1943 and 1949. It took fifteen years or so for their full impact to be felt. *L'Espace littéraire* (1955) and *Le Livre à venir* (1959) delved more deeply into the same themes. A novelist unfamiliar to all but a few readers, Maurice Blanchot focused his thinking not on the individual works he presented in his critical articles, but on *the act of writing.* Each review is an essay in the form of a paradox opening up a continuously renewable inquiry into the dual activity of writing, and writing about writing. "Let us suppose that literature begins when we start asking questions about it." This is how, in *La Part du feu,* Blanchot phrased the problem that for him served as an inexhaustible source of philosophical reflection sustained by readings of Mallarmé, Hegel, and Heidegger. It was not Sartre or Bachelard, but Blanchot whose thoughts on the conditions and paradoxes of the critical discourse cleared the way for the "vanguard" criticism of the sixties.

Blanchot believed the act of reading validates the book while annulling both author and reader: "In a way, the book needs the reader . . . in order to assert itself as an object without author and also without reader." For the critic, it is not a question of explaining, interpreting, or evaluating. It is a question of discovering the wellspring for the discourse unfolding in the book. Literature for Blanchot is not a series of works but a nascent language, a collection of signs negating reality, a void, an absence. Blanchot's philosophy is haunted by antimonies: absence and presence, being and nonbeing, empty time and fullness, wandering and staying in one place, life and death, solitude and communication, nonsense and authenticity, the possibility of writing and its impossibility. The writer is born of the death of a man disappearing into the void made by the act of autoprojection outside life that we call writing. The writer dies when *the book* is finished, and is reborn with the "need to write," a dialectic that will never be finished. Only the reader can turn the book into a completed "work."

Blanchot himself "validates" certain books in this way, awarding them honored status in the "literary space" cleared by the "language on language" of Blanchot the reader: Mallarmé, to be sure, also Hölderlin, Kafka, Beckett, René Char. Blanchot's contact with the works of these writers gave full scope to his inquiry into the nature of literary existence seen as an autonomous human production that is divorced from reality, and not as a commentary on that reality.

Against a background of Hegelianism, Blanchot was stating a problematic of the production of literary language in its dual writing-reading aspect. Unlike Sartre, Blanchot insisted on the determining role of reader, not author, in constituting what, in the course of this process, *becomes* literature—but what is not literature until the process begins. Blanchot rejected all of the contemporary critical modes, demonstrating the inadequacy of their assumptions, but not suggesting new ones. But his definition of "literary space," of the literary work's status as a "linguistic object," and his suppression of the author and of the reader's ego, broke with the romantic critical tradition that persisted in defining a literary work—as did Sartre—in terms of a story: society's, the author's, or literature's. Following in a tradition begun by Mallarmé and Valéry, Blanchot prefigured questions that were raised by the critics of the sixties—Genette, Todorov, Ricardou, Kristeva, and Sollers—who also attempted to solve them.

The New Critics, 1952–70

As far back as 1944, Henri Hell, codirector of the review *Fontaine,* was already complaining of "a certain pseudo-philosophical-poetical tendency that was miring literary criticism deeper and deeper in the swamp of vapid and pretentious gibberish" (*Fontaine* 32). To the layman, the image projected by literary criticism during those years appeared to corroborate this judgment. However, the difficulties presented by the language of criticism were due not to the fact that it didn't make sense but to the plethora of current critical systems, each with a terminology of its own. These terminologies rested on theories defining the act of criticism which were themselves, in turn, directly or indirectly linked to conceptions regarding the literary phenomenon that frequently were mutually exclusive. Often they were borrowed from other disciplines—sociology, psychoanalysis, anthropology, linguistics. The categories employed, for example, in Freudian criticism, were foreign to the linguistic or neo-Marxist. And there were some critics, furthermore, who attempted to combine elements from different systems, or to invent systems of their own. Only rarely did a book of criticism appear without a lengthy preface explaining the author's personal critical method, and justifying his choice of terminology—an idiosyncratic one, more often than not. Occasionally critics actually created their own terminologies, with the text under discussion serving merely as "raw material." These vocabularies fell in and out of fashion with a swiftness as disconcerting as the aggressive intolerance with which their appearance in the critical kaleidoscope was sometimes greeted. The war of terminologies was not always in ingenuous one. At stake in some cases was the ideological conflict between spiritualism—latent or overt—as characteristic of traditional critical attitudes based on Christianity or neo-Hegelianism, and uncompromising neo-Marxist materialism. In the rhetoric of neo-Marxism, attacking or destroying the traditional language of criticism was equated with attacking the foundations of "bourgeois" culture and preparing the way for social revolution; which explains the repercussions this critical controversy had on education and its influence on literary syllabi at every level.

The source of this plethora of systems, theories, and terminologies was undoubtedly to be found in the painful awareness on the part of France's younger generation that, intellectually, post–World War II France was imprisoned in an ideological framework that had become outmoded. This would also explain the violent attacks on the "dead language" of academia. But it was not until this polemical barrage reached its apogee between 1964 and 1967 that the criticism controversy was finally perceived as a conflict between the "bad guys"—rigid, authoritarian academic criticism—and the "good guys"—the nonacademic, daring, trendy, "new" criticism. And yet important studies written by academics—Georges Blin's *Stendhal et les problèmes du roman* (1959) and *Stendhal et les problèmes de la personnalité* (1958), for example—broke the ground later cleared by the "new criticism." It was actually *inside* the universities that the various new critical trends first developed. But they were scholarly, even pedantic, and produced research of little if any interest to the nonspecialist.

The years 1952–65 witnessed a proliferation of critical studies accompanying the proliferation of critical methodologies and an attempt on the part of the critics, in turn, to sort them into some kind of order. Subcategories multiplied, and meta- or diacriticism became an active branch in the field of criticism with the proposal that it be divided into various classifications: psychoanalytic, phenomenological, existentialist, Marxist, thematic. During the sixties a new factor emerged in the course of debates like the one organized in 1964 by the Marxist group Clarté on the theme, "What purpose literature?" and a colloquium like the one held in 1966 at Cerisy-la-Salle questioning the usefulness of any critical methodology whatsoever. A new generation of young intellectuals, following in the wake of Roland Barthes, theorized, delivered exposés, debated, and organized colloquia, attempting in the process to free themselves from methodological chaos by adopting a form of textual analysis inspired by structural linguistics. Based originally on the work of Saussure, structural linguistics also drew on work by Mallarmé, or even Valéry, and addressed the problems of "writing," how a text is made and how it works; this new discipline replaced interpretation of a text with analysis of its *structures*. Structuralism soon broke into splinter groups, however, and despite the attempt at terminological documentation and normalization represented by a publication such as the *Dictionnaire encyclopédique des sciences du langage* (Oswald Ducrot and Tzvetan Todorov, Le Seuil, 1972) this movement seriously reinforced the proliferation of terminologies.

Beneath the already complex surface of this critical scene, latent conflict could be discerned. To cite just one example: anthropologist Lévi-Strauss's rationalism versus the antirationalism of Bataille, both exerting an influence on the "critical vanguard," their respective attitudes each representing a deeply ingrained tendency in Western thought which, following the upheavals of 1914–18, had come into acute conflict. But ever since the days of Aristotle a more generalized conflict had divided the field of criticism: on one hand, the need for systematic sets of rules by means of which literary production can be codified, with each individual work approached as an object to be described and classified; and, on the other, subjective response to a work explored from within and submitted to an act of interpretation that will reveal its meaning or lead to a better understanding of the author behind the text—or in it. A third tendency, represented by Derrida's work on pure writing (*L'Ecriture et la différence, De la grammatologie,* and *La Voix et le phénomène* in 1967; and *La Dissémination, Positions,* and *Marges de la philosophie* in 1972) opened up avenues which after 1970 appeared—temporarily perhaps—to be a logical continuation of the other two. In general, however, the distinguishing mark of modern, as opposed to traditional, criticism has been its refusal to attribute definitive meaning or content to any text. To modern criticism, a text is a text, no more.

Serious criticism in the seventies, whichever of these paths it chose to follow, invariably dealt with the process by which meaning is generated. Methods were based on certain axioms: that language is a system of signs, and that this system is polysemic (i.e., that every signifier—a word or group of words—can transmit many different messages, or signifieds); that language functions through the intermediary of three great impersonal and analyzable mechanisms: (1) its own rules of production and transformation, (2) the myths, political ideology, and philosophy organizing the social reality of the collectivity whose language it is, moral and religious representations included, and (3) the deep libidinal structures common to all human beings, whose function was discovered by Freud and which introduce into the interplay of human relations a hidden syntax underlying the overt syntax of the language. The traditional idea of the *author* was deprived of its power by these axioms; once a creator, he was now merely a scribe, leaving the romantic notions of "genius" also open to attack, and leading to suppression of the "I," which was transformed from "subject" to grammatical function.

Panorama of Critical Practice, 1970

In 1952, and for about fifteen years thereafter, the field of criticism was
dominated by the so-called *thematic* or *phenomenological* criticism. This
school of criticism was influenced by Bachelard and the early Sartre and also
incorporated suggestions from psychoanalysis. Phenomenological, or
thematic, criticism posited the presence of a consciousness—the author's—
serving as the originating principle of the text, the center for its organization
and production. The phenomenological critic attempts through his reading
of the text to achieve a state of total identification with this originating
consciousness, which implies the existence of an essence shared by every
human consciousness, each individual human consciousness being a separate manifestation of it. By means of a sort of intuition, the critic is led in the
course of this process to a discovery of the "origin" or pivotal point at
which the lived experience of one individual "ego" (the author's) is trans-
muted into language (the text). This is the point at which "ego becomes
writer," i.e., begins to elaborate a coherent literary language. Reading the
text reveals the modalities of this language: temporal representations or
reiterated figures such as the circle (Georges Poulet); groups or interrelated
words suggesting an unconscious penchant on the part of the writer for
particular kinds of movement (flight, for example), particular materials, or
particular forms (Jean-Pierre Richard); or organization based on a dialectic
of the hidden and the obvious (Jean Starobinski). These configurations or
groups constitute a kind of matrix, a shared thematic or basic language that
connects an author's various works to one another. Uncompromisingly
subjective, thematic criticism more than any other is a kind of literature
about literature.

Psychoanalytical criticism applied to literature was slow to gain a foothold in France. Its methodology was explained with clarity by Charles
Mauron, who had been attempting since the twenties to find ways to use
psychoanalysis as a tool for criticism. In 1963, in the introduction to his
book *Des métaphores obsédantes au mythe personnel,* Mauron succeeded in
formulating methods of "psychocriticism" and their limitations. Like the
thematic critics, Mauron also attempted through the reading of an author's
complete works to uncover networks of association or configurations of
repeated, obsessive images. He compared different texts by the same author
until the outlines of that author's personal myth began to emerge through
the various motifs. Mauron's model for his interpretation of these myths
was a Freudian one. Falling into abeyance for a time, psychoanalytic interpretations of literature returned with renewed vigor to the scene when
psychoanalyst Jacques Lacan pointed out the analogy between what the
libido does to circumvent the superego's censorship of its self-expression,
and such familiar rhetorical devices as metaphor and metonymy (metaphor
being the substitution of one image for another; metonymy the substitution

of one term for another contiguously, as it were, related to it; and both being parallels of the double meanings found in dreams and in the kinds of things patients say while under analysis).

Socioliterary criticism, referred to as genetic structuralism by its most famous French practitioner, Lucien Goldman, drew for its inspiration on the Marxist aesthetic theories developed by a Hungarian, Lukács, who was little known in France before the sixties. Sociocriticism is based on the Marxist concept of individual mental structure as a reflection of the social group to which it belongs. A writer is merely the man who most clearly reflects the mental structures or "vision" of his group. It therefore becomes the critic's task to determine the writer's position in his own group, and the group's position in relation to society as a whole. The problem here is not—as it was for the naive Marxism of the thirties—a literary text's *content;* the problem is the interplay of social relations transposed by means of the text from the real structures of society, as perceived by one of its collectivities, into an imaginary one. From the sociocritic's point of view, the literary text is thus a unique social document. For the psychoanalytic critic, the ultimate goal is understanding man; for the sociocritic, it is understanding society.

Formalist and *structural-linguistic criticism* is based on the work of Ferdinand de Saussure. Directly inspired by the linguistic studies of Roman Jakobson and Noam Chomsky, by Propp's work on the transformation in the Russian folktale, and by the work of Lévi-Strauss, formalist criticism set out to create "models" or systems of abstract relations that would account for the dynamics of genres or literary types, as Lévi-Strauss had done in his efforts to explain the many different myths of various Amerindian tribes *(Anthropologie structurale)*. This type of literary criticism, in its diverse manifestations, aimed to analyze the novel or, to use a broader term, "narrative discourse" (Jean Ricardou); or to formulate a new poetics (Gérard Genette, Tzvetan Todorov); or to conduct research into semiotics or linguistic analysis of the text as a meaning system (Julia Kristeva, Philippe Sollers). It was frequently practiced in the form of intensive microanalysis of individual words and phrases.

The Paradigmatic Trajectory: Roland Barthes

In a series of works spanning a twenty-year period starting with *Le Degré zéro de l'écriture* in 1953, Roland Barthes, less a literary than a Marxist-inspired social and cultural critic, sounded the successive keynotes of the *nouvelle critique,* formulating better than anyone its scientific aims. Influenced in the beginning by psychoanalytical methodology (Michelet), Barthes in his essay *Sur Racine* combined psychoanalysis with structuralism; he then became interested in formalist analysis, and later in semiology, which he applied to structural analysis of the various codes of narrative discourse in his book *S/Z,* an essay on Balzac's novella *Sarrasine.* Barthes, in

a rich variety of critical works, combined theory with practice, demonstrating the development of a mind in perpetual movement, eager to surpass
itself, assimilating and then using research by linguistic specialists like Emile
Benveniste, or philosophers like Derrida. More than anything else Barthes
was a brilliant, if not always infallible, seminal figure bursting with new
ideas, new theories, methods, techniques, and terminologies. In addition, his
numerous essays, articles, prefaces, book reviews, and interviews (*Essais
critiques,* 1964; *Critique et vérité,* 1966) present a coherent philosophy of
the problematics of literature and criticism. No understanding of today's
critical vanguard, its accomplishments and aspirations, its myths and prejudices, would be possible without an understanding of the intellectual itinerary followed by Roland Barthes. The last stage of this journey, begun about
1970, went from *Sade, Fourier, Loyola* to *Le Plaisir du texte* (1973). During
this period Barthes repudiated what he called his "euphoric, scientificized
dream" and attempted simply to analyze the pleasure a literary text gives to
the reader. The focal point of his argument is a basic distinction he makes
between the rarely produced "writerly" text, that is, the text that *could* be
written today; and the "readerly" text, which reflects the general culture in
a commonplace way, is easy to read, but does not require participation or
"coproduction" of the reader as the "writerly" text does. He then describes
the "pleasure" afforded by the "writerly" text, which is a kind of game
played with the impulses and linguistic skill of the reader. An example of the
"writerly" text would be, according to Barthes, *Lois,* by Philippe Sollers.
Ideally, literature should be a combination of the "readerly" and the
"writerly." These final texts by Barthes are highly subjective and perhaps
symptomatic of a certain lassitude on his part in reaction to the current
plethora of abstract discussion, and an attempt to return to the affective
values of the literary art.

The radical change in the analytical methods and in the vocabulary of
criticism that occurred between 1950 and 1970 was highly disconcerting to
critics who had been trained during the first half of the century. As a result,
there was a complete—if perhaps only temporary—break between these
critics and the so-called *nouveaux critiques.*

Each of the opposing groups tended, however, to rekindle interest in
books that had previously remained in the shade: Raymond Roussel's
books, for example, or the work of Antonin Artaud, the latter's essays on
the theater published by the *Nouvelle revue française* having been the only
things of his to enjoy public appreciation. Both critical camps supported
Lautréamont, Kafka, and Sade. It is interesting to note, however, that the
most significant critical debates centered on the most "classic" writers of the
past: Racine, Baudelaire, Flaubert, Mallarmé.

Another major critical contribution of the period was publication of the
great uniform editions comprising both the classical heritage and the literature of our own time, an endeavor on which foreign and French scholars
alike collaborated. There were annotated critical editions of complete works

published in the refurbished Bibliothèque de la Pléiade (Balzac, Baudelaire, etc.); Dumas's complete plays published by Minard-Lettres Modernes; vast amounts of correspondence: Sainte-Beuve, Mérimée, George Sand, Mallarmé; the complete works of writers like Bataille and Céline; fresh presentations of the previously published and publication of the previously unpublished—notebooks, miscellaneous texts; all of which broadened the base and destroyed the unnecessarily narrow boundaries of academic literary history. Literary theories and literary abstractions were put to the test, but one question still remained unanswered: what *is* this vast literary space, and how does it really work?

Historiography and Literary History

The brand of literary history bearing Lanson's name was based on the same fundamental principles as those developed by nineteenth-century historians. But historiography itself has evolved since then, partly under the influence of new interpretive and analytical methods using statistics and computers. The event-centered history of practitioners steeped in nineteenth-century rational positivism is slowly being replaced by a more complex conception of the historical process. In 1929 a group under the aegis of Lucien Febvre and known as the "Annales Group"—from the title of the review they founded—bent its efforts toward the in-depth study of processes that link together the economic phenomena, social structures, and cultural forms of a particular place at a particular time. Some years later Fernand Braudel (*Ecrits sur l'Histoire,* 1958) established three dimensions of history: (1) the short-term history of surface events, i.e., the "microstructures" approach dear to the great historians of the nineteenth century; (2) the longer-term history of social and intellectual change; and, at a deeper level, (3) "macrostructure" history of whole geographic regions, such as the Mediterranean world, what changes in them and what remains the same. Historians have turned increasingly to the study of communities, villages, or small towns, investigating the exact conditions of life and trade that regulate community life.

French historians have made a considerable and an innovative contribution to historical studies. In fact, for serious readers intellectually curious about the past of their own countries, it has frequently seemed that historical studies might be replacing the great sociological novels. The old concept of linear history was superseded by a new concept of multiple structures and time levels; and the conventional idea of progress by explorations of synchronic cultural systems operating on the vertical, as it were, but responding to underlying population movements giving rise to the surface events of microhistory—studying the lives of twenty million Frenchmen, in other words, in order to grasp the resulting epiphenomenon that was Louis XIV.[1]

[1]P. Goubert, *Louis XIV et vingt millions de Français* (Paris: Fayard, 1966).

There was plenty of room in these complex patterns for literary history, with the individual literary work appearing not so much an isolated event as simply one manifestation among many others of a given historical period's style.

It may well be that future historians will define the preceding half-century as the age of the ideologue. In any case, the burgeoning of critical theory and critical research has thrown confusion into the literary world; a contributing factor has been the substantial entry onto the scene of a vigorous literary internationalism with academic connections, especially in the United States. The respect accorded to contemporary literature, the warm reception foreign writers and professors receive, the viability of current research, and the accessibility of works from every part of the globe have all contributed to considerably increasing the size and changing the nature of the public for French writers. Whether read in the original French or in translation, certain contemporary French works became "classics" for thousands of students in other countries even before their French counterparts learned about them. The criteria for publication changed, reflecting a vast literary network of international scope. The "Paris try-out" was no longer the sole nor perhaps even a necessary determinant of how well a book would do, how long it would last, and how many copies it would sell. It is difficult to foresee the long-term influence this new circumstance will have. At the moment it seems to be providing, through a stringent process of selection, a corrective to the huge numbers of books flooding the Paris market. Other, unpredictable factors may also come into play in the future that will favor Oriental or Francophone works, for example, at the expense of French ones: this will depend on academic syllabi, on which books happen to get translated, and on changing intellectual fashions. French writers are in an uncomfortable position, caught between the expectations and demands of the "closed circle" described by Nourissier and a foreign public scattered far and wide. To add to their problems, in France, as elsewhere, new research and new directions in critical methods have transformed in disconcerting ways the fine, familiar, ancient edifice of French literature they once believed they were entering.

Four

The Literary Space

12

A Change in
Topography

Former surrealist André Thirion, writing half a century
after the fact, remarked that the "tone" of the twenties was
set by Gide, Morand, Valéry, Giraudoux, Cocteau, Max
Jacob, Roger Martin du Gard, and Larbaud; in other
words, by men who represented the "new spirit" of the
pre–World War I era. From this matrix was born, under
the impact of dada, the most dynamic of all the postwar
movements: surrealism. Gaining in strength with the passage of time, surrealism created a rupture in the field of
literature. It injected into the literary circuit texts that
dominated the period not only by their quality but also by
their very nature and by the peremptory tone of the
theories they represented. Yet the success of the surrealists
betrayed their complicity with the era they denounced. The
fact that the surrealist movement was symptomatic of a
deeper trend was not lost on André Breton, who in 1922
declared, "Actually I do not believe that cubism, futurism,
and dada constitute three distinct movements, but believe
that all three belong to a more general movement whose
exact scope and significance we do not yet understand"
(Les Pas perdus). It is our belief, in fact, that the intellectual
attitudes of the post-1950 vanguard were, despite their
denigration and denial of subjectivity in any form, merely
chastened and more circumspect versions of an uninter-
rupted itinerary begun in 1910 that may have reached
the end of the line with those attitudes.

The intervening fifty years witnessed this movement's
complete revolution of the literary scene; the old hierarchies were overturned, leaving behind a sense of vacuum.
Examined retrospectively from the standpoint of 1975,
however, this sense of vacuum seems to have been more
rhetorical than real.

Without attempting to redefine the concept of literature,
we can assume that works gain admittance to the "literary

space" because the quality of the writing is considered by critics to be valid and the work then becomes a part of the literary domain. Literature, therefore, is anything that at any given moment is accepted as literature. Judged by this definition, there has been no period richer than this one in literary works.

These were the years when Proust, Gide, Claudel, Valéry, and—always a case apart—Colette reached full maturity. Works by these authors have secured a place for themselves among the great literary works of the Western world. The generations growing up beside them jockeyed with each other for space rather than succeeding one another gracefully. There was innovation in every literary genre. Novels proliferated: François Mauriac, Jean Giraudoux, Jules Romains, Georges Duhamel, Roger Martin du Gard, Louis Aragon, then Georges Bernanos, Jean Giono, Julien Green, and then André Malraux and Céline; also the lesser-known Marcel Jouhandeau, Raymond Queneau, Henri Bosco; and, finally, Sartre, Simone de Beauvoir, Marguerite Yourcenar, and Camus endowed the novel with substance and great diversity. The novel was also adapted to more arcane usage in works by Jean Cayrol and Julien Gracq, in Maurice Blanchot's strange books, and Raymond Abellio's even stranger ones. By the time the ink began flowing on the subject of the *nouveau roman* and the *nouveau nouveau roman*, works by Samuel Beckett, Claude Simon, and Jean-Marie Le Clézio had already found their own public—a limited one perhaps, and no doubt the same one that closely followed the novel-to-novel development of Michel Butor, Alain Robbe-Grillet, Marguerite Duras, and Robert Pinget and was absorbed in the successive stages of Nathalie Sarraute's progress toward perfecting her original narrative technique.

Establishing diachronic perspective in regard to a body of literature with which we are still surrounded is difficult, however. As far as French literature is concerned, we can note that the years 1952–70, which corresponded to the vigorous outpouring of Francophone literature, were considerably less rich than the era that preceded them—a period of great fertility. The great literary figures had disappeared from the scene and no one took their place: there were no obvious successors to Saint-John Perse, Giraudoux, Malraux, Sartre, or Camus. For a historian surveying the immense diversity of this literary production, bound at times to err through omission or because it is impossible to read with care everything there is to read or to take in everything the critics have to say about it, who therefore can adopt only partial, provisional, and disputable positions, what stands out today is the anarchic and diminished aspect of a literature which seems, temporarily no doubt, to be suffering a profound disturbance. Although the development of French literature during this time may in a general way have conformed to the periods we have outlined, individual works frequently escape them altogether. It would be dangerous to draw overrestrictive boundaries. We will therefore attempt, first, an overview of this literary space, and then go on to analyze its modulations in detail.

The first highlight was the renaissance of *the theater*. The French stage was transformed by a brilliant constellation of directors who also participated in the international theatrical movement, renewing every aspect of the dramatic arts. With Claudel, Giraudoux, Cocteau, Armand Salacrou, Jean Anouilh, Sartre, Henry de Montherlant, Camus, and later Samuel Beckett, Eugène Ionesco, Arthur Adamov, and, to a lesser degree, Roland Dubillard, François Billetdoux, Romain Weingarten, Fernando Arrabal, literature and drama formed a new alliance and reached a new public.

Poetry emerged from its retrenched position as many new works were created and gradually found a place in the sun. Pierre Jean Jouve, Jules Supervielle, Saint-John Perse, Henri Michaux, Francis Ponge, Paul Eluard, Jean Tardieu, Louis Aragon, Jean Follain, André Frénaud, Yvonne Caroutch, René Char, Pierre Emmanuel, Yves Bonnefoy, Joyce Mansour, Alain Bosquet, Philippe Jaccottet, Denis Miège, Robert Sabatier, Jean-Claude Renard . . . Where should we stop? During the period under discussion, more than three hundred poets worthy of note were published in France, their names succeeding one another from generation to generation. And how many were the unclassifiable, or unconventional works like those by Georges Bataille, Michel Leiris, or the belatedly recognized Jean Paulhan? Publication of a major body of unrecognized work like Paulhan's can change our entire concept of literature—as has been noted by T. S. Eliot and, after him, by Philippe Sollers.

Within the broader area of literature, diaries, memoirs, autobiographies, short stories, and essays—frequently of a high standard—were also recognized as forming distinct "genres." It therefore seems safe to say that a considerable gap existed between the ritual predictions announcing the death of one "genre" or another, such as the novel, or even of literature in general, and the unquestionable wealth filling the literary space. There were some French writers who between 1920 and 1970 went to great lengths in their explorations of the vast resources and possibilities offered by language and literary structure. They were no longer willing to recognize any constraint on vocabulary, syntax, or form that would restrict the widest possible deployment of discourse. But no single writer explored all of these avenues at once. And there were many who remained faithful to the old codes that had been so frequently denounced; still others settled for more or less personal compromises. There are many different approaches we could take to this vast network of literary texts, but there is no way we could reduce it to homogeneity.

With the disappearance of literature's conventional contours came the disappearance of its hierarchies. The trailblazers and masters who had served to polarize the literary aspirations of their time and give direction to efforts at literary renewal died off. The only "visible" tendencies were the extremist ones. The center collapsed. Confusion reigned. Confronting each other head on were innumerable contradictions and incompatible conceptions of the value, nature, and function of literature. Any attempt to identify a single trend as the most important would perforce ignore or neglect other works of equal interest. There is undoubtedly some connection between this proliferation of styles, modes, and forms of expression, and the shrinking place occupied in the minds of the "informed" public today by literature. The familiar landmarks are gone. Literature has indeed changed course. Literary codes that remained in force until midcentury were disrupted. This explains the disproportionately favorable public response to criticism, at least to the interpretive kind, as opposed to its hesitation before the literary texts themselves. And, in a situation where the familiar forms and categories were blurring, should not language, the basis common to all literature, be a primary concern of writers? And should not continuity also be primary, and the way continuity is ensured by means of language? This is where the tensions exhibited by "modern" writing practice come from, and it explains the almost obsessive attention this new "modernism" has received.

The catalyst for this process of disruption was dada and surrealism, two movements which in our view were really one, acting not so much through their somewhat naive theories as through their productions, which cast doubt on the effectiveness of both literary and ordinary language as a tool for representing reality. The ultimate beneficiary of this catalytic action seems to have been the *Tel Quel* group, despite the latter's efforts to dissociate itself from surrealism, a movement whose idealism and ignorance of the principles of dialectical materialism it deplored (see *Tel Quel* 46).

Dada and Surrealism: The Disrupters

The *history* of the surrealist movement in France has long since been written. Each of its phases was marked by manifestos and texts from the hand of André Breton. Since the 1945 publication of Maurice Nadeau's *Histoire du surréalisme*, there has been an accumulation of studies regarding every aspect of surrealism. Writings originally intended as ephemera have been rediscovered and painstakingly reedited. Critics have explored the literary and philosophical antecedents of the movement; its theories, myths, mystifications, and contradictions; its successes and its failures. "There have perhaps been movements richer in individual genius," noted "second-string" surrealist Julien Gracq, "but the substance of surrealism had a brilliance and a variety whose equivalent I have never seen elsewhere" *(Lettrines)*. This explains its enormous impact. In the beginning, surrealism was not so much a movement as a rallying point for an amorphous group of artists and poets attracted by the passionate intransigence of André Breton's personality, and moved by hatred for anything rigid or conventional. As new recruits replaced old campaigners alienated by the dissensions and cliquishness that were shattering the communal life of the group, it became possible to distinguish successive waves of adherents from one another.

Three phases in the history of the movement that has influenced every generation of writers from 1925 onward could perhaps usefully be identified. We will omit—as they themselves would—writers who lived for a time in the surrealist fold but attempted to remain independent of Breton's personal influence even while they retained the initial attitudes that eventually spread far beyond the official confines of the group.

Surrealism began to take form between 1920 and 1924, at first in symbiosis with dadaism, which Breton, around 1922, was moving away from. It came of age in 1924 with publication of the *Manifeste du surréalisme* and the "collective action" review, *La Révolution surréaliste*. The crucial works testifying to the extent of the group's shared commitment to its cause and the scope of its enterprise appeared between 1926 and 1928: Breton's *Nadja*, Aragon's *Le Paysan de Paris*, Robert Desnos's *La Liberté ou l'amour!* and René Crevel's *L'Esprit contre la raison*—texts and manifestos that all easily held their own as literature. With Eluard's *Capitale de la douleur* and Desnos's *A la mystérieuse*, surrealism took the field of poetry by storm. It was during this period that surrealism exerted its strongest attraction on other small groups, and grew by forming passionate allegiances or more precarious alliances.

Between 1925 and 1929 began the schisms and dispersions that were to grow more acute during the thirties: Antonin Artaud, Roger Vitrac, Raymond Queneau, Georges Bataille, Michel Leiris, strong personalities all, each decided to go their own way, as did Aragon and those like him who had rallied to Marxism. Breton also alienated the young writers on the *Grand Jeu*, one of whom, at least, René Daumal, subsequently turned out to be a fine writer. At the same time, however, Dali, Buñuel, Marcel Jean, Pieyre de Mandiargues, Joyce Mansour, René Char, and, later, Julien Gracq, were joining the movement. Despite these reinforcements and its increasingly large international audience, surrealism began to lose its initial momentum. The *Second Manifeste surréaliste* (1929) and Breton's speech *Qu'est-ce que le surréalisme?* (1934) revealed the vicissitudes and vexations of those years. In 1938, however, the first great international exhibition of surrealism took place in Paris. Subsequent exhibitions—especially those in 1947, 1959, 1965, and 1974—demonstrated an increasingly favorable response to surrealism on the part of the general public. Surrealism had become an active cultural catalyst, but it lost its old role as insurgent.

Despite support from Benjamin Péret, who in a vehement pamphlet, *Le Déshonneur de poètes*, sounded the iconoclastic note of early surrealism in an attack on the poetry of political commitment consecrated in an anthology entitled *L'Honneur des poètes* (1943), André Breton was on the defensive when he returned to Paris after World War II. The new circle that formed around him was a clique rather than a militant clan. From then on, only isolated works, and Breton's personality, attracted attention. The scattered surrealist slogans adorning the wall of the Sorbonne in 1968 were symptoms of nostalgia and not of a rebirth. The two reviews, *Le Surréalisme au service de la révolution,* in 1930, and *Minotaure,* in 1933, had exerted a clear-cut impact on the public; this was not the case with any of the reviews Breton launched after 1945: *Néon, Médium, Le Surréalisme même, La Brèche.* A 1966 Cerisy-la-Salle colloquium on surrealism, while providing proof that poets faithful to Breton's doctrines still existed (Philippe Audouin, Claude Courtant, Henri Givet, Alain Jouffroy, Annie Le Brun, Gérard Legrand, Jean Schuster, and others) served mainly to emphasize the extent to which Breton's style of writing had spread through the literary mainstream. It could be claimed, as a matter of fact, that the interpretation of dadaist and surrealist texts, and an understanding of the qualities that made them distinctive, only became possible with the advent of the *nouvelle critique,* thus bringing to a close the movement that began in 1916.

January 1920 was a landmark in literary history. This was when dadaist spokesman Tristan Tzara, arriving from Zurich, and Francis Picabia, arriving from New York via Spain, met in Paris. The convergence of these two already legendary personalities and the small group of young poets— Breton, Aragon, and Soupault—that had been strongly influenced by Tzara's *Troisième Manifeste du dadaïsme* (1918) proved to be explosive.

Newly launched by the three young French poets, the review *Littérature* was hardly distinguishable, except for a hint of insolence, from all the other little magazines. Like Apollinaire, Cendrars, and Marinetti, these poets yearned to create a "modern" art. They were simultaneously heirs to Lautréamont and Jarry's violent verbal insurrection, and to a poetic tradition stretching back through Mallarmé and Rimbaud to Baudelaire. They respected Valéry and Gide. *Littérature* began venturing onto other paths, however, and these proved rewarding. Late in 1919 *Les Champs magnétiques* appeared in its pages, a collection of texts written by Breton and Soupault, working together under "dictation" from the unconscious. Inspired by the work of Freud, Breton was experimenting with automatic writing, a technique employed by psychiatrists. The idea was to transcribe words as they occurred spontaneously to the mind, and to do so— theoretically at least—without the conscious intervention of the person doing the transcribing. *Les Champs magnétiques* was the overture to the surrealist drama, asking a number of questions about the nature of language that remain unanswered. Its publication passed completely unnoticed.

It was dada that gave the *Littérature* team its taste for blood and infused it with the energy it needed to penetrate chaotic post–World War I Paris to the bone, galvanizing the discontent and the aspirations of much of the "1925 generation." Dada was nihilist by conviction, and in the course of its heady rebellion it fell in love with its own freedom. Creating scandal and heaping derision on the "enlightened" Parisians—zestfully accomplished through a series of manifestations that took place in 1920 and 1921—was only one aspect of the disruptive mission of dada that its practitioners regarded as a sort of reverse "civic-mindedness" (Crevel). But the rebellious gestures yielded startling inventions, of which Marcel's urinal/objet-d'art and Picabia's erotic, parodic machines were emblematic. The sense of anxiety that ran through this period, and that had been diagnosed by Nietzsche, provided the counterweight for dada's complete freedom with words and forms. Dada was a craft, its practitioners untrammeled "fabricators of the fantastic." A completely novel outpouring of the "infinitely grotesque" (Aragon), a bizarre fund of ideas that were often outlandish, and humor that was often (though not always) black began to make their appearance in art and literature. Probably endemic, this current lying just below the surface of literary history emerged to provide the literature of our own time with one of its most distinctive characteristics. Dada revived Alfred Jarry, and the spirit of dada still presides over the activities of the "Collège de Pataphysique" founded in 1948 under his aegis. It was not by pure chance that the Collège de Pataphysique provided the setting for meetings between a young Boris Vian and rank beginner Eugène Ionesco with Raymond Queneau and two old-time dadaists—Marcel Duchamp and Max Ernst. Pataphysicians are mystifying demystifiers, opposed to all seriousness and any kind of system; advocating "a science and an art that would enable everyone to live as though he were an exception, representing no law but his own." The spirit of dada remains alive today in the works of such disparate authors as Queneau, Henri Michaux, Jean Tardieu, Jacques Prévert, Boris Vian, Eugène Ionesco, and many more.

It was dada's willful "antiseriousness" that in 1922 led to the break—later to prove temporary—with Breton's faction. The latter also cultivated dada's provocative attitudes and its playfulness, but did so with a purpose: to change the world.

Breton's sense of mission was motivated by his discovery of the autonomous properties of language. But the "dictated" texts of *Les Champs magnétiques,* and those of *Poisson soluble,* which later accompanied the 1924 *Manifeste,* distinctly differed from dadaist texts. They were organized according to the rules of syntax. The same was true for hypnotic state "speech," for the transcriptions of dreams, and for games like *cadavre exquis* or parody proverbs. In the latter case, syntax was actually guaranteed by the rules of the game. But the words that were structured by this syntax gathered themselves into startling and "singular sequences." These texts functioned in defiance of the convention requiring that, if they were not to earn a verdict of nonsense, they must be "accurate reproductions" of the coherent, real world supposedly being referred to. As Michel Riffaterre has pointed out (in *Le Siècle éclaté,* I, 1974), whether or not these texts were actually dictated by the subconscious is immaterial; the important thing is the *effect* they have on the reader, the initial readers being, of course, the "transcribers" themselves, men who at first saw what they were doing as "inspired stenography" (Crevel). They were discovering that the "system of signs" making up a language does not rest on "objective order." The representative function of literature was being called into question. The literary stakes were changing position. One step further and it became possible dimly to grasp that reality assumes the form proposed by language, and not vice versa. The limits of vocabulary and association permissible in a literary text had been breached. Poets, of course, have always been more or less consciously aware of doing this. What had changed was the new importance given to this subtext, and to the means for giving full rein to its expression.

The first surrealist manifesto stated the basic myth serving as the mainspring for the group's activities. This was the Paradise of Childhood Lost myth, or Rousseau's myth of natural man alienated by his social environment. It had been given new form by Freud, who oddly enough is made more accessible through a reading of Hegel. According to Breton, in any case, modern man is imprisoned by the conventions of rationality, and the utilitarianism of a petty, calculating, narrow-minded society without honor and without imagination, existing in a state of mediocrity imposed on him by the rules of language. The barrier cutting him off from the subconscious in which his own inner life is rooted must be demolished, so that he can recover the full potential of his spirit. "Reason" must be relegated to its proper place in a richer psychic process, a more complete mode of knowing. What kind of reason, asks Crevel, would persuade a man to live inside, to confine himself inside, a tiny plot of exploitable reality? We must strive for "total recovery of our psychic force through the only means available to us, a headlong descent into our own inner being" *(Second Manifeste)*. Surrealist texts refer us to a context that is hidden. For them, writing is the instrument for "systematic illumination of what is concealed."

The surrealist injunction to pursue total emancipation of individual behavior with steadfast conviction, both in writing and in the everyday world, led perforce to schisms within the group and to the production of highly individual texts. But in the beginning the surrealist experiment was a communal effort, and with its accumulation of apparently gratuitous verbal associations it opened the door onto a new world rich in myths and images that seemed to the group to signify unlimited creative possibilities. Love, liberty, happiness, a life made to the measure of man: the young surrealists practiced what they preached, and the generosity of their collective myth explains why they entertained such fervent hopes for social revolution; they projected onto the level of society as a whole the concept of liberation they pursued on the level of the individual.

The new way the surrealists looked at the world of dreams, the world of reality, and at eroticism, swelled their language with new richness; and their great faith in the revolutionary potential of poetry was contagious. Having given a new dimension to language, they believed that through language they could give a new value to life, reintegrating the marvelous with the ordinary. Although the "marvelous" in surrealist terms seemed occasionally to be merely willful or factitious, the best of the surrealist writings offer the reader an overwhelming experience in which the imaginary and the ordinary are juxtaposed in a rich outgrowth of images. For the surrealists, language was freed from its referential, realistic, narrow role; but it nonetheless opened onto a world of metamorphosed objects and beings recreated to the measure of their own desire. But when the surrealists proclaimed that poetry is inherent to all human behavior and lies within the reach of every individual, and that its roots are to be found in unconstrained subjectivity, they opened wide the floodgates on a wave of formless and mediocre texts. First Aragon and Eluard, and then Breton, recognized the problem, emphasizing the purely experimental nature of some of the exercises the group was engaged in. Also, because the surrealists followed the symbolists, whom they had rejected, and elevated poetry to the privileged status of both a way to knowledge, like science, and a way to salvation, they doomed themselves to failure; and this is part of the explanation for their subsequent efforts to demystify their theories and reduce the poem to a simple fact of language.

Surrealism nevertheless restated old problems in new terms: what part of poetic creation, for example, depends on inspiration, and what part on hard work? In what does the poetic phenomenon really consist? And what is the reader's relationship to a text that is enigmatic, "open," and equivocal? The number of works devoted to poetics that owe their inspiration to surrealism is considerable. Because surrealism construes poetry as a sort of errant essence that uses language as its plaything, "poetry" and language that is merely nonutilitarian appear to be one and the same thing. The prose/poetry categories no longer strictly apply and begin to blur. It therefore follows logically that experimental poetics has ultimately interested novelists as much as it has poets. These heirs to surrealism have been distinguished from their predecessors, however, by the fact that their experiments have been confined to *elaborating texts,* and have not ventured into Breton's brand of metaphysical speculation. When the realist tradition, with Sartre as its spokesman, reasserted itself, literary development was presided over by language as experience—one of surrealism's initial concerns—and *metaphysics* gave way to *epistemology.* The surrealist hope that life's great antinomies could be resolved through the intervention of startling imagistic leaps or the hazards of "objective chance," "signs" of vaster horizons, came to seem but a brilliant fiction. The surrealists had not *looked for meaning* in their new language; starting in 1924, they had *attributed meaning* to it. This turned things upside down and they knew it: the language of the poet is the token of "another reality," one that is instituted by it. More surely than the "definitive dreamer" or the "explorer" of the early manifestos, a poet is a man of reality because he is a man of language. Surrealism must, therefore, be one kind of humanism.

Although undeniably sinning against certain accepted practices, rebelling against realism and the "accurate copy" side of the novel, the surrealists were nevertheless unable, themselves, to escape the historical, literary, and, indeed, social determinations which, through language itself, impregnate the surrealist view of thgs. The dualism represented by playing linguistic games with form vs. searching for a linguistic "other world" coexisted but were not resolved in the dada-surrealism symbiosis. The surrealists believed the poetic spark that illuminates the "hidden reality" is struck by a juxtaposition of unlikely images. It is only in the mind of a reader that this spark can be kindled. Poetic substance is therefore virtual. The surrealist poets wanted their readers to read the same way a poet writes. This takes practice.

Today these poets have found readers who understand them—many readers, in fact, who are sensitive to the beauty of the spectacle deployed by language. These readers have patiently explored the interplay of relationships and tropes making up each text and communicating it. Today, interest in surrealism is thus, paradoxically, primarily literary. One thing is certain, in any case: surrealist texts cannot be submitted to traditional critical criteria. The rules of the game have effectively been changed, and standards of evaluation are now a matter of individual readings supported by meticulous textual analysis. The *nouveau roman,* at least in its second phase of attempting to create new kinds of readers rather than new kinds of stories, is a direct descendant of this aspect of surrealism.

The Contribution of "Tel Quel"

The review *Tel Quel,* with Philippe Sollers at the helm and Julia Kristeva its most famous theoretician, has provided the motive force behind a literary movement whose true impact it is too early to evaluate (see *Tel Quel* 44). In 1958, when Sollers was just starting out as a novelist, he aligned himself with André Breton and surrealism. He then quickly broke away again, just as Breton had once repudiated the theory and practices of the *Esprit nouveau.* But the bonds between the two groups were obvious. As the surrealists had once extolled Marx and Trotsky, the *Tel Quel* group now extolled Mao; as Breton had once rehabilitated Sade and Rimbaud, Sollers and his group drew attention to Bataille and Artaud. Both groups claimed Jarry, Lautréamont, and Hegel as their antecedents. As surrealism once had done, *Tel Quel* devoted much of its energies to the concepts of desire and eroticism in the largest sense, and its avowed intent was also to transform the relation between man and the human condition by transforming language.

At first the activity of the *Tel Quel* group was concentrated on the novel. But soon this activity overflowed the borders of a single genre to include the entire concept of "literary discourse." Drawing heavily on theories and methods borrowed from the social sciences, linguistics and psychoanalysis among others, *Tel Quel* examined on both the theoretical and the practical levels some of the most firmly established conceptions regarding literary creation, and it did so with a single goal in view: to give new direction to the entire literary enterprise. The groundwork for this undertaking had been laid during the fifties through the efforts of a few novelists concerned with renewing fiction techniques and creating new narrative forms. Although they were all very different from one another, all of them—Nathalie Sarraute, Samuel Beckett, Marguerite Duras, Claude Simon, Robert Pinget, Alain Robbe-Grillet, Michel Butor, Claude Ollier—were involved in issues that were essentially traditional in nature. A second wave of writers—Jean-Pierre Faye, Philippe Sollers, Jean Ricardou—formed themselves into a militant avant-garde, drawing from the first group's technical essays theoretical principles that subsequently swung back again and influenced the thinking of the people who had initiated them in the first place. Thus, as Léon Roudiez has noted *(French Fiction Today)*, between the years 1960 and 1970 a certain unity was perceptible in the concerns of a fairly large group of French writers. The concerns were no longer confined to the fictional framework that had originally inspired them, and they included a sort of rationalizing ideology—not to say mythology—that could be classed among the "axiomatic logics" the group back at *Tel Quel* was in the process of denouncing.

In fact, in our opinion this movement escaped the closed circle of the *Tel Quel* editors (Sollers, Julia Kristeva, Marcelin Pleynet, Denis Roche, et al.) and returned from a fresh angle to the initial project of surrealism, which was to point philosophy and society in a new direction by presenting new ways of organizing literary texts. This line of thinking is primarily addressed to the problem of literary creation, and proposes working hypotheses rather than solutions.

This group of writers inherited from the "modern" tradition a *denial of all established forms and all aesthetic principles,* accepting only the basic axiom that a text is a verbal structure; beyond that, their individual positions on what this structure *means* were far from unanimous, the Marxist neopositivism of a Ricardou running head on into Sollers's more complex schema. In *Drame,* for example, Sollers presents a conflict in which different modes of literary creation are pitted against one another at the frontiers of language: the articulate order of "ready-made" language against the profound, erotic impulse that motivates writers, the desire to "disarticulate" articulated order, to destructure it, pillaging it in order to "open" the text to new linguistic relations. *Drame* is a transcription of the mysterious turnings in this journey from impulse to act of writing, and an attack on the bonds that imprison man and confine him inside a specific linguistic space. The mystery presented by the drama (action) of literary creation itself remains unresolved.

Although these writers' downgrading of subject and content represented a break with traditional poetics, they maintained their affiliation through their tendency to see in the practice of literature a means to knowledge—if only through the exploration of linguistic potential—and the rationale for a subversive style of life. However, theirs was not the dadaist aim of introducing nonmeaning into language; nor, as with the surrealists, of exploring the "stately avenues of dream." What they wanted was to "articulate" a new reality. The act of "writing" becomes action writing—a drama, as the title of Sollers's text would have it. In the theater of language, energy is released, impersonal, revolutionary, erotic energy which, because of the violence of its desire to say something other than what is being said already, provokes displacements in the relations between words; disjunctions and ruptures that shatter established connections between the word-as-sign and the object to which it refers. A new text emerges, contaminating the original one, assaulting it, minimizing it and going beyond it. Here is where the reader comes in, his responsibility being to submit to the same violent process in order to resituate himself in the new "articulation" and, consequently, to "produce" the meaning of the text.

The purpose of this brief attempt to explain theories which are often abstract and always in a state of mutation is to underline the fact that dada and *Tel Quel* are linked by the continuity of a single theme: the struggle against a rule-dominated language which in its turn dominates the individual. This theme, expressed as a generalization and somewhat arbitrarily applied to all human relations, appears to reflect not so much a social, as an aesthetic malaise, that of the artist who has inherited an ancient culture rich in traditions, and who seeks to make his own way through this cluttered terrain. It is easy to identify certain ideological oversimplifications. Categories too vague to serve, such as "realism," "bourgeois society," "formal code," are little more than facile abstractions on a level with the hypothetical "reader." But it cannot be denied that, amid the reigning cultural confusion of our time, this movement, like surrealism before it, has affirmed the necessity and the worth of creative writing. "He who writes has something to do with everything"; "Either write or be written"; and "In writing we meet death": in saying these things, Sollers expresses himself in aphoristic forms linking him, perhaps without his being aware of it, to the rhetoric of the classics.

This trend toward "opening up" language and literary form into areas that exist, paradoxically, beyond limitations that were once considered absolute has affected the old categories and classifications which, with deceptive simplicity, allowed writers and readers alike to recognize clearly defined modes of literary activity. "Today I am on the verge of being free to write a book, the book of all books, unclassifiable, belonging to no specific form, that may be a novel, poem, and criticism all at the same time," noted Sollers (*Le Figaro littéraire*, 22 September 1962). This most striking aspect of this movement is the extreme subjectivity characterizing attitudes and opinions regarding theories and texts that are supposed to be rigorously depersonalized, and the return to questions of the writer's didactic purpose and social role.

The *Tel Quel* group has defined the role it intends to play as an avant-garde movement. Given its position historically and socially, it proposes, in a more circumscribed way than Sartre once did, to transform from within the ideology of lower-middle-class intellectuals so as to bring them closer to the proletariat. However—and here we stumble upon a disconcerting contradiction—the proletariat in question is not the actual proletariat as it is, but a virtual proletariat "as it will be" (*Tel Quel* 52). Basing its work on this ideology, *Tel Quel* sought to formulate a single coherent intellectual framework that would combine the concepts of Engels, Freud, and Lacan, but still remain faithful to dialectical materialism. While acknowledging the existence of a specifically linguistic dialectic, *Tel Quel* nevertheless attributed only relative autonomy to it. The group believed that the material realities of a given society are imprinted in the subconscious and in the impulses of the id, and will reappear in that society's language. Written texts, and systematic analyses of them, will thus expose the complex generative processes of "creativity."

Despite the political inflexibility of these positions, they are not free of contradiction. In light of a concept such as "virtual proletariat," for example, it might well be asked whether the ambitious goals and the esotericism are not the result of a specific historical situation. The young intellectual theoreticians of *Tel Quel* lived in expectation of a revolution whose coming is continually deferred. Clinging to their faith in the reality/dialectical-materialism equation, they use this myth in their search for a way out of the contradictions of the modern world. In the last analysis, they are experiencing—and their work confirms—not a break but a reintegration with society.

"Of the men who feel the need to act," said Francis Ponge (*Entretiens avec Philippe Sollers*, 1970), "there should be but two kinds: the real militants, that is, the political militants, who influence human societies . . . and the patricians, who concentrate on changing the *patterns* we use to see and understand ourselves in the world." With the *Tel Quel* group, it seemed that the conflict between militants and patricians, which had once broken up the surrealists and had always fueled so much controversy, was finally coming to an end. *Tel Quel* opted for a place among the patricians. By 1975, its influence was clearly on the decline.

Literary Genres: A Desire for the New

Today, nothing is more hotly discussed than the question of literary genres, and nothing is in a state of greater confusion. When a writer like

Cocteau classified his works under such headings as "theater poetry," "novel poetry," and "criticism poetry," it was not in order to be conspicuous. Although the three categories novel, poem, and play may still serve as the framework for today's poetics, it is a somewhat precarious one. Other "genres" intrude: the essay, the autobiography, the short story. Drama, because of the basic elements that go into making a play—stage, actor, audience, text—will probably always be a fairly easy category to define. But what is the appropriate way to approach the various texts that fall under this heading? Tragedy, comedy, and drama are increasingly labeled merely "play." Other classifications have been suggested, in which works would be arranged according to types—epic, lyric, satirical, etc.—that have been recognized and defined by critics. And there have been other, even vaguer, distinctions: traditional writers, innovators, "discoverers," *nouveau théâtre* playwrights, *nouveau roman* novelists, new poets.

The desire for experimentation that motivates modern literature has given rise to a multiplicity of divergent works impossible to classify with accuracy. Maurice Blanchot believed the literature of the future ought to be "unclassifiable and uncategorizable as prose, poetry, or novel" *(Le Livre à venir)*. Sollers expressed the same hope, one which appears to have been realized by writers as different from one another as Georges Bataille, Michel Leiris, Francis Ponge, Henri Michaux, and Michel Butor.

In any case, more and more writers are breaking with the past and looking with suspicion on threadbare conventions. Several conflicting trends are in evidence: contempt for the facile coupled with disdain for the over-aesthetic; a sustained inquiry into the rules governing art and at the same time a need to get away from them; appeals to the reader combined with disdain and even outright hostility toward the public; the desire for objectivity and a return to total subjectivity. Finally, just when the artist began demanding *carte blanche* (Cocteau), i.e., complete freedom, he also became concerned with the constraints of the *code*.

For all its deficiencies, we still adhere to literary classification by genre, because so far none other has managed to prevail. Addressing the question of literary genres in their *Dictionnaire encyclopédique des sciences du langage* (1972), Ducrot and Todorov note that a new typology of "literary discourse" reflecting the structural typology of discourse in general seemed called for, but they add, "Inasmuch as this typology is generally still relatively underdeveloped, it is preferable to approach its study from the point of view of the literary genres." They point out that, as far as these genres are concerned, "throughout history, two radically different approaches can be observed. The first is inductive: a given period is studied, and through this study, the existence of genres is *noted*. The second is deductive: a theory of literary discourse is formulated, and through this theory the existence of genres is *postulated*." Neither approach is fully satisfactory today. We will, however, be using the traditional deductive method.

13

The Novel:
A Form with
No Frontiers

In a work entitled *Roman des origines et origines du roman* (Grasset, 1972), Marthe Robert notes that "the novel as we know it today is a relatively recent form, no longer connected in any but the loosest way to the tradition from which it springs," and she labels it the "undefined form." The novel form is "lawless," a characteristic also noted by Gide, because fictional narrative can take many forms, there are many different traditions of the novel. In this connection, Marthe Robert draws attention to the "imperialistic" nature of the novel: "A novel can take literature and do anything it likes with it; there is nothing to prevent the novel from employing and adapting to its own ends description, narrative, drama, essay, comment, monologue, or dialogue; and there is nothing to prevent the novel from being, either alternately or simultaneously, a fable, a story, an apology, an idyll, a chronicle, a tale, or an epic; there are no rules and no constraints governing choice of subject, background, time, or space; the only law it usually obeys is the one determining its status as prose, although there is nothing obligatory about the prosaic vocation, and a novel may, if it likes, include poems or simply be 'poetic.'"

Between the Wars: The Novel Evolving

In the surrealist manifestos, Breton denounces with particular vehemence the realistic approach and psychologism of the novelist. "The days of romantically fabulated psychological literature are numbered," he declares, accusing of tedium the descriptive passages realistic novelists use to authenticate their stories by establishing a specific background. Breton was merely restating an already centuries-old theme. Baudelaire before him had questioned the effectiveness of the realist aesthetic and the positivist concept of reality. The great innovating novelists who began to make reputations for themselves in the twenties (Proust, Gide, Joyce, Virginia Woolf, Thomas Mann, Kafka) all based their work on the principle, shared with the other arts, that there will be a new apprehension of reality corresponding to each new era, hence a new relation to reality and, for the artist, a need for new forms. Each of these novelists rejected in particular the mechanism of psychological causality as a structural element in "moving carpet" plots, as Gide called them.

The iconoclastic wind of the *Esprit nouveau* was blowing on the novel. In *Cornet à dés*, Max Jacob parodied the novelistic style. In the four novels he published between 1918 and 1924—*Le Phanérogame, Le Terrain Bouchaballe, Flibuste ou la montre en or, L'Homme de chair et l'homme de reflet*—he created fictions in which the logic and conventions of the skillfully tailored novel were replaced by games with language and the imagination. Blaise Cendrars, in *Moravagine* and *Dan Yack,* spun out epic-burlesque frescoes that were not dissimilar from the silent film scenarios he found so fascinating. In his eight novels, from *Suzanne et le Pacifique* (1921) to *Choix des élues* (1938), Giraudoux threw reality completely overboard. Plot became nothing but a tissue of frank and unabashed fiction involving transparent characters in imaginary situations. The important thing was Giraudoux's *attitude* to his world, his faith in the power of language to communicate through its very texture a happy—if not a naive—vision of existence. Underlying Giraudoux's work was his conviction that language shapes the relation of the individual to the inner self, to other people, and to the world; that when we decide what to say, we decide how to be and what will become of us. This was a reversal of the axioms of realism and naturalism.

Although the novel as a "bourgeois" art form was periodically denounced as old-fashioned and trite, it was actually developing and diversifying: there were picaresque novels, neo-epics, fables, and utopian novels. *Experiments with form* constituted the major trend of the period. The great novelists of the twenties gave increased flexibility to narrative technique through their concern with psychological, or metaphysical, truth—their faithfulness to their own experience and their own knowledge of reality. Writers and readers alike adapted effortlessly if belatedly to the new techniques: one story told from several points of view; interplay between "narrative viewpoint" (that of the person telling the story) and that of his fictional characters; interior monologues copied after the stream of consciousness; different temporal schemes; unpredictability of action.

Surrealism had of course severed plot from the contextual network of social, psychological, and cultural determinations that make it an "observed" fragment of the real world. The logic of action and the function of character were changed as a result. Fictional pieces by the surrealists were brief and did not become widely known; they cannot be reduced to a single model except for one thing: in them a "narrator" follows his double on unpredictable yet necessary journeys whose twists and turns are marked by *signs,* configurations that elude the laws of causality and form chains of signifiers with no signified. The important thing is not the development of a plot with a beginning, a middle, and an end, but the emergence of an enigmatic pattern imprinted within the field of the real. A well-known example is *Nadja,* by Breton: a random meeting with an ambiguous character (Nadja), a clairvoyant prostitute, reveals to the narrator (André Breton) that they are surrounded by a mysterious network of forces, a kind of "magnetic field" Nadja is "plugged into" as it were. The surrealist narrative thus becomes a field of potentiality, with the main character a stranger even to himself, a knot of virtual relations waiting to be deciphered. The "Who am I?" opening Breton's narrative is the leitmotif of all surrealist narrative. Something mysterious enters the scene, an alien, fragmentary "me-he" that begins a dialogue with the "me-I" of the narrator, displacing the protagonist of the novel. The language becomes problematical.

Giraudoux also played games with language, but he never questioned its ability to endow life with meaning and then to communicate this meaning to others. The first man to have done so appears to have been Raymond Roussel, an obscure experimental writer whose career began in 1897 and ended in 1936 with the posthumous publication of *Comment j'ai écrit certains de mes romans.* Painstakingly voiding the act of writing of any preestablished goal, Roussel, as he explained it, started from an external stimulus of some kind: an object, often a very small one, such as the label on a bottle of mineral water *(La Source);* or a word, like "billiard." The initial motif, or sign, becomes the key opening a series of possibilities to the creative process through a kind of proliferation, generating a word sequence or a text composed of phonemes but bereft of any context save their own phonic or graphic associations: the word *billard,* for example, through the process of paronomasia, yields *pillard* and other, similar words, "The words between the lines on that old billiard ball"—the substitution of a single consonant completely changes the meaning. Puns, double-entendre, and wordplay of other kinds have always been part of the literary arsenal. The novelty here is their use as a dynamic, self-generating system for producing a text that is random and, outside of the self-generating process, meaningless. On a purely lexical level, Roussel's work illustrates another experimental avenue that was to affect the novel: his attempt, not to transform technique in order to bring narrative closer to the real structures of experience, but to *create structures so that they could later be examined for what novelties they might reveal.* Roussel anticipated one of James Joyce's more complex innovations.

Polymorphous the novel may be, but the overwhelming majority of novels published in our time have belonged to categories that were developed in the nineteenth century. Whether based on the story of individual lives or on society as a whole, they revolve thematically around the relations individuals have with each other and how they react to their social code. To oversimplify a little, we can say that, in this type of novel, what the characters do reveals their psychology and that interactions between them triggers events which in turn reveal the moral values of their milieu. Novelists have constructed thousands of variations based on this model. Good examples of the traditionally structured novel would be the works of Roger Martin du Gard, particularly *Les Thibault,* and Marguerite Yourcenar's *Mémoires d'Hadrien,* a fictionalized first-person narrative based on real events; also *L'Œuvre au noir,* a historical novel in the tradition of Flaubert.

The appearance of a new aesthetic was announced with the publication in the thirties of a series of new novels. One year apart, in 1932 and 1933, respectively, Raymond Queneau and Louis-Ferdinand Céline each published their first novel, *Le Chiendent* and *Voyage au bout de la nuit.* The two important new developments in fiction represented by these works were not placed in the proper historical perspective until the sixties. The same was true for Maurice Blanchot's novels, the first two of which, *Thomas l'obscur* and *Aminabad,* were published in 1941 and 1942 respectively, the latter being the year which also saw publication of Albert Camus's *L'Etranger* following Sartre's *La Nausée* in 1938. Going back even further, two books published in 1927 and 1928, Georges Bataille's *L'Anus solaire* and *Histoire de l'œil,* both unappreciated at the time except among a small group of initiates, did not reveal their virulence to the broader public until forty years later. Two more modest works from 1938–39, Nathalie Sarraute's *Tropismes* and the first novel by the then unknown Samuel Beckett, *Murphy,* published in London, also failed to attract any notice.

Within the decade of the thirties it is thus possible to distinguish *two lines of development* in the novel. One was followed by those novels that, while cautiously modifying their narrative style, still remained faithful to the aesthetic of *subject* and *mimesis;* and the other was followed by those novels more or less openly breaking with that tradition. Camus's *L'Etranger* struck a sort of equilibrium between the two tendencies. But there were few novels of any importance published during the interwar period that did not exhibit some kind of novelty.

The Experimental Novel from 1950 to 1970: New Techniques

The importance of the experimental novelists of the fifties—Samuel Beckett, Michel Butor, Alain Robbe-Grillet, Nathalie Sarraute, Claude Simon, Marguerite Duras, and, to a lesser degree, Claude Ollier—lay in the fact that they were aware of the new literary trends, they used them to forge new literary techniques, and they put these new techniques systematically to work in the composition of their novels. Their break with the past was not a break with the form of the novel in general. They willingly acknowledged the influence of their predecessors: Balzac and Flaubert, Proust, Dostoevski, and Joyce. Among the second wave of new novelists, Jean Ricardou and Jean-Pierre Faye belonged to another tradition, the one going back to Mallarmé. What all of these novelists did want to break with, however, was the Sartrean, philosophical-political, "committed" novel and its aesthetic of neorealism. The value of literary tradition, for them, resided not in its function as a model to be imitated, but as something to be confronted and surpassed. They made the same demands on themselves in relation to their own work. Early works were often fairly traditional, structurally, but they moved progressively further and further away from the original model. Quite a distance separated Butor's first novel, *Passage de Milan,* from *Où* (1971); and Marguerite Duras's first popular novel, *Un barrage contre le Pacifique* (1950), from *Amour* (1972). Discussions inspired by the explanatory and theoretical articles of the fifties were also, occasionally, preceded by technical innovations on the part of established writers like Jean Giono, or else followed by successful modifications in the work of someone like Louis Aragon.

The extent of the need for renewal is indicated by the number of novelists who embarked on this same venture, either in the wake of the early innovators, or on their own (Marguerite Yourcenar, Marguerite Duras, Jean-Marie Le Clézio). But there was also a risk involved: that these already esoteric works might sink into the morass of a new orthodoxy. By 1975 it was still as difficult to assess the literary significance of these experiments with form as it was to weigh their social significance. It is no less difficult to identify the unifying thread holding them all together. The many critical studies devoted to the *nouveau roman,* published primarily in the United States, have generally elected to approach each of these authors separately. And, in fact, the structure of each individual work should be analyzed in detail, something it would be impossible to do in these pages. We will therefore confine ourselves to a very brief analysis of two or three of the novels in question.

Two separate tendencies affected the structure of the novel. Novelists under the influence of surrealism effected a disjunction in their works between the adventures their characters embarked on, and society. Other authors, yielding to the social and political pressures of their time, abandoned the descriptive, objective attitude of the novelist in favor of adopting a *position* and *explaining* it. As Sartre has noted, every novel implies a metaphysic, but usually not an explicit one; nor, as in the case of Proust, one presented as the fruit of a single character's experience in relation to his own story. French novelists writing from the twenties to the fifties—Catholics like Mauriac, Bernanos, Jouhandeau; nonbelievers like Romains, Malraux, Sartre, and Camus—all constructed their novels in the light of a particular interpretation of the human condition they were trying to communicate. They subordinated the social context to the metaphysical context, and individual, particularized character to the face of mythic "man" or woman. Because the novelist's purpose is to render life more intelligible through an examination of the human being's knowledge of nature and of his own place in the world, the *subject* and *plot* of the novel no longer have any but incidental value; the important thing is the context, or intellectual framework in which the explanation takes place.

Without relinquishing the old codes and structures of realism, the novel became didactic and laden with metaphysical significance. Novelists presented the same image of themselves as they had in the past: recorders of reality, but of a reality illustrating a personal mythology. The last famous example of this trend in the novel toward the allegorical is Camus's *La Peste*. What the novelists of the fifties were reacting against was this didactic aspect of the novel, and what they set out to do was not to *interpret* a specific reality, but to use the narrative in order to *create new structures,* i.e., new ways of telling stories and, therefore, of conceptualizing reality. This mythology of structure was followed by the idea of the self-generated narrative based on the linguistic dynamic corresponding to various stimuli such as numerals, shapes, and pictures. The narrative then becomes the self-contained progress of the pen inscribing words on the surface of the page. The focus of attention moved from problems of representation to structural schemas, and then to the associations and resonances arising from the fabric woven by the words. This shift is clearly visible in the evolution of Claude Simon as he passed from *Palace* to *Histoire,* and in Robbe-Grillet's as he passed from *La Jalousie* to *Dans le labyrinthe.*

The Fictional Idiom: Queneau, Céline, Sarraute

Almost simultaneously, in 1932 and 1933 respectively, Céline and Queneau launched an attack on *literary language* from two different points of view. Through his study of Chinese, Queneau had become aware of the considerable distance—less, of course, than in China—separating the literary from the spoken language in France. His experience reading the works of Joyce and participating in the antics of the surrealists focused his attention on the linguistic nature of stylistic effects, a discovery he illustrated in *Exercices de style* by describing a single meaningless act ninety-nine different ways. Queneau created a language for himself, using slang, neologisms, compound words, puns, and, even more distinctively, phonetic and syntactic transcriptions of popular speech. The best-known example of this is the "doukipudonktan" from *Zazie dans le métro*. This language generates a kind of whimsical verbal comedy which was also used to good effect by Boris Vian, and which in the case of both writers served as the counterpoint to a somewhat negative vision of humanity.

Each of Céline's novels represented a further development in his attempt to transform narrative discourse into a dynamic vehicle—in his words, the "emotional rails"—that would carry the reader toward the flux of emotions that had engendered the novel in the first place. Though called the language of everyday speech, it is actually a language skillfully calculated to imitate the rhythms and locutions of everyday speech. After *Guignol's Band I* it becomes increasingly disconnected, punctuated by the suspension points that became Céline's trademark, going from scatology to invective and from invective to insane fantasy and including everything in between. Céline's style is the creative tool responsible for one of the most powerful bodies of work of our time, one that endows a purely negative vision of the historical epoch and of humanity as a whole with an epic dimension that belies it. Like Joyce, Céline obtained parodic effects through the juxtaposition of "incompatible" narrative styles, a penchant that reappeared in the writings of Jean-Marie Le Clézio, who also used this kind of linguistic billowing to create similar fluctuations of viewpoint in his novels: modulating from the ordinary to the lyrical or epic according to the emotional mode required by the action.

Starting with *Tropismes,* Nathalie Sarraute's efforts were bent toward the invention of a language. The problem as seen by Sarraute is how to render the concealed magma of emotions, retreats, advances, and repressions generated by human contacts before the individual consciousness meets them with the kinds of everyday banalities that are traitors to, rather than translators of, the turbulent and elusive depths they come out of. By progressively eliminating the personal references distinguishing "he" from "she" and the marks separating "this" from "that," and also by eliminating the differentiation between conversation and the nonverbal exchanges she calls "subconversations," Nathalie Sarraute translated the network of social intercourse and the fierce and farcical microdramas of social life into a "ceaseless whispering" of language. Her text is a kind of rhythmic and musical verbal mimicry of the modalities of psychic life.

The outstanding characteristic of the experimental novel in the fifties was the creation by novelists of their own narrative discourse, one that deviated from literary norms. In some cases, as with Samuel Beckett and Marguerite Duras, it is the narrative discourse and this alone that gives their work the coherence formerly provided by the plot. This means the reader-critic must find the poetic proper to each individual work, just as he would do for a poem.

Narrative Structures

Roquentin, the antihero of *La Nausée,* discovers, among other things, that between reality and the way we represent reality to ourselves there occurs a dissolution of continuity; and, in particular, that the very concept of *adventure* or *story* has more to do with the *narrative organization* of experience after it happens than it does with the experience itself. In arriving at this conclusion, Roquentin destroyed the axiom requiring fiction to be modeled on reality. But then, what kind of structure should novels have? At the beginning of the twentieth century, this was the question facing Gide and Proust, Thomas Mann and Virginia Woolf; but it was James Joyce whose work served as the inspiration for new experiments in the structure of the novel.

In the April 1922 issue of the *Nouvelle revue française,* Valery Larbaud explained the formal structure of Joyce's *Ulysses,* and how it was based on strictly observed rules; of the eighteen episodes in the book, each one corresponds to one hour of the day and to one particular organ of the body—to name only two such correlations. Raymond Queneau, in a volume of critical essays entitled, *Bâtons, chiffres et lettres,* acknowledges his debt to American and English novelists, especially to Joyce, for having taught him that there is such a thing as a technique of the novel. In his own very first novel, *Le Chiendent,* for example, he imposes a set of complex constraints on himself, based on numbers: there are seven chapters containing thirteen sections, with the last section performing a special function. But other rules are involved as well—symmetry and what might be called "assonances," correspondences between situations and characters similar to those between the rhymes in a poem, specific narrative frameworks: an episode with dialogue after an episode of stream of consciousness after an exchange of letters. Robbe-Grillet's novels continued developments along the same lines—limitations of place, time, theme, and motif *(La Jalousie, Dans le labyrinthe);* so do those by Butor, who explained the structural constraints in his *Degrés,* and by Jean Ricardou, who did the same thing for his *La Prise/Prose de Constantinople.*

In these books, several different structures are at work simultaneously, and the coherence of the story depends on the coordination between them or, as happens in Butor's *L'Emploi du temps,* on the failure of an attempt to coordinate them—the attempt, at least undertaken by a character in the book. In *La Modification,* one such structure limits the space: a third-class compartment on a train; the time: twenty-one hours and thirty-five minutes in all; and the distance: Paris–Rome. A second structure is created by the superposition of several temporal planes, the main character having already made the trip more than once before; a third is established on a dream level, involving a series of mythic associations; and so on.

The variety in these structural schemas is infinite, and, even when carefully premeditated, they can pass unnoticed by the reader. When they are too complicated, they can transform a novel into a riddle to be puzzled out; and if the only "textual pleasure" to be had is deciphering the novelist's chosen system of organization, the best-intentioned reader may find it a slim one.

A continuous narrative strand runs through the novels of Samuel Beckett, in each of which a character-writer (Molloy, Moran, Malone, the monologuist in *L'Innommable)* continues a story unattached either to time or to space. And it is always the story of a journey, the journey of a wandering and infirm vagabond, perhaps one and the same as the person doing the writing. Between the stories a web of resonances, but never of exact echoes, is woven, and these resonances suggest other works by other authors: Dante's *Inferno*, the *Gospels*, various philosophical systems. There is nothing fictional about this universe, no points of reference beyond the vague connotations that emerge from the text itself. Concrete, imbued with sardonic humor, Beckett's fiction develops a sort of minimal epic, in the sense of the term minimal art—figurations whose precise modes of linguistic or structural articulation no critic has so far been able to identify but which simulate the schemas of an unending quest, one that is constantly re-embarked upon and continually interrupted by the pauses during which the motionless scrivener returns to his task.

Blanchot's novels too—there are about ten of them—involve "obscure" characters who recur with increasing anonymity in each book, pursuing quests that also remain obscure in nature. Places have no name, journeys are labyrinthine, cities contain strange buildings that hazily take shape as they are approached. A secret mythology apparently presides over unexplained encounters and wanderings, unexplained exchanges of words.

Thematic Elements

It would be impossible to draw up an inventory of fiction themes within the limitations of this survey. We will therefore confine ourselves to noting just a few of the thematic elements which in our view are representative of the era.

An entire thematic issued from surrealism, based on the *dynamics of the dream* and the *impulses of the libido,* which freed the novelist and his characters from the grasp of reality. This thematic fostered a narrative *tone* of anguish, poetry, and mystery. Quest, alienation, the bizarre and unexplained adventure, transgression—these were some of the motifs it employed. This gave new life to the adventure novel. Under this heading fell the works of Julien Gracq, particularly *Le Rivage des Syrtes,* and those of Henri Bosco (who incorporated Rosicrucian tradition), André Dhôtel, and Henri Thomas. Also belonging in this category were Robert Pinget's early novels and the robustly erotic stories of Pieyre de Mandiargues, which occasionally—as in *Le Lys de mer* and *La Motocyclette*—drew on astrology. The motifs of quest and alienation occur throughout the fiction of the fifties and sixties, providing the motive force for the novels of Marguerite Duras, for example. The libidinal motif emerged with the canonization of the Marquis de Sade, was more confidently asserted with Bataille's *L'Histoire de l'œil,* and burst out of bounds with works like Henry Raynal's *Orgueil anonyme;* other examples were Guyotat's *Eden, Eden, Eden* and the more cerebral libertinism that inspired *Histoire d'O* (Pauline Réage, pseudonym), as well as the blatant sensuality of Monique Wittig's work *(Le Corps lesbien).*

A third major theme attained a sort of paroxysm in the work of Céline, but also provided the backdrop for many other novels: the theme of *contemporary society's dereliction*. It gave Céline's work both of its structural constants: its frenzied representation of the human animal's madness, irresponsibility, weakness, and cruelty; and the equally frenzied denunciatory monologues delivered by a protagonist who is both observer and narrator, and through whom Céline creates his own legend. Céline passed as a realist only because the concrete language he forged for himself misled his readers. In fact, the representation of reality was forced in his hands to undergo the violent and baroque distortions of satiric epic.

This worldly irresponsibility is a basic *motif* of the Christian, or neo-Nietzschean, novel, like those of the young Montherlant, one of whose themes was the impossibility of life within the limitations of the ordinary.

The ancient individual-versus-society antagonism was internalized in the metaphysical novels of authors who were either Christians or freethinkers, and there it engendered the *tortured conscience motif* and a thematic of salvation—i.e., of transcendence through an act of consciousness resolving the *internal conflict*. Here intentionality is threefold—diagnosis and description, followed by a prescription involving personal commitment—and determines the highly subjective quality of the writing. The objective progress of the narrative is interrupted by flights of eloquence and lyricism. This metaphysical attitude underlies the *theme of evil* with its motifs of despair, revolt, hatred, and violence (suicide, crime), and the *theme of salvation* with its corresponding motifs of grace, love, and conflict—both internal and external—in novels by Mauriac, Bernanos, and Jouhandeau. Each of these novelists presents in a slightly different light the twists and torments concealed in the darkness of the soul and projected in the drama of behavior.

Several of these tortured-modern-conscience novelists were Roman Catholic: Mauriac, Bernanos, Green, Jouhandeau, Joseph Malègue. Postwar anxiety and nostalgia for tried and true values guaranteed them an attentive audience, from which Mauriac in particular benefited. The novelists in this group, whether believers born and bred or, like Green, converts haunted by a sense of sin, dealt above all with *individual destiny,* even when dealing as Bernanos did, with the destiny of all mankind.

The essential drama of Christianity is between salvation and the forces of the supernatural, and this also has the effect of opening the novel up to the mysterious and the unforeseen. Sustained by a structured metaphysical vision and ontology, Christian novelists can more easily free themselves from conventional narrative forms and develop each in their own way. In his autobiographical novel *Augustin ou le maître est là,* the story of a long pilgrimage toward salvation, Joseph Malègue remains faithful to the aesthetic of the realistic novel. Mauriac, on the other hand, filled his novels (*Thérèse Desqueyroux,* 1922; *Génitrix,* 1923; *Le Noeud de vipères,* 1932) with opaque, hallucinated characters in the grasp of an absolute destiny whose significance they do not recognize. Their dramas unfold against landscapes highly charged with an intense symbolism, a Paris and a Bordelais transformed to harmonize with the state of their souls.

In novels and in virulent pamphlets punctuating political events accepted by the public with what he considered criminal unconcern, Bernanos, the literary heir to Léon Bloy, proclaimed his horror of the modern world. Over a twenty-year period half a dozen novels from *Sous le soleil de Satan* (1922) to *Monsieur Ouine* (1946) describe a world beset by evil and sinking into bestiality. Evil, for Bernanos, is not an abstraction. Evil is the presence of Satan triumphant among us, transforming living beings into dead souls. The hero of Bernanos's world is the priest, the symbol of Christian man, locked in combat with Satan, wresting souls from him and leading them to salvation. From this point of view, the story of the humble priest in the village of Ambricourt, the hero of *Journal d'un curé de campagne,* is exemplary. Often chaotic, tormented, and violent, Bernanos's writing overflows the formal codes of fiction. Bernanos's own voice, his boundless rage against a world that daily repeats the massacre of the innocents, endows his writing with its hallucinatory force.

In the novels of Sartre and Camus, *evil* is located in the metaphysical subconscious that has overtaken the entire body social: this is reflected in the basic structure of their early novels. In each of them a "banal" protagonist experiences a violent awakening following an event or series of events; through this dawning consciousness, or epiphany, he becomes detached from "other people." This is what happens to Roquentin in *La Nausée,* and to Meursault in *L'Etranger.* This new insight is the last stage in the discovery of a dimension of existence that the author, through the intermediary of his story, is also trying to reveal to the reader. In this way the *coherence* of the Catholic as well as the agnostic novel is achieved—not without a hint of tautology, since the novel's outcome is already inscribed in its initial premises.

The *tortured conscience of modern man* theme reappears in another form in the novels of Malraux: against a background of violent action—jungle expeditions, revolution, civil war—to which the characters have committed themselves; they "think through" their situation and *examine* their actions, each character representing one of several possible responses to events. These novels become one vast examination of the meaning of the human adventure, in itself a quest mirroring the adventure or action being described. The fascination exerted by these novels is explained by the ambivalence of their *motifs* of alienation, rebellion, and violence. The affliction of Bernanos's village priest turns out to be sainthood; Roquentin's panic turns out to be liberating; Meursault's death sentence reveals the value of life to him; and the defeat of revolutionaries Kyo and Katow (in Malraux's *La Condition humaine*) forms the basis for their authentic greatness. But although these novels dispensed with traditional psychological analysis, they contain all the other attributes of traditional fiction: specifically described locale; distinctive characters with well-defined roles; plot and "suspense"; resolution.

The theme of a *happiness* made to the measure of man and seen from the dual perspective of pre-1914 futurism and socialism underlies Jules Romains's *Les Hommes de bonne volonté*. Singing in praise of the city, Romains claimed that the fulfillment of the individual—which is a form of happiness—resides in the increased intellectual energy and technical power of men when they are gathered into increasingly concentrated communities. Containing neither hero nor psychological analysis, his vast fresco features more than a thousand people absorbed in their daily life and concrete occupations over the course of a quarter of a century (1908–33) in the huge collectivity represented by France. Romains's characters participate in a shared destiny whose epic-poetic dimension is inscribed in the changing face of a mythical Paris evoked in five broad descriptive frescoes: Paris in 1908, 1918, 1922, 1928, and 1933. There are successes, failures, and aberrations, but no tragedy. The only really important thing is what a recent critic has called Romains's own "visionary hindsight." Significantly, this vision became progressively darker after Romains began publication of his novel in 1932; his sunny optimism was severely tested by current events.

The world of Jean Giono, a wholly imaginary one, in the beginning evoked a pretechnical society whose members participated in the life of the cosmos, their joys and their sorrows following the great rhythms of nature, offering them the possibility of living a fully human life—à la Giono. These novels have their source in literature (Homer, the Bible, Melville) and in folklore (the legends of the Manosque region of France); it was through misapprehension that they were ever considered to be merely stories about peasants. An increasingly sure master of subtle and diverse narrative techniques, Giono used the sense of wonder at all forms of life—human life among others—as a basic theme of his novels. This main theme informs the motifs of nature's *presence,* not as mere spectacle, but as the very element from which the people in these novels draw their profound feeling for the changeless order of things and their respect for life, for everything alive, for their own existence, and for that of other men.

The two themes identifying happiness with the character's participation, through all of their senses, in the life of the cosmos and in a feeling of solidarity with other men also shaped the works of Camus and Saint-Exupéry. In a very different vein, and with unbridled invention, Raymond Queneau's preposterous plots and comic-strip characters pull the reader into a free-floating world, a sort of "Sunday off from life." This phrase was borrowed by Queneau for the title of one of his novels *(Dimanche de la vie)* and comes from Hegel, who used it to describe his impressions on looking at the genre paintings of Flemish art. These touching and carefree images of daily life, however, are a far cry from the ones Queneau gives to his lovable but zany characters whose inconsequence rests on philosophical concepts of considerable depth.

These themes were relegated to the background—temporarily perhaps—by contemporary political events. During the period immediately following World War II, people responded to the horrifying impact of "I-was-there" or "Lazarus" literature (Jean Cayrol), good examples being Cayrol's own trilogy *Je vivrai l'amour des autres* and Pierre Gascar's *Le Temps des morts*. The concentration camp experiences recounted by these authors precluded any theme based on the idea of happiness. The latter reappeared in more conventional novels that were well received by the reading public of the sixties and seventies (poet Robert Sabatier's successful trilogy: *Les Allumettes suédoises, Trois Sucettes à la menthe,* and *Les Noisettes sauvages*).

The theme of *world travel* broadened the imagination's geographical scope. North Africa, the United States, South America, and the Far East yielded various fictional motifs: the physical pleasure of the exotic and of movement to the rhythm of great express trains or automobiles (Cendrars); escape from the oppressively narrow confines of French life and the broadening of personal horizons (Montherlant); the love of danger and heroism, and the need to surmount the physical responses of the human animal (Malraux); confrontation with another civilization (Morand); or, for Claude Ollier, the "objective correlative" provided by traveling into the foreign territory of unwritten history. The *heroism theme* of Malraux's *Les Conquérants* was drained of its mystique in Céline's *Voyage au bout de la nuit* and Claude Lévi-Strauss's *Tristes tropiques,* both of which denounced the lyrical illusions of the colonial adventure in the face of sordid reality, a theme that was to recur in the novels of Marguerite Duras *(Un barrage contre le Pacifique).*

Another theme makes its appearance in Breton's *Arcane 17.* In this book, the rocky tip of Canada's Gaspé becomes a *text to be read,* to transcribe into words, and hence, with all of its spatial and temporal dimensions, to incorporate into the reader's consciousness. From the beginning, all of Butor's work is an expansion on the theme of the "genius of place" with its cultural overlay and the ways in which this overlay defines and reveals the inhabitants. The source of fiction, for Butor, is in the effort he makes as "scribe" to arrange the text in various ways—serially, thematically, typographically, through word distribution on the page—that will situate his character, thus himself, in relation to the spatial and temporal structures of a specific place. The locales Butor chose became increasingly complex. At first they were urban (an apartment building in Paris, an industrial town in England, a compartment on a railway train, a Parisian secondary school). But with *Mobile* Butor raised his sights. He tried to create texts representing the United States, Niagara Falls, Arizona, a Zuni Indian festival in New

Mexico, or public monuments like the basilica of St. Mark in Venice. Butor's ambition of deciphering the structure of these locales and then rendering them in a verbal equivalent led him to abandon every conventional element of the novel except for the narrator-object-text relationship. Each time, the text relates the successive stages of awareness; an objective configuration existing in the outside world is explored in all of its many cultural aspects until the author has deciphered its meaning in terms of his own spiritual itinerary. Each text is therefore both a journey toward the outside world and an internal itinerary opened up by the act of writing. This style of writing gave birth to a myth of the city that took a new form with Robbe-Grillet. Robbe-Grillet's consecration of the collective erotic myths, fragmentary but violent and obsessional, associated for example with the city of Hong-Kong, produced *La Maison de rendez-vous,* and another set of myths produced *Project pour une révolution à New York.* The big modern city, murderous and hallucinatory, also serves as both background and protagonist for Le Clézio's visionary novel *La Guerre.*

After Proust and Gide, the theme of the genesis of narrative discourse became a major one with Blanchot and Beckett. It has ceased to be explicit and is difficult to spot. It is now incumbent upon the reader to discover its development for himself by identifying the network of associations that served to point the text in a certain direction from the very first words. During the sixties, this theme tended to obliterate all others as far as the experimental novel was concerned, and to be esoteric and stereotyped. There is no reason to believe, however, that this "new enscripting" was particularly congenial to the hypothetical reader to whom it was addressed. There is also no particular reason to believe that the premises of this new, much discussed organization of the novel are even to be found in it.

The Writers' Progress: Jean Giono and Louis Aragon

The novel, like other art forms, was becoming emancipated; structurally, it frequently moved away from the predominant forms of naturalism or psychological analysis. We have already noted above the characteristic traits of the experimental novel in each historical period. The work of some novelists, however, spanned the entire half-century and followed all of its meanderings. In our view, two examples of this phenomenon would be Giono and Aragon, with Aragon exhibiting greater breadth in the variety of his narrative structures. In both cases, stylistic changes in the writer's work were closely related to the repercussions current events had on his private life.

With his *Trilogie de Pan* (*Colline, Un de Baumugnes,* and *Regain,* 1928–30) Giono had an immediate impact on a reading public that shared his aversion for a civilization it believed responsible for the disaster of World War I. Conditioned by a youth spent reading the Bible and Homer, and listening to Provençal tales told at the fireside, he transposed into the novel the form and style of the oral tale, transforming his native Provence into a semilegendary realm peopled with beings halfway between peasantry and poetry; against a background of the recreation of the world, Giono set down words and actions in which simple, solid values resumed their place in contrast to the morals of a humanity he saw as decadent. This beginning-of-the-world universe, its joys and its labors, also its sorrows—love, death—belonged to the old utopian tradition calling for a return to primordial nature where mankind can once again find happiness. A second series of novels—*Le Chant du monde, Que ma joie demeure,* and *Batailles dans la montagne*—had epic qualities. In both series, the stories are generated by a single, detached voice recounting vast events unauthenticated by any other source, but from which Giono, blending together the real and the imaginary, drew an ethic for his contemporaries to use.

On two occasions during World War II, Giono's uncompromising pacifism drew unfavorable attention: first as a conscientious objector calling for resistance to the draft; and second as a collaborator. Giono abandoned his role as moral guide. In his third series of books, which began to appear in 1947, the affirmative, sometimes even messianic, voice of the omniscient narrator is gone. In *Les Chroniques,* which Giono was still working on when he died, the single narrator is replaced by many narrators taking over from one another from volume to volume. A sort of collective memory, riddled with doubts and moving in zigzags, weaves a text in which people, places, times, and events blend together; mythic lives are caught by the words but are never held. The novel representing the hinge between the two sides of Giono's work, *Le Hussard sur le toit* (1951), is one of his best; and the narrative schemas of *Les Chroniques* foreshadow the concerns of the *nouveau roman.*

Toward the end of his long and varied literary career, Louis Aragon began to see everything as a novel. *Le Roman inachevé* (1956) is a collection of poems; texts that could not be categorized became novels—*Henri Matisse, roman* (1971), *Théâtre/roman* (1974); a major text entitled *Le Fou d'Elsa* (1963) was a "romance" if not strictly speaking a *roman,* combining all kinds of forms—poems, letters, narration; also a "novel" according to Aragon were the critical reflections of *Incipit* (1970). In other words, for Aragon, all discourse is fiction. And it was as a novelist that, fifty years earlier, Aragon had made his début with *Anicet ou le panorama,* a parody of the picaresque novel. Within the limitations of the present work we can only briefly indicate the phases Aragon went through in the course of his career, emphasizing the importance of this master novelist for whom our own era is "the century of the novel."

Aragon's first prose writings were influenced by the experiments of the surrealists, whose precepts he never rejected. After joining the Communist Party, he turned to the novel. He adopted the aesthetic and the narrative methods advocated by Zhdanov, which he justified in *Pour un réalisme socialiste* (1935). His first group of fictional productions, written to reflect the "real world" (four novels and the five volumes of *Communistes,* a novel that was never completed), conformed with exceptional verve to Zhdanov's dicta.

After Stalin's death, Aragon's *Postface au monde réel* announced some reservations regarding his aesthetic faith—but not his politics. A new phase in his development opened with *La Semaine Sainte* (1958) and was confirmed with *La Mise à mort* (1965) and *Blanche ou l'oubli* (1967). There is a change in the relations between author, character, and text. The present-day problematic of writing makes its appearance. It is no accident that Antoine, the hero of *La Mise à mort,* already a double of the author's, splits again, turning into a "virtual man" that his own elusive double, Alfred, a reflection in a mirror, drives insane. Text or mirror, only virtual images are reflected back to the author, casting doubt on his own existence. In *Blanche ou l'oubli* the main character is a linguist who, like the author, was born on 3 October 1897, who becomes confused with him and gradually aware of "existing inside the words." Here Aragon touches on one of the essential themes of today's avant-garde literature. Through the intermediary of characters who exist "inside the word," he poses the problem of the relation between the subject and what the subject says: "Who am I? I am he who speaks and cannot help speaking about himself." For Aragon, the "storyteller" is someone who nevertheless continues to speak "the great dream that belongs to us all and that cannot go astray." In this way Aragon the novelist adhered both to the surrealist endeavor of his early years and to the overall development of a period that frequently returned to romanticist themes, attempting to use them as an expression of the collectivity's experience.

Tales and Stories

The line separating the novel from the novella and the novella from the short story or the folktale is difficult to establish with accuracy. Other types of short piece (recent works by Marguerite Duras; *Comment c'est* and *Le Dépeupleur* by Samuel Beckett; Robbe-Grillet's *Instantanés;* the surrealists' writings) complicate the problem of definition. As René Gadenne has pointed out, in an attempt to identify the structural specifics of the genre (*La Nouvelle française,* 1974), a certain amount of confusion has also reigned ever since the nineteenth century as to the exact usage of the terms "tale" and "novella." The same is true for "story." But in the twentieth century, the word "tale" has generally been used to designate a short narrative in which elements of the fantastic are involved. Collections of tales have become increasingly rare and are frequently intended for the juvenile market: Marcel Aymé's *Contes du chat perché,* André Dhôtel's tales, and even Supervielle's collection *L'Enfant de la haute mer et autres contes,* with the exception of the title story, all fall in this category. But the most brilliant storytellers of all have undoubtedly been the Francophone Africans, whose inspiration is drawn from a secular oral literature transmitted by *griots* (native sages). The collections of folktales retold by Birago Diop, one of the foremost Senegalese writers and learned from a *griot* attached to his family named Amadou, son of Koumba, another *griot,* have become classics. *Les Contes d'Amadou Koumba, Les Nouveaux contes d'Amadou Koumba,* and *Contes et Lavannes* breathed new life into a traditional form. Other, less well known storytellers such as Jacques-Marcel Nzouaïnkeu and Benjamin Matip, and the Senegalese Ousmane Socé have been able to transpose into the French language—as Diop did—the charm and poetry of these tales from another world, thus enriching the realm of the imaginary from which all stories are drawn.

The *short story* form tempted a greater number of writers, but it has remained a minor genre substantially unchanged from what it was in the nineteenth century. Gadenne makes a distinction between the "incident story," concentrated on a single episode, and the "instant story" in the style of Chekhov or Katherine Mansfield, which evokes a momentary feeling. He notes the preference of twentieth-century short story writers for the instant story. Many writers who have made their reputations in other media have been lured by the flexibility of the short story form. Critics have tended to judge short stories in the total context of a given author's work rather than as a separate genre (Sartre's *Le Mur;* Camus's *L'Exil et le Royaume).* Three writers, Marcel Aymé, Georges Simenon, and Marcel Arland, have made outstanding contributions to the short story genre; other, lesser-known examples are Larbaud, Morand, Mauriac, Giono, Bernanos, Jouhandeau, Benjamin Péret, Pieyre de Mandiargues, Boris Vian, Marguerite Yourcenar, and Françoise Mallet-Joris—and many more.

Marcel Aymé published six volumes of collected short stories, among which the best known are *Le Passe-muraille* and *Le Vin de Paris.* Taking meticulously observed situations from everyday life—the black market, wartime rationing—as his points of departure, Aymé switches back and forth between reality and fantasy without ever relinquishing the rational tone in which the story is being told. Georges Simenon built some seventy short novels around the figure of Police Inspector Maigret, classics of detective fiction which in terms of their style and the quality of their psychological insights rightly belong in the realm of literature. But the only author of fiction to have written short stories almost exclusively was Marcel Arland, who, with more than one hundred stories to his credit, illustrates the great variety of a form often treated as the novel's poor relation.

Autobiographies, Memoirs, Diaries

Since the rise of what has been called the "prose of ideas" in the eighteenth century, and particularly after the romantic period, a body of prose works, often considered of minor importance, has developed on the fringes of the traditional genres. Having broken with mimetic and formal constraints, they represent a massive intrusion of the "me-I" into literature. This kind of writing, concerned primarily with *self-expression,* has in fact, clearly aided by the existentialist preoccupation with personal experience and psychological analysis, tended to dominate the literary field for the last half-century; included in it are autobiographies, memoirs, confessions, and personal essays.

There is hardly a single writer who did not in some way contribute to this so-called intimate literature, which reached particular brilliance with Gide. Any list would have to be a long one and would include, among others: François and Claude Mauriac, Alain, Julien Benda, Gabriel Marcel, Georges Duhamel, André Maurois, Francis Carco, Jean Guéhenno, Claude Lévi-Strauss, Henri Bosco, Pierre Emmanuel, Violette Leduc, François Nourissier, Georges Simenon; also, and no doubt more notoriously, Sartre with *Les Mots,* Simone de Beauvoir with her four-volume collection of memoirs, and Malraux with his *Anti-Mémoires.* The extent and diversity of this body of work explain recent attempts at research and critical definition; good examples of these are Alain Girard's books *Le Journal intime* (1959), and Philippe Lejeune's *L'Autobiographie en France* (1971).

The lines of demarcation between these different forms, and between autobiography and fiction, are still fluid, however. For example, Cendrars in his autobiographical prose works—*L'Homme foudroyé, La Main coupée, Bourlinguer*—has created a copy of himself and his world with a mythic quality equal to that of his long journey-poems and his novels. Marcel Jouhandeau, in his fiction, is only very thinly disguised as the three successive characters the narration revolves around: Théophile, the child; Juste Binche, the adolescent; and Monsieur Godeau. Elsewhere he has created other mirrors of himself: in *Mémorial* (six autobiographical volumes) and in his diaries *(Journalier),* which he started publishing in 1961 and which do not differ substantially from his previous work in either style or content. The most flagrant case is that of Jean Genet, who in publishing his autobiography, *Journal du voleur,* clearly stated his intentions: to give mythic dimension to the "obscene" lives and ruined human beings he was celebrating, while at the same time creating his own legend. He had already confronted the "honest citizens" around him with his own legend as an outcast in the four novels that established his success as a writer: *Notre-Dame-des-Fleurs, Miracle de la Rose, Pompes funèbres, Querelle de Brest.*

Simone de Beauvoir's novel *Les Mandarins* was also closely connected to her memoirs, in which the passage from autobiography to straight chronicle was imperceptible and fragments from her diary were also incorporated. Sartre, too, included pages from his diary in the novel *La Nausée*. The overlapping between various modes of expression in this prolific personal literature explains to a degree, perhaps, the severity with which other writers banished the "me-I" from everything they wrote.

The Essay

The essay can take any form and exists on the fringes of every genre; it has also been marked by the massive intrusion of the "I" into literature. It has formed the matrix, during this fifty-year period, of French intellectual life, a fact borne out by the success of a collection such as Gallimard's "Idées" series, comprising expository essays, literary essays, political essays, philosophical essays, personal essays, occasional essays, and essay-manifestos. Today, however, the essay is in retreat before the interview and the published proceedings of various colloquiums. In its isolation it has tended to fade from the literary scene. One result has been the recent practice of collecting essays in one volume and giving a distinctive title to it: *Prétextes* by Gide, *Variété* by Valéry, *Situations* by Sartre, *Actuelles* by Camus, *Répertoire* by Butor.

Essays in literary criticism, a heritage going back to Sainte-Beuve, subjective and frequently reflective, developing a critical point of view in relation to a literary work or a literary theme, abounded during the period between the two world wars and then began to be less common. The essay-manifesto, on the other hand, presenting a political or ideological literary position, produced extremely important texts: Breton's manifestos and the dadaist manifestos; Antonin Artaud's statements collected in *Le Théâtre et son double;* Sartre's "Présentation des Temps modernes" and *Qu'est-ce que la littérature?* Nathalie Sarraute's *L'Age du soupçon;* Roland Barthes's *Le Degré zéro de l'écriture;* Robbe-Grillet's essays collected in *Pour un nouveau roman*—these were the signposts in a genre that deserves a whole study to itself. The lyrical essay in the style of Barrès is rare today, but outstanding examples of this genre are Camus's *Noces à Tipasa* and the pieces collected in *Eté,* especially *La Mer au plus près*.

However, the kind of essay that appears to have the best chance of surviving is still the one presenting itself as a search for lucidity in the style of Montaigne. In the twenties, a brilliant practitioner of this type of essay was Henri de Montherlant, who developed the grand themes of self-discovery in a language that was eloquent and concrete, rich in contrasts, comparisons, and symmetries. Antoine de Saint-Exupéry was also an essayist who in his novels—*Courrier Sud* and *Vol de Nuit*—as in his philosophical pieces—*Terre des hommes* and *Pilote de Guerre*—was primarily concerned with finding spiritual extensions of the events he had experienced.

Looked at from a certain angle, Sartre's entire literary output, starting with his treatise *L'Etre et le Néant,* is one great attempt to make his own inner reality coincide with his experience of the world. Camus, on the other hand, used his philosophical essays to isolate a single theme (a sense of the absurd in *Le Mythe de Sisyphe,* contemporary overemphasis on the Promethean revolt in *L'Homme révolté*) which in his view was invisibly molding the mind of modern man. In order himself to escape its grasp, he examined its impact and its limitations. For Camus, the essay was therefore both an exercise in lucidity, and a therapy. Simone de Beauvoir's international reputation rests on two didactic essays whose social implications were wide-ranging: *Le Deuxième sexe* and *La Vieillesse.* Finally, the *research essay,* both personal and socially significant at the same time, combined with autobiography, produced one of the great documentary texts of our time: Claude Lévi-Strauss's *Tristes Tropiques.*

Out-of-Bounds: "La Zone off-limits"

The "Zone off-limits" Michel Leiris talks about is beyond classification and refers to the kind of literary experiments illustrated by the work of two writers we will hold as exemplars: Georges Bataille and Leiris himself. Both belong to the turbulent generation born between 1895 and 1905; both were influenced by surrealism, and both were attracted to ethnology, Leiris conducting his ethnological research in Africa, Bataille plunging into the study of Sade, Hegel, and Nietzsche. Both were influenced by Freud, and both explored Oriental philosophy in various forms. Both were profoundly interested in the arts, and especially in painting. This particular configuration of interests was not exceptional among the writers of a generation that was no longer willing to uphold the official cultural norms undermined by the war, but internalized nonetheless and begging to be exceeded. But in order to enter this "off-limits" zone of experience, they had to do violence to themselves. Transgression is a theme shared by all of them, along with the rejection of any system capable of organizing what they wrote a priori.

The writings of Georges Bataille elude any accepted concept of literature; in them the boundaries between the literary and the nonliterary (scatology, pornography, political economy) are erased; the text presents unfinished sentences and blank spaces, begins in the middle, includes fragments of a story, an autobiography, and poems that continue in other places in other texts. Starting with *Histoire de l'œil* there is also an excess of erotic and scatological fantasy; its presence and incongruity disturb the sensitive reader who senses that this complex figuration of characters and episodes refers to some area of the beyond, impossible to grasp. The narrative, monstrous in terms of ordinary rationality, seems to be a sort of exhorbitant Buddhist "koan." Bataille absorbs into his discourse, where they dissolve, the most disparate literary modes, in effect placing himself "out of orbit" and into regions of psychic experience that language cannot reach but can only mimic: the void that is death, madness, horror, and excess where the man of flesh and blood confronts his mythic face made sacred. What Bataille attempts to do is to translate his inwardly experienced sense of nonself, the unsayable, the impossible, a nonform, into another kind of nonform.

Leiris's enterprise is of a different kind. It takes place on the level of everyday life and is offered as experimental autobiography. In his postface (1946) to *L'Age d'homme* (1939), which is where this experiment began, Leiris places his project among the various manifestations of that personal literature of which, as he emphasized, there was so much. He distinguishes his own work from the rest in terms of his attempt to combine the strictest respect for documentary accuracy with experiments in form designed to establish a wholly new literary genre, completely outside the traditional ones—a *major* genre, in his view, and today the only authentic one. Leiris defined the rules of his genre in a work entitled "La Littérature considérée comme tauromachie" (Literature as a bullfight). Public ceremonial and ritual, the practice of literature should involve the writer in a dangerous combat, a stylized game whose rules he respects. One of the rules of composition Leiris set himself was the meticulously accurate transcription of his psychic experience. From *L'Age d'homme* through *Biffures, Fourbis, Fibrilles, Frêle Bruit* are scattered fragments of autobiographical narrative; disparate impressions, memories, anecdotes, and dreams are strung together but left unexplained. The resulting texts are like a collection of hieroglyphics lacking a syntactic code.

To the names of these two authors who attempted to go beyond the limits of traditional genres we might be tempted to add Michaux, Artaud, perhaps the Butor of texts like *Où*, also Sollers, and lastly if more remotely, Beckett and Céline in his late works.

14

Poetry

Of all the areas of literature, poetry is the most difficult to define, either socially and historically, or according to quality, quantity, and tendency. Poetry is kept alive in innumerable and often ephemeral little magazines, at poetry conferences, and in small temporary groups, all of which have only recently been documented with any regularity by the Centre d'information et de coordination des revues de poésie. But it also lives in the works of poets who from volume to volume, sometimes over a span of half a century, pursue their inner development and the transformation of their poetic vision. Every poet tries at first to find a voice in his predecessors, whose language he must destroy before he can find his own; and yet it is rare to find the tone that will run through a poet's entire body of work absent from his very first poems. In the following pages we can only make a start on the kind of study that would be required if we were to identify all the different faces of poetry and the accomplishment of every poet worthy of interest.

Furthermore, from the time when, at the end of the nineteenth century, "verse came under attack" (Mallarmé), the very concept of poetry and what makes a poem has been constantly expanding. Surrealism divorced the concept of poetry from all its associations with the forms of traditional versification. For a certain number of writers like Bataille, the word "poetry" designates any text that does not conform to the conventions of the traditional genres. Although the prose poem has been with us for over a hundred years, it began to take on new forms. For example, in the work of Francis Ponge and Henri Michaux, and in Butor's work starting with *Mobile,* in which linguistic forms are less important than the relations established within a verbal assemblage whose sonic structures are not particularly important; and the recent works by Marguerite Duras in which just the opposite is the case, where the rhythmic structures constitute the predominant mode of expression.

Finally, during the period in question, there has been no single conception of either the nature or the function of poetry, no poetic theory that, even in the surrealist period, predominated over all the others. Every poet has had his or her say in prefaces or articles concerning the function of poetry and the role of the poet in the modern world. Or else, following Mallarmé and Valéry, they have transformed their own poems into the story of how they were written. Here we can indicate only briefly a few of the theories formulated by the poets themselves on the nature and practice of their craft.

Every decade or so, anthologies make a new attempt to sort and classify material in the area of poetry, usually hovering between a selection that may be considered too arbitrary and a collection that cannot be exhaustive no matter how hard it tries, but in which any clear-cut idea of current trends will be lost. The usual solution is to combine chronological arrangement with a division according to theme. This is what Serge Brindeau did in his five-hundred-page anthology devoted to French poets, *La Poésie contemporaine de langue française depuis 1945* (1973), which gives insights into the field of poetry that are useful if fragmentary. Brindeau's work, like the present one, is intended to serve merely as an invitation to the reader to make further explorations of his own. Obviously the only way to learn about poetry is to read poems. Every poem must be read individually. The literary critic-historian can give only a very limited idea of what the poetry produced over the last half-century is like, and the task becomes riskier the nearer we get to the present. It would be impossible within the limits of this work to describe the stylistic characteristics of each poet: the inherited, the shared, the individual. Elsewhere we have already noted the technical innovations employed by poets even before 1914 in an attempt to divorce the poem from linearity and then from the page itself, either by transformations in the typographical disposition of the poem or by proposing poems whose development was purely phonic (Pierre Garnier's spatialism, Isidore Isou's lettrism, Henri Chopin's phonetic poetry); there was also the effort dating back to dadaism to subvert the syntax of poetry. We will not go over them again in this section. The reader is referred to the bibliography, and particularly to the works of W. Theodor Elwert, *Traité de versification française des origines à nos jours* (1965), and to *Le Vers français au XXe siècle* (1967), edited by Monique Parent, regarding problems of verse technique. Although modern versification is presumably "liberated," a major segment of contemporary poetry has not parted as much from the traditional poetic structures as a century and a half of revolt against their constraints would seem to indicate: "The innovations in contemporary poetry," concludes Elwert, "have been syntactic and stylistic, at times graphic, but not metric." Language, as the linguists have always insisted, does make some demands of its own.

The Poetic Lineage: A Survey

In 1920, confusion reigned on the poetic scene: avant-garde leader Apollinaire was dead. Many poets who had been writing before 1914 (Romains, Duhamel, Morand, Cendrars) decided to try the novel, a genre for which there was a wider public. Claudel's work was beginning to gain an audience, and he and Valéry were destined to become, in the eyes of the French, the two great poets of our time, both of them in traditions going back to the nineteenth century, with Valéry the heir to Baudelaire and Mallarmé, and Claudel to the lyricism of Victor Hugo and Rimbaud. Both represented an extension of the romantic poetic tradition. Valéry rightly perceived, in the "poetic sphere" of the interwar period, the "resonance" of Baudelaire's work. But the grandiloquent rhetoric of romantic lyricism as transmitted by Claudel also reappeared. It is still possible to detect, from one generation of French poets to the next, the stylistic tension between the type of verse characteristic of Claudel, and the fixed forms cultivated by Valéry.

There was a third trend, itself subdivided into three somewhat different approaches to poetry. It was the trend that had been represented by Apollinaire, also the literary descendant of Baudelaire, via Laforgue and Rimbaud, and it dominated the French literary scene during this period; its three facets were represented, respectively, by Max Jacob, Pierre Reverdy, and Blaise Cendrars, all active presences in the post–World War I literary world. These three poets were modernist and futurist, following the style set by Apollinaire, and their aim was to steer French poetry into the maelstrom of the twentieth century and divorce it from its subservience to both the symbolist metaphysics and the humanitarian concerns of Jules Romains and the Abbaye poets. Bent on demystification, Max Jacob employed the resources—and often the absurdities—of unconstrained language, attacking the rules of poetic rhetoric with nonmeaning; Cendrars attempted to transform into poetry the rhythms and the beauty of the modern world *(Du monde entier; Au cœur du monde)* and their reverberations in the mind of the poet ("Everything is color, movement, explosion, light"). The continuity of a poem by Cendrars is the result of the kinetic speed with which—as in Apollinaire's *poèmes-promenades*—impressions, sensations, and souvenirs unfold and overlap, giving an effect of spatial displacement based on the rapid succession of a series of images according to an apparently improvised rhythm. The concentration of Pierre Reverdy's poetic language puts him closer to Mallarmé; he also moved away from the symbolist dualism (image-idea; physical world-mental world; poem-reality; poem-metaphysic). Reverdy's poetry binds together disparate elements into configurations of images whose unity is provided by a single intense perception—often one of expectation or premonition of disaster—revealing an unspoken presence at the empty center of the poem from which the poet's own presence seems lacking.

These were the contradictory tendencies that coexisted and overlapped with one another in the poetic vortex of the half-century 1920–70: the aesthetic of poetic unity, harmony, and coherence, and the anti-aesthetic of the disparate and unexpected; fidelity to traditional forms and attacks on their usefulness; the great lyricism of harmony with, and celebration of, creation (Claudel) and the orphic poetry of descent into the inner self and of chaos vanquished through the painstaking composition of the song (Valéry); and the poem of incompleteness, of glancing perceptions and inexhausted reality (Cendrars). The "I" of the poetic discourse it abandoned (Reverdy), or objectified (Valéry), or parodied under a thousand different and often jeering masks (Jacob), or asserted (Cendrars); poems were variously presented as controlled entities, or as fragmentary sequences. On one hand, the cult of formal perfection was held to be the sole justification for the activity of the poet-artisan (Valéry); on the other, the poet saw himself as a prospector at the formless frontiers of culture (Apollinaire); and so forth.

By 1950 it may have seemed to some observers that Valéry and Claudel belonged to an era in the history of poetry that was past, but a retrospective look at the situation of poetry as it developed during the fifties does not entirely confirm this opinion.

Our division of this period into three sections is particularly relevant in regard to poetry. The poetic continuum was twice interrupted by political events. An underlying unity was temporarily eclipsed by more immediately visible surface manifestations. In the immediate postwar environment of 1920, a group of precocious young poets—the surrealists—was catapulted into notoriety at the expense of their predecessors. The Second World War caused a reaction that created a chasm between poets: poetry written on the subject of the painful events being experienced by the country often had recourse to traditional forms. Contributing the landmark works of poetry to this half-century were four distinct generations in the lineage of French poetry. First came four poets of stature; Pierre Jean Jouve, Saint-John Perse, Jules Supervielle, and Pierre Reverdy, all born between 1884 and 1887, published their first important collections of poems around the year 1925—*Les Mystérieuses Noces* (Jouve, 1925), *Anabase* (Perse, 1924), *Gravitations* (Supervielle, 1925), and *Les Epaves du ciel* (Reverdy, 1924). Both Jouve and Supervielle were poets whose lyric abundance flowed unabated over the course of their long lives. Perse, out of respect for his diplomatic career, kept silent after the publication of *Anabase* until 1942, when he began a series of great lyric poems that over a period of twenty years earned him a place among the major poets of his time. Reverdy, less influential and less prolific, stood in contrast to his three contemporaries.

They were followed by the generation of poets born at the turn of the century, between 1895 and 1903, which produced a host of innovators and some checkered careers. Besides the poets associated with dada and surrealism—Tzara, Eluard, Breton, Desnos, and Pérot—this generation included other original, independent figures: Antonin Artaud, Raymond Queneau, Jean Tardieu, and the popular Jacques Prévert. It also included two extremely innovative poets, Henri Michaux and Francis Ponge.

Each of these poets too was to find his own individual voice during the productive years of the twenties: Tzara, with *De nos oiseaux*, 1923; Eluard with *Mourir de ne pas mourir* and *Capitale de la douleur*, 1924 and 1926; Breton with *Clair de terre* and *Poisson soluble*, 1923 and 1924; Desnos with *La Liberté ou l'amour*, 1927; and Péret with *Le Grand Jeu*, 1928. Although Artaud's *L'Ombilic des limbes* and *Le Pèse-Nerfs* (1925, 1927) were published during the same period, their author did not gain recognition as a poet until the sixties; Michaux, his originality confirmed with the publication of *Mes propriétés* in 1929, was not really discovered until the forties, the years when Ponge also became known, although he had indicated his presence as a poet long since with the publication of *Douze Petits Ecrits* in 1926. This collection was the first concrete evidence of a unique and painstakingly matured poetic enterprise which made Ponge, in the view of *Tel Quel* a quarter of a century later, the exemplary avant-garde poet. It was not until much later, with *Les Ziaux* (1943) and *Monsieur, Monsieur* (1951), respectively, that Queneau and Tardieu assumed their rightful place among the poets of this amazing generation. With a few exceptions—Artaud, Péret, Michaux, Ponge—almost all of these poets eventually abandoned their clamorous revolt against classical prosody and made frequent use of fixed forms with precise syntax and limpid wording.

The generation of poets born between approximately 1920 and 1925 began to take the floor after 1950. In his 1956 *Anthologie de la poésie nouvelle*, Jean Paris identified them and attempted to define their stance, which was singularly different from that of the *nouveaux romanciers*, or new novelists. These were poets, still living today for the most part, who took exception by and large to the antiliterary aspect of surrealist poetry and aligned themselves with the lyric tradition of the romantics. In their poetry we find a reemergence of rhythms reminiscent of Victor Hugo, and experiments with condensed poetic language reminiscent of Mallarmé.

These poets were consciously reasserting their ties with a tradition *within which* they sought to discover a new language, as had their predecessors born at the turn of the century. Intervening between them and the surrealists were some extremely worthwhile independent poets who either had been influenced by surrealism and gone beyond it but never repudiated it, or had drawn on other sources for their inspiration—the Bible, in the case of Jean Grosjean and Patrice de La Tour du Pin; and in the case of Pierre Emmanuel, to an even greater extent, the example of Pierre Jean Jouve. We find the same kind of opposition within this group of poets as in the earlier group, an opposition between verbal expansion of the poetic discourse represented by Jacques Charpier, Jean Laude, Charles Le Quintrec, Jean-

Claude Renard, Robert Sabatier, and Claude Vigée; and the tendency toward verbal density represented by Edith Boissonnas, André Marissel, and
Robert Marteau—André du Bouchet is another example, a poet who pushed
this tendency to its extreme limits. This style of verbal density owed as much
to Baroque poets such as Sponde as it did to Baudelaire, Mallarmé, or
Reverdy. A new turning in this tradition was announced in 1960 by one of
the poets of this generation, J.-P. Faye.

The generation of poets born in the thirties and just beginning to publish
around 1955 found its voice about 1960. Notable among them are Marc
Alyn, Michel Deguy, Yvonne Caroutch, Pierre Oster, Marcelin Pleynet,
Denis Roche, and Jacques Roubaud. This generation was split down the
middle. On one side are poets like Alyn, Caroutch, Deguy, and Oster, who
did not attempt to move away from prosodic tradition but sought to renew
poetic language and poetic themes; and on the other are poets like Pleynet,
Roche, and Roubaud, who experimented with poetic forms and gave first
priority in their poems to problems of form—an attitude singularly reminiscent of Paul Valéry's. When Jacques Roubaud created the "sonnet to
end all sonnets" by submitting the sonnet form to permutations based on
the rules for the Japanese game "Go," he created a text whose sequences can
be read in three different ways. When in collaboration with a team of poets
from different countries—Octavio Paz, Eduardo Sanguinetti, and Charles
Tomlinson—he composed a Japanese "renga," he resembled Paul Valéry,
whose concern was also to create consciously controlled form. The same
concern for form probably also lies behind the favor enjoyed by other fixed
Japanese forms such as the *tenga* and the *haiku,* the latter having also been
briefly popular around 1920. Jean Pérol, although he entitled his collection
of story-poems *Ruptures,* felt himself as strongly attached to the French
tradition as to the influence of Japan. Exploration of the subconscious
seemed to be losing ground in favor of a concern for craftsmanship—
unheard of since the twenties—and for the perfect (finished) form, and this
concern perhaps signaled a return to a formal aesthetic.

At the same time, various forms of descriptive poetry were reappearing,
such as Butor's *Illustrations,* or Ponge's poems; and also narrative poems,
such as those of Robert Champigny, who rescued the narrative that was
being abandoned by the theoretician-practioners of the *nouveau roman.*
These types of poetry also seemed to mark a return to poetic objectivity and
a new pact with language. It was the pact repudiated by Denis Roche when
in 1972 he announced his simultaneous break with poetry and with the *Tel
Quel* group, perhaps feeling, as Jean Vaché had felt half a century earlier
and for other reasons, that the practice of poetry is absolutely "inadmissible."

A skilled translator of Ezra Pound and E. E. Cummings, an art lover, and
a partisan of Kandinsky's theories, Denis Roche was an active participant in
the *Tel Quel* discussions from 1964 on. Mindful of the Marxist writer's role

in a bourgeois, capitalist society, he decided, along with his *Tel Quel* cohorts and in accordance with the views they held at the time, to work toward social change by denouncing through "miswriting" the fraudulence of the established literary structures ("La poésie est inadmissible," 1968). Between his first collection of poems, *Récits complets* (1963), and *Le Mécrit* (1972), he did in fact develop a theory of poetry based on his study of Kandinsky's techniques in which the poem was seen as a production of purely abstract forms devoid of any semantic resonance (i.e., any communication of feelings, impressions, or ideas) and any aesthetic purpose. The poem's sole function, according to his theory, was to convey, through the tensions, movements, and collisions it created on the page, the presence of some kind of activity at play. Perhaps owing to the resistance of the language to this kind of willfull abstraction, Roche ultimately renounced his attempt to transform language into mere "raw material."

We might also note that this "discontinuous poetry" was subordinate, as far as most of the last half-century's poets were concerned, to the *long poem*, its sustained development and familiar resonances.

This brief survey can give only an abbreviated image of the amazing variations evidenced by a poetic language moving between the patrician rhetoric of a Saint-John Perse and the vulgar rhythms of the doggerel imagined by Queneau; between Char's solid verbal brilliance and the melodic variations of virtuoso Bosquet; and between Supervielle's "Song" and the complex harmonies sought by Jean-Claude Renard.

Other names could easily be added to the total picture: André Frénaud, Jean Follain, Eugène Guillevic, René-Guy Cadou. The patriarchs are now securely in their places: Jouve, Supervielle, and Saint-John Perse. In the following generation: Eluard, Char, Michaux, Ponge; now Bonnefoy. It is around these names that the following brief thematic study will be organized, in which we will also indicate, if need be, each poet's own concept of what he does. In general, however, and opinion to the contrary notwithstanding, most poets prior to the sixties were not particularly interested in theorizing.

Thematics: Change and Continuity

From time immemorial *the self* has been considered the origin—if not the source—of the poetic act. From the time of the romantics, the self and its states of consciousness and perception have been the preferred poetic subjects, and in many cases they still are. The self in this sense is conceived as a basic given, a center of consciousness perceiving the emotions that affect it, and that color how it sees the world; these emotions are: love, boredom, joy, anger, etc.

The lyricism of a poet like Eluard can be seen up to a certain point as belonging to this tradition. But for the surrealist poets, the position of the self in relation to the poem had changed. The *goal* of the poetic enterprise, for these poets, and not its source, was the revelation and liberation of an unknown self and, simultaneously, the *unveiling,* in the *light* of language, of the world the self inhabits. The poem is a *verbal* realization of the miraculous overlapping of the inner self and the outer world which, for Eluard, was the shape of love. It is the beloved woman who opens up the path to this level of existence because, in the surrealist mythology, woman's intuitive powers link her in a profounder harmony to the forces of the subconscious. Love, an irrational state of being, is also a "lyrical state of being" favorable to the "intellectual debacle" (*Notes sur la poésie,* Breton and Eluard, 1936), which is the source for the "integration of the conscious self with the inner self." The poem awakens the poet to full awareness, an awareness whose continual renewal is contingent on "love/poetry." However, Eluard very early made a distinction between poetry and the verbal flow of automatic writing. A poem for him was the direct consequence of an act. A deliberate, conscious act. But the failure of the surrealists to attain unity of the self through the poem was subsequently violently attacked by Artaud. What Artaud saw in language, once it had been freed of logical constraints, was the presence of dangerous, nonhuman forces repudiating the self and leading to its destruction. Eluard's sexualized, creative self became for Artaud the prey of Eros the destroyer; and this Eros, for him, was but one of the many masks of death.

Michaux believed, "There isn't one self! There aren't a dozen selves! The self is nothing but a delicate balance." And the Henri Michaux whose name is on the cover of his books is actually only an ephemeral configuration of disparate elements whose random and discontinuous modes of existence he projects indefatigably, an activity enabling him to "emerge" from chaos and retain mastery over himself. Ponge ignores the self and concentrates on a different problem: "How can we demonstrate verbally the basic relation between man and the objects around him?" (Jacques Garelli, *La Gravitation poétique*). With these words Ponge is breaking off from a long tradition. By ignoring the self, he is also ignoring all the themes—anguish, metaphysical quest, rebellion against the human condition—generated by the idea of self, calmly proceeding to a celebration of "Objoy": the pleasure of feeling at home in the objective world. "The silent world is our only homeland."

It is contemporary poetry, therefore, more profoundly than the novel, that has reflected our era's attitudes and doubts concerning the self and what it really is. Only rarely has there been a poet left unaffected by this question. A strong sense that this destitute "self" was really of little importance inspired the cavalier tone of an entire school of poetry illustrated by the works of Queneau, Tardieu, and Bosquet.

With Saint-John Perse the poet was still a patrician made sacred by his lyric gift; if, because of that, he was also an outsider, he was nonetheless a witness participating in the adventure inscribed in his poem. But for Breton the poet was a liberator and a forerunner of the man of the future. At the time of the German Occupation, poets became witnesses of "France's agony" and its sufferings, transforming history into legend as Aragon was doing; but the poet as creator gradually gave way to the poet as artisan, bowing to the demands of his "raw material."

One of the most persistent poetic themes was the *Christian mystery*. Jouve's real career as a poet began, according to him, with a double conversion, to Christianity and to psychoanalysis. In the center of all his poems, from *Mystérieuses Noces* on, lies the Christian drama of sin and redemption, but this theme is expressed the most powerfully in the lengthy and obscure poem *Sueur de sang*.

The highly individual synthesis Jouve operated between Christian sin and Freudian id modified the Christian frames of reference. Using an extremely complex system of symbols, Jouve tied the Oedipal conflict to the Christian theme of guilt and wrongdoing. Evil is depicted as one with the sexualized being represented by the poet who experiences in his subconscious the anguish of the Fall, the expulsion from paradise and the awareness of inner conflict. Jouve shows death and sexuality in league to obstruct the paths leading to redemption. The progression of the poem is a *via dolorosa*, a path of carnal sacrifice consented to in anguish and in the "bloody sweat" of a cruel crucifixion, but one that must take place so that the desperately sought reconciliation with the Father will come to pass.

A return to first causes is the natural impulse of both the Christian conscience and Freudian analysis. This impulse gives Jouve's poem its dynamic flow and also, because of the Freudian principle of multiple symbolism, allows Jouve to incorporate into his poem a large variety of myths and mythic figures: the descent into death and the reascent toward life suggest the myth of Orpheus, and the theme of obsessive sex offers the faces of legendary femininity. Jouve has used all of this to produce a dense poetic text in which the sumptuous flow of language veils the peculiarity of the poet's obsessions.

The new generation of poets to emerge after World War II included many other individuals who also chose the Christian mystery as their theme. In the early part of his career as a poet, Emmanuel, inspired by Jouve, incorporated into the drama of the fall, the incarnation, and the redemption, numerous other myths, such as the Promethean myth; but for Emmanuel as for most of his contemporaries, evil meant the terrestrial evil represented by tyranny past and present, "monstrous incarnations of the sin we all share" and from which only the continually renewed drama of Christ and the Crucifixion can deliver us. The Bible, a rich source of symbolic and mythological figures, exerted a strong influence on Emmanuel, whose initially obscure language gradually became more transparent.

Christian poets, if happy in their faith, have also discovered in *the world* a sumptuous text in which the nature of their God is revealed to them. Supervielle, however, saw the world, its spaces, objects, and beings as so many familiar friends, and it is from this familiarity, he claimed, that the inner song serving as the source for his poems sprang. For Supervielle everything was both familiar and mysterious: the inner landscapes of memory as well as the outer landscapes of the real world with their trees, their pebbles, and their gardens; life as well as death; and the strange and preoccupied god to whom he occasionally addressed his words, though unsure as to whether or not this god existed. This theme of a friendly and familiar world cropped up again among the post–World War II poets, but this time something new had been added: a sense of the world's vulnerability. No previous generation had felt as deeply the imminence of a "silent world" as did for the space of a few years the generation Emmanuel called "the children of Hiroshima." As Bosquet had already pointed out, the relation between man and his world was changing. Human vulnerability was now, for the first time, being shared by the whole world. A similar attentiveness to the joys the simplest contacts with the world can give enabled several other poets to "construct" their own domain: Edmond Jabès, Rouben Melik, Armen Tarpinian, Claude Vigée, and the very subtle artist Philippe Jaccottet; in the latter's work an acute sense of the world's beauty is allied with complete naturalness to a sense of the extreme fragility of each living creature, each thing, and each moment of happiness.

For René Char, poetic substance was furnished not by the world but by the earth, and a very particular part of the earth—l'Isle-sur-Sorgue in the Vaucluse region of France. Through it, he situated himself as a conscious man, a man for eternity and a man for the moment, living, through mind, at the frontiers of a reality that is inhuman and disturbing. In Char's poems fire, water, earth, air; fish, fowl, river, harvest; death and love; light and shadow create a linguistic universe rich in allusion where the complexities and paradoxes of human experience confront one another: "The only place where we can live is in the in-between, right on the hermetic line separating the light from the dark." Char believed a poet is someone who, through the rigorous use of language, reconciles man with this fully apprehended situation.

A *journey*, as Cendrars saw it, is something that takes place on the surface of the earth. For the surrealists, the journey is an interior one; and the journey back to origins or roots—usually childhood—the favorite metaphor. In Saint-John Perse's *Anabase* the journey takes the form of a vast expedition and conquest, a cyclical adventure begun over and over again. *Eloges,* written before 1914, by its very title and also with its first word, "Palmes," announced a poet of celebration. Perse revived the Pindaric ode, enlarging it until it achieved the dimension of the ritual, ceremonial epic he was to make his own. The three great poems by Saint-John Perse— *Anabase, Vent,* and *Amers*—celebrate the adventures of men, continually impelled forward by mysterious forces, who at each successive stage resume a collective task that is slightly different for each individual: to institute and organize the conquest of man represented by human culture in all of its forms. The "winds" bearing these men forward into the unknown blow within them, making them strangers and perpetual exiles on earth. Exile, journeying's other face, was Perse's first theme when he was young, "Crusoe's exile from his island, when he had returned to live among men"; and, in *Eloges,* the poet's own exile, far from the Caribbean island where he had grown up. Finally, the poet's exile in 1940 when he was forced to leave his country, an exile he accepted as one of the laws of the human condition—and of human greatness. For Perse, who, as a matter of fact, seldom defined the nature of his own activity (as he did, for example, when he received the Nobel Prize), a poet is a man of memory and of presence experiencing as intensely as possible the journey made by mankind, recognizing its continuity beneath all of its manifestations, *one* of which is the inscription of this adventure in the written form of the poem.

The *quest,* a private, mysterious and sometimes painful quest, is the principle theme in the poetry of Bonnefoy who, through the patrician tenor of a richly allusive and symbolic language, belongs to the line of poets tending toward the hermetic, a line including Char and Perse, and Mallarmé. According to Bonnefoy, his quest is not a metaphysical one. It is the quest for that single instant when the poet, in a particular *terrestrial spot,* hovers on the *brink* of a revelation, in the *presence* of a reality that transcends the visible. In *Arrière-Pays* (1972) Bonnefoy explains this search for a physical *place* that the experience of unity regained should transfigure—this quest for a lost Eden which, according to Bonnefoy, is similar to the gnostic quest. The search for a "place," and the mysterious "Ordeals" that accompany this search in the guise of linguistic metaphors transcribe the gradual progression toward the *place* at which the movement of the poem will rest motionless inside an area of writing that is completed. The adventure narrated by the poem is the arduous adventure of the artist seeking a vision and throwing light onto its ends and its beginnings. Here the voyage is a refusal to be exiled, and evidence that exile has already occurred.

Poetry, Revolt, and Activism

For the dadaists, the act of writing was an act of pure aggression; its weapon was irreverence. But the surrealist *revolt* against the constraints imposed by the symbolic forms of accepted art had something Nietzschean about it. According to Nietzsche, the artist destroys traditional forms in order to create new combinations just for the fun of it. There was also a Promethean aspect to surrealism, a legacy of the romantics. There were two sides to the surrealist revolt, the subversion of language being first of all a tool used by the surrealists for the purpose of attaining a postive goal:

liberated man. Surrealist irreverence was addressed to social institutions and except in certain special circumstances was not an essential theme of surrealist poetry. *Marxist philosophy,* on the other hand, furnished the inspiration for a rather traditional antibourgeois school of poetry, although it, too, had two sides to it (Aragon's *Front rouge*). Marxist poetry was both polemical and pious, and Marxist poets thought of themselves as political activists. None, however, was successful in reconciling poetry with the theme of political activism. None, except in very special circumstances, was able to create poems whose political effectiveness was certain. A single poet, and one who did become popular, anarchist, iconoclast, and dada-influenced Jacques Prévert, successfully employed certain surrealist methods to evoke and then ridicule the social realities he attacked—a difficult combination. Henri Pichette was another poet who in his early work attempted to create a rhetoric of total revolt *(Apoèmes),* but he was only partially successful and did not try again.

The Spanish civil war, World War II, the German Occupation, and the detonation of the atomic bomb inspired a few great poems repudiating the violence that was unleashed by these events: *Placard pour un chemin des écoliers* (Char), *La Marche dans le tunnel* (Michaux), *Combats avec tes défenseurs* (Emmanuel); and, on a less elevated level, Aragon's *Le Musée Grévin,* which with the *Nouveau Crève-cœur* was political down to the ground. In the atmosphere of occupied France a poem like Aragon's *Crève-cœur* or Eluard's famous litany *Liberté* were able to galvanize the latent feelings of society and perhaps to inspire the people who read them to begin or to continue taking an active role in what was going on. But French poetry after Mallarmé has addressed itself increasingly to a public of initiates. Even as they proclaimed their revolutionary fervor, French poets have given up trying to use their poems as effective political weapons in the conflicts of their time. It is primarily in the area of textual and linguistic theory that modern poets have been active.

The poet's commitment to poetry is often itself considered to be a gesture of revolt, one which has been accompanied among the poets of our own time by a need for self-affirmation, as Claude Vigée pointed out in his book *Révolte et Louanges:* love versus violence, freedom versus tyranny, hope versus despair. It may be for this basic reason that attempts to recreate a poetry of political revolt—renewed in 1950 by the young Marseille poets connected with the review *Action politique*—have not been successful. It is also for this reason, perhaps, that the poets at *Tel Quel* who became militants started with political controversy but ended with linguistic controversy—the exact opposite of the course followed by the surrealists in the twenties. In any case, the great poetry of politics and rebellion was created not in France but by the Francophone poets of Africa at the dawn of decolonization.

The primary concern of French poetry, from dada to Denis Roche, has been man, his language, his powers, his destiny; his relations to himself, to others, and to the elements and the objects that surround him. A love of words, said Ponge, is the path to poetic creation, and poetic creation is the same as self-creation. Although the major poetic themes of this period have clearly been the traditional ones modulating the poetry of the Western world, their resonances are no longer the same. With the possible exception of their esoteric and paradoxical efforts to force language beyond language and into another language, today's poets have gradually abandoned the Promethean attitude: they do not present themselves as *seers*. They are reluctant even to call themselves poets. This is a poetry which, even when expressing faith in the Christian promise of immortality for the self, is firmly rooted in the concrete. In spite of its excesses and, occasionally, its pretensions—especially its tendency to abstraction—French poetry seems in all of its variety to have assembled the elements of a new mode of discourse poets can use to relocate themselves in relation to their past and, beyond that, to bring them to that *brink* of revelation, to borrow Bonnefoy's phrase, at which they stand today.

A-lyrical Poetry: Henri Michaux and Francis Ponge

Leafing through a volume of poems by Michaux, *Plume* preceded by *Lointain intérieur,* for example, is instructive. The volume offers a disparate collection of texts drawing on various kinds of genre: a series of anecdotes featuring a fictitious character named Plume; a letter addressed by a "she" to a "you"; two one-act plays; some aphorisms; and, couched in the documentary tone of natural history manuals, miscellaneous descriptions of fantastic animals; a section of "poems" in free verse; a selection of brief anecdotes modeled on the objective rhetoric of the human interest news story but featuring the "I" who is telling the story; and a postface signed H. Michaux. According to Michaux, this is a book not made by the author: "Reader, as so frequently happens, what you are holding here is a book the author did not make." And this non-I, nonauthor, suggests to the reader that he make a book of his own.

Each separate text in the volume is split into short paragraphs or phrases, articulated with all the syntactical apparatus of logic, or casually, and as if inevitably, juxtaposed with one another. Each fragment involves a dual "I" who is inside the text but who talks about the text when speaking to the "you," presumably the reader, who is supposed to exist with the "I" simultaneously in the universe of the text and in the "real" world. It is to this "you" that the "I" appeals to corroborate the validity of his reactions.

The situations in which this "I" involves the reader do not, however, offer any basis for judgment: "I raised a tiny little horse where I live. He gallops round my room. He takes my mind off things." "I found him out walking in the corridors of the hotel with a little animal that eats locks." "Over the course of an interminable life of hard knocks, I found a great peace." The "tiny little horse," "the animal that eats locks," this "great peace" set off by the indefinite article, which gives it concreteness, introduce us into the teeming imaginary world of Michaux. Whenever Michaux takes up paint-brush or pen, "encounters" of this kind immediately start to proliferate, imposing themselves with authority, but always in new guises. The animal that eats locks will no more emerge from the brief text in which he is described than the illustrations in the Larousse will abandon their allotted position in the dictionary. Michaux does not suffer from the "unity fixation." He is a poet who never says the same thing twice, and who defines himself *in opposition* to others. *Contre!*—a poem from the collection *La Nuit remue*—is both a poetic manifesto and a sort of mime-drama trans-posing into writing the violent, almost physical inner turmoil leading to the inscription in exterior space (the page or the canvas) of a new form. In his essay *Emergences-Résurgences,* from the collection "Les Sentiers de la créa-tion," Michaux describes how this works in relation to his craft as a painter.

The poem *Contre!* is made up of free verse stanzas that are swept along on a wave of sarcasm, imprecation, and violence. Its aggressiveness is obvious from the very first line: "I will build you a city of rags, that's what I'll do . . ." his rebellion is directed against "Parthenons," "arts that are Ara-bian and Ming," in other words, against the symbols of a supposedly higher order of things. Against the world of geometry, order, and cement, the rebel creates a city of rags and fortresses of smoke, tremor, and vibration; a sort of verbal-object city built upon the ruins of civilization. The "I" of the poem believes that from this violence will come salvation; and he expresses this violence by means of a truculent vocabulary: "braying at the frozen snot noses of the Parthenons"; stuffing them with "broken-down mongrels." But the poem stops short with a final rebellion against this "I"'s own miserable body: "pissing, pain-in-the-ass, fucked-in-the-ass carcass . . ." This "oppo-sition" vocabulary aimed against the grandiose perspectives evoked by the vaguely diabolical image of the rebel, prepares the way for the moment when he turns that violence on himself, unmasking the craven insubordinate beneath. There is a superego in the poem whose ferocity attenuates the rhetorical excess of the initial outburst. The exorcism of humor acts as a kind of self-destruct mechanism on the *verbal content* of the poem, but it also complements the impulse transcribed in the poem, the rise and fall of an energy both destructive and creative. The total effect is obtained through an accumulation of violence in the vocabulary, imagery, rhythm, and syntax of the poem. The rage of the "I" confronting the "you" he finds so exasperat-ing makes an appeal to a "we" the poet seeks to involve in his enterprise. Unceremoniously begun on a note of visceral fury, the poem fills out and becomes a sort of Mephistophelian or Promethean assault. These mythic connotations are polarized by the archetypal image of the rebel, the founder of the city. The words "to be counter," "to construct," "to construct counter to," and "to act counter to" are the generative vocables of the poem.

However, this magician "architect" persona is only one of the identities that inhabit Michaux, one that the poet apparently disavows in his "post-face" where he asserts these "pieces . . . were made . . . a day at a time . . . not in order to construct something but simply to preserve it." But, for Michaux, "construct" implies calculation, and calculation is the reverse of invention: "In this book even the words I have invented and the animals I have invented were done so 'uncontrollably' and not constructively according to what I think about either language or animals."

It is obvious that Michaux belongs to the tradition in French poetry that since Baudelaire has taken the most inaccessible perceptions, the ones most alien to so-called normal consciousness, explored them as far as they possibly could be explored, and made them the material of poetry. What Michaux observed and then recreated verbally is physical and organic life in all of its multiplicity and freed from constraints of any kind, as well as the changes in perception it causes. One result of this was the lucid, almost obsessional attention he gave to the changes in his own perceptions of the world caused by drugs, and of his own perceptions of himself after becoming the object of their action. But he broke completely with the lyrical forms associated with this tradition, and with the connection between poetry and song. The first thing he did was to remove the "I" in order to objectify it and to rid it of its privileged role in the text, scattering it among a multitude of beings of every sort appearing and disappearing with each new text. But there also seems to be an inherent unity in the work as a whole, an intertextuality *within* which a seamless thread runs from one text to another, each individual text being frankly presented as fictitious. Always consistent is the never ending gesture transforming experience into fiction.

Michaux has given various, and at times contradictory, explanations of his activity as painter and poet. At times he described it as exorcism and therapy, something physical through which he could rid himself of his sufferings, his emotions, or the obsessions that possessed him. He also described painting and writing as activities by means of which he could impose some proof of continuity on his fleeting and elusive sense of self. Nowhere does he mention any aesthetic consideration or, theoretically, any concern for communication; nowhere does he pretend to be gifted with any special faculty: "What I do, anyone could do." And in fact, owing to the perennial presence of that other "you" in the body of the text, it is to an equal that the poet's words are addressed, and one to whom, through the intermediary of his constantly reiterated fabulation, he reveals himself. Michaux knows all the tricks that language can play, but he trusts language, except when it reaches the borderline beyond which it becomes system and theory, antilife. Using concrete language and exerting strict control over the coherent grammatical release of words relating the a-logical in a logical manner,

Michaux reduces to absurdity verbal constructions that supposedly "adhere" to some kind of reality. And it is from this "absurd" process of construction, paradoxically," that the reader's essential pleasure comes, once he has allowed himself to become involved in the phantasmagoria of the best of Michaux's texts.

Ponge, on the other hand, was a constructivist. He did have a method, an individual, practical art of poetry. He has often described his aims and his method—his "metatechnique"—from the punning *Dix Courts sur la méthode* ("poèmes courts, cours), to *Entretiens de Francis Ponge avec Philippe Sollers* (1971) and *La Fabrique du Pré*. The latter text, published in the series "Les Sentiers de la création," presents various drafts of the poem *Le Pré,* which Ponge worked on for four years. As this text indicates, Ponge, unlike Michaux, was not a poet of impulse but a craftsman, a poet-artisan. Ponge's adventure, based on the emotions that give rise to words, developed slowly. When the collection *Le Parti-pris des choses* (1942) was published, marking the first stage in this adventure, Ponge had spent fifteen years working on the texts included in it. Originally a poet of Mallarméan persuasion, Ponge ultimately broke completely with this model. "I recognized," he said, "that I could never express myself." It was at that point that Ponge rejected the metaphysical themes and decided to "stick with things." Confronted with the dizzying abyss that is man, Ponge wrote, "I cast my eyes on the nearest object, the pebble lying at my feet, and if it, too, opens on an abyss, at least this one is much less dangerous than the abyss of man, and by means of the expression at our command, it can be closed again." From that point on, the problem as Ponge, who "ached to express things," saw it, was to meet "the challenge things present to language."

The *things* Ponge deals with are all things of this world, each individually observed, from matchstick to sun above, from cake of soap to meadow to towel on the towel rack. All are familiar, none has any magical role to play; they carry no message. They should be moved into language, "not in order to disturb, but to reassure." Ponge's early texts were in the form of rather brief prose "essays," but subsequent ones became progressively longer, employing the resources of typographical spacing and grouped in stanzas of unequal length. His aim never varied. Using his method, he sought through language to provoke "the emergence of the most ordinary objects into the human world, where they could be grasped by the mind of man. Mutual acquisition of corresponding qualities. A new world where men together with things will come to know harmony in their relations with each other.

For this to occur, a sort of ascesis must first be undergone: everything known about objects must be forgotten, every idea we project a priori on them, so that we can look at them with new eyes. Next, in order for the object to emerge into human consciousness we must see what language can do, but not through a process of description in the ordinary sense of the word. Ponge's procedure is to assemble what he calls an "obset," i.e., a text that is as singular and specific as the original object. Ponge starts with an initial association, into which he then brings the object as a *name*, that is as a *vocable*, making it a part of a particular linguistic interplay: "La pluie, dans la cour où je la regarde tomber, descend à des allures très diverses." "L'âne se tient ainsi à un bout de la ligne et refuse d'abord d'avancer."[1]

In Ponge's system, each object makes its entrance into the world of language in its own way; and this way is determined by an initial impression that aroused in the poet the *desire* to put the object into words. This verbal emergence in turn controls the unique form that will be taken by what Ponge calls, in regard to knowledge, more specifically, the "volubility" of the object; that is, the linguistic machinery it sets in motion within the mysterious depths of the language. Ponge sets out to explore these networks of resonances methodically: he adjusts etymology, clichés, literary associations, homophones, and homonyms through successive approximations until the initial vocable bursts into a sort of final throb, the obset-text, which brings to a close its function as a celebration of the object. Thus, above: the rain-object is celebrated in an obset that has taken the form of a rhythmic, perfectly regular, circumscribed verbal unity; whereas the object-mule, "braced" at first "under its circumflex accent," proceeds "under duress" through a series of stops and starts toward its destination.

Ponge worked hard but happily at putting together these word structures, with no other goal, he was known to have said, than to "give people a good time." It was Ponge's belief that the function of poetry is "to speak and, perhaps, to speak in parables." And he believed his own role was to accomplish a sort of fusion (which he compared to orgasm) between the two worlds he identified as our only homelands: the silent world of objects, and the inexhaustible French language whose quality he celebrated, "the francicity," as he called it, of the language he loved. Ponge believed that human consciousness is born from the interaction between objects and words that his own verbal cosmogony, rife with humor and with love, recalls. As a rhetorician, Ponge has affinities with Malherbe, and as a poet, with Horace; but the Ponge who found salvation in the practice of a carefully controlled language rebounding from objects onto him is without a doubt a contemporary man.

Neither Michaux nor Ponge wanted to change the world. Each of them, in different ways, sought somewhat impersonal, almost anonymous forms of poetic expression free of any concern for meaning. Gone were symbolism, correspondences, the language and the great perspectives of metaphysics. What they created, however, were controlled and indisputably literary forms. With each of them, the relation of the writer to language took the

---

[1]No translation for this passage is given in the text, since the argument depends on the rhythm in French. In English—"The rain, in the courtyard where I watch it fall, comes down at different speeds," and "The donkey stands at the end of the rope and refuses at first to go forward"—the author's point cannot be made.

form of humor. This reaction is a natural one in an artist who realizes the limitations of the linguistic medium he has inherited and who destroys it through parody or integrates it into different kinds of structures. Each of these two poets also used their texts to open, through language, a spatial, rather than a temporal dimension, which was perhaps indicative of the transformation in contemporary consciousness analyzed by Butor. And each of them saw writing as a physical activity, a sort of alchemy by means of which the text "devours its own substance" (Genette).

There is no place for these two poets under the traditional generic categories. They require and they justify the critical concept of "text," a term that reminds us the divisions into genres has never covered more than a part of the literary field. Ponge transcended mere opposition to the classical tradition—which had itself become traditional—in the name of freedom to be creative within the linguistic framework. Michaux also conceived of the text as what Ponge called a "parable." Michaux's version of this parable was gestural, Ponge's descriptive. It would seem that with these two writers the tradition pioneered by Baudelaire, Mallarmé, and Rimbaud, and described by Marcel Raymond (De Baudelaire au surréalisme) and Albert Béguin (L'Ame romantique et le Rêve), had been left behind.

15

The Theater

In May 1975, *L'Express* described the Festival Mondial du Théâtre in Nancy in the following words: "Fifteen hundred actors, forty acting companies, thirty thousand spectators; 'teeming,' 'explosive,' 'disturbing,' 'tonic/stimulating.'" It is good to evoke in contrast the year 1920 and the reopening by Jacques Copeau, after the interruption of World War I, of the small, intimate, austere Théâtre du Vieux-Colombier. Copeau was carrying on a revolution in the theater that had begun in Europe in the latter part of the nineteenth century and culminated in events like the festival in Nancy. From the beginning, this revolution overflowed the confines of national boundaries: there were Stanislavsky, Nemirovitch, and Dantchenko in Moscow; Reinhardt in Berlin; Fuchs and Eiler in Munich; the Englishman Gordon Craig; the Swiss Adolphe Appia; and, in France, Antoine and Lugné-Poe. But their impact on the customs and repertoire of sophisticated Parisian theater—the "red and gold théâtre du Boulevard" referred to by Cocteau—was negligible. It was not until the transformation of the Parisian cultural climate in the twenties, added to the persistence of a few "men of the theater" like Copeau, that a fresh departure was possible.

In 1920 the only viable theatrical activity in France was in Paris, and it was to Paris that the directors who had been inspired by Copeau took their companies and in Paris that they settled. Fifty years later, however, there was an active theatrical life not only in Nancy but in Lyon, Saint-Etienne, Toulouse—in all kinds of provincial towns, where the theater was sometimes more daring than its Parisian counterpart. The summer festivals (in Orange, Avignon, or the Marais in Paris) also contributed rhythms and modes of existence to theatrical life that were unknown in 1920. The very theatrical space had changed—the hall containing a stage with actors on it became more flexible, and drama was played in vast open-air spaces like the Papal Palace in Avignon or, for a time, in the abandoned stalls of Les Halles in Paris as well as in cafés *(cafés-théâtres)* or in very small theaters or "in-the-round."

Throughout this period of evolution the French theater experienced one of the richest phases in its history. In the course of one half-century it was decentralized and also, to a degree, internationalized. The French theater public today is not the same as it used to be—Parisian, sophisticated, middle-class. It is made up of people who are really interested in the theater, theater buffs and students, some of them specializing in experimental theater; it is also an international public and one that, in general, is infinitely better informed and more selective than the old one was. On the whole, this new public is not so much interested in a play's *text* as in the quality of its production. Theater today is not conceived as a branch of literature but as various media existing beyond the confines of literary space. The key figure in the contemporary theater is the producer-director. Paradoxically, Copeau, who sought to heighten the effect of quality texts, wanted just the reverse. No dramatic form either old or new, however, is excluded from the stage a priori: the main consideration is the interpretation and theatrical conception incorporated in any given production. For the first time since the Middle Ages, the way a play is produced has become more important than the text. It is impossible, therefore, to study the theater solely from the literary viewpoint.

There were several factors at work in this transformation, which occurred in two phases: the first ran from 1920 until about 1950. It was characterized by a group of producer-directors who created a new atmosphere in the theater, encouraged fresh talent among playwrights, and formed a new public for their work. A second phase began under the effect of two separate developments, both of which, however, were a result of the profound upheaval France experienced because of the country's defeat during World War II. The first of these developments was the government's concern regarding the paucity of cultural life in the provinces and among the working class. As a result, through the intermediary of the Direction des Arts et des Lettres, the administration increased the subsidies traditionally allotted to the theater since the time of Richelieu; it also adopted a policy of cultural dissemination and decentralization from which the theater greatly benefited. The second of these developments was the break on the part of a small group of playwrights—no doubt influenced by the feelings of the time—with the dramatic techniques and the themes of their predecessors, creating new forms of dramatic expression, variously referred to as nontheater, theater of the absurd, theater of ridicule, which required new production techniques.

The Government and the Theatrical Revolution

Jacques Copeau was a man of letters, a critic, and a playwright who approached the stage with a set of principles that were considered and unyielding. Reacting against the sumptuous theatrical decors the Ballets Russes had made fashionable before 1914, and also against decors in the naturalist style, Copeau sought a return to the austerity of the "bare stage." He set out to rehabilitate not only the theater but also the craft of acting. He created the Ecole du Vieux-Colombier for the purpose of training his own company. The actors were not to aim for stardom. They were to devote themselves to their vocation, master a difficult craft. Copeau taught his actors discipline, dignity, professionalism; and it was due to Copeau that the popular image of actors—larger-than-life, doomed to perdition—was replaced by a completely different one. Actors had always enjoyed prestige, but now they were respected as well.

Copeau thought of the theater as a rite of participation. He had the Vieux-Colombier stage rebuilt, replacing the seventeenth-century "shadow box" with an architectural format that brought the stage closer to the audience and made it more flexible. He eliminated painted sets and instead used lighting in the ways advocated by Appia and made possible by electricity. As far as repertory was concerned, Copeau wanted above all to end the divorce between literature and the stage. He revived great works from the past—the Elizabethans, Heywood and Shakespeare; the classics, especially Molière—which had traditionally been the domain of the slightly rigid, somnolent, and conventional Comédie-Française, and also attempted to attract new writing talent. Another of his aspirations was to realize a dream that had been born with the turn of the century, the dream of a popular open-air theater that would not be subject to the influence of Paris—which he considered harmful. There is scarcely a theatrical innovation in our time that was not either foreseen or inspired by Copeau. Although Copeau was forced to leave Paris in 1924 because of financial difficulties, his ideas continued to serve as the inspiration for an important group of producer-directors—Louis Jouvet, Charles Dullin, Jean Dasté, Michel de Saint-Denis—who in their own turn trained a third generation of great directors, including André Barsacq, Jean Vilar, Jean-Louis Barrault, Marcel Herrand; and then a fourth: Roger Blin, Roger Planchon, Jean-Marie Serrau, Georges Vitaly, among others.

After 1920, new companies began to spring up beside the commercial theaters and the Comédie-Française. Four of them gradually came to dominate the theatrical scene during the interwar period: the ones headed by Dullin (1921), Jouvet (1922), Georges Pitoëff—a Russian who settled in Paris—(1922), and Baty, who in 1921 founded La Chimère. Each one had his own conception of the theater. Together they formed a cartel, providing each other with mutual support against the spirit and conventions of the commercial theater. In 1926 Copeau was able to write with some justification, "For the time being, theater people—directors or producers—are ahead of writers in their thinking. Theatrical directors today have reached a point at which they are just waiting for writers to catch up with them."[1]

This marked the successful conclusion of the initial revolution in the theater. When people talked about the theater they no longer referred to the *théâtre du boulevard* or even to the *avant-garde*, but to "repertory theater" and "experimental theater." Jean Giraudoux remarked, drawing attention to this new development, "A new public was prepared for what was happening: increasingly it included musicians ready to come to terms with the theater, if the laws of the theater could obey the most basic law of music, which is the law of distinctions; and it increasingly included the well-read, who asked nothing better than to see, and to support, their favorite novelists on the stage; . . . and including, finally, an increasing number of women . . . A new corps of actors has been created. All the old words that in France had once been associated with the word "actor"—Bohemian, down-and-out, flashy, star, poverty-stricken failure, brilliant success, nobody, and somebody—were now replaced by a more normal vocabulary: culture, conviction, ensemble playing . . ."[2]

The expectations of the new public were soon met by a number of writer-dramatists. Although the prestige of the individual actor—and especially, perhaps, of the individual actress—remained strong, the director now often was associated on an equal footing with the playwright: Jouvet-Giraudoux; Barrault-Claudel; Barsacq-Anouilh; Blin-Beckett; Victor Garcia-Arrabal. Instead of writing their plays for a particular star, as they once had done, playwrights now often wrote for a particular director who, like Roger Planchon, would eventually create his own distinctive repertoire; other directors created their own distinctive type of spectacle, as Barrault did with his adaptations of Rabelais and Nietzsche, or improvised, as Ariane Mnouchkine did with her company.

After 1945 the French government, anxious to reintegrate dramatic art into the cultural life of the nation, gave official support to some of the new developments sought by the producers—not, however, without stirring up bitter controversy. This official action took two forms: decentralization, i.e., the creation of permanent repertory companies and dramatic centers in the provinces and in the suburbs of Paris (Guy Rétoré's company in Ménilmontant; the Théâtre de la Commune in Aubervilliers; the Théâtre Gérard Philipe in Saint-Denis; the Théâtre de l'Ouest Parisien—or TOP—in Boulogne Billancourt; not to mention numerous companies on the outskirts of Paris, the most famous of which is Ariane Mnouchkine's Théâtre du Soleil). The Maisons de la Culture located in various French cities began to

[1]See *Revue générale* 115 (1926).
[2]*Oeuvres littéraires diverses*, 596; talk delivered in 1931.

participate actively in the implementation of this program in 1961 (starting with Le Havre and Bourges). And back in the center of Paris the Théâtre National Populaire, which had been vegetating since the time of its inauguration in 1920, began to take on new life in 1951 under the direction of Jean Vilar. These theaters are subsidized by national and municipal government in order to facilitate access for people belonging to all social and economic levels. This "popular theater" conceived during the Occupation and born after the Liberation is not "popular" in the sense of coming from the people; it is a form of cultural activism, a disinterested way of making the theater more democratic.

The centers for dramatic art are professional theaters that are required to justify their existence by the quality of their programs and their ability to attract the public; in addition to them, permanent repertory companies have also been established, generally as a result of local initiative, and often taking the form of traveling "shows." There have also been "Young Companies" springing up almost everywhere and participating actively in the summer festivals. Political crises such as that of May 1968 notwithstanding, this effort triggered the second phase of the revolution in French theatrical life. It focused attention on the *public* and the role of the theater in relation to it. While popular theater has in general not been successful in reaching the working class, it has nevertheless achieved what it set out to do: it has attracted a new public of young people, members of the lower-middle and merchant class. The producers, who are usually idealistic and often Marxist, have tried to initiate their public in the great French theatrical tradition, and also to play a revolutionary social role. The popular theater has been responsible for questioning the theatrical conceptions which had more or less consciously been the guide for producers and playwrights between 1920 and the fifties.

Theatrical Companies

In 1970, four differing conceptions of the theater existed which, for the sake of simplification, we can associate with three names—Artaud, Brecht, and Copeau—and one event—May 1968.

From 1920 until 1950, avant-garde theater in general accepted the idea of communion and catharsis, a dramatic conception linked to the Aristotelian tradition as it evolved through Nietzsche and Mallarmé. Seen in this light the theater is a kind of ceremonial or collective rite with the effect of cleansing the public of its petty anxieties or individual problems, allowing it to participate, through the intermediary of the characters onstage with whom it identifies, in what Mallarmé called "the essential drama" of the human condition. The public internalizes the emotions and attitudes it sees on the stage. This joint participation uniting the audience in a single shared emotion is purified and controlled by the aesthetic quality of the play from which it springs. The goal is therefore to create a drama based on character and conflict. An autonomous universe is brought to life onstage in which contemporary conflicts are transfigured and contemporary feelings are illuminated. Giraudoux, a prime example of this aesthetic, believed the spectator requires of the playwright that he "reveal his own truth to him, that he confer on him, so that he may organize his own thoughts and his own feelings, that secret of which the writer is sole depository: style." In this view, the theater, by achieving a fusion of life with art, is a theater of language, antinaturalistic, metaphysical, obliquely didactic; it reconciles the spectator with his own life and ennobles his dilemmas by universalizing them. In a constantly evolving secularized society, this kind of theater would serve as a cohesive force, a link with the past and a means for initiating people into the structures of the real world. In short, the theater is the perfect instrument of culture. It is this conception of the theater that in 1945 served as the inspiration for the pioneers of popular theater, and from this conception arose the brilliant literary theater that was to flourish for almost thirty years.

Artaud and the theater of cruelty. Artaud also believed the theater should effect a catharsis, but a catharsis of a different kind. Artaud held a personal and intransigent conception of the theater as *action*. Influenced by Jarry, employed as an actor by Dullin and then Pitoëff (who in 1927 founded an ephemeral Théâtre Alfred Jarry), and briefly allied with the surrealists, Artaud was also fascinated by pantomime, which was being revived by Etienne Decroux. The opportunity he had to see the Balinese theater company during the 1931 Exposition Coloniale in Paris enabled him to develop his ideas on the theater, which he then expanded in a series of essays written between 1931 and 1933 and collected in a volume published in 1938 that twenty years later was to have an enormous impact, *Le Théâtre et son double.* Artaud broke with everything the Cartel believed in and did not respect the playwrights it had encouraged. He believed theater in the Western world was "petrified" and that it needed to return to its sources in order to come alive again—not its Greek source, but its source in the ceremonial theater of the Orient. Artaud believed Westerners refuse to make contact with the obscure and violent forces of life. He believed they repress them, turn a blind eye to them, and become exiles from a part of themselves. Oriental theater, on the other hand, unleashes these forces in the spectator "in a kind of virtual revolt" so that they can be exorcized.

This conception of the theater is important because of the dramatic principles Artaud adduced from it. First, that words in the theater are ancillary: "Dialogue, a thing that is written or spoken, has no place on the stage, it belongs in books." The language appropriate to the stage is a language of gestures, movements, postures, and objects; characters are "signs." Speech must become rhythm, incantation, outcry. Action must touch the audience's feelings directly, in order to release primitive states that have been repressed—eroticism, fear, etc.—until they reach the level of paroxysm. "I propose a kind of theater in which violent physical images will crush and mesmerize the sensibilities of audiences gripped in a vortex of forces greater than they." In this theater, named by Artaud and intended by him to be a "Theater of Cruelty," the verbal text gives way before a "language of the physical and the concrete." Superstitious faith in the text and the dictates of the author had to be "renounced." This was a return—but in a completely different spirit—to the "slice-of-life" formula of dramatic representation, but this kind of play was one that could live only as a function and emanation of the stage itself, and it was the kind that inspired Apollinaire's *Mamelles de Tirésias* and Cocteau's early essays, both authors looking for a new theatrical language, one that would be the opposite, in a word, of what Copeau was trying to do.

Le Théâtre et son double influenced a major current of dramatic thought, which still waxed strong in 1970 and was in tune with the theater of revolt characteristic of the years 1951–55, a trend that went by many names: a-theater, antitheater, theater of the absurd, experimental theater, metatheater, theater of ridicule. This school of thought also questioned the role of verbal expression, and hence the role of the text, in the theater; and, because it was successful, it relegated the type of drama it was repudiating firmly to the past.

Bertolt Brecht and political theater. It was only belatedly that Bertolt Brecht's plays and his theories of the drama had any real impact on France, when his *Berliner Ensemble* company took part in 1954, 1955, and 1957 in the Festival International de Paris. Brecht, who was playwright, producer, and director of the company he founded, created plays that illustrated his ideas. He was a Marxist who believed the purpose of the theater is to make the playgoers understand the nature of the social context they live in, and what their own responsibilities are, so that when they leave the theater after a play is over, they will have been stimulated to think and, later, to act. A typical Brecht play tells a fictitious story that unfolds in a series of episodes located in past history but whose main themes connect the story to the contemporary social and political context—for example, war in *Mother Courage*. Brecht rejected all notions of identification and catharsis. He believed the opposite, that a play should introduce a certain distance between stage and audience prompting critical reflection. Demystifying and frequently satirical, the text with Brecht resumed its central position, but its function had changed. It mimicked and schematized onstage things that were susceptible of inciting the audience to judgment—judgment not of the play but of the reality represented by the play; Brecht, like Artaud, rejected the identification of actor and character.

May 1968. After 1968 a fourth tendency emerged in the French theater: the attempt to create action theater or theater of the event, "happenings" that replaced texts written by playwrights with a collection and montage of documents or texts based on an event such as the Algerian war; or with the *collective work* of an acting company creating its own "script," and soliciting audience participation. Here the important thing is the production and the effect of spontaneity it creates.

These four conceptions of drama (the 1920–50 avant-garde represented by the pioneering work of Copeau; Artaud's Theater of Cruelty; Brecht's political theater; and post-1968 "happenings") each rested on a different way of looking at the relations between playwright, producer-director and his actors, text, staging, and audience. But none of them questioned the basic *necessity* for theater, or the theater's indispensable role in the life of the community.

The *popular theater* triggered a controversy that affected all of these attitudes. Generally speaking, the producers of popular theater were imbued at one and the same time with the conventional aesthetics of the stage, and with enthusiasm for Marxism, i.e., they were certain that they had a mission to "change the world." To them, a militant theater politically involved in contemporary problems seemed imperative and, hence, a break with the aesthetic tendencies of modern theater. Should popular drama, as Romain Rolland believed, really be written *for* the people? Or should it, as the partisans of the *Living Theater* believed, come *from* the people? And is it possible, in any case, when attempting to form a new public for dramatic art, to eliminate traditional theatrical conventions entirely? And to what degree precisely do these conventions belong to an archaic "bourgeois" culture? When people go to the theater, do they really want to see current political problems on the stage? What kind of repertoire does the public want? What are the conditions most favorable to theatrical development? There is no simple format (traditional theater, avant-garde theater, bourgeois theater, political theater, literary theater, theater happenings) that can account for the enormous diversity of the dramatic works appearing over this fifty-year period. And yet it is clear that in 1970 the situation Copeau complained of fifty years earlier was once more in evidence: a dearth of new writing talent. Does the life of dramatic art ultimately depend on literature after all?

An Evolution in the Theater: General Tendencies and Individual Works

In the drama, more clearly than in any other form of literature or art, the lines of demarcation between the era's cultural phases are discernible. Three distinct phases emerge.

From 1920 to 1938, an enormous number of plays in every imaginable form, style, and tone were produced in Paris, making it the theatrical capital of Europe. It was about 1925 that the main trends of a new theater began to emerge, which was to leave the spirit and forms of pre–World War I theater far behind it.

During the Occupation, a new generation of playwrights made its appearance for which the stage was a means for throwing some light on the controversies and intellectual upheaval created by events.

The period 1952–55 was as crucial a time for the drama as the twenties had been. It was during these years that a new group of playwrights appeared who completely rejected every trend and every preoccupation of the two generations that had preceded them. This *nouveau théâtre* acquired an international public and then petered out, leaving no real legacy behind.

A *tentative movement* toward political theater followed but did not become permanent. Theater audiences were growing and becoming better informed, but playwrights became less assertive, and less certain of what direction to follow. A half-dozen names at most come to mind, and even these are not well known outside of France.

1920–38: Modernism

In 1920 the reigning post–World War I spirit was one of "release" and of reaction against the conformity of the "home front." The public's tastes were also changing, and this had a profound effect on the conventions of the commercial theater and the authors—Alfred Capus, Robert de Flers and Gaston de Caillavet, Henry Bataille—who sustained it and who passed swiftly into eclipse. Although the quality of what appeared on the stage varied greatly, audiences for both the commercial theater and for "directors" theater exhibited the same tastes: they wanted *comedy,* in all of its forms, and intimate dramas tinged with the melancholy of illusions lost when dreams confront reality. The theme of disillusion was the most common. The king of the commercial theater was Sacha Guitry, and he remained king until his death, embroidering countless variations on the theme of the seducer (a Parisian man of the world) who is himself seduced. After 1922, however, the year Dullin produced *La Volupté de l'honneur,* it was Pirandello who dominated the French stage, tying together the scattered dramatic themes then current and exerting a profound influence on other playwrights. Pirandello's plays explored the private and complex world of the inner self, the fluctuations of personality and the strange workings of the conflict between illusion and reality. Pirandello attacked the very concept of personality that had for so long sustained the idea of theatrical character, and in doing so he employed a strategy that was not unfamiliar to other innovators. Like Cocteau, Pirandello claimed there is a specifically stage reality, that the artist creates a reality "more real" than the sketchy reality of life; that all truth is subjective and relative; that no human "situation" is static and definable; that personality is an imprecise and fluctuating thing. Pirandello undermined those conventions most dear to bourgeois drama, causing the latter despite certain successes (Henri Bernstein, Edouard Bourdet) to become outmoded.

Farce during this period became more poetic, and more varied. Jules

Romains's classic farces *M. Le Trouhadec saisi par la débauche* and *Knock ou le Triomphe de la médecine* enjoyed great success. But other forms of farce were more indicative of the times and sketched the outlines of the things that lay ahead in the theatrical revolution of the fifties.

In 1921, Jean Cocteau's *Les Mariés de la Tour Eiffel* and Roger Vitrac's *Victor ou les Enfants au pouvoir*—a play that did not become popular until it was revived in 1962—made use dramatically of elements that were visual. In his depiction of a middle-class wedding reception taking place in a restaurant on the Eiffel Tower, Cocteau created what he called a "poetry of the theater." He gave concrete form to images that had been slumbering within the clichés of everyday language. His marionette stage is populated with phonographs that talk and cameras that have lions and ostriches popping out of them instead of "little birds." And what Vitrac did was to create an incongruous situation by showing the evolution onstage of a child-giant, the Victor of the title, who at nine years of age vastly surpasses the drab adults surrounding him in his ability to understand what is going on. In another vein, Fernand Crommelynck also brought to a farce like his *Cocu magnifique* magnificent resources of language, its incongruity introducing into farce an element of ambiguity foreshadowing some of the developments in drama that were to come, as did the short, "surrealizing" plays of Breton or Aragon.

Other French playwrights of this period were less daring and restricted themselves to minor formal innovations. For example, they often abandoned the old division of a play into acts, preferring a series of tableaux. They also rejected the flawless rhetoric providing logical explanations for the action. They created plays in which a dialogue of indirect allusion emerges from a silent background (Jean-Jacques Bernard) or seems itself to be a kind of silence in which true feelings are hidden (Denys Amiel). They eliminated the logical markers articulating the development of the action. Henri-René Lenormand—a playwright famous between the two world wars, though forgotten today—transposed psychological conflicts from the conscious to the subconscious; and Charles Vildrac (whose *Le Paquebot Tenacity* was popular in 1920) was inspired by Chekhov and staged intimate dramas dealing with ordinary people, while Jean Sarment revived a style of sentimental comedy reminiscent of Musset.

In 1928 Giraudoux's first play, *Siegfried,* produced by Jouvet, played to an enthusiastic Paris audience, which for twenty years longer and well beyond his death (with *La Folle de Chaillot* and *Pour Lucrèce,* both produced posthumously) Giraudoux continued to dazzle. Popular as a novelist with a small élite, Giraudoux absorbed what the as yet little known Claudel had brought to the theater: the creation onstage of an autonomous universe that transfigured and illuminated everyday life. Although they exhibit wide variations in terms of form, Giraudoux's fourteen plays all belong to a single aesthetic vision, one that visibly influenced authors as various as Jacques

Audiberti, Jules Supervielle, Jean Anouilh, and Jean-Paul Sartre when they wrote for the stage. And it was primarily against Giraudoux that the play-wrights of this period reacted. All of Giraudoux's plays were myths, either freshly created or reworked; and his staging was more festival than sacred rite. Giraudoux exploited every resource of the language to transport his audiences into an *imaginary* world, "a microcosm" reflecting the various real life attitudes and conflicts represented by his characters. Rife with allusions and analogies of an often whimsical nature, Giraudoux's plays create an atmosphere rather than developing specifically delimited action. Giraudoux took legend as his canvas, and on it he represented in dramatic form the conflicts they implied, creating an occasionally prophetic interplay of forces illuminating the dilemmas, the frailties, and the sensibility of his time. After the brilliant and paradoxical *Siegfried,* a play constructed around the theme of the contrast between the French and the German sensibilities, Giraudoux's other plays, notably *La Guerre de Troie n'aura pas lieu* and *Electre,* dealt with the larger themes of collective violence: civil war and international war. Giraudoux's plays broke every conventional formal rule (for example, the development of realistic action or psychologi-cal motivation). They forced audiences to let themselves be carried away by what they saw on the stage. Giraudoux believed playwrights are "magi-cians" whose primary responsibility is to "bewitch." They must tear the rational French spectator away from the boundaries of his everyday life. For the space of two hours, they must appeal to the sensibility, the imagination, and all of the senses so as to open the way for the audience into a mythic realm where the forces that control human destiny will be revealed. Although as dramatists they were very different, Giraudoux and Artaud both agreed about the inhumanity of those forces confronted or unleashed by the characters in their respective plays: Hector and Ulysses; Electra and Aegisthus; Siegfried or Amphitryon. The underlying theme of all Giraudoux's plays is the unresolvable conflict between man's noble aspira-tions, and reality as it must be lived. These plays dominated French theater between the two world wars.

Jean Cocteau, from *Les Mariés de la Tour Eiffel* to his final play, *Bacchus* (1951), gave the French stage eleven plays and four adaptations. Cocteau remained consistent with his original viewpoint concerning the "poetry" of the stage, from the beginning of his career making a distinction between the "show," or exterior form of a play, and its meaning. He believed any form of "show"—romantic drama, bourgeois drama, comedy of manners, tragedy—could coexist with any other. Cocteau did not subscribe to the opinion that there is a "modern" art appropriate to every historical period and, like all great directors before and after him, worked toward the forma-tion of free and open taste. In *Orphée* (1926) and *La Machine infernale* (1934) he reworked familiar myths and reinterpreted them in terms that were modern and Freudian. The central character in each of these two plays is searching for his own identity, and the complexities of his various levels of consciousness are represented on the stage in the person of symbolic characters, or the form of symbolic objects.

The Anxious Thirties:
Metamorphosis of the Bourgeois Theater

Armand Salacrou and Jean Anouilh were devoted stagecraftsmen who wrote plays, for Dullin and Barsacq respectively, that were accessible to the public because they took certain elements of bourgeois drama and reworked them. For both of these playwrights a play was a dynamic entity that "involved" its author and expressed his own private world. They reflected, in a more direct way than either Giraudoux or Cocteau, the anxiety characteristic of the thirties. It was in the early thirties that Salacrou began to make a name for himself with plays like *Une femme libre* (1934) and *La Terre est ronde* (1934). Basically, these plays belonged under the heading of bourgeois drama: in general both sets and characters were based on a middle-class environment, and plots revolved around adultery or money. But Salacrou had been influenced by surrealism. For him this reality of the everyday opened up onto the unknown. Long before the word became fashionable, Salacrou already had a keen sense of the "absurd," of the metaphysical void lurking behind the everyday. The *technical experiments* Salacrou undertook in an attempt to communicate this outlook made him a precursor of things to come: Salacrou believed that my manipulating time, all that is hidden will be revealed. This is why he destroyed the linear sequence of dramatic action. He used flashbacks, and split personalities—i.e., confrontation and dialogue between a character and his other self in a given moment of time; he even went so far as to make the life of his characters progress backward from death to birth *(Sens interdit)*.

It was actually Jean Anouilh, however, who with more than thirty plays to his credit, starting with *Le Voyageur sans bagage* (1937), clearly dominated the French stage during the thirties. It was also with Anouilh that we see the paradox of the so-called avant-garde theater developing. Ever since the turn of the century, producers and critics alike had been seeking a form of drama capable of reaching a large public. But commercial success and dramatic worth appeared to most critics to be mutually exclusive. Just when people were beginning to discover Molière the entertainer beneath the mask of Molière the textbook moralist, critics were moralizing on the subject of Anouilh the entertainer. But Anouilh's plays, in all of their great diversity going from a slight entertainment such as *Le Bal des voleurs* to the vast historical fresco of *Becket, ou l'honneur de Dieu,* partook of the intense and joyous life that is dramatic creation itself. Rife with a multiplicity of characters and situations, the theme of Anouilh's drama is playacting, in all of its forms, and the confrontation with reality. Anouilh, to use his own classifications, wrote black plays, rose-colored plays, grim plays, and costume plays, all of which deal with the conflict between reality and the impulses of dream or emotion. It is as a result of this conflict that Anouilh's characters—possible, impossible, comic, pathetic, tragic, historical, or invented—live and die. In this universe the critics have identified two kinds of people: the "pure"—usually young—and the "vile"—adults stained by compromise—and a thematic of negation. The "pure" refuse to play the game of life. This seems somewhat simplistic when we consider the complexity of a world in which everything is possible, but when once a choice has been made, everything else is eliminated. When an Anouilh character says yes, he is also saying no. In any case, Anouilh's plays are a locus of conflict, trials, decisions, and characters who are all *imaginary*, hence his whimsy.

Around these major figures another body of dramatic work grew up whose dominant note was poetry; a *poets' theater* attempted to succeed onstage. For Jules Supervielle, for example, the stage was an extension of his poetry, a world of legend where dream mingled with invention, humor, and sober reflection *(La Belle au bois, La Première Famille, Le Voleur d'enfants, Schéhérazade)*. And at the same time, between 1919 and 1939, Michel Ghelderode was creating a drama of violence and ridicule based on eroticism and death and inspired by the paintings of Brueghel, Bosch, and James Ensor. Three of these plays, *Fastes d'Enfer* (1924), *Hop Signor!* (1931), and *Escurial* (1927) were revived at a much later date in Paris (1947, 1948, and 1949, respectively) and served as a prelude to the *nouveau théâtre* of the fifties.

The War Years: The Drama of Ideas

In contrast to the eclipse it suffered during World War I, French theater during World War II remained active, despite material difficulties and censorship. The decade of the forties witnessed the disappearance of Giraudoux (1944), but also, and more significantly, of the great producers—Pitoëff, Lugné-Poe, Copeau, and Dullin; they were followed in 1951–52 by Jouvet and Baty. This was the time Henry de Montherlant, Jean-Paul Sartre, and Albert Camus were making their debut as playwrights, with Jean-Louis Barrault and Jean Vilar succeeding the producers of the old Cartel.

Although individually very different as playwrights, Montherlant, Sartre, and Camus all put the main *character* back on center stage; and all three rejected the mythical situation and characters in favor of characters and situations drawn either from current events or from history. They took French theater in the direction of a new psychological realism, but within the framework of dramatic structures that were more often than not far removed from the conventions of bourgeois drama that Sartre ultimately favored. Montherlant and Camus worked toward a revival of tragedy. What

Montherlant wanted was to rediscover the austere outlines and spare language of classical drama and to bring to life onstage the conflicts and fate of complex, proud, and violent characters refusing to bow to the values of their society. From his first play, *La Reine morte* (1942), to his last, *La Guerre civile* (staged in 1965), the dozen or so works written by Montherlant for the theater constitute an ensemble of high literary worth standing outside the main trends of his period. Camus concentrated on an exploration of the possibilities and the limitations of man, and his plays deal with the irreducible hiatus between thought and action. Camus's dramas are tightly wound around tragic antinomies within which man the absurd struggles to find unity.

Sartre's brilliant plays are molded in forms that are immediately accessible. Sartre used the stage not so much to *explore* the conflicts of his contemporaries as to create an "effective theater" that will have an impact on the public. Situation, conflict, action, and language are all used in the service of Sartre's concept of the social role that politically involved literature should play. He believed the theater should be in direct contact with current events; and that at the same time it should be structured according to his own philosophy, which was in essence dramatic. Sartre has clearly stated his own aims: a drama of "extreme situation," i.e., of situations which force the characters to reveal themselves under circumstances where they have only two possible choices, one of which is death. Sartre's plays are dramatic realizations of a psychological and philosophical system. But because what Sartre described was the concrete world of the here and now, his plays are anchored in a neorealism belied by the flowing verbal rhetoric of his characters. In Sartre's best plays, such as *Huis clos,* thesis and theatricality are balanced and fused in the language. In his weaker ones, the philosophical argument destroys the drama. Seven of Sartre's plays, from *Les Mouches* (1943) to *Les Séquestrés d'Altona* (1959), sustained a "theater of ideas" not unreminiscent of George Bernard Shaw and Henrik Ibsen.

These playwrights were absorbed in the political conflicts of their time and they attempted, as Giraudoux had done, to stage major public issues, but they did so without Giraudoux's imaginative sleight of hand. As foreshadowed by the plays of Christian existentialist philosopher Gabriel Marcel, French theater by midcentury had become as somber and intellectually demanding as the political events of the time.

There was also a peripheral French theater playing on the stages of the avant-garde that with Jacques Audiberti, Georges Schéhadé, and Georges Neveux prolonged the theater of the interwar period and was lively, nonrealistic, and idiosyncratic. And with Pichette's *Epiphanies* and *Nucléa* the violent rhetoric of revolt burst for a moment onto the stage, without, however, inspiring the revolution some people were waiting for. But the poets and playwrights of the human condition—heirs, to a man, of Giraudoux and Claudel, the latter having finally been brought to the stage by Jean-

Louis Barrault—used language as the basis for their dramas. And it was language that Artaud attacked, and that the French theater of the fifties rejected.

"Antitheater": A New Kind of Drama

The revelation of a new kind of drama based on a new way of using the stage occurred in 1953 as a result of the controversy following production of *En attendant Godot,* a play written by the then unknown Irishman Samuel Beckett. This and other plays by Beckett, Ionesco, and Adamov raised questions concerning dramatic structure, the function of language, and the nature of action; in addition, other avenues were being explored by Jean Genet and Jean Tardieu.

"Antitheater," also known as "theater of the absurd," has been the subject of ample analysis, notably by Emmanuel Jacquart, in *Le Théâtre de la dérision* (Gallimard, 1974). Here we will only briefly recall its major characteristics: minimization of scenery and action; minimization and depersonalization of characters, who are given no social identity and often no name; the use of clowns, marionnettes, and robots reminiscent of Guignol, mime, or the circus; minimization of dialogue, each of these playwrights employing it in his own particular way. Certain characteristics were shared by all of these dramatists—for example, dissociation of word from gesture, words from meaning, dialogue from situation. Parody, satire, and irony were much in evidence. Characters became passive, and action disappeared from the stage. Plays were based on verbal exchange within a static situation, or on the disintegration of the characters within a mobile one. The scenery, composed of specific concrete objects, as in the German expressionist theater, often represented imperfectly repressed psychological states. No *meaning,* and no *interpretation* of the action was ever given. Each of these authors, however, eventually went his own way, Beckett toward even greater minimization of dramatic elements, Ionesco toward broader themes and larger framework for his plays, and Adamov toward the kind of political theater inspired by Brecht.

In four masterly plays, *Les Bonnes, Le Balcon, Les Nègres,* and *Les Paravents,* Jean Genet created what has been referred to as the "theater of the possessed." In these plays the world of the outlaw is shown in opposition to the world of established power, the relation between them effected through the spell cast by masquerade. In this dramatic world a language that is ceremonious and dangerous reigns supreme. The individual characters resemble priests officiating at a Black Mass; Genet recreates its subversive and mystical ceremonial with skill and determination. At the other extreme we find Jean Tardieu, who in his short plays experimented with abstract theater based on the similarities betwen drama and music (*La Sonate; Conversation-Sinfonietta;* and *L'ABC de notre vie,* which was in the form of a concerto), in an effort to discover new formal structures to take the place of the discredited structures of the past. Tardieu's experiments were similar to those being undertaken in the plastic arts and in music and concentrated on dramatic *form* rather than *content*. As Tardieu himself once pointed out, his plays are really *Action Poems*.

The Uncertain Sixties

By about 1960 the themes and the stage language of these innovators had been assimilated by French theater. The successors of Beckett and Ionesco, none of whom were French (Pinter, Albee, Dürrenmatt, Peter Weiss, Gombrovicz), were warmly welcomed in Paris, where they continued to employ the methods of their predecessors, while at the same time demonstrating a tendency to restore a social or psychological dimension to the theater. The French public showed that its tastes were eclectic: vaudeville was as popular as Brecht; Feydeau was a smash hit. As a result of the expansion of theater in the provinces, there was a large crop of new directors—Gérôme, Planchon, Blin, Serreau, Vitaly, Reybaz, Mauclair, Polierei—to carry on the work of the older generation. The two names dominating the theatrical scene were Anouilh and Ionesco. A tentative move toward political theater (early indications of which were Sartre's *Nekrassov* and Marcel Aymé's *La Tête des autres*) was represented by Adamov's later plays, the works of Armand Gatti and the posthumous production of two farces by Boris Vian *(Les Bâtisseurs d'empire* and *Le Goûter des généraux)*. François Billetdoux, Roland Dubillard, and René de Obaldia maintained the "poetic" theater tradition, in both its nostalgic and its comic vein. Three novelists—Robert Pinget, Marguerite Duras, and Nathalie Sarraute—attempted to give psychological drama new form. There was only one playwright, Fernando Arrabal, a Spaniard by birth whose work is reminiscent of Jean Genet's, who obviously set out—in what he called "panic theater"—to create his own highly erotic, rebellious theater of cruelty. It is hard to tell today where the French theater will be tomorrow, but that it will evolve toward new ways of making use of the basic elements of the stage seems certain.

Conclusion

In 1970 no major identifiable literary trend was in evidence, apart from the explosion of feminist literature that was just then beginning to seek appropriate outlets. This phenomenon spotlighted retrospectively a body of literature that had often been neglected by the critical establishment: the woman's voice. Works by Colette and by Simone de Beauvoir were seen in a new light. Names like Marguerite Yourcenar, Simone Weil, Nathalie Sarraute, Marguerite Duras, Violette Leduc, Monique Wittig, and Hélène Cixous became reference points in this movement. An essential fact that had been made obvious by the emergence of Francophone literature, was noted anew: that literary space, like any other, can never be inflexibly established once and for all. Whenever people talk about "the death of the novel" or "the death of literature," they are creating an abstraction out of the fluidity of literary space, out of that extreme plasticity which is continuously generating new groupings, opening up new perspectives, and, like the very space we live in, showing us new configurations with every passing day.[3]

[3]The author wishes to thank the Macmillan Company, New York, for kind permission to use in this chapter certain exerpts from her book *Twentieth Century French Drama*, written in collaboration with Alexander Kroff.

Five

The Literary Personalities of a Half-century in Transition

Introduction

The presiding spirit of this half-century has been a turbulent and unquiet one, but also provocative and self-confident. Theoretical speculations and formal experiments of the most audacious kind have proliferated, often sharing with each other only a taste for adventure. At a deeper level, however, we can observe some constants in the literary field: an increasingly keen awareness of the planetary and even cosmic context in which mankind finds itself today; a new and as yet ill-defined psychological and metaphysical viewpoint; a feeling of discontent with a literary enterprise that has become problematical. It seems to us that during this period, more than at any other time in history, writers have bitterly debated the limitations of language, while at the same time exploiting its resources to the utmost. They have frequently assumed the paradoxical position of simultaneously rejecting the language of the collectivity because of its function as an instrument of social constraint, and attempting to achieve. total subjectivity by pushing the arbitrariness of writing to the point of incommunicability in order to reach a collective or noncoded area existing outside the boundaries of the unreliable ego.

If it is true that, to be considered modern, a period must be characterized by the disintegration of commonly accepted stylistic norms and the development of highly diversified individual styles, then our own period is modern in an even profounder way than was the modernism advocated before 1920 by the futurists. There has not necessarily been any single poetics connecting individual works to one another. This has made the chapter that follows a difficult one to write. In it we shall be referring to some of the literary works which, from decade to decade, seem to us to have illuminated the intellectual climate of the time while also in large measure contributing to its creation. But the defining characteristic of that intellectual climate has been its diversity. In order not to oversimplify, we have chosen two figures of comparable stature but antithetical nature from each decade, hoping in this way to adduce indirectly the many intermediary nuances coloring a literary spectrum that is never all black or all white. It goes without saying, however, that although we attribute a high value to their literary work, we are not attempting to establish a hierarchical classification in which they are placed at the top of the ladder in relation to their contemporaries. We have selected the particular writers we did because of their *representative* value and because at a given moment in time their work coincided with an intellectual and affective climate of which it served as both emblem and expression.

From the twenties we have chosen Jean Cocteau and his implacable antagonist André Breton; for the thirties, André Malraux and Louis-Fernand Céline. For the forties, the similarities and dissimilarities between Simone de Beauvoir and Albert Camus, we feel, deeply illuminate the vicissitudes of the generation that gained prominence between 1942 and 1945; the crucial role played by Sartre has already been mentioned. After 1950, no single literary figure stands out this clearly. But it seemed to us that the development of two writers, Claude Simon and Marguerite Duras, and the different phases they went through, offer the best illustration of the spirit of those years. This is not a classification according to generation: Claude Simon belongs to Camus's generation, and so does Marguerite Duras; Céline belongs to Breton's. The criterion is the moment their work first began to have an impact on the public, a specific moment that the total span of a writer's development greatly exceeds. Cocteau's first poems and his final play, *Bacchus,* were separated by fifty years.

The very way in which a work touches the public will vary, and will partake of the literary configuration of its time. It was Breton's personality rather than his works that first gained him fame, for example; his major texts are still little known (with the exception of the *Manifestos*), and *Fata Morgana, Arcane 17,* and *Ode à Charles Fourier* were not published until the forties. In Cocteau's case, on the other hand, we might say that both the man and his work sold from the start. Céline's reputation did not begin to take off until 1965. And the tiny circle of initiates that follows the work of Claude Simon or Marguerite Duras tells us as much about that particular literary climate as the vast audiences Malraux, Simone de Beauvoir, and Camus were able to reach.

16

The Twenties:
Jean Cocteau and
André Breton

In 1920 Jean Cocteau and André Breton were both active members of the dadaist group that created the scandal at the Palais des Fêtes. Forty years later Cocteau was a member of the French Academy, and Breton, who for ten years past had almost stopped writing completely, was recognized as the uncontested master of several generations of poets and a man who had given a movement of astounding fecundity its initial impetus. Both had held the center of the Parisian stage during the twenties, and both, always highly controversial, constantly exhibited an irreducible nonconformism that with Cocteau was cavalier, and with Breton, moral. Both withstood the violent political passions of the forties: Cocteau, who remained in France, because the untrammeled anarchy of his behavior caused the small clique of Parisian collaborationist writers to look upon him with suspicion. His plays were outlawed. Breton, by definition an implacable enemy of all constraint and an intransigent anti-Nazi, was forced to go abroad, first to Mexico and then to the United States. Neither participated directly in the Resistance, and so they remained on the periphery of political vendettas. Cocteau unintentionally created a ripple of scandal with his last play, *Bacchus* (1952), which Mauriac chastized for its subversiveness because of its lack of respect for the Christian religion. But by midcentury, both were being left behind by the literary movement. Breton still enjoyed considerable prestige, in contrast to the somewhat affectionate indifference with which Cocteau was regarded. It was a fact, nonetheless, that after the brilliant role they had played during the twenties the increasing politicization of culture left them in the shade.

Their careers intersected only briefly, around 1920. They both, however, shared some of the ideals characteristic of the time, mainly a desire to point literature in new directions and a keen sense of the interdependence of the arts (painting and film) and literature. And both were equally fascinated by the impact on the imagination of their generation exerted by the discovery of the subconscious and its burden of egocentricity and ambiguity. Toward the decade's end, when Breton (in *Nadja*) asked the question "Who am I?" he was in fact echoing a doubt to which Cocteau's play *Orphée* furnished a response. But the frame of reference in which this doubt was expressed and the philosophical methods of the two writers were not the same; the major and even the minor points of difference between them contained in latent form the various elements which, because of their dissociation, were ultimately to result in some of the divisions we have already noted in the subsequent development of French literature.

By the year 1920 Cocteau was no longer just a beginner. He had just celebrated his thirtieth birthday. *Parade* had opened three years earlier, and Apollinaire had called attention at the time to the ballet's pioneering role: he saw in it "a kind of surrealism . . . the point of departure for a series of expressions of the New Spirit . . . that is bound to seduce the elite and promises to revolutionize our customs as well as our art in a spirit of universal joy." It was the joy of invention rather than the spirit of rebellion that distinguished Cocteau at this stage; he reacted to art, not to society.

Cocteau, a precocious imitator of the neo-Symbolist poets, broke away from this influence after his first three collections of poems, and turned to nonliterary masters for his inspiration—to Diaghilev, Satie, and Picasso, among others. Under their influence he seemed to gain awareness of the craftsmanship involved in art, and of the plasticity of the various media. He always remained a *practical* artist for whom the object of the creative act is a *production* designed for public consumption. It seemed self-evident, to the young man who had witnessed public reaction to the performance of *Le Sacre du printemps,* that a production should also be designed to create scandal. For Cocteau, however, scandal was not an end in itself; it was simply the sign that certain aesthetic taboos had been breached.

Cocteau's relation to the dada group could never be anything but tenuous. He believed that art is always a performance and must have an audience. Not just any audience, either, but the "elite" referred to by Apollinaire, limited in Cocteau's view essentially to those circles in which worldly Parisians mingled with "performers" in some sense of the word: clowns and prizefighters as well as artists; aristocratic patrons of the arts and wealthy hostesses; stars of the stage; literary figures, painters, and composers; Coco Chanel, Edith Piaf, and Jacques Maritain. This was not so much snobbery on Cocteau's part as legend would have it; it was more a particular way of looking at life. For Cocteau, life was a perpetual invention, a creation of new forms whose ultimate purpose is art. Cocteau was always in continuous motion, producing a play, decorating a wall, making a film, supporting and launching some newly discovered talent—"Les Six," Radiguet, Al Brown, Jean Marais, Jean Genet. Cocteau's life was his studio, and he was always at work in it.

It is not surprising, therefore, that a life whose vicissitudes and obsessions were almost instantaneously transformed into subjects for literature or art should present what amounts to a cinematographic record of the characteristic experiences and attitudes of the time: the first airplane flights (Le Cap de Bonne-Espérance); the sinister "long vacation" represented by the war (Thomas l'imposteur); adolescent crisis (Le Grand écart); homosexuality (Le Livre blanc); and all the other sexual impulses uncovered by Freud, such as incest, and their opposites—sexuality and death, for example (Les Enfants terribles, Les Parents terribles, La Machine infernale); the impossibility of conversion to Catholicism (Lettre à Maritain). "For half a century," wrote Michel Décaudin, "Cocteau, because of the way he lived and the diversity of what he did, was at the very center of the artistic and literary movement of his time. His omnipresence and his omnicuriosity made him one of the most sensitive indicators of what was happening in society, in literature, in theater and film, as well as in music and in painting."[1]

But was he an indicator of everything that was happening? That would be saying a lot. Cocteau's participation in the great movement of revolt that characterized his era was more apparent than real. He never questioned either the social order or literature. He was not interested in "changing the world."

Three constants distinguish Cocteau's apparently heterogeneous work. First, the highly visual quality it shares with the plastic arts and painting, and particularly with dance, which explains why Cocteau was able to let himself go most freely in film. This quality prejudiced him in favor of art-as-performance (art designed for an audience). His aim was to provoke, astound, or scandalize. Second, Cocteau shared with his artist friends a conception of art as craftsmanship; he enjoyed inventing freely and making free use of literary and other forms which he employed in idiosyncratic ways. This polymorphism earned Cocteau an undeserved reputation as an aesthete whose technical virtuosity concealed a void. But his virtuosity was a problem, the constant temptation to mass-produce literary objects: a romantic drama following a bourgeois drama; a fairy tale after a classical tragedy with Freudian overtones. It was redeemed by the fact his work was centered on painful reality—the poet's "existential dilemma," the enigma of an ego threatened with dispersion but successfully reassembled through the practice of art.

Cocteau's work is in fact based on the myth, inherited from the romantics, of the outcast poet, victim of a fate dedicating him to suffering and exile, the price he must pay for the mysterious activity that he serves as agent rather than initiator. But with Cocteau, drugs and Freudianism had made the notion of the subconscious a familiar one, and he transformed the romantic myth in terms of obsessive fantasy figures invading the poet's ego and holding power over the "key" to his existence. The theme of a quest for

[1]Jean Cocteau, La Revue des lettres modernes, 1972, 3.

identity, and unity, runs through an entire current of literature illustrated by the works of Proust and Gide; here it is reworked, but in a new way. Cocteau's world was haunted by the "double" of the German romantics that was fashionable at the time, and also by an obsession with the three-pronged trap of fate, death, and beauty in which the poet is caught.

Performance and spectacle, whether occurring within or without, whether experienced or created, were the preferred elements of Cocteau. In preference to the language of psychological analysis, he chose the elaborate and enigmatic language of his own hallucinatory fantasies transformed into myths of his own making. It was these myths that gave Cocteau his contact—if only fleeting—with some of the principal themes of his time. In his autobiographical notes—especially in *Journal d'un inconnu*—Cocteau explains the origin of these myths, which were already apparent in the war poem *Discours du grand sommeil* and an early story, *Le Potomak*.

Cocteau, in his own inner world, transformed his emotions into stage sets and fetishes—statues, decks of cards, a snowball, mirrors, a horse—that often had their roots in memories of his childhood. He then transformed these fragments of a personal imaginary universe into myth; they sustained a legend he sought to free himself from through the act of writing: "Hidden, I am hidden beneath a cloak of fables: they stick to me like tar only worse," he said, or, "I am a lie that speaks the truth." Even in his lyric poems the structure Cocteau employed was visual and basically dramatic: a series of tableaux; elaborations on indefinitely varied forms, or the use of familiar forms once and then never again; a language of analogue and image translating a subjective drama into concrete terms—these traits gave Cocteau's diverse work its underlying unity.

An imitator in his early work of the neosymbolist poets, Cocteau later turned to the modernist impressionism to which some of his first pieces, and notably his first novel, *Le Grand Ecart*, belonged. To this impressionism belongs his "critical poetry," reminiscent of Paul Morand, and sometimes of Max Jacob or Giraudoux because of its speed, its tendency to ellipsis, paradox, allusion, and wit; and also because of its idiosyncracy: "Mirrors would do well to reflect a little longer before sending back images." "Greece had a blind face. Egypt looked forward sideways." "The gimmick is art." "Rimbaud and Mallarmé are Adam and Eve. Cézanne is the apple." The tone of Cocteau's writing oscillated between the two extremes, both enigmatic, of hallucination and wit; just as his stage sets oscillated between abstraction and dream (nightmarish landscapes, or enchanted, fairy-tale gardens). Like Morand or Jacob, Cocteau maintained an attitude of skeptical mockery in relation to the polished language of the typical man of letters, drawing away from them in order to learn from masters who were not literary: Diaghilev, Satie, Picasso, Chirico. *Parade* and *Le Bœuf sur le toit* had no need of words. Cocteau served his apprenticeship as a man of the theater with these two ballets, and with them he discovered his personal artistic vision.

Between 1920 and 1932 Cocteau made his name in every genre at once: he produced six volumes of verse, four novels, two plays, and three adaptations, "modernizing" *Romeo and Juliet, Antigone,* and *Oedipus Rex;* he also produced seven works of "critical poetry," in which critical reflections were mixed with day-to-day chronicle *(Portrait-Souvenirs)* and autobiography; and, in addition, the first of his nine films, *Le Sang d'un poète.* Out of this total were some obviously successful achievements: *Plain-chant* and *Opéra* (poems); *Thomas l'imposteur* and *Les Enfants terribles* (novels); *Les Mariés de la Tour Eiffel* and *Orphée* (plays); *Le Rappel à l'ordre* and *Opium* (critical reflections and autobiography). The variations of form from one work to another within the framework of a single genre is striking. Cocteau, however, classified everything he wrote under the general heading of "poetry," thus emphasizing a deeper coherence linked to his basic "approach" *(Démarche d'un poète),* which was already discernible in 1932.

From 1933 until the 1952 production of his last play, *Bacchus,* Cocteau concentrated primarily on theater and film. Then came two collections of poetry, *Le Chiffre sept* and *Clair-Obscur,* and two autobiographical works, *La Difficulté d'être* and *Journal d'un inconnu,* marking a period of introspection foreshadowed by his revival of the Orpheus theme in a film. Because Cocteau's successes with a sometimes recalcitrant public came mainly through his plays and films, we will concentrate on the theater in our attempt to give a rapid summary of his work.

For Cocteau, plays were "big transmitters you put on the stage" to communicate in visible form that which is veiled by the more secret language of a poem, or of a "waking dream"; his films and his novels—notably *Les Enfants terribles*—emerged from this concept. The theater also offered Cocteau the most favorable conditions for creating a synthesis in which the impulses impelling him toward art might achieve a balance. A theatrical renaissance was one of the cultural facts of the interwar period—perhaps of the entire period under discussion—making Cocteau's work in this area particularly significant in terms of his times. As a young virtuoso swept up in the fashions of the moment, Cocteau expressed in visual terms, in *Parade,* a rudimentary aesthetic of performance he was subsequently to develop in greater depth, and to which he always remained faithful: in this ballet, three variously costumed dancers appear before a closed circus tent, while two managers in the guise of phonographs made of colored cardboard vainly indicate that the performance is really inside the tent. The ballet's basic elements are functional: a sense of spectacle is supposed to grow from their invisible relations to one another. They could easily be replaced as need be by elements with other connotations—bourgeois, legendary, fairy tale—according to the code desired. The work's "modernism" resided less in the visible figures and more in the invisible order controlling their apparent anarchy: this ballet, as a visible spectacle subject to invisible control, represented an early sign of an as yet indecisive constructivist "postmodernism."

Les Mariés de la Tour Eiffel is characterized by a wealth of invention that is playful but controlled: all the arts, and all the current artistic fads, are brought into play. In it we see a puppet show whose theme, a traditional wedding breakfast, is modernized by the background of the Eiffel Tower, a juxtaposition echoed by the music accompanying the play, modernizations of traditional melodies composed by "Les Six." The whimsical and unpredictable dynamics of the situation emerge as if spontaneously from the latent images behind the threadbare clichés of its language. Taking form before the spectator's eyes, these images begin to move about. The play is a linguistic machine not dissimilar to Picabia's self-destruct machines. With good-humored wit it parodies and takes apart the myths of the petite bourgeoisie. Its wordplay and logic of the absurd give it much in common with the productions of the dadaists and the exercises of the surrealists, but its spirit was not the same: Cocteau set out deliberately to create an organized, stylized spectacle. Scenery, music, commentary, movements of the actor-puppets, inconsistencies, and trickery were all arranged in order to create a single impression of antic absurdity. In so doing, Cocteau drew heavily on the ideas and wordplay he admired in Lewis Carroll's *Alice in Wonderland.*

The same kind of transition from the literary to the visual presides in a different key over the "contractions" Cocteau effected on such hallowed texts as *Romeo and Juliet, Antigone,* and *Oedipus Rex.* In this he was a precursor of Artaud, who a dozen years later was to attack the reverence that locked classical texts into scenic and linguistic conventions long outmoded. When dealing with *Antigone,* a play he greatly respected, Cocteau made the costumes and scenery create the desired atmosphere of expectation and anguish, while reducing dialogue to the bare minimum necessary to advance the action. This reduction of language relative to the other elements of the play places Cocteau at one of the aesthetic extremes of his time and was the prelude to some of the things he was to undertake later on: his "combinatoires" and textual interplays.

Cocteau's development was based not on dada but on the modernist New Spirit. According to Radiguet, and under his influence, between 1921 and 1923 Cocteau realized that the time for games was over; and it was just at this time that Breton began to detach himself from the dadaist movement. But Cocteau continued to experiment with form. No longer satisfied with being simply the agent of new, unexpected verbal and visual juxtapositions, a kind of "magician" or "joiner" as circumstance required, he began looking for ways to make the interior spectacle to which *Parade* had referred into a visible one. The dadaists and the budding surrealists were not fooled; they realized there was a gulf between Cocteau and themselves, and they did not treat him kindly. Two of Cocteau's works marked this crucial moment, which also coincided with the end of the great period of general release that had followed World War I: *Poésie* (1924) and the play *Orphée* (1926). In *Poésie,* a collection of poems written between 1916 and 1923, we can follow Cocteau's development on two levels: theme and form. The poem *Le Cap de Bonne-Espérance*, for example, which is dedicated to the aviator Garros, makes daring use of typographical, syntactical, and even phonetic dislocations by means of which Cocteau creates a movement on the page analogous to that of an airplane in flight. *Plain-Chant* (1923), on the other hand, returns fixed classical forms reminiscent of Malherbe. Cocteau never lost his taste for magic, but after *Clair-Obscur* and *Orphée* he sought to express himself in ways that "would not hit people between the eyes with their novelty."

Certain themes recurred in Cocteau's poems that gradually built up a subjective and personalized linguistic code: the airplane inspired analogies between the flight of the pilot and the flight of the poet, both of whom obey invisible laws. Because these laws exist, both pilot and poet can move in an extraterrestrial element where human life is seen from new viewponts; among the elements constituting Cocteau's personal mythology we find: the acceleration of takeoff, the noise of the invisible propeller that becomes visible only when it slows down for landing.

In the second poem of this collection, *Discours du grand sommeil,* a kind of inverse image of the airplane's motion is given that is linked to images of the war and colored by an obsession with death: the image of the deep-sea diver exploring inner darkness. From the two images taken together emerges the angel figure, dweller within the confines of the human world but linked with the unknown—a figure who, like the propeller on the airplane, only becomes visible when touching ground. The angel's harsh beauty is a trap. It delivers the poet to the supernatural forces surrounding the human world. Thus he becomes the poet-victim, the uncertain messenger of the unknown inside him.

An early expression of this myth is given in the play *Orphée* and reiterated later in three of Cocteau's films. But from that time on it was myth that resided in the center of Cocteau's work and gave it its coherence. No matter what story Cocteau used for his scenario or what dramatic code he chose to go with his scenario *(Renaud et Armide),* or in some cases to go before it *(L'Aigle à deux têtes),* his plays thenceforward belonged to the same world of myth and hallucination in which there always lurked the threat of chaos that sustained, and also destroyed, his fictitious "creator-children," *les enfants terribles.*

Orphée is Cocteau's key work and the expression of a conception of art in which several more or less traditional attitudes meet: that in order to become a poet, man must pass metaphorically onto the other side of the mirror separating the everyday world from the world of darkness; he must face death and lose himself in the chaos from which the poetic work and the demands it makes on him will save him. In one way this conception goes back, through the intermediary of Rimbaud interpreted in the light of Freud, to the romantics and beyond. When, however, the poem—whether dramatic or any other kind—is conceived as a verbal machine, it recalls Valéry; and the notion of art as an ascetic rite of purification through language *(Orphée, La Machine infernale)* is reminiscent of Mallarmé. For Cocteau, art nevertheless remained the expression above all of a subjective experience, of the ambiguous and incomprehensible human condition. Cocteau saw the human universe, with its categories of time, space, and causal order, as a tiny, local domain surrounded by the vast and obscure world governed by invisible forces that control the fate of the individual. He represented this concept onstage in the nocturnal décor for Oedipus's meeting with the Sphinx *(La Machine infernale)*.

In the scenery for this play, a vast darkness surrounds the narrow, illuminated spot on the stage where Oedipus encounters Anubis and the Sphinx, and in this dark space echo the increasingly distant voices of the gods. The infernal machine on which the fate of Oedipus depends is elusive but implacable. At this point Cocteau reminds us of Kafka's *Trial* and his vision of the world as "absurd." But with Cocteau there is no social structure or historical circumstance involved: Cocteau's Oedipus is the eternal man of myth in the classical tradition. Any being or any object can be the agent for these inhuman forces whose presence will be revealed by a slight "shift" in perception. Cocteau believed poets are the beings most open to perceiving this inhuman presence, which manifests itself like an electric current: both shock, perhaps a mortal one, and illumination; sacred terror, and beauty. From the poet's contact with this mystery a "poetry-fluid" is generated that it is the artist's function to "tame" by means of the "vehicle" fashioned by him: "To make things simple, let us call this fluid: poetry; and: art, the more or less successful exercise of taming it." The writer's primary responsibility, therefore, is to develop *techniques* through which he can capture and communicate the experience that has disturbed him. At this point the craftsman takes over from the divinely chosen, eternally damned romantic poet. He escapes from the chaos threatening his life by substituting for the dark world of the gods the controlled world of form and artistic order. What places Cocteau squarely on the modern side of his century, is the clarity with which he stated the question of the ambiguous relation between the artistic "vehicle" and what that vehicle must capture, which is mystery. Cocteau saw the work of art as created around a center that is not there. The line of demarcation separating him from Proust or Gide is clear.

Everything in Cocteau's view of art was bound to have a highly irritating effect on Breton, a man for whom conscious literary artifice and the work of art as a showpiece were despicable caricatures of what poetic activity should be. Breton believed a poet must shed the shackles of subjectivity in order to reach the "sublime point" beyond self where opposites—life/death; self/other; self/world; past/future—cease to exist. Breton rejected the practice of literature; Cocteau found his salvation in it. And Breton denounced the social world where Cocteau lived like a "mindless prince"—a prince who also saw himself as a victim—whose laws he transgressed (by taking drugs and practicing homosexuality), a mode of behavior of which Breton disapproved.

Cocteau, in fact, fell between two generations, the generation of the last great classics—Gide, Proust, Claudel, and Valéry—and the generation of the surrealists, who were his juniors not so much by age—Cocteau was seven years older than André Breton—as by his precocity: as a young Parisian man about town his social class, his talents, and his homosexuality earned him early entry into the glittering world of *la belle époque* then at its height, and which was always to remain his preferred milieu. But the anguish of wartime and the real chaos of everyday life—of his life—led Cocteau toward the awareness born of desperation symbolized by Vaché. He became obsessed with death and with the "uselessness of everything," both characteristic obsessions of the twenties in general. Like Gide before him, he turned toward the tradition that sees in literary expression both salvation and the true language, though *purified by art*, of a profound and problematical inner self.

After 1921, Breton like Cocteau sensed that the postwar period of "decompression" was nearing its end. In 1922, when he suggested organizing a "national congress for determining the directives of the modern spirit," which did not take place, and when he claimed that "man holds in reserve within his own mind an unknown reality on which the future of the world probably depends," Breton was addressing a different facet of the human myth than Cocteau had done. Breton believed "literature is a sad road" that can lead anywhere, but that poetry "must lead somewhere." In the last analysis, it must lead not only the poet but all of humanity back to paradise regained. It was this Promethean enthusiasm of Breton's that involved him in the kind of theorizing that the success of the Russian Revolution in 1917 and the ideology of the Communist Party gave new form to: the theory of the relation between the activity of the poet and the activity of the militant . revolutionary. For Breton the commitment of the poet is an absolute that brooks no compromise; in the area of politics, the same thing was true for the militant. During the twenties, Breton was the foremost exponent of a form of exigence and anguish whose virulence and nature were foreign to Cocteau.

Breton may have been anti-Christian, but he was a visionary even so. He had inherited the mystical tradition of a Logos, a sacred text—originally the Bible—long since lost or shrouded in mystery. It is this lost text that Breton attempted to find and that he deciphered in *Arcane 17,* using as his starting point a geographical location and a natural phenomenon, the Rocher Percé at the tip of the Canadian Gaspé Peninsula. Breton's inquiry was addressed to the world, and not to his own inner self, and even less to literature.

In the twenties, Breton was first an author of manifestos and the leader of a group of militants. He employed with a fine assurance the two traditional weapons of satire: praise and vituperation; overwhelming agreement and outrage. He deployed a rhetoric based on flowing rhythmic periods that contrasted sharply with Cocteau's elliptical style. Breton's ego may have been at odds with his time, but it was in solid agreement with himself, as shown by the haughty tone of his "Confession dédaigneuse": "Absolutely incapable of accepting the destiny reserved for me, afflicted at the highest level of my conscience by an absence of justice for which in my view original sin is no excuse, I carefully avoid adapting my own existence to the ridiculous conditions of common existence here on earth." Breton's flowing phrases" contrast with Cocteau's allusive and laconic ones, as does his peremptory tone with the Parisian taste for wit. What had happened was that after 1920 Breton assumed the mantle of the romantic poet with a mission, a powerful myth stretching all the way back to the tradition of the enlightened visionaries, or great "seers."

The declaration quoted above makes ironic use of biblical terminology (original sin; here on earth), recalling the Judeo-Christian tradition Breton rejected but to which his entire philosophy belonged. Breton was seeking an original language with its vast gamut of nuances that modern man, because of his devotion to rationalism, has lost. The eruption into language that has been liberated of a flash of imagery was for Breton a sign that there does exist some continuous linguistic presence which is merely occluded, not spasmodic or discontinuous.

At the time of the Surrealist Manifesto, this linguistic "hinterland" had a fairy-tale quality. Breton's "new" language in the beginning unveiled a realm of the marvelous that seemed to have come down in a straight line from Chrétien de Troyes and the medieval romance and to have little in common with Breton's proposed goal. The myths Breton created—the fairy-woman mediating between man and the real world; his "signs" (key objects and encounters revealing and delineating the contours of desire and the destiny of man to himself)—were private.

Breton's assertion that man holds in reserve within his own mind an unknown reality on which the future organization of humanity probably depends, gave a humanistic foundation to his enterprise; but it appears oddly gratuitous. The key words in the surrealist enterprise were from the beginning held by Breton to be: poetry, love, and liberty—in other words, complete happiness. The anticipated goal preceded the means employed to gain it: no particular method was designated a priori for "conducting the surrealist enterprise" *(Manifeste)*; but the motive force for this enterprise was identified in advance: "desire with no constraints." These statements of Breton's made him the catalyzer for the scattered tendencies dada had momentarily mobilized; they proposed a plan of action and a goal: "to free poetry at any price from the constraints that are eating it away"; and held out "hope for the great formless beyond" (Char), which had also been shared by the major utopian thinkers of the nineteenth century. These statements also answered the current need to escape from confusion. We

have referred elsewhere in the present work to the activities of the surrealists, and to Breton's role, in painting as in poetry, as an innovator and
talent scout. What we want to emphasize here is Breton's *own development*,
and the line of demarcation that separated it from Cocteau's.

After 1923, Cocteau effected a reconciliation between the two aesthetic
principles of avant-garde "modernism" and tradition; for him, literature
was always to remain the expression of subjectivity confronted by nothingness. What Breton wanted, on the other hand, was to put an end to this
alienation of the individual, to achieve something beyond the sterile nihilism
of a Jacques Vaché. His contacts with the dadaists led him to think of this
enterprise in terms of a collective adventure. After *Poisson soluble* it was
clear that what Breton dreamed of, and aspired to, was a condition of fusion
between the spirit and the world in which the individual would be re-
absorbed into the whole.

Breton's political protests were a form of revolt against everything pre-
venting this fusion: social constraints as much as the binary categories of
traditional logic and their divisive effect on the field of consciousness. *Poisson soluble* also marked the first appearance of the alchemist, one of the
poet's alter egos. Although Breton had originally aligned himself with psy-
chiatry in order to give his redemptive myth a soundly documented scientific
foundation, he was always more the son of Eliphas Levi than of science. The
synthesis effected by Cocteau was between two contradictory attitudes of
his time, which were represented by the poet-artisan dichotomy. Breton's
synthesis was between two contradictory imperatives of the same period:
the reconciliation of absolute objectivity with absolute subjectivity; the reconciliation of the real world and man's consciousness beyond mere positivism or idealism, a dichotomy the existentialists also sought to transcend.

Breton's real interest, however, from "La Confession dédaigneuse" to
Arcane 17, was the adventure pursued by the great esoteric adepts, whose
tradition he revived. Breton's dream plunged him into a past symbolized by
the five-pointed star that became his own emblem and that from the time of
ancient Egypt had been the emblem of all those seeking a return to first
causes. Breton wanted a language freed from any contemporary cultural
control to corroborate his vision and to reveal, beneath the cryptogram of
immediate, everyday life, the configuration of the paradisical. "Perhaps," he
wrote in *La Confession,* "what we are trying to do is to restore substance to
form." With the emancipation of man, in this context, goes the revolt
against time; with the pursuit of "true life" the denial of family, country, and
work, i.e., of social reality; and with the search for the "marvelous in the
everyday" a denial of "empty time," or habit.

Breton's most profound aspiration was to free himself from every trace of
the constraints of everyday life. It was in order to fight this "crust" of habit
that he adopted his state of permanent revolt against "life as given." He
belonged to a tradition going back a long way, and he knew it. His refusal to

conform to ordinary social life drew him toward political revolution, and he experienced in his own person the profound contradiction opposing, on the one hand, the necessity for fighting constraints of any kind and, on the other, the imperatives of a political party for which all spiritual activity had to be subordinated to the materialist dialectic of progress. Breton's socialism was sincere and practiced without reservation; but there was nothing to distinguish it from libertarian utopianism.

It was this social reality that Breton was brought up against at every turn and at each stage of his life, from the 1914–18 war to the Riffian war, from the Russian Revolution to the rise of fascism, the Spanish civil war, and the outbreak of World War II in 1939. It explains the uneven course run by a life in which ruptures succeeded readjustments, each of them highlighting the importance of a specific historical moment. By joining the Communist Party, Aragon and Eluard were reasserting the humanitarian tradition in modified form. "The time has come," wrote Eluard, "when poets can and must acknowledge their profound involvement in the life of other men and the life of the community" (L'Evidence poétique). They believed the poet should speak for the man in the street. For them, poetry assumed a functional, fraternal value that was later to be enhanced by the Resistance movement. Their poetry drew on the sources of familiar, traditional prosody. But neither Eluard nor Aragon espoused Breton's philosophy at its deepest level, any more than did the thousands who practiced automatic writing, that "literary science of cause and effect" denounced by Breton in Point du jour (1934).

Breton never abandoned his original goal, and when he returned from America after World War II it was still the same: "to transform the world, change life, and completely refashion human understanding outside political organizations of any kind." At least one portion of his program, "to refashion human understanding," coincided with the goal of the existentialist and the structuralist Sartre and Lévi-Strauss, respectively. The utopian dream of transforming the world was taken over by Marxism. After the thirties, this facet of surrealism became dated. But its other facet, its appeal to the traditions of the occult, continued to influence the work of prose writers like Julien Gracq, Henri Bosco, Michel Butor, and Abellio; and of poets such as Yves Bonnefoy, among others. It is here that Breton succeeded in tapping one of the deepest and most invisibly present currents of the half-century. And by his inflexible and disordered resistance to political organization—to *exterior organization* of any kind—Breton embodied the hesitations and scruples of a philosophy which was in essence totalitarian. He believed the surrealist quest required total commitment from each individual engaged upon it: "Every artist must reembark *alone* on the quest for the Golden Fleece."

Breton's work is known primarily through his Manifestos, and Breton the man as the spokesman for a group. But in the course of its development his work presented both increasing breadth and undeniable continuity. A burst of writing would frequently be inspired by a specific circumstance—an encounter of some kind—that somehow put the poet on the alert; for example, the encounter with the young woman, Nadja, with a book, the works of Fourier; with a landscape, the Rocher Percé in the Gaspé. The encounter would then graft itself on to a latent affective state of the poet's, forming a sort of incline for his thoughts to follow. Then, in their spontaneous progress down this incline, his thoughts would set into motion, from echo to echo, and analogy to analogy, the activity Breton called imagination from which poetry springs. In *Nadja* the imaginative area opened up by the stimulus of the encounter is relatively restricted and the mystery to be elucidated somewhat transparent. But after 1940 the area of imaginative resonance widened. New geographical locations and new natural phenomena opened new horizons to Breton, a world made to his measure: the Sicilian mirage known as the "Fata Morgana," New York lit by the aurora borealis, the immensity of the Rocher Percé and the birds living on it in the Gaspé, the Grand Canyon and the Pueblo Indians of New Mexico. Through the intermediary of these particular encounters, all of Breton's previous experiments led up to a cycle of poems which, written between 1942 and 1947, belonged to a traditional genre: the grand philosophical epic poem in prose or verse—*Fata Morgana, Arcane 17, Ode à Charles Fourier*. These poems are in the same line as Chateaubriand's meditations and opened an avenue later followed, for example, by Michel Butor's experiments in capturing the "genius" of places and deciphering the meaning of the human reality inscribed in them.

By this time Breton had become fully master of a language that was dense and symbolic, and he used his situation as an exile as the basis for an examination of his own destiny and that of all who at that time were being swept into the vast maelstrom of the current conflict. His inquiry follows a course set by the complex of images stimulated by the spectacle of one specific, grandiose manifestation of natural forces. It develops organically in a dynamic movement whose flow links the poet's meditation on his own affective situation to the configurations of his past life and the major historical circumstances that have changed the course of his life and the lives of all mankind. "Arcane 17" is a card in the Tarot, and for Breton it is the numeral on which his destiny depends. To him it represents a positive destiny linked to the beneficent forces of the cosmos. He sees it as a sign that under the aegis of three forces—liberty, love, and poetry—humanity will be able to achieve happiness. The "cri de Mélusine" in *Arcane 17* is the expression of a spiritual victory.

In his later work it was from woman, more than from imagination, that Breton expected mankind's salvation to come. From the fairy-woman or child-woman still close to the original Garden of Eden and, in her humanized form, able to open to man the way to poetry. But the question

Breton asked in his later work was still the same: What future is man making for himself? He refused to accept the idea that human beings are incapable of creating a life for themselves equal to the one they crave. They need only allow the mythic man living on poetry to emerge. The apparent hermeticism of these three final poems is dissipated in the light of their biographical context and of the esoteric writings Breton was referring to. They are actually profoundly coherent. Breton had posited the authenticity of poetic language on a collective psychism that "speaks through the poet and is of concern to all humanity." There is an almost epic quality to these last works of Breton's. In them an equilibrium is established between the breadth of the vision he proposes, and the urgency of the surrealist injunction. But it was always from the individual that Breton expected salvation to come, from each individual's freedom to live according to his own desires: "this is the price of poetry," an exceedingly individual enterprise.

In *Le Surréalisme et la peinture,* written in 1928, Breton articulated the goal of the surrealist movement: to substitute for the images in art that reflect nature, images that reflect a model found inside man. For Breton the purpose of a work of art was not aesthetic, and he was completely uninterested in the plastic values of the kind of painting he advocated; what did interest him was what the work of art had to reveal in terms of the human psyche. His own work culminated with *Arcane 17* in a unification of the two great surrealist myths that in pictorial form had appeared in canvas after canvas during the interwar period: the theme of the fusion between the male and the female principle, and the theme of the primordial unity of creation, which are symbolized by the Androgyne and are to be found in *Minotaure* on page after page (see particularly the article by Albert Béguin, "L'Androgyne," no. 11, 1938). This ancient and universal figure is linked to the themes of perfection, unity, and resurrection. Breton adds to it the myth of the redemptive value of the female principle. In *Arcane 17* we find Breton's final articulation of the role of the poet-artist: to reconcile these two principles by assimilating, himself, "everything that makes a woman different from a man" in order to become a complete being. The accomplishment of this resolution on a personal level apparently brought to an end Breton's initial revolt. He seems to have found that profound harmony with the All for which he had always yearned. And *Arcane 17,* in the last analysis, takes its place in a long literary tradition going back to a distant past.

The authors we will be dealing with in the next chapter, André Malraux and Louis-Ferdinand Céline, also wrote works that were characterized by this tendency toward the epic and a similar broadening of consciousness; but they did not share the preoccupation with "self" underlying Breton's work as much as Cocteau's.

17

The Thirties:
André Malraux
and Céline

Publication of Céline's *Voyage au bout de la nuit* and Malraux's *La Condition humaine* made it clear that fiction style had undergone a change. The surrealist movement had set out to instill new life into the imaginary by plunging into the subconscious; Céline and Malraux created the imaginary on the basis of current social and political reality. Both were Parisians and both came from a background of lower middle class or small shopkeepers; both were born into families that were not needy but lived in dismal areas of Paris; both were largely self-taught; and both were prey to violent feelings of revolt against their surroundings. Although Céline belatedly took up a profession, the practice of medicine, Malraux from the age of twenty on refused to work at anything except the semi-clandestine erotic book trade and publishing, which he was to practice sporadically throughout his life. Both were profoundly affected by the historical events that marked their lifetime, and, in the works of both, history, fiction, and autobiography are inextricably mingled.

History serves as the anchorage for their fictionalized tales, which are based on contemporary events they have experienced themselves but which in their books are enlivened by narrative power of great lyric intensity. It was therefore natural that Céline and Malraux should choose the novel as the vehicle for what they had to say; but it was also natural that in order to adapt the novel form to their own lyric, epic register, they were obliged to dislocate some of its narrative codes. Céline's tone differed radically from Malraux's, however. Céline chose a "vindictive" mode that ridiculed and stripped bare the usual styles of writing in order to commemorate the stupidity of the human species in a great, burlesque epic; it is human stupidity that holds the center of the stage in Céline's work, and the derisory vanity of human stupidity that he emphasizes the most. A fierce, paroxystic, parodying humor animates a flood of language that keeps the writer in a permanent state of rebellion.

Malraux, on the other hand, built a fictitious stage on which the drama of history is acted out against a backdrop of cosmic void. On this stage the makers of history confront one another, experience self-doubt, and replace the silence of the gods with the sound of their own speech. In Malraux's novels, history is the stage on which heroes are defined. The voice of the author, whose aim is to create a myth of redemption more eloquent than the silence of the cosmos, takes on an apocalyptic tone. Céline and Malraux both witnessed what to them was the death of a civilization: the great civilization of the Western world; but their respective points of view were diametrically opposed to one another. For Malraux, the value of Western civilization is based on lucidity and determination and a denial of biological fatality and meaningless death. For Céline, this kind of desire for transcendence was a source of delirium, a madness impelling man to destroy his own body and his links with nature and to divorce himself from the wellsprings of life. The men who were heroes for Malraux were delirious madmen for Céline.

Although a large part of the total output of both authors was written after World War II and even, as happened with Malraux, occasionally changed its form (going from novels to metaphysical essays on art, and then to a lengthy rumination on the past), the basic direction of each man's work remained the same. For the average reader, the average reader of the time, in any case, the image of Céline and Malraux, respectively, is the one they projected during the thirties, a period when political feeling ran high. It was not until 1960 that this began to change. Now the eclipse suffered by Céline after 1945 turned in his favor. Meanwhile Malraux, increasingly absorbed by the legend of an era that was nearing its end, became more remote.

"The thing that made us different at the age of twenty from our masters was the presence of history," stated the seventy-year-old Malraux to his biographer, Jean Lacouture, an opinion he expressed repeatedly when he was around that age. And history, in the guise of war, had indeed hit Céline very hard when he was twenty: in 1914 he was one of the earliest of the wounded (the number rose to three million); he was ever afterward the implacable enemy of war. Malraux, seven years Céline's junior, confronted history at about the same age, twenty-two, while traveling in Indochina trying to earn a little money: it was then that he witnessed the rebellion fomented by the colonized peoples of the Far East against the European colonists. A trip Céline took to Africa made him aware of the same thing. Starting in the thirties, however, the same set of historical circumstances led the two writers in two diametrically opposed directions.

When *Voyage au bout de la nuit* was published, it was well received by leftist intellectuals, who read it as the kind of attack on the capitalist system the latter deserved; but when Céline returned from a trip to Russia, he stepped into the political arena: *Mea culpa* proclaimed his hatred of communism and of everyone—specifically, Jewish capitalists—involved in the Stalinist "plot" to start a war. In two virulent pamphlets, *Bagatelles pour un massacre* and *L'Ecole des cadavres,* Céline employed a defamatory tone and an abusive rhetoric that was exaggerated and gratuitous, which catapulted him into the role of prime *antagonist* of the traditional values of liberal society. At a time when Jews were being mercilessly persecuted in Europe, the unforgivable excess of these denunciations earned Céline a place on the list of personalities to be liquidated after the Liberation, even though he had not engaged in any compromising activity with the Germans during the Occupation. He was exiled for seven years, seventeen months of which were spent in harsh imprisonment, and his books were banned—eight years of silence. Then came the series of unprecedented works which only on the very eve of his death broke through the barrier of hostility most French people had erected around his name. In the space of less than ten years Céline published four completely unclassifiable works—*Féerie pour une autre fois I et II, D'un château l'autre,* and *Nord,* as well as the unfinished story *Rigodon,* all of which burst on the literary scene like so many time bombs. Taken together they present the story of a burlesque Götterdämmerung: the fall of the Reich seen through the adventures of a ragtag group of fugitives, Céline, his wife Lily, their cat Bébert, and an actor named La Vigue (Le Vigan). Céline in these works resembles the Cendrars of *Moravagine,* but in a framework of "reality," not fiction. The literary era that had begun in 1928 with *Les Conquérants,* by the then young Malraux, was brought to an end as much by these narrative-chronicles of Céline's as by the *nouvelle vague* novels of the younger generation.

While Céline was fleeing for his life to Germany, Malraux was fighting at the head of a brigade in Alsace. He was participating in the last of the adventures that were to make him, in the eyes of his contemporaries, both heroic conscience and exemplary protagonist of a history whose legend he was also in the process of recording. Before his trips to Indochina, Malraux as a young man had not been particularly concerned with history, and he was never to show concern for politics except from afar. But, in contradistinction to Céline, everything he became involved in after publication of *La Condition humaine* reverberated in intellectual circles far beyond the borders of France. In 1920 Malraux cited as his literary masters two literary personalities of the time, Max Jacob and Pierre Reverdy, and it is in the style of that time that he wrote *Lunes de papier,* a whimsical, "crazy" work, according to him. But his "true masters" were the men at the *NRF,* especially Gide, Valéry, and Claudel. It was not long before he himself became an associate of these famed literary arbiters. Malraux was a voracious reader, and he quickly acquired enormous cultivation, particularly in the plastic arts; he was also possessed by the demon of adventure.

Art, and sometimes strangely romantic adventure—the search for the

Khmer statues in the Indochinese jungle, the search by plane for Queen Saba's Palace in the desert—were the twin passions of the young Malraux, along with a need to judge himself in terms of the times he lived in. This confrontation with his own time is what Malraux called history, an amalgam of spectacular events with which he became involved, in imagination or in fact, and that he represented in his writings in order to illustrate the impassioned metaphysic he called lucidity. In *Les Conquérants* a new décor replaces the Paris of rooms that are opened or closed, the fetishes, and magic signs. In this new work, loudspeakers, sirens, uprisings, plots, and—prominently—the landscape of a violent and heroic Orient transport its readers outside the boundaries of the things they are used to. The literature of the exotic, which had been dying out, here found a new field in the novel: the exalted struggle for an ideal freedom totally untinged by ambiguity. Malraux had rediscovered the basic patterns of the *Chanson de Roland;* he told his story from only one side, that of the insurgents responsible for the strike in Canton and Hong-Kong in 1925.

The story begins with a radio broadcast, "A general strike has been declared in Canton," and it continues in the style of a newspaper report written entirely in the first person present by a young Frenchman, an eyewitness. Malraux's characteristic style is already in place in this novel. The story's point of reference is a violent historical event presented in a series of episodes strung together like a film. In passages of dialogue that are rapid and incisive, the characters involved in the action discuss what has been happening from hour to hour, what their strategy should be, what historical significance it all has, and what meaning for them. For a few brief moments they stake their own lives on History in action, and in a series of dramatic ellipses they define their answers to the great, ultimate question: in the secular world of today, what must man do in order to escape the void?

If we compare *Les Conquérants* to three novels by other authors that came out at the same time, it is easy to see how far it was from the typical novel of the twenties. The three examples might be *Le Temps retrouvé*—crowning the lengthy progress of *A la Recherche du temps perdu*—*Les Enfants terribles,* and *Nadja;* all three, even *Nadja,* were anchored in a world that was familiar, and even Parisian.

Les Conquérants answered the same need to break with the past as surrealism, but in another way. Malraux had created a highly romantic confusion between the real and imaginary, between the destiny of the world and that of the individual; the "I" of *Les Conquérants,* who is easily mistaken for the author himself, introduced readers of the book, through their identification with him, into a story taking place in an almost legendary world. What Malraux had created was an exalted model of the romantic hero whose lineage stretched in a straight line back to the heroes of Corneille, but whose concerns were of a different kind. Malraux realized this himself. In the "Postface" to *Les Conquérants,* written twenty years later for the

"Bibliothèque de la Pléiade," he acknowledged: "But it is only superficially that this book belongs to history. It has managed to keep afloat all these years not because it describes this or that phase of the revolution in China, but because it describes a heroic type in which an aptitude for action is united with culture and lucidity. These values were indirectly linked to the European values of the time." Malraux's concern for the state of culture was not dissimilar to Drieu La Rochelle's, and was a continuation of the concerns of Barrès and Maurras.

In *Les Conquérants,* Malraux based his story on his own experience as an obscure young journalist who for one year edited a militantly anticolonialist newspaper in Saigon called *Indo-Chine,* transposing it into the broader framework of narrative history, recounted by others and reinvented by him. This larger framework suited his own avid desire to escape from mediocrity and play a role, a passion that had launched him originally out into the jungle tracks of Indochina. The theme of *Les Conquérants* is the archetypical one of the encounter between the neophyte and the hero. The hero is embodied by the central character in the book. The same structure is apparent in Malraux's second novel, *La Voie royale,* a fictional transposition of the unedifying but true story of how the Banteai Srey Temple statues were stolen. And the same structure reappears throughout the meanderings of Malraux's *Antimémoires:* in the author's meetings with Nehru, de Gaulle, and Mao. It is actually conceivable that it was a similar need for heroism that at this same period attracted thousands of young Germans to Nuremburg, and young Italians to the fascist brigades. The yearning for heroism that with the romantics had pitted the individual against society was reversed, collectivized, and endowed with ideology: whether this ideology was fascist or communist made little difference.

Malraux's growing importance between 1926, when *La Tentation de l'Occident* was published, and 1933, when *La Condition humaine* won the Prix Goncourt, cannot be measured solely in terms of bulk in this nevertheless fairly abundant body of work: two essays, the short "crazy" story, and three novels. However—crazy story apart—Malraux's basic narrative mode did not change but continued unbroken from one work to the next, with *La Tentation de l'Occident* falling somewhere between the essay form and fiction. A single, eloquent voice expresses a single passion. The characters in the books represent the metaphysical points of view fighting for supremacy in Malraux's visionary and extremely mobile thinking. The function of the historical event is to serve as a point of reference for them, to fill the void where thought confronts nothingness. Action, individual at first and then collective, is the form taken by Malraux's revolt against the fact of nothingness. And the work's impact derives from the persuasive force of an argument which, in the uneven, Pascalian confrontation between man and nothingness, attempts to reverse the terms and weight them in favor of man. Malraux's apprehension as he scrutinizes the face of European youth, from the time of *La Tentation* on, explains the urgency of his appeal to heroic values. This is the source of the tension present in his style, of its ellipses, and of its almost exclusively sensational nature which, because of its stylistic intensity, conveys a noble aura of the tragic. For, as in the tragedies of classical times, it is tragedy that provides the stuff of life to Malraux's characters. The stakes are immediate, and also absolute.

The subject of *La Condition humaine* is Chiang Kai-shek's 1927 march into Shanghai, and the liquidation of the communist groups that had helped him do it. In this novel, Malraux's narrative model remains very much the same, but the fictional characters, historical events, and characters' action, anxieties, and fates are more skillfully integrated in terms of creating a powerful story. This story revolves around the two poles of an axis joining the original insurgence of the clandestine communist groups against a government being upheld by the colonial powers, and the ultimate defeat and destruction of them. Each of the two periods of intense action is interlarded with passages of dialogue in which the characters define and reveal themselves, and they are separated by an episode in which two of the militants take a trip and, while they are on it, become aware of the fate that awaits them. At the end of the novel there is a kind of epilogue suggesting a new cycle is about to begin that will throw fresh light on their apparent failure. The action of the novel is cyclical and atemporal, and revolves around the central episode. Malraux's aim was to divorce history from linear sequence, and thus to give it the quality of a myth.

There is a more mature sense of historical reality in this book, one which, illuminated by the visionary Marxism Malraux believed in at the time, gave to his characters—the communist leaders of the insurrection—a more palpable substance and related their cruel fate both to the ancient myth of Prometheus, and to the myth of Christ: their death reproduced the pattern of ritual sacrifice of the redeeming hero, but Marxist teleology saved them from absurdity and offered as consolation the reality on earth of an ideal fraternity.

With this novel the work and the legend of Malraux—a legend that he himself had fostered—became one. The youthful Malraux's mythomania became an established fact: he—as distinct from his imaginary alter ego—had never participated in any of the events described in this book. But from then on, alter ego and man blended into one. Malraux became the man of his legend and the man of his fiction: the antithesis of Céline. Malraux was a militant antifascist, he commanded a republican escadrille in Spain, belonged to the French Resistance, and was colonel of the Alsace-Lorraine brigade. To his novels he added numerous occasional texts, speeches, or articles written as propaganda during the war and virtually as eloquent as his fictional works, *Le Temps du mépris* and *L'Espoir*, the last novels he ever published with the exception of one that was never completed, *Les Noyers de l'Altenburg*.

L'Espoir is a fictionalized chronicle of the first months of the Spanish civil war. Because of the abundance and diversity of its characters, its sequential development and a broader, more varied orchestration of its basic themes, *L'Espoir* may be the most "durable" of Malraux's five novels, although it is not as popular as *La Condition humaine*. His imagination had been enriched and his characters humanized by experience. Even the title of the book—*L'Espoir*—seemed to indicate that the themes of anguish and meaninglessness had been set aside. Malraux's motto, "Take the broadest possible experience and transform it into (human) consciousness," could also have been Breton's. But the thing that separated the Malraux of the thirties from Breton was the fact that Malraux saw this experience in terms of History—with a capital H—and made no distinction between this "consciousness" and his own personal myth. Breton sought to apprehend the unknown by plunging into the depths of his own consciousness, discovering within it the basic configurations of a universal myth. Malraux took a personal myth and gave it the face of universality.

To the idea of "history as destiny" Malraux opposed a counterhistory, a history of heroes whose actions illustrate man's conquest of his own destiny, of heroes who at the cost of their lives transpose conflict from the level of nature to the level of culture. "All life created by the gods is destined for the void; everything to have survived the void—forms, ideas, and gods—has been created by man": for Malraux, the gods are those forces, chance and necessity, over which man has no control, either within himself or without. Malraux based the ethical hierarchy of his characters on this man-god opposition, with man assuming control over a domain formerly reserved to the gods. When Malraux began to experience history directly, instead of imagining it, he abandoned the novel and pursued his myth in his reflections on art as antihistory, i.e., antidestiny.

Malraux's novels are an indictment of the gods, and an affirmation of the greatness of man, an exaltation of the spiritual values of a culture he believed was disappearing. Malraux embodied in both his life and his novels the neoromanticism of an entire era, and he articulated the anxiety felt during this era because of the historical catastrophe that had escaped human controls. Malraux's call for action and lucidity was the remedy of desperation, a battle fought by the rear guard. The combination of a body of work and a man's life both dedicated to a stand *against the inevitable*, in fact against the very idea that there is such a thing as the inevitable, made Malraux the hero of the absurd. Starting with *La Tentation de l'Occident*, the urgency of the message he felt he had to convey severed him from the esotericism that had been the bane of his earlier works and forced him to choose a style of writing which, in contrast to surrealism, placed his novels in the mainstream of traditional realism and guaranteed them a contemporary audience.

Individual destiny was, for Malraux, merely a "ripple on the surface of

History"; but for Céline, who as a physician tended the poor until the day he died, it was an all-consuming concern, and his entire work is a brilliant, increasingly savage variation on a single theme: the relentlessness with which contemporary man seeks to destroy himself. From *Voyage au bout de la nuit* on, this concern is translated into a writing style of visionary realism artfully following the modalities of a vast Rabelaisian anger frequently intermingled with the Homeric laughter Céline is shaken by when he contemplates the enormity of the havoc being wreacked on the human race. Malraux's *themes* influenced the existential novel and found echoes at times in some poets belonging to the generation born in 1925, like Bonnefoy or Claude Vigé; but Céline's *style* had as profound an effect on a whole line of writers, both in the United States and France, as James Joyce did.

"In the History of time, life is just momentary intoxication and Truth is death." This aphorism appears in the first thing Céline ever wrote, which was his thesis, a biography of Semmelweis the physician. Céline from the start confronted head-on a circumstance that Malraux refused to accept. Writing was for Céline, however, as art was for Malraux, a kind of anti-death, an "intoxication whose source lay in the emotion clutching the writer before the spectacle of life. Céline judged the literature of his own day harshly, much as Julien Benda had *(La France byzantine)*. He imputed to romanticism the "feminization" of French culture, reproaching literature with the complaisant subjectivism that was also denounced by Malraux in *La Tentation de l'Occident*. He reserved special scorn for "leftist" writers: "As bourgeois as can be, every single one of them, in intention, and at heart, frenetic lovers of the bourgeois ideal." Sartre said much the same thing in *Qu'est-ce que la littérature?*, but at greater length. It was a mold that Céline and Malraux, by living their lives a certain way, both set out to break. *Voyage au bout de la nuit* contains a sustained and virulent parody of various literary aesthetics. Thus the young Musyn, in the practice of his art, possesses a gift for "giving a certain dramatic distance to his insights," because "the foreground in a painting is always offensive and the demands of art require that the work's focal point be located in the distance, in the ungraspable there, refuge of lies, of dreams created from fact." When Céline writes, he puts everything in the foreground, savagely attacking those distant refuges where what he would call lies and others might call myths are hiding—lies or myths that make us forget Céline's credo that the "Truth" of the human condition "is Death."

Céline develops the life/intoxication metaphor along a gamut running from "frenzy" to "transport," terms that, as a physician, he uses two ways. If we can trust the French dictionary, the "frenzied" *(frénétique)* individual is "a madman seized with violent delirium caused by an acute cerebral defect." Céline's novels are filled with frenzied individuals—at their most extreme, homicidal maniacs—and it is they who cause catastrophes of all kinds. They are individuals dedicated above all else to abstract ideas, and it is their aberrations, according to Céline, that afflict the collectivity with all the virulence of an epidemic. Céline's preferred frame of reference for his vast, panoramic novels is this frenetic civilization. At the other extreme we find the intoxication of creativity, a humble activity engaged in by the writer whose model for Céline is the dance. The activity of writing is a "transport" in two senses of the word: a state of ecstatic possession, of being carried away emotionally; but also a literal carrying away of people or things by means of a vehicle—in this case, language. For, according to Céline, "in the beginning was emotion," not the Word. And so he tried to find a dynamic syntax with "a special kind of melodius, melodic tone" that would mimic the flow of this emotion backward and foreward. The vehicle of transport is narrative, that "emotive subway train." For the reader as for the author, narrative is a journey.

With *Voyage au bout de la nuit,* Céline immediately found, if not yet his fully matured style, at least his tone, and a narrative structure which, although still traditional, opened the way for more daring experiments. He used the picaresque form, but he introduced a note of fundamental ambiguity into it. In the prologue the story is begun by a narrative voice and concerns a protagonist who is this same narrator as a younger man. This naive initial voice addressed to the reader creates the illusion of a running dialogue accompanying the story, beginning in the prologue and continuing throughout. Céline presents us with an open narrative, instead of a closed, self-contained one, thereby establishing a dual complicity between reader and narrator, narrator and protagonist. The narration is presented as an autonomous field of reference that the narrator is drawing to the reader's attention: "Just a fictitious story," says the narrator of *Voyage,* a story "on the other side of life." The work of literature is presented as that autonomous block of writing described by Derrida. But, because Céline uses the different phases of his own life as the model for his story, he casts an ambiguous light on what he means by "fictitious" and on both narrator and his protagonist. In his two first novels the protagonist Ferdinand Bardamu remains in the foreground, playing the classic role of the picaresque hero who recreates a frame of reference for each new episode.

This frame of reference is defined by the conventions of the traditional novel as reality. And it was to this reality that the novelist directed the attention of the reader. But Céline's prologue undermines these conventions. There is nothing but words—as with Proust, the words of the narrator. In the chronicles he wrote later, Céline did away with a distinct protagonist altogether; the narrative "I" assumed all the roles: the self actually experiencing events; the self carried away in a "delirium" of writing, borne on the railway tracks of emotion; and the "I" representing the character who emerges from the language of this delirium. Ferdinand the picaresque hero is replaced by Louis-Ferdinand Destouches, clown, physician-victim, persecuted martyr. Less coherent, shot through with digression, this narrative is nonetheless amply sustained by the vigor and shock value of a language that is skillfully dislocated, insulting, hallucinatory, hilarious, and vindictive, which Céline uses to deliver himself of reality, transporting it "to the other side of life." The dance has become a sarabande.

Céline's first two novels, however, *Voyage au bout de la nuit* and *Mort à crédit*, both of which adhered fairly closely to the style of conventional realism, were the ones that impressed the reading public of the thirties, and it was on them that his reputation was based. The two books are presented as a two-stage account of the life of Ferdinand Berdamu, a Parisian from the lower middle class. The chronology of the two volumes is reversed: the events in *Voyage au bout de la nuit* take place after the ones in *Mort à crédit*. *Voyage* is constructed like a diptych. The first section is an exploration of the human condition presented in three parts: war, in which the civilization of Europe is crumbling; conflict with nature in the jungles of Africa; and the antinature of modern times, the mechanized urban civilization of the United States. The second section of the diptych describes in day-to-day detail the disintegration of a lower-class population caught in the net of industrialization and the big city created by it.

Céline's main character, Ferdinand Berdamu, is a callow medical student the author sends off to war on a kind of bet. When he emerges from this initial ordeal, Ferdinand has acquired a healthy fear of, and contempt for, the "frenetic" type of human being and is prepared to do anything to save his own skin. Céline then sends his hero off to Africa in the employ of La Compagnie Pordurière: his post is lost in the middle of the jungle, and when he reaches it, he finds himself prey to another kind of frenzy, that of the uncontrolled nature all around him, which attacks his body with all the relentlessness of the enemy canon in the war. This homicidal delirium comes from the tropical forest. Ferdinand sets fire to the shack he is living in and starts on a journey backward in time, in the course of which he is sold as a slave, crosses the Atlantic on an ancient galley, the *Infanta Combitta*, and lands on Ellis Island. Here begins his journey across America, which ends in Detroit. He is taken in by a beautiful and wise prostitute named Molly, and with her he finds a brief respite from hatred and fear. But, like Ulysses, he must return to his Ithaca, Paris.

In the diptych's second section, Berdamu is a scruffy physician ministering to the poor in Rancy, and he draws up an inventory of the bodily ills of his patients and the moral swamp into which they are sinking, prisoners of urban decay. The city also seems possessed by a determination to kill human beings—by suffocation. Spreading like a cancer, it attacks the vital tissue of the countryside, destroying souls along with bodies. Here again, Ferdinand, in the course of his continuous flight, finds refuge from that decay; he becomes physician to an insane asylum; and he also finds happiness with Sophie, a beautiful nurse. Like Candide, he turns his back on the world and decides to cultivate his own garden.

At each of these stages Céline sets up a confrontation between Berdamu and Léon Robinson, a lonely derelict sunk even deeper than he in contempt and disgust, who until the day of his death shares all of Berdamu's adventures with him. Robinson is a typical deserter: first he deserts from the army, in the strict sense of the word; next he deserts his shop counter in Africa after looting it. He sinks to the bottom of the human ladder and reappears in Detroit among the "workers of the night," nocturnal sweepers who clear away the detritus that accumulates from the activities of the day; he next appears as the clumsy killer who misses his victim and mutilates himself. He finally turns away in disgust from the only happiness available to him— union with young, practical, sentimental Madelon, who in exasperation at his indifference shoots him dead with a single shot from her revolver. Robinson is the Outsider par excellence, a man born of the brutal uprooting his participation in the war meant for him. A half-bandit, half-exile with no responsibilities, he is a reject of postwar society. His is the fate the crafty Ferdinand constantly risks and constantly evades, thanks to the refuges provided for him by his infallible sexuality: Lola, Musyn, Molly, Tania, and Sophie in turn cast their spell on him; as do the hordes of lovely New Yorkers and the huge fantasy images projected onto the screens of cheap movie houses.

For Céline there is an intimate connection between writing and erotic fantasy, and both stretch their fragile nets between two opposite poles: intoxication and Truth; life and Death. He has inscribed within the concrete texture of his narrative the theme that preoccupied Blanchot and Bataille and furnished Robbe-Grillet with the keystone of his aesthetic. Broadly speaking, *Voyage au bout de la nuit* is actually a kind of turntable on which the themes and forms of the past are pointed toward the new direction fictional narrative will be taking in the future. On one level the book is a vast allegory of the human condition, particularly, given the nature of this condition, of the absurd ways in which human beings behave. Throughout the novel, as in the medieval allegory, places, events, and objects are emblematic; certain motifs underline their meaning: slaughterhouse, shooting gallery, the old boat belonging to the colonists that is riddled with leaks, the temple to the great god Dollar, the underground vault with the mummies in it ... And yet this allegory is submerged beneath the rich overlay of the narrative, and the throng of characters with all their idiosyncrasies, gestures, ways of expressing themselves—a gesticulating, haranguing throng engulfing Ferdinand.

The human throng that for Malraux assumed the form of a murmur in the Shanghai night, of raised voices veiled in shadow coming from a prisoner-of-war camp *(Les Noyers de l'Altenburg),* or of hieratic Spanish peasants *(L'Espoir),* for Céline was the very substance from which his novels were made: soldiers and their officers, the piteous, exploited peoples of the colonies and their despicable masters, the rich and the poor—all were subjected to the same impartial scrutiny by the physician, who saw them as physical beings, vulnerable physical beings made of flesh and blood and every one of them in the process of physiological decomposition. Into the space separating this danse macabre from the equally classic theme of human folly was born Céline's delirious laughter and the phantasmagorical parodies with which he illustrated the various types of insanity manifested by the madman running around on the loose and observed through the eyes of Ferdinand. From this dual point of view comes the ambiguity of the novel.

On this level, *Le Voyage* is a novel of initiation, a sort of "education" *(Bildung)* of the young, postwar European. In the course of the narrative, Ferdinand assumes, in turn, all the roles that devolve on the classic picaresque hero: the student who has dropped out of school; the soldier who is by turns boastful and cowardly; the scapegoat; the parasite; the physician without a practice.

In *Mort à crédit* Céline abandoned the allegorical form, and he never again returned to it. *Voyage au bout de la nuit* established the parameters of his own novelistic universe and constituted his first attempt to deploy a new language. *Mort à crédit* is the burlesque and brutal tale of Ferdinand's childhood years. In it, Céline perfected the stylistic tool that was to become his trademark: the insertion of an idiosyncratic piece of punctuation into his texts—the three suspension points. In *Voyage* these three dots only appear in the dialogues, indicating breaks, hesitation, and ellipses in speech. In *Mort à crédit* they become an inherent characteristic of Céline's style, indicating the sudden rush of emotion before the brutal and unbelievable spectacle of an insane reality. Words disappear almost before they have been uttered, others rush in to fill the gap and push them aside; Céline had created his emotional railway track. But the distance between the character of the young Ferdinand and the verbal power exhibited by the narrator was considerable, nonetheless. By doing away with transitional characters like Ferdinand in his *Chroniques,* Céline was able to achieve greater narrative consistency.

In *Voyage,* Céline forces the reader to make a distinction between Ferdinand's story and the presentation of the story, a task he assigns to the narrator. In his postwar chronicle-novels, however, all the narrative elements of the novel—characters, plot, theme, place, in short the entire referential field—are integrated into a single network of proliferating language. The picaresque form and the autobiographical novel of the thirties is replaced by a narrative-monologue. But the mechanisms impelling that emotional subway train down the track are the same: they are summed up in the effort of one individual—now seen to be Céline himself—to escape, through words, from the huge, homicidal delirium of an insane world.

The hieratic world evoked by the chastened language of Malraux and the teeming, unkempt throngs that emerge in the lyrical, satirical, and scatological language of Céline form a sort of literary counterpoint to one another.

But they share a common source: the sense of an imminent catastrophe that will lead the Western world—and France in particular—into total disaster. From this common source came the inflated rhetoric of exhortation practiced by Malraux, and of denunciation practiced by Céline. Their message was an urgent one. In both writers, that urgency created a block that interfered with the objective-subjective balance along their entire narrative axis. Their representations of reality became representations of how reality resists meaning. At the heart of their novels was ambiguity. Both authors, Céline even more than Malraux, paved the way in the thirties for the dualistic adventure of the post–World War II novel. They foreshadowed both the ideal of political involvement and the experiments undertaken by criticism to reexamine the basic nature of the novel in every way. But if, as Philippe Sollers believes, the novel "is how society talks to itself," then society, in the confrontation between Malraux and Céline, was talking like a schizophrenic.

18

The Forties:
Simone de Beauvoir
and Albert Camus

Coming ten years after Malraux's *Condition humaine* and Céline's *Voyage au bout de la nuit*, Camus's novel *L'Etranger* and Simone de Beauvoir's *L'Invitée*, which were published approximately one year apart, seemed out of phase with the political realities of the time: war, defeat, and the Nazi Occupation. The story these two novels have to tell takes place outside of current events and is scaled to the lives of individuals, avoiding the vast perspectives that involve all humanity. They present, in contrast to the intense subjective and emotional presence of Malraux and Céline, the impersonality of stories that are at least superficially circumscribed and objective.

The reason these two novels are located outside of current events is in part that they were begun before the debacle that brought to an end an attitude of mind often referred to by Simone de Beauvoir in her *Mémoires:* a stubborn optimism that persisted despite disdain for the "mystifications" of bourgeois politics. At the time, Camus, who had been a militant communist for two years, was more involved in politics than Simone de Beauvoir, but he shared the same optimism, the result, in his case, of a vague faith in a collective future based on the postulates of Marxism—although it was not long before he separated art from politics.

Later, when social and historical events did furnish the frame of reference for their writing, Beauvoir and Camus still maintained a distance between what was actually happening and their fictitious representations of it in novels or plays. Their early technical and stylistic choices were a return to Gide's theory of "attitudes" that place the individual in relation to the events of his time and illuminate their complexities.

Unlike Malraux and Céline, both Beauvoir and Camus were conditioned by a university education, and their approach to the act of writing betrays a certain detachment. Their respective concerns overlapped and belonged to the intellectual climate known as existentialism. Both were atheists, and both felt the same need to free themselves as much from the nihilism and contempt exhibited by Céline as from Malraux's visionary romanticism.

The fact that Simone de Beauvoir's ideas were deeply intertwined with Jean-Paul Sartre's is common knowledge and remained unchanged until about 1970, when Beauvoir realized the consequences, for her, of the feminist theses she had developed twenty years earlier in *Le Deuxième Sexe*. Camus was impelled by the same need to give his philosophy a solid intellectual underpinning but the direction his philosophy followed after the thirties separated him from Sartre's brand of existentialism. He did, however, share one fundamental trait with Beauvoir that Sartre did not: the quest for self-fulfillment not uncharacteristic of an interwar student world enjoying the fruits of the artistic and intellectual explosion then taking place and the more liberated life style inaugurated by it. For Camus, a man of the people, and for Beauvoir, a woman, admittance to the literary world was self-fulfillment of the best kind.

When history erupted into their lives, they did not see it as Malraux's grandiose drama, in which heroic figures play out humanity's destiny and their own; they saw it as a source of profound frustration. Both recognized that, in the course of the three periods we have identified, history interrupted their lives. For both there was a "before" 1939 and an "after" 1944–45, underlined by Beauvoir's two titles for the central volumes of her *Mémoires: La Force de l'âge (The Prime of Life)* and *La Force des choses (Force of Circumstance)*. Both writers made their appearance in the literary arena during the decade of the forties, which was also a determining factor in the formation of their personalities as writers. In a period spanning less than ten years, from 1942, when *L'Etranger* was published, through 1951, when *L'Homme révolté* appeared, Camus produced the major portion of his work and had entered a new phase that was cut short by his death. Only nine of the more than twenty-two works eventually published by Simone de Beauvoir came out before 1950. But *Les Mandarins,* which won the 1954 Prix Goncourt and, after 1958, *Les Mémoires* both stem from the forties, which are thus doubly present and viewed from a double perspective. Beauvoir has said that it was the shock of the 1939–40 political events and the revolt they made her feel that transformed a literary vocation that had been virtual into the active practice of writing. Camus and Beauvoir together give us a dual perspective on the years of crisis they lived through themselves.

However, their works cannot be reduced to any ideological pattern and are in fact radically different in terms of purpose, style, and point of view. Beauvoir saw her work increasingly as, in essence, cultural observation, while Camus saw his in relation to a literary tradition and an aesthetic.

The Politically Committed Writer: the Constraints of Ideology

When *Les Temps modernes* came into being, Simone de Beauvoir held a respected rank among leftist Parisian intellectuals; by 1970, she was much more: the most famous woman writer of her generation in the world, and a figurehead in the women's liberation movement. Her unique status among her contemporaries came as a result of the coincidence of her own career with a social movement of great importance. At the source of her success was her stubborn determination to remain true to her fundamental conception of what a writer should do: to recreate direct experience and communicate it to the reading public so as to help them in leading their own lives.

For Beauvoir this meant, first, gaining insight into the general significance of a particular experience, which implies an intellectual act; and, second, of elucidating this meaning through use of an unequivocal style, a project which is essentially a didactic one. Beauvoir's medium is therefore prose, a style of prose she saw as a transparent system referring back unequivocally to reality. The literary forms she adopted were traditional, and her style was realistic; there is basically no difference between the various forms she employed. Her two nonfiction treatises, one on the status of women and the other on old age, are simply more systematically documented than her other works.

Simone de Beauvoir's literary output can be divided into four areas: fiction (four novels, a collection of short stories, one play); philosophical, critical, and polemical essays; four volumes of memoirs; and two massive nonfiction treatises. But her entire body of work can be considered as constituting a single intellectual autobiography. Beauvoir herself has lent authority to this view by defining for each volume of her memoirs the original impulse lying behind it. It is possible to look at all of her work in terms of her autobiography, which she began when she was about fifty years old and finished fifteen years later on the brink of old age. Each volume of the *Mémoires* is one part of a unified project: to reveal the successive insights through which Beauvoir gradually uncovered the sociocultural myths hiding social reality and which in her view tend to dictate modes of behavior to the individual consonant with the bourgeois scheme of things. She contrasts these with her own *direct*—existential—experience of life, a truth which ipso facto repudiates falsehood.

Simone de Beauvoir wrote *Le Deuxième Sexe* after experiencing in her own life the constraints imposed by the myth of female inferiority; and she wrote *La Vieillesse* when she began to feel the first symptoms of old age in herself. The massive, scholarly aspect of the work and the immense amount of research with which it is documented reflect the threefold aim of the writer: to confront the social myth with the reality of direct experience; to denounce falsehood; and to inspire action. This was the pattern of all her work after *L'Invitée*. In this she demonstrated punctilious fidelity to Sartre's definition of the *committed writer*.

But in the *Mémoires* this same commitment raises questions concerning ambiguity of viewpoint. Beauvoir's first work, *L'Invitée*, is constructed in relation to two separate fields: first, the experience of jealousy, and, second, the existential schema of interrelations between the self and the other that Sartre was defining at the time in *L'Etre et le néant*. This was an abstract, theoretical schema based on the axiom that the relation between self and other is conflictual, a response to the master-slave, dominate-subordinate relation described by Hegel. In *L'Invitée,* the structure of the drama taking place between the three characters depends on this schema in a reworking of the classic jealousy theme, which, however, remains beneath the surface. Because it does, the plot of the novel acquires a sort of mysterious inevitability. Beauvoir had staked out her area, the relation of the self with the other—one of the most fertile if not the only area of all fiction. The impact of the direct experience, tempered by an organizing principle, created a powerful and coherent work of fiction.

After *L'Invitée,* however, the underlying intellectual schema appears to precede the lived experience. The fabric of subsequent texts was impoverished as a result, with the existential theme—no matter what it happened to be—running up against a context of political principles by which it was diminished, and which the author herself appeared to find boring. When Beauvoir adopted the Marxist schema, with its vocabulary, her arguments became more peremptory: every individual or collective circumstance, even old age, is shown as the result of the inhuman attitudes and criminal intentions of bourgeois society. Even the *Mémoires* raise questions as to their validity as a document. As in Sartre's autobiography, *Les Mots,* Simone de Beauvoir's evocation of her youth is couched in terms of a satiric denunciation of bourgeois culture from a political point of view. The *Mémoires* belong among the works of self-criticism through which Simone de Beauvoir marked out the path of her own intellectual itinerary and made it exemplary. It was an itinerary that led not to literature but to ethics and, ultimately, to a negative political commitment.

In Simone de Beauvoir's work there is another thematic strand that has been identified by the critics: the theme of happiness, viewed as harmony between the self and others, and the untrammeled explosion of feeling symbolized by the act of celebration, the greatest celebration of all being the collective celebration of the 1944 Liberation. The reverse of this theme is Beauvoir's ill-contained revolt against death. Critics have underscored the moral and intellectual constraints imposed on Beauvoir by the need to adhere to a set of political beliefs and to rationalize everything in terms of it. Her aphorisms and didactic arguments ill disguise her desperate impatience with the "force of circumstance," a force in conflict with the continuation of the harmonious life the author knew before 1939, and which for her constituted a kind of happiness where anything is possible. But the underlying message projected by her work is an ambiguous one: only rarely does real life coincide with human systems and human aspirations. The feeling that everything human beings do is meaningless will always be with us, no matter how hard we try to get rid of it. Beauvoir's austere yet utopian existential program for putting the life and philosophy of the individual to the test of sociopolitical reality may have provided Beauvoir herself with a life and a philosophy whose vectors were strictly parallel to Sartre's, but it seems to have introduced into her work a conflict that was perhaps unconscious and saved her from pedantic didacticism. In all of Beauvoir's fictitious works it is the women, faced with a masculine universe absorbed in politics and action, who ask the great metaphysical questions. A feminine discontent disrupts the world of masculine theories and "grand designs": Françoise, the heroine of *L'Invitée,* experiences the impossibility of the triangle, even though theoretically it has been accepted; Anne, in *Les Mandarins,* casts a cold eye on the post-1945 demise of all the fine intellectual and political dreams of the Left. Unattainable happiness and love, the approach of old age and death, and the passage of time are the themes sustaining a visceral anguish more eloquent than the themes of liberty, choice, and responsibility. The unique, and at the same time representative, aspect of Simone de Beauvoir's work was the result not so much of her progress from "bourgeois" idealism to existentialism and then to Marxism as of her refusal to indulge that underlying sensibility, and her determination to give positive form through her writing to the flood of events that swept through and overturned her own microcosm, in order to give to this act of writing a new cultural relevance.

Art and the Constraints of History

Albert Camus's career, unlike Simone de Beauvoir's, did reach its height between 1942 and 1944. *L'Etranger* and *Le Mythe de Sisyphe* both received warm acclaim. They were followed by two plays: *Le Malentendu,* which put the Parisian public off balance, and *Caligula,* whose success was due to its star, Gérard Philipe. A second group of works, published between 1947 and 1951 and including *La Peste,* two plays entitled *L'Etat de siège* and *Les Justes,* and another essay, *L'Homme révolté,* confirmed a reputation which was nevertheless beginning to elicit certain reservations. In response to *L'Homme révolté* the political controversy surrounding Camus's positions was made public on the initiative of *Les Temps modernes.* In 1956–57 a third group of works was announced by the appearance of *La Chute* and *L'Exil et le royaume.*

Camus, who was a professional journalist, also published numerous editorials and articles on current politics; in 1950 he collected the most important of these in the three-volume *Actuelles.* The posthumous publication of Camus's *Carnets* (notebooks), followed in 1962 and 1965 by a carefully edited and documented edition in the Bibliothèque de la Pléiade of his complete works, which in turn was complemented by the appearance of some of his unpublished works (among them an early, unfinished novel, *La Mort heureuse*) in the *Cahiers Albert Camus,* made it possible more than ten years after his death to appreciate the continuity of a body of work that is more varied and more substantial than it seemed to be at first, and with a high literary quality that emphasized its unity.

There is no other purely *literary* work of this period that immediately attracted a comparable bulk of critical commentary from every quarter; the critical works that have accompanied and extended Camus's writings are still growing in number. Criticism of Camus's work was first directed by Sartre, in an article on *L'Etranger,* toward an abstract interpretation of the story. According to him, *L'Etranger* was an illustration of the philosophical argument in *Le Mythe de Sisyphe,* an essay dealing with "the absurd." And it was on Camus's philosophy, measured either against orthodox or Sartrean Marxism, or against classical logic, that early criticism of his work fell—which somewhat falsified its true scope. Camus criticism gradually freed itself from this initial approach and an increasing number of critical studies dealing in particular with Camus's stories, emphasized the many different levels of his fictional works.

Yet the interrelations between Camus's individual works had been indicated by the author himself when he grouped them in successive blocks, and in his notebooks, when he collected them under a series of titles: the cycle of the Absurd; the cycle of Revolt; the unfinished cycle of Moderation he was working on when he died; and a projected final cycle—Love. Each separate category was further distinguished by being placed under the aegis of an emblematic figure from mythology: Sisyphus, Prometheus, Nemesis. In this way Camus showed that his writing was ordered according to a diachronic perspective and followed an itinerary with each separate stage also presenting a distinct theme.

As with the first two cycles, each additional cycle was to include a story, plays, and an essay. Camus explained this arrangement according to genres thus: "I use different genres when I write so as to avoid confusion. I have written plays using the language of action, essays using a form that is rational, and novels dealing with the mysteries of the human heart" ("Dernière Interview," *Essays,* Pléiade, p. 1926). He was proposing three different approaches, none replaceable by either of the others, even though all are united by a single theme. This classification requires a synchronic perspective.

Within each cycle, in fact, the "rational" essay appears to follow rather than to precede the other forms of writing, and to be developed according to a special kind of dialectic. For example, as the foreword to the essay *Le Mythe de Sisyphe* indicates, Camus examines in it a sort of *mal du siècle,* a latent nihilism Camus diagnoses and then sets out to exorcize by transposing it from the level of semireflection to the level of full consciousness. After this reasoned and fully substantiated diagnosis comes the myth. We are given the image of Sisyphus, pushing his heavy boulder uphill, condemned by the gods to climb the hill over and over again because, each time he almost reaches the top, the boulder falls back down again. This image puts the finishing touch on the analysis in the body of the essay where the classical paradoxes of the human condition are presented, which Camus designates by the single term "absurd." The term "absurd" refers, according to the young Camus, to the impasse in our secularized modern world that any philosophy of the absolute, or the whole, will come up against. Camus sees in this the origin of the nihilism that devalues life. He uses the myth as a way of displacing the problem. He proposes to himself and to the reader that they cease confronting the insoluble paradoxes of man's *fate,* and turn instead toward something that can be grasped in the here and now: man's *happiness.* A modern Sisyphus must be *imagined*—that is, invented—who is happy.

In *L'Homme révolté* Camus was also able to reach beyond his theme in this way, but less easily. Here Camus examines the hold exercised on the imagination of Western man by the Promethean theme of liberation. To achieve this liberation requires a rebellion against the constraints imposed by "the gods," that is, by the natural and the social order. Camus traced the ways in which this initially liberating rebellion eventually leads to the to-talitarian ideologies—whether nihilist or socialistic—that have punctuated modern history and in his view developed into the inhuman political tyran-nies, fascist as well as Stalinist, that are negations of the very liberty and justice they originally set out to attain. Claiming that the end justifies the means, they no longer recognize any limitation of their enterprise. This essay also concludes with a brief, ironic narrative summing up the story of the modern Prometheus. Beneath the mask of the mythological hero, Camus discovers another mask covering the face of a Caesar who deals in mystification and lies and is absorbed in the egocentric and sterile enterprise of turning himself into a god. It is at this point that the theme of revolt engenders a countertheme, a positive one: creative revolt, with the activity of the artist serving as one example of it.

Intellectually, both essays conform to the basic rhythm of Camus's work, to his personal dynamic; a theme is explored, its limits are reached, it opens up onto a new point of departure. The concept of removing successive masks is inherent in Camus's philosophical approach and reflects a disposi-tion toward the Nietzschean view. In the words of Zarathustra, an artist creates many masks for himself embodying the thousand impulses of a single sensibility.

In a way, all of Camus's fictional characters, from the deskworker Meur-sault in *L'Etranger* to the engineer Arrast in *La Pierre qui pousse,* are intimately linked to the inner "Dionysian" life of Camus the artist. The most powerful of these characters create themselves, and their story, solely through words, that is, through the text. The first words of Camus's first and probably most enigmatic novel, *L'Etranger,* have become famous: "Mother died today. Or, maybe, yesterday."[1] With these words, the autonomy and presence of the speaker are imposed immediately on the reader. Camus varied the form of these apparently self-creating works, carefully selecting the narrative style appropriate to each one. After Meursault's story came the third-person story of *La Peste,* told in a language which is carefully controlled. In this book an eyewitness describes a plague epidemic in Oran, Algeria. At the end of the story the man reveals that he is a physician from Oran named Dr. Rieux, and that he was the person who organized the fight against the plague. After this book came the monologue-dialogue of the protagonist in *La Chute:* "penitent judge" Jean-Baptiste Clamence and his conversation in an Amsterdam bar with someone he encountered by chance and whom he turns into his own alter ego. This monologue was followed by a short story entitled *Le Renégat,* a lengthy inner lamentation on the part of the renegade priest of the title, a lament which loses itself in the desert that surrounds him.

For the short stories published in the book *L'Exil et le Royaume* (with the exception of *La Renégat*) Camus used the third-person narrative, but he sought the same effect of narrative autonomy as in the works written in the first person. From the interior structure of each story, even those that are— apparently—the most realistic, such as the account of a strike *(Les Muets)* or the dilemma of a schoolteacher in the Algerian hills *(L'Hôte),* there more or less insistently emerges a dimension which is not solely that of the reality (usually Algerian) in which the characters are geographically located. The titles of the stories are clues, and so are the landscapes in which the characters, welded to a specific place and a specific climate, evolve: Clamence is a prisoner of the mists and the concentric canals of Amsterdam; the schoolteacher in *L'Hôte* is held captive in the no-man's-land of the Algerian hill country, halfway between the world of the colonists and the world of the nomadic Arab tribes. We could cite many other examples.

The unity of tone and multiplicity of thematic resonance in these texts appears to present the reader with a meaning that goes beyond them but is never made explicit. Even when Camus openly declares the allegorical nature of the text, as he does in *La Peste,* the behavior of the characters and the structure of the story leave certain areas of obscurity that cannot be completely explained either in the context of the German Occupation of France, to which we are referred by Camus, or in the metaphysical context of man's fate perceptible in the background. The plague, a tangible form of evil that is here made to represent all the other forms, retains both its specificity and its opacity. *L'Etranger, La Chute,* and particularly *La Renégat* have never yielded to exegesis of any kind.

Camus's narrative takes place in the realm of myth and, like any other

---

[1] *The Stranger,* trans. Stuart Gilbert (New York: Knopf, 1973).

myth, it is charged with ambiguity and ends with a question rather than a conclusion. Meursault, the man-condemned-to-die, having assumed the most universal attributes of the human condition, is not, within the limits of the story, put to death. Clamence may begin his accusation-confession all over again the next day; and in Renegade's lament no one can untangle the part that is real from the part that is illusion. Camus revived Gide's type of narrative style, which itself had its origins in Nietzsche, by embuing it with a richer and more highly concentrated poetic density and thematic direction.

Camus was less successful with the stage, in spite of his passion for the theater and his long experience in it. His stage adaptations of various works, some already belonging to the theater and some, like the two most famous—*Les Possédés* and *Requiem pour une nonne*—taken from novels, were more successful than his own plays. His partial failure cannot, therefore, be explained by lack of skill. Of the four plays by Camus staged between 1944 and 1949–50, one, *Caligula*, was a success; *L'Etat de siège*, a sort of lyrical "mime-drama" combining song, pantomime, crowd scenes, and an array of various scenic devices, was a failure; *Le Malentendu* and *Les Justes* enjoyed a tepid *succès d'estime*.

Camus's ambition as a playwright was to put tragedy back on the stage. In *Le Malentendu* he also seems to have sensed the new direction French theater was taking. The action takes place on a stage that has been reduced to a sort of abstract space, a room in an inn. It is sustained by three main characters—mother, daughter, and unrecognized son, whose return home after a long absence automatically sets in motion a weighty ritual of murder. All of the action takes place under the eyes of an aged deaf-mute manservant who utters only one word, "no," in response to a desperate appeal from the sole survivor, the outsider, the wife of the sacrificed son whose belatedly discovered identity leads to the death of the two murderesses. Hieratic gestures and a sibylline dialogue composed of allusion and "misunderstood" signals suggest the kind of tragic conflict the play was intended to represent: the struggle between repressed emotion and deliberate action inspired by the conscious and imperious desire of the two women. They kill the travelers so that they can steal the money they need to reach at last the sun-filled country of their dreams.

Because of its economy of means, *Le Malentendu* stands as something of a model of Camus's dramatic method. The play's tragic irony resides not in its climax—the double suicide of mother and daughter—but in the moment of awareness that precedes it, when, too late, mother and daughter recognize in the murdered stranger their son and brother. All of Camus's three plays, although superficially very different from one another, share the same basic structure: one main character, or several—the Emperor Caligula, the innkeepers in *Le Malentendu,* the Russian terrorists in *Les Justes*—react to an intolerable situation by initiating a course of action to change the status quo; but once this process has begun they are caught and, losing control of the initial mechanism, discover their failure in a moment of desperate lucidity just before death. The sense emerging from Camus's plays of a "modern" tragedy springs from the disparity between the human logic underlying an action that is voluntary and the consequences this action entails. Camus's tragic protagonist does not disobey the laws of the gods, for here there are no gods; he yields to what we might call the "existential" temptation to assume responsibility for unbridled freedom in the pursuit of justifiable ends. He embodies the hubris of modern man according to Camus. All of Camus's plays raise the question of the limits inherent in the paradoxes defining "the absurd." His plays, like his fictional works, contain a critical philosophy from which the logic of the dramatic action flows. This logic has often escaped playgoers, unfortunately, but it gives the three plays their emblematic value. They illustrate better than the essays and the stories the author's attitude toward the tragic reversals that the reality of man's fate inflicts on his aspirations, even in the case of the most generous of men, such as Kaliayev, the poet-terrorist in Les Justes.

Camus's theater is literary and consciously experimental, falling within a tradition that goes back to Greek tragedy. Camus altered the conventional relations between character, plot, and climax in an attempt to give the action a meaning that would reflect his own perception of the semiunconscious dilemmas and blind alleys modern philosophy finds itself up against.

Sartre once noted, in an article on L'Etranger, the strangeness, for a Parisian, of a literary world embued with the exotic sensuality appropriate to the Algerian, Mediterranean landscapes evoked in the story. Camus's work and his artistic sensibility did, in fact, have their source in the dual reality of the slums of Algiers and the sumptuous countryside of Algeria. In Camus's two earliest published works—L'Envers et l'Endroit and Noces à Tipasa—this dual reality is presented right from the start as the two poles of Camus's universe. It was in Algiers that Camus, a dozen years before L'Etranger was published, began his triple literary career as playwright, novelist, and essayist. And it was in Algiers that he belonged to a group of writers— which included Claude Fréminville, Gabriel Audisio, and, later, Jules Roy, and Emmanuel Roblès from Oran—determined to open the way for the "new Algerian culture." The sensual and intellectual climate of Camus's work is the product of those years.

Camus's active participation in the Resistance, and in the "History" he both witnessed and made, affected his work more violently than it did Simone de Beauvoir's, and darkened its tone. This history dictated the direction followed by the Cycle de la révolte. For Camus, who suffered a relapse of tuberculosis in 1946, working in the politically charged atmosphere following the Liberation was difficult. It was only after a ten-year struggle comparable to the experience described in La Peste that the short stories in L'Exil et le Royaume appeared. In the words of Nietzsche, one of his masters at the time, Camus from the very beginning of his career had chosen to "work in chains," i.e., to accept the constraints of a strict form. His models were the classics. He stood apart both from the surrealist aesthetic and from the existentialist trend toward making form subordinate to achieving the broadest possible popular appeal. Although in works like *L'Etranger, La Chute, Le Renégat,* and *Le Malentendu* there were occasional foreshadowings of the future directions to be taken by French drama and the French novel, Camus's own work followed an entirely different path. And it was perhaps the rigor with which he pursued his goal of grasping whole a reality he experienced with all the passion and sensuality of a young Algerian in the grip of intense beauty that explains the quality of his work and its unprecedented popularity with a public for which he made no concessions as a writer—any more than he did for himself.

Simone de Beauvoir, faithful to the existential aesthetic, created a fictional style in the tradition of realism, but without the central consciousness that functions to organize and interpret the story. She presents her story through several consciousnesses, the conversations and reactions of each character serving to define his or her individual existential "project." Beauvoir kept psychological analysis out of her books, replacing it with the schemas of existential psychoanalysis, which control and explain the actions and the relationships of her characters. *L'Etranger, La Chute,* and *Le Renégat* illustrate more clearly a new relationship between author, reader, and text. Camus's philosophy calls every system of interpretation and every system of political ideas into question. With *L'Etranger* the reader is faced with a text that at first seems to come from a character firmly rooted and defined according to accepted conventions; and yet it is never possible to locate this narrator precisely in relation to the events he describes. Sooner or later the question arises: Who is speaking? And to whom? Camus has divorced the *temporal level* of the story being told from the temporal level of the events taking place. The status of the protagonist becomes problematic. The story does not come to any conclusion: an appeal has been made. The ambiguity of the protagonist and what the protagonist has to say becomes even more obvious in *La Chute* and *Le Renégat.* Both the character and the character's story emanate from a discourse that has no validation other than its own and is articulated by means of linguistic and thematic associations within the text itself; the logic of the text is no longer the logic of reality. The text is presented neither as a representation of observed reality, nor as a representation of reality as reflected by a subjective consciousness; it is presented as the deployment of ambiguous language, as language "interplay," a fiction concealing and at the same time revealing a fictive and problematic subjectivity. It is no longer possible to distinguish the story from how the story is being told. To the reader has devolved the task of locating this discourse so as to identify, i.e., to create, the narrator and the significance of what he is saying. Camus does, however, maintain the consistency and continuity of the discourse necessary for making the postulate that it comes from a single "speaker" seem believable. Camus's narrative technique has something in common with the *nouveau roman*. But his chosen subjects maintain the primacy of a meaning obliquely concerning the reality in which the reader lives.

19

1950–70:
Marguerite Duras
and Claude Simon

Le Square was the book that in 1955 drew the attention of the reading public to novelist Marguerite Duras. Her career had begun in 1943, and this was her seventh novel. And it was with *Le Vent,* his fourth novel, that Claude Simon achieved his first success. Also, it was with this novel that he joined the innovators on the editorial board of Les Editions de Minuit who were determined to break with the past and who launched the literary movement that seems to have reached its simultaneous apogee and decline with a 1971 colloquium on the *nouveau roman.*

The writers who had made their reputations after 1940 faced a period of serious crisis coinciding with the end of the great era of existentialism and the beginning of a dual reaction to it. One portion of this reaction was political and ideological; the starting signal for it was Marcel Aymé's novel *Uranus* (1948). The other portion was literary, and it likewise had two sides to it. One group of young writers was turning toward the past, the past of the twenties and the style of nonchalance represented by Radiguet; an example was Françoise Sagan and *Bonjour Tristesse.* The other group, the Editions de Minuit authors, was also seeking to renew their ties with tradition, but with the tradition represented by Gide, Proust, and Valéry, writers who believed the craft of literature must have an accompanying theoretical framework. The original "pioneers" of the group, Alain Robbe-Grillet, Nathalie Sarraute, and Michel Butor, have been amply studied since, both as theoreticians and practitioners of the *nouveau roman.* Samuel Beckett's reputation can also be gauged by the quantity of works he has inspired. The same is true of Ionesco. Falling somewhat behind is Robert Pinget, whose work has pursued a brilliant and abundant course, even though it has been the subject of less critical commentary. But we have chosen Marguerite Duras and Claude Simon for our discussion here, not only because of the quality of their work, but also because its development from decade to decade has conformed, in their respective cases, to the dual literary trend of the period.

Neither Duras nor Simon is particularly interested in theory, but both have occasionally talked about their own work during interviews; Simon has taken part in some colloquiums on the *nouveau roman,* and in his *Orion aveugle* (1970) he describes and shows how his text spread out and organized itself while he was in the very process of writing it; but he has no general theory of the novel to offer. Marguerite Duras has maintained her distance from colloquiums and collective theoretical work and has manifested her aversion for the theoretical hullabaloo that accompanies debate on the subject of the novel. In her view, what novelists need is "a sense of man, not a concept"; and she considers the proliferation of theory to be an aberration of the masculine brain. "Man," she has said, "must stop being a theoretical imbecile" *(Les Parleuses).* And yet is is her work, more than any other, that has accomplished the *destructuralization* of narrative demanded by some of the theoreticians. In contrast to this, Claude Simon's work procedes step by step toward a method of "production" for fully articulated texts organized on the basis of certain initial premises and according to principles of composition that he has explained at length.

"There was an entire period," Marguerite Duras has said, "up to the time of *Moderato Cantabile,* when I was writing books I no longer recognize." Thus does she repudiate her early work. She distinguishes three periods in her own development: the six novels and the short stories written between 1943 and 1958 that she no longer recognizes; the three novels *Moderato Cantabile, Dix Heures et demie du soir en été,* and *L'Après-midi de Monsieur Andesmas,* which wera written between 1958 and 1962 and inaugurated her experimental period; and, finally, the five works that followed: the trilogy *Le Ravissement de Lol V. Stein,* a kind of matrix text, *Le Vice-Consul,* and *L'Amour,* with their respective epilogues, and the films *La Femme du Gange, India Song,* and *Le Camion.*

Claude Simon's work can be divided in almost the same way. First, three novels that still conformed to familiar models; then five large works inaugurated by *Le Vent* and concluding with *Le Palace* (1962). After a silence of five years, a new phase began with *Histoire* and continued with three "novels" and one text, *Leçons et choses* (1975), which illustrated, five years after *Orion Aveugle,* how a text is woven together and how it can be "diverted" in the process.

Looking back from 1970, the three phases Duras and Simon recognized in their own work were diachronically analogous. During an initial phase ending in the late fifties, both adapted to their own uses the techniques of the realistic novel that were based on autobiography and received new impetus under the influence of the American novel. Then came a second, experimental phase, but one in which some elements of traditional narrative were retained: plot, character, a context the reader can recognize. Here is where the difference between their two styles of writing becomes apparent, along with their respective ties to two separate currents in the twentieth-century novel: Duras belongs indisputably if indirectly to the line going back to Virginia Woolf; Simon's ties are more explicitly to Joyce and Faulkner. The works written during this second phase of their development earned the two authors the attention of the critics and a public that was small at first but increased. Following this phase came a period of more profound change when, in the view of the two authors themselves, their books retained only the remotest connection with the novel. Claude Simon's participation at this time in various debates dealing with the *nouveau roman* guaranteed him a continued if limited audience; but Marguerite Duras, by her own account, suffered from the silence that greeted her work.

In retrospect, the development of the two writers appears as a continuum, despite the successive breaks introduced by each new work. *Le Square,* for example, foreshadowed the experimental period in Duras's work that began with *Moderato Cantabile,* just as *Histoire,* from the technical point of view, was a transition between *Le Palace* and *Triptyque.*

On the thematic level this continuity is striking and its origins biographical. Duras's characters are haunted by a "somewhere else" reflecting a sensibility conditioned by the "somewhere else" that was the author's life as a child raised on the banks of the Mekong River. Living within her is a submerged landscape, the "river of pain," famine, and misery that flows from Cambodia to Calcutta. Attached to this landscape are the underlying themes of Duras's work: the haunting memory of this suffering; her need to be absorbed by it; her obsession with death; and her hatred of colonialism (see *Les Parleuses*). Her major theme of feminine erotic desire is expanded within it. Marguerite Duras's interest in film must have grown naturally out of the ever-presence of this dream landscape.

The obsessive presence in Claude Simon's novels is the war: the Spanish civil war (four novels, notably *Le Palace*); the disastrous defeat of 1940 *(La Route des Flandres); France after the Liberation (Gulliver);* the First World War; and, in the more distant past, the battle of Pharsalus, in the novel by the same name *(La Bataille de Pharsale)*—the "I" in this story reads Julius Caesar's account of the battle while traveling through Greece. Besides its recollection of the Spanish civil war, *Le Palace* also evoked the Spanish penetration of South America. This fragmentary presence of collective history is part of the personal, autobiographical "tangled magma" from which Claude Simon drew his novels. The continuing presence from one book to the next of a single geographical region, the southwest of France; a single family; and a single character exploring the thousand labyrinths of a single memory, "telling," "telling itself," a fragmented story that is never entirely "put together," allows the reader glimpses of a real field of reference fading in and out before his eyes.

After *Histoire,* the fictitious narrator and (in theory) producer of the text for which he has provided the point of departure and whose inner development he follows, disappears. All that remains is a man holding the pen who, starting from his desire to write and his relation with one or more incongruous, juxtaposed objects, inaugurates a "text," a fabric woven of words and growing on the surface of the page through a complex interplay of semantic, metaphoric, and phonic associations. Writing becomes an adventure, a drama of linguistic interplay expanding and ordering itself into unforeseen combinations.

Although the context changes, both of these writers bring us back to the initial action of an author holding a pen. Their enterprise raises the question of the relations of the writer to a language that has returned to its "transporting" or, as Duras might put it, its "ravishing" function. When Duras and Simon entered their experimental phase, around 1955, both gave up trying to situate their novels in relation to a realistic frame of reference, even though both at first continued to employ the usual elements readers expect to find in a novel: characters, plot, point of view.

Duras's novels through *Détruire, dit-elle* present superficial stories and situations that are transparently simple. Their plots are easy to summarize: a housemaid and a door-to-door novelty salesman meet by chance in a public square, talk to each other from 4:30 until nightfall, separate to meet again, or not, later in the week *(Le Square)*. Four French people on a trip, a couple and their child accompanied by a woman friend, spend a night unexpectedly in the hotel in a small town in Spain where a man is wanted by the police for killing his wife. While the husband and the woman friend yield to irresistible desire, the deserted wife attempts without success to be of some help to the murderer *(Dix heures et demie du soir en été)*.

Claude Simon's novels can also be said to belong to these "novels of memory" (Jean Rousset) in the Proustian tradition to which two of Butor's four novels belong—*L'Emploi du temps* and *La Modification*—along with several of Pinget's novels, *L'Interrogatoire,* for one. A single character, located in time and space by the author, journeys back from association to association through a specific past his current situation brings to life again, but in incoherent fragments that seem to conceal a mystery of some kind. For example, in *La Route des Flandres,* Georges, a repatriated prisoner of war, in the course of a night spent sleeping with Corinne, the wife of his cousin and superior officer killed under his eyes during the 1940 debacle, recreates in a kind of continuous interior monologue the chain of events, emotions, and questions coalescing around his relationship with this cousin. In *Le Palace,* a character whose memory at times overlaps with Georges's, returns to Barcelona fifteen years after having stayed there as a student, and the same process unfolds. A patient reader can reconstruct the exact chronology of the events presented in the story in relation to historical time.

With Duras, however, there is nothing to explain what is happening to the protagonist—always a woman—snatched from her middle-class environment by some cataclysm and thrust into the imaginary world of the novel. Thus the harmonious world of Anne Desbaresdes, a woman who is rich and happy, mother of a little boy she loves, is torn apart by the sound of a revolver going off during a crime of passion. This revolver shot opens up a breach within her, which ignites the violent and devastating desire for a boundless love, a passion experienced to the death *(Moderato Cantabile)*. The existence of Lol V. Stein, a young middle-class woman who has everything she could want and is engaged to be married, is devastated in the same way when her fiancé, Michael Harrington, deserts her for another woman, Anne-Marie Stretter, at a dance. "What is perfection," said Valéry's Faust, "if not the denial of all we desire." It is against this denial, an enterprise that is Faustian and mortal (the other facet of denial being hunger, the desire for life) that Duras rebelled, in her life as in her works. For her, the necessity for literary experimentation must be seen in this context. Breaches must also be opened in the ordered sequence of language and narrative so that the unsaid, the denied, can rise to the surface and invade articulated language. Conventional syntax and accepted cultural forms suppress one mode of discourse so that another may be imposed; it is this false order that Marguerite Duras, in turn, sets out to suppress.

This unformulated discourse gradually comes to light in the somnambulistic behavior of Duras's characters, whose individual personalities are concentrated in the incantationlike use of a name: Anne Desbaresdes, Lol V. Stein, Anne-Marie Stretter; in the settings they inhabit; and in the rare words they utter.

Duras's texts rely on the musical properties of language—word placement, use of leitmotif—to create a rhythmic continuity replacing syntactic continuity. Its function is to "ravish" the reader, abducting him away from his routine surroundings and transporting him into that boundless, limitless reality that is human "denial." The separation between the two worlds is made apparent in the two musical phrases between which the characters in the *Vice-Consul* oscillate, inside the protective walls of their Calcutta embassy: the blues number *India Song,* its score folded shut on the Vice-Consul's piano in Paris, and the monotonous cry of a beggar woman punctuating her long journey from Cambodia to Calcutta.

Through her disarticulation of the "perfect" structures of fictional narrative, Marguerite Duras attempts to tear her characters away from the determinations of tradition, from the Faustian, masculine fictions that define them. Her female characters are, in her words, "riven from without, pierced by passion." It is therefore through them that the "river of pain" and of life overflows, erodes, and bears away the "reassuring" structures of the West, as the beggar woman's singsong undermines the constrained forms of sonata, waltz, and other kinds of musical composition. The captivity of the woman and the writer inside bourgeois settings that are narrow and isolated (villas behind iron gates, luxury hotels, resort towns, embassies) is the text "imposed" on the suppressed mode of discourse; and Duras pursues the destruction of this "imposed text" to its limit. In *Amour* there is no longer a story of any kind. On a desolate beach between sea and a deserted city named S. Tahla—could it be the S. Tahla of *Le Ravissement?*—three characters are outlined. One walks back and forth on the beach, another is a woman sitting down and referred to as L.V.S.—could it be Lol V. Stein? The third character is a traveler-observer who has made a pilgrimage of return—could it be Michael Harrington, who once deserted Lol V. Stein? There is no way of telling. Everything remains suspended in this end-of-the-world or beginning-of-the-world landscape which nonetheless recalls the distant figures of other stories. All of Marguerite Duras's books were oriented progressively toward the constitution of the *minimal text* in order to obtain, it would seem, somewhat in the manner of Beckett, that undifferentiated human consciousness beyond the limitations of the "self," expressed in the monody of the "Woman of the Ganges." Duras's fundamental theme is the alienation and denial at the heart of a ruined society, the theme of the Other toward whom the act of writing thrusts the writer. It is almost always the feminine consciousness that has been alienated and must be delivered or deliver itself.

Claude Simon's experiments took another direction, toward what British critic Stephen Heath has called "retextualization." Simon, a painter, approached the problem of formal narrative organization from the point of view of painting. As a writer, how could he contain and channel the chaotic, proliferating chains of associations presented to the memory? Having read extensively in Proust, Joyce, and Faulkner, Simon clearly distinguished three levels in the "novel of memory": the disparate events, objects, and people collected in the memory of one person; the narrator's attempt to follow the course of events responsible for collecting them there; and the work of the writer in imposing order on them.

Since the reality that Claude Simon himself experienced was the absurdity and meaninglessness of human life, he could not impose a teleological order on this work of rememoration—a finality like the one leading *A la Recherche du temps perdu* or *La Modification* to a final resolution. Like a Baroque painter who groups together figures from different periods in time on a single ground in his altarpiece, Claude Simon imposed certain *spatial* constraints on the dynamics of these rememorations, directing their progression along certain vectors he represented graphically.[1] Once an initial situation had been established, he could follow "word by word" the associations generated by the disparate offering of memory, turning them into catalysts for setting in motion, in the thoughts of a narrator, the interplay of associations from which the dynamics of the narrative will come. Serving as such

---

[1]"La Fiction mot à mot," *Le Nouveau Roman: hier, aujourd'hui*, II (coll. 8/10), 73–96.

catalysts in Simon's works have been pigeons, torn posters, the Palace that is absent from a public square in Barcelona, or the series of postcards the narrator of *Histoire* finds in an old bureau drawer.

At this point fiction takes possession of the memory, the past becomes the "present" when it is being written about, and the narrative coalesces around a few "hubs" (Ricardou); one of these hubs, for example, is a dead horse in *La Route des Flandres* that serves four times as a point of return for this cloverleaf novel. They are "tentative" stories, "fragments" snatched by the act of writing from a history that is half erased. This kind of writing no longer conforms to the tradition postulating a *narrator* addressing a reader who accepts the convention that what is being said comes from someone. The Story and how it is being told are divorced from both author and narrator, with the latter groping for his own identity among the networks of relations being revealed to him. Claude Simon's notoriously long sentences and his use of the present participle indicate, in his words, the "enpresent-ing" role of writing. The text is constructed as it goes along, following the path of memory and associations whose significance remains hypothetical but which do build up a psychic landscape similar to the groupings found on altarpieces.

Here the writer's task is conceived as the *transfer* into language, and the recombination into a new textual arrangement, of the "debris" *(Leçons de choses)* of memory. The narrator "Georges," whose legend is created on the basis of the real life of Claude Simon, disappears with the final word of *Histoire:* "me?" From that point on, Claude Simon's experiments were with wordplay (phonic associations, puns, metaphors, metonymy that was usu-ally based on something visual but was also occasionally based on super-position: umbel-umbrella) or with an "object theme" (a painting, a calen-dar).

Each in their own may, Marguerite Duras and Claude Simon both fol-lowed the evolutionary curve of the experimental novel: both progressively minimized character and plot; both attempted to find a new "formaliza-tion" for fiction. They ended up at opposite poles from one another. At one extreme was the quasi silence of *Amour* and the recourse to film in order to open perspectives onto that deep level of sensibility which Duras believes preexists all fiction and eludes language. At the other extreme is Simon's creation of self-generating texts whose coherence resides precisely at the points where the average reader sees nothing but inexplicable dis-continuities. But they have one thing in common—their constantly re-affirmed belief in the relationship of mutual exchange between the self who is writing and the text being written, between experienced reality and its "translation" into language that must be transformed. The self is diffused throughout the text, it is not present in the form of a self-contained, auton-omous subject who judges a world outside himself or creates a self-sufficient world around him. The author has acquired new modesty. A narrowing of subject matter in the case of Duras, and an extension of it in the case of Simon, have displaced the traditional field of action of the reader.

Conclusion

For this brief summary of French writing from Cocteau to Claude Simon one might almost be tempted to undertake the kind of experiment Simon tried in his novels from *Vent* to *Histoire,* following from decade to decade the imprint made by French history on the sensibility of our era as reflected in the French literature of the period. It has been a deep one, of that there can be no doubt; clearly, there is no writer of this period whose literary enterprise has not been determined in part by a keen awareness of his historical situation. This is true even for those who, like the *nouveaux-nouveaux écrivains* of the sixties, set out to divorce literature from its representative and referential function. Attitudes have changed, are changing, and continue to grow. It follows that the relation between fiction and its modes of expression will also change. The concept writers have of their own function, the vocabulary they use to describe it, the form they give to what they write, and the style they choose will always be closely related to the way they see themselves in the world.

Abandoning for a moment the diachronic perspective, a difficult one to establish for a period still this close to us, we could approach these works all together, as though they constituted a synchronic series in which each individual work is defined in relation to the others. Certain themes are echoed back and forth from one work to the other. Two predominate: history, with its related themes of fate and time; and an all-encompassing enquiry into human consciousness and the nature of the self, frequently accompanied by the related themes of death and creation. Absorption in the self fades, however, and is replaced by speculations concerning that mythical creature inherited from the nineteenth century, man, and also "the new man."

In this context, certain obsessions can be discerned: the beast, for example. It is the beast in man that was stalked by Malraux, and man's irremediable decline into bestiality that was prophesied by Céline; beasts appear in hundreds of images and metaphors in Claude Simon's novels, and a bestial image is evoked by Marguerite Duras's hordes of starving beggars. Beasts and bestiality, violence, eroticism, and death haunt a literature that is neutralized—naturalized we could perhaps say—by the ordering of written text. It is a literature also haunted by the dream or the hope of new forms of affection and friendship binding human beings together: Breton, Malraux, Camus, and Duras each developed this theme in their own way.

It would seem that for writers, writing is still something beyond man, something through which man can transform himself. Beginning with Breton, French writers appear to have set themselves the task of *creating* a hypothetical, potential experience for their readers, rather than *recreating* a conventional and familiar one. Poetry, said Breton, is insubordination; and prose, perhaps, investigation. Rebellion and quest are, of all the forms taken by literary discourse, the two most common during this period, which explains the uneasy relationship this discourse maintained with its own past, and with the canons that designated and defined it as literature.

An Inconclusive Conclusion

In the course of the present work we have clearly distinguished, first, the extremely rich period whose literary production accompanied, and in various ways reflected, the "modernist" ferment of the twenties. Most of these works can be placed within the framework of a literary tradition they were reinterpreting. The modernist era was followed, next, by a period of retrenchment and relative sterility which perhaps will later be seen as a period of gestation. Historically, however, this period of retrenchment coincided with the hiatus of which World War II was a consequence perhaps more than a cause. Haunted by the history of great empires and how they fell, people began to talk about decadence, a somewhat unsatisfactory term. The doubts expressed during this period regarding the function of literature were a reflection of the uncertain future facing the Western world and the effect this had on French attitudes. Our third and last period has been called "neomodernist" and includes all the new literary works launched on a vector running, very approximately, from 1950 to 1970: at this point its impetus began to peter out, just as it had with Symbolism around 1910. From 1920 to 1970 we have followed from decade to decade the changes in the literary field perceptible today. Not until about 1985, perhaps, will the physiognomy of the fifty-year period as a whole begin to emerge with sufficient clarity to be interpreted more definitively.

Having come to the end of our retrospective journey, we may, however, risk a look toward the future. Between 1970 and 1977 the literary scene had already begun to change. Certain terms linked to the overall category of "modernism" have recurred from chapter to chapter and punctuated the present text: change, doubt, breaking out of established forms and structures, and, lastly, "deconstruction"; or again: text, writing, discourse, code, language. Other terms have emphasized the transition from unity to diversity, singular to plural: polysemy, critical languages, Francophone literatures, paraliteratures, mass media. Today we also speak of "homosexual literature" or "feminist works." This is another way of saying that French culture, under the pressure of social transformation, has opened to the concept of diversification, while, at the same time, conflict among various political dogmatisms has been considerable. No single ideology has prevailed. Every "discourse" has been the subject of doubts and harsh criticism. "Modernism" has in fact been the product of a new political awareness. It is linked to a keen sense of the problematical nature of all forms of expression, and of the conditioning necessary before any form of communication is possible. This awareness has given rise to the two inseparable aspects of a single question striking at the very source of the literary enterprise: What status should be given to the subject, the "I"; and what relation should be established with the language?

This questioning may eventually run its course, however, and be replaced by the need for some kind of affirmation. From the point of view of society as a whole, there are certain groups clamoring to be heard—women, for example, and minorities. The renewed need to speak or to write, seems to indicate that writers are once again seeking a more spontaneous, more immediate relation with their language and their readers. The "scientific" phase of postmodernist criticism seems to be veering toward a broadened yet more precise awareness of both the assumptions underlying the dual activities of reading/writing, and their limitations. But a text, as a text, is in itself irrefutable. And the "pleasure of the text," whatever we mean by it, no less so. The "naive" reader, making direct contact with the text, comes before the reader who is laden with theories; and, in an occasional reversal of roles, it is the former who can accuse the latter of naiveté.

There are certain themes, however, which, though conjectural, do lend themselves to reflection. French literature, in the course of its long history, has known periods of growth followed by periods of inactivity that were later seen to be times of gestation. But the post-1950 literary controversy had its roots in another going even deeper: the controversy surrounding culture itself. French literary life for almost four centuries had rested on *reading,* and on critical commentary on a group of "classic" texts transmitting both a concept of how to live and how to write, and constituting the ideal of "high culture." With the democratization of education and the new orientation of a civilization in which reading was becoming a marginal activity, this ideal tended to disappear.

Seen in this light, the importance attributed to the text by small groups of marginal intellectuals, writers or critics, appears as a sort of defense mechanism; and the position they assign to that mythical reader as symptomatic of it. In point of fact, this attempt to make reading an activity for the elite few reveals perhaps better than anything else the retreat of the writer before the rise of a new public. A hasty appeal to experimental techniques that were still untested—psychological, sociological, and linguistic—in order to bolster up this effort, and the proliferation of dubious critical jargon completely mystifying to the average reader, tended to create a new cult of the literary text. It may be some time before the harmony between society and literature that seems to be the prerequisite for a productive literary life can be restored. For the time being, this prerequisite is lacking, or appears to be. But we are perhaps too close to our subject to be able to discern, beneath the ripples on the surface, the currents developing at a deeper level, for the process linking the literature being made to the people who will read it is a complex one. And the contradiction is great when the writer, through the esotericism of his language, divorces his public from his work, even while rightly proclaiming his readers to be indispensable to the viability of the text. But perhaps the demands placed on their readers by these new writer-theoreticians will create a better-informed, more highly critical, keener public, which will give rise in turn, as in the Renaissance, to a new kind of writing, a literature tailored to the final years of the twentieth century, which for us are still shrouded in darkness but are rich in possibilities both inconceivable and singularly imminent.

The great task of our era has been to redefine the reality in which we live. The teaching of French literature has undoubtedly placed a disproportionate emphasis on transmitting a system of values no longer significantly relevant to the new structures of the contemporary world. This perhaps explains the present state of affairs: a proliferation of systems for interpreting literature and indecision as to the form this literature should take; the coexistence of two distinct brands of literature—the books people read but nobody talks about, and the books nobody reads but everyone comments on. In any case, the vigor of the controversy that for the last twenty years has surrounded literature seems to us a sure sign of its central role in that ill-defined whole we call culture.

Dictionary
of Authors

Abellio, Raymond, pseud. (Georges Soulès). 1907–

Graduate of Ecole Polytechnique, engineer with the *Ponts et Chaussées*, politician. Elected to administrative committee of SFIO, drafted in 1939. Prisoner of war, released in 1941. Joined Eugène Deloncle's Mouvement Social Révolutionnaire (MSR). After World War II, retired to Switzerland. His first book, *Heureux les pacifiques*, came out in 1946 and was awarded with Sainte-Beuve prize the same year. Abellio published two more novels, *Les Yeux d'Ezéchiel sont ouverts* (1950) and *La Fosse de Babel* (1962). He was also the author of several essays on gnosticism, the science of numbers and the phenomenology of being: *Vers un nouveau prophétisme* (1947); *La Bible, document chiffré* (1950–51); *Assomption de l'Europe* (1954); *La Structure absolue* (1964). In 1975 he published a collection of reminiscences, *Les Militants, 1927–1939.*

Adamov, Arthur. 1908–70

Born in Russia, where his family owned oil wells in Baku. Educated in Geneva, moved to Paris in 1924. Frequented surrealist circles. During the Vichy regime was interned at a camp at Argelès. In 1946 published *L'Aveu*, an account containing the main themes of his theatrical work. In 1950 his play *La Grande et la Petite Manœuvre* was produced at the Théâtre des Noctambules. In 1953 he published volume 1 of his dramatic works *(La Parodie; L'Invasion; La Grande et la Petite Manœuvre; Le Professeur Taranne; Tous contre tous);* and in 1955 volume 2 *(Le Sens de la marche; Les Retrouvailles; Ping-Pong);* an increasingly powerful theater of political involvement was announced by volume 3 in 1966 *(Paolo Paoli; La Politique des restes; Sainte-Europe);* volume 4 was published in 1968 *(M. le Modéré; Printemps 71).* Adamov also wrote numerous essays on the theater: *August Strindberg dramaturge* (1955); *Ici et Maintenant* (1964); and a collection of reminiscences—*L'Homme et L'Enfant* (1968). A leader in the *Nouveau théâtre* (with Ionesco and Beckett), Adamov turned after *Paolo Paoli* toward writing plays of social satire.

Anouilh, Jean. 1910–

Born into a family where the father was a tailor and the mother a violinist, Anouilh, "the poor man's Giraudoux," began his career as secretary to Louis Jouvet. In 1928, his first play, *L'Hermine,* was produced at the Théâtre de l'Oeuvre. After his meeting with Barsacq and Pitoëff in 1937, he produced *Le Voyageur sans bagage.* Following the production of *Antigone* at the Théâtre de l'Atelier in 1944 he went on to write fifteen plays that earned him a reputation as one of the greatest names in the French theater. Anouilh divided his dramatic works into *Pièces roses (Le Bal des voleurs; Le Rendez-vous de Senlis; Léocadia; Eurydice)* published in 1949; *Pièces noires (L'Hermine; Le Sauvage; Le Voyageur sans bagage, Médée)* published in 1958; *Nouvelles Pièces noires (Jézabel; Antigone; Roméo et Jeannette), Pièces brillantes (L'invitation au château; Colombe; La Répétition ou l'amour puni; Cécile ou l'école des pères)* published in 1951; *Pièces grinçantes (Ardèle ou la Marguerite; La Valse des toréadors; Ornifle ou le courant d'air; Pauvre Bitos ou le Dîner de têtes)* published in 1956; *Pièces costumées (L'Alouette; Beckett ou l'honneur de Dieu; La Foire d'empoigne)* published in 1960; and the *Nouvelles Pièces grinçantes (L'Hurluberlu ou le réactionnaire amoureux; La Grotte; l'Orchestre; Le Boulanger, la boulangère et le petit mitron, Les Poissons rouge ou Mon Père ce héros)* published in 1970.

Aragon, Louis, pseud. (Louis Andrieux). 1887–1982

Born in Paris, in "les beaux quartiers," Aragon was drafted at the age of twenty into the medical corps. In 1919 he founded the review *Littérature* with André Breton, joined the dadaist movement, and became a leader in the surrealist movement. In 1928 he met Elsa Triolet, whom he later married. After attending the Congress of Revolutionary Writers in Kharkov (1930), he broke with the surrealists and embarked on the course of politically committed literature. He was a member of the Communist Party and editor of *Ce Soir* until the newspaper was banned late in 1939. He was again drafted at the time of the Second World War. He became the major poet of the Resistance. After the Liberation, he resumed editorship of *Ce Soir* and *Lettres françaises.* A member of the Central Committee of the French Communist Party in 1950, he was active as a political militant while at the same time publishing the bulk of his work as a writer.

Aragon's first poems, *Feu de joie,* appeared in 1920. He followed it with publication of *Le Mouvement perpétuel* (1926) which was influenced by the surrealist aesthetic; *Persécuteur persécuté* (1930) and *Hourra l'Oural*

(1931), marking his conversion to Marxism; *Le Crèvecoeur* (1941), *Les Yeux d'Elsa* (1942), *Le Musée Grévin* (1943), *La Diane française* (1945), and *Le Nouveau Crèvecoeur* (1948), on the Resistance; *Les Yeux et la Mémoire* (1954), *Elsa* (1959), *Les Poètes* (1960), *Le Fou d'Elsa* (1963), and *Les Chambres* (1969), collections in which he turned toward more traditional versification.

The successive phases evident in his poetry are also evident in his novels: *Le Paysan de Paris* (1926), influenced by surrealism, followed by the social realism of *Les Cloches de Bâle* (1934); *Les Beaux Quartiers* (1936); *Les Voyageurs de l'impériale* (1942); *Aurélien* (1944); and *Les Communistes* in six volumes (1949–51). In a return to classical forms during his final phase, Aragon combined his vision of history with his vision of his own history: *La Semaine Sainte* (1958); *La Mise à mort* (1965); *Blanche ou l'oubli* (1967).

Aragon also published numerous essays, among them: *Traité du style* (1928); *La Peinture au défi* (1930); *Servitude et grandeur des Français* (1945); *L'Homme communiste, I* and *II* (1946–53); *Matisse, apologie du luxe* (1946); *Journal d'une poésie nationale* (1954); *Littératures soviétiques* (1955); *Avez-vous lu Victor Hugo?* (1954); *Les Collages* (1965); *Je n'ai jamais appris à écrire ou les incipit* (1969).

Arland, Marcel. 1899–
Fatherless, Arland had an unhappy childhood. It was in books and in a contemplation of nature that he found a refuge for himself. After completing his secondary education at the Collège de Langres, he went to Paris, where he became involved with the surrealist movement. In 1920 he founded an avant-garde review, *Aventure*. Shortly thereafter he published his first collection, *Terres étrangères* (1923), and joined the NRF, over whose destinies he presided for half a century. Some of the more memorable titles in his considerable body of work are *Etienne* (1924); *Monique* (1926); *Les Ames en peine, Edith,* and *L'Ordre,* which earned him the Prix Goncourt in 1929; and collections of short stories published over a span of time stretching from 1932 to our own day and placing him in the front rank of contemporary short story writers, who were few in number: *Les Vivants* (1934); *Les plus beaux de nos jours* (1937); *La Grâce* (1941); *Il Faut de tout pour faire un monde* (1947); *L'Eau et le Feu* (1956); *A perdre haleine* (1960); *Le Grand Pardon* (1965). Innumerable essays and works of criticism could be added to this list, among them: *Anthologie de la poésie française* (1941); *Avec Pascal* (1946); *Chronique de la peinture moderne* (1949); *Marivaux* (1950); *La Prose française* (1951); *Essais et Nouveaux Essais critiques* (1952); *La Grâce d'écrire* (1955). In 1952 he was awarded the Grand Prix de littérature by the Académie Française, and in 1960 the Grand Prix National des lettres. In 1968 he was elected to the Académie Française.

Arrabal, Fernando. 1932–

Arrabal was born in Spanish Morocco. In 1936, during the Spanish civil war, his father was arrested and disappeared. Arrabal spent the rest of his childhood in Madrid with his mother and brother. In 1950 he won a scholarship and moved to France. He became ill, and this is when he wrote his first plays. In 1958 J.-M. Serreau produced *Pique-nique en campagne*. Published that same year was *Théâtre I (Oraison; Les Deux Bourreaux; Fando et Lis; Le Cimetière des voitures);* in 1961 *Théâtre II (Guernica; Le Labyrinthe; Le Tricycle; Pique-nique en campagne; La Bicyclette du condamné);* in 1965 *Théâtre III* and *Théâtre IV (Le Grand Cérémonial; Le Couronnement; Concert dans un oeuf; Cérémonie pour un Noir assassiné);* in 1967 *Théâtre V (L'Architecte et l'Empereur d'Assyrie);* in 1969 *Théâtre VI (Le Jardin des délices; Bestialité érotique; Une tortue nommée Dostoievski);* and in 1972 *Théâtre VII (Deux Opéras* with music by Luis de Pablo and Jean-Yves Bosseur). Arrabal also published several novels, *Baal-Babylone* (1959); *L'Enterrement de la sardine* (1961); *La Pierre de la folie* (1963); and *Fête et rite de la confusion* (1967).

Highly erotic, Arrabal's plays have been referred to by the author himself as *Théâtre panique*.

Artaud, Antonin. 1896–1948

Artaud began to suffer from nervous disorders early in life. In 1920, with the help of Lugné-Poë, he began his career in the theater and subsequently acted under directors Gémier and Dullin. After his first poems were rejected by the *NRF,* he initiated a correspondence with Jacques Rivière concerning the problem of literature and its impossibility. In 1924 he edited the third issue of *La Révolution surréaliste.* Shortly afterward *L'Ombilic des limbes* and *Le Pèse-nerfs* were published. In 1927 he broke with the surrealists. He then participated in the creation of the Théâtre Alfred Jarry and the Théâtre de la Cruauté. He gradually developed a number of texts published in 1939 under the title *Le Théâtre et son double.* In 1934, *Héliogabale ou l'anarchiste couronné* was published. After the failure of *Les Cenci,* staged at Les Folies Wagram, he traveled to Mexico and began to show signs of mental derangement. He was repatriated by way of Ireland, institutionalized in 1937, and then transferred to Rodez, where he was given electroshock treatment by Dr. Ferdière. In 1946 he stayed at a sanatarium near Paris. On 13 January 1947 he gave a talk at the Théâtre du Vieux-Colombier. On 3 March of that year he died of cancer in a hospital in Ivry. It was not until about ten years later that the importance of his theories on the theater began to be recognized and that his complete works emerged from obscurity to attain, by 1970, international fame. Artaud's *Selected Writings,* translated by Helen Weaver and edited with an introduction by Susan Sontag, was published by Farrar, Straus and Giroux in 1976.

Audiberti, Jacques. 1899–1965

After working briefly as a law clerk in the Justice of the Peace's office in his native Antibes, Audiberti went to Paris in 1925. He got a start as a journalist and became involved with the surrealists. In 1929 he published his first collection of poems, *L'Empire et la Trappe,* which won the Prix Mallarmé and was soon followed by *Race des hommes* (1937). He wrote about ten novels of which *Abraxas* (1938) and, especially, *Le Maître de Milan* (1950) will be remembered. But Audiberti's reputation rests primarily on the richness and abundance of his work for the theater. His first play, *Quoat-Quoat,* was produced in 1945. Volume 1 of his collected plays was published in 1948 (*Quoat-Quoat; Les Femmes du boeuf; Le Mal court*); volume 2 in 1952 (*Pucelle; La Fête noire; Les Naturels. du Bordelais*); volume 3 in 1956 (*La Logeuse; Opéra parlé; Le Ouallou; Altanima*); *L'Effet Glapion* in 1959; volume 4 of the collected plays in 1961 (*Cœur à cuir; Le Soldat Dioclès; La Fourmi dans le corps*); volume 5 in 1962 (*Pomme, pomme, pomme; Bâton et Ruban; Boutique fermée; La Brigitta*); and, finally, *La Poupée* in 1969.

Aymé, Marcel. 1902–67

Aymé, the youngest child in a large family, was raised by his grandparents. A poor student, he was considered a "real dumbell." He did his military service following World War I in occupied Germany, and afterward held a number of different jobs. During an illness suffered in 1925, he began to write. In 1926 he published his first novel, *Brûlebois,* which won the Prix Renaudot. In 1930 he was awarded the Prix Populiste for *La Rue sans nom.* But his first real success was with *La Jument verte,* published in 1933, a lively novel on political life in a small provincial town. He went on to publish many novels, tales, and short stories, among them *La Vouivre* (1943), *Les Contes du chat perché* (1939), and *Le Passe-muraille* (1943). After 1948 he concentrated primarily on the theater, writing satirical plays aimed at the cruelty and stupidity of mankind (*Clérambard,* 1950; *La Tête des autres,* 1952).

Bachelard, Gaston. 1884–1962

Bachelard started out as a minor bureaucrat in the Post Office Department and in 1912 obtained his *Licence ès-sciences* in mathematics. He was drafted in 1914 and spent thirty-eight months at the front. When he returned, he studied for his *Agrégation* in philosophy, and then for his doctorate, for which he wrote a thesis entitled *Essai sur la connaissance approchée* (1928). His work is a consideration of the new rationalism: *La Valeur inductive de la réalité* (1929); *Le Nouvel Esprit scientifique* (1934); and *La Formation de l'Esprit scientifique: contribution à une psychanalyse de la connaissance objective.* In a denial of dualism, Bachelard attempted to reconcile the poetic and the scientific spirits. To this end, and under the influence of Jung, he wrote *La Psychanalyse du feu* (1938), but also *La Philosophie du non* (1940); *L'Eau et le Rêves* (1942), L'Air et les Songes (1943), *La Terre et les rêveries de la volonté, La Terre et les rêveries du repos* (1948), but also *Le Rationalisme appliqué* (1949), *L'Activité rationaliste de la physique contemporaine* (1951), *Le Matérialisme rationnel* (1953); *La Poétique de l'espace* (1957), *La Poétique de la rêverie* (1961), *La Flamme d'une chandelle* (1961).

Barthes, Roland. 1915–80

Son of a naval officer, Barthes spent his childhood in Bayonne. His early writing was published on the literary page of *Combat*. He was a lecturer at the universities of Bucharest and Alexandria, after which he joined the CNRS, where he devoted his energies to lexicography and the research on social signs and symbols. In 1962 he was made Directeur d'études at the Ecole des Hautes Etudes. A landmark date was 1953, when *Le Degré zéro de l'écriture* was published. In this work Barthes introduced the now classic distinction between "language," "writing," and "style." In 1957 he published *Mythologies,* in which he applied the basic concepts of structural analysis to everyday reality. Pursuing his research on language, he became a seminal figure in the *nouvelle critique* and in 1965 published *Eléments de sémiologie,* followed in 1967 by *Système de la mode.* His *Essais critiques* appeared in 1964, *Critique et Vérité* in 1966, with *Sur Racine* and *Les Nouveaux Essais critiques* in 1972. Concentrating more specifically on "textuality," he continued his work of linguistic deciphering with *S/Z* (1970); *L'Empire des signes* (1970); and *Sade, Fourier, Loyola* (1971). Third phase: *Le Plaisir du texte* (1973), *R.B. par lui-même* (1975). He strongly influenced the *Tel Quel* group. He was named to the Collège de France in 1976. In 1981, *Le Grain de la voix: Entretiens 1962–1980* was published posthumously.

Bataille, Georges. 1897–1962

After attending l'Ecole des Chartes, Bataille joined the surrealists. In 1928–30 he founded the review *Documents* with Michel Leiris, André Masson, and Georges Limbour. When he broke with Breton, he published *Un Lion châtré.* In 1936–37, with Georges Ambrosino, Pierre Klossowski, and André Masson he founded a review whose first issue bore the title *La Conjuration d'Acéphale,* and also created the "Collège de sociologie" with Leiris, Caillois, Monnerot, and Klossowski. After World War II he launched the review *Critique* while employed as a librarian. He published fiction and poetry, including *L'Abbé C.* (1950) and *L'Impossible* (1962); theoretical works, including *La Part maudite* (1949), *La Littérature du Mal* (1957), *L'Erotisme* (1957), and *Les Larmes d'Eros* (1961); a summa atheologica, *L'Expérience intérieure* (1943); *Le Coupable* (1944); and *Sur Nietzsche* (1945). The violent eroticism of a body of work that remained obscure until the late sixties is the expression of a mystical philosophy in which the concept of sin and the obsession with death lead to a quest for the absolute.

Beauvoir, Simone de. 1908–

Born into a comfortable middle-class family, Simone de Beauvoir, after a conformist childhood, lost her faith at the age of fourteen. She followed the path of rebellion from then on. She met Jean-Paul Sartre while she was studying for her *Agrégation,* which she earned in 1929. She entered the teaching profession and did not leave academia until 1943, the year her first novel, *L'Invitée,* was published. At the time of the Liberation she became a member of the first editorial board of *Les Temps modernes.* During this period she published a number of essays, *Pyrrhus et Cinéas* (1945); *Pour une morale de l'ambiguité* (1947). The system of morality outlined by de Beauvoir was one of freedom, but not without equality, and it formed the basis for her book *Le Deuxième sexe* (1949), an important essay on the condition of women. She became a Marxist because Marxism "de-alienates" man and delivers him from his chains, and in *Les Mandarins* (1954) she logged the day-to-day progress of the intellectual Left. This novel earned her the Prix Goncourt. Her publications over the years included *Mémoires d'une jeune fille rangée* (1958); *La Force de l'âge* (1960); and *La Force des choses* (1963), a sort of lengthy autobiography in which she recounts her struggle for freedom and the futility of trying to escape from the human condition. *Une mort très douce* (1964), *La Vieillesse* (1970), and *Tout compte fait* (1972) also belong to this autobiographical sequence. An important text on Sartre's death, *La cérémonie des adieux,* followed by *Entretiens avec Jean-Paul Sartre, aout–septembre 1974,* appeared in 1981.

Beckett, Samuel. 1906–

Irish novelist and playwright Samuel Beckett writes in French as well as English. His profoundly original work has gained an international audience. A friend and translator of Joyce, in 1928 Beckett was lecturer in English at the Ecole Normale Supérieure de Paris. In 1930 he published *Whoroscope* (a poem), followed by an essay on Proust and a novel, *Watt,* which he later translated into French. In 1935 he moved to France and shortly afterward published *Murphy,* in London. In 1945 he submitted his first text written in French to the review *Fontaine.* He wrote a novel, *Molloy* (1951), and a play, *Waiting for Godot,* that made him famous when it was produced in 1952. He continued writing novels: *L'Innommable* (1953); *Comment c'est* (1961); *Watt* (translated in 1969); and *Mercier et Camier* (1970); and successfully staged his plays *Fin de partie, Actes sans paroles,* and *Tous ceux qui tombent* (1957), and *Oh! les beaux jours* (1963). Primarily recognized as one of the leaders of antitheater, his fiction having earned him more slowly but just as surely a place among the major writers of his day, Beckett won the Nobel Prize for literature in 1969.

Bernanos, Georges. 1888–1948

This versatile man led an adventurous life. Educated by the Jesuits, he entered the Notre-Dame-des-Champs seminary for boys, and then went on to earn a *licence* in letters and law. He was a militant in the Action Française movement and edited the royalist weekly, *L'Avant-garde de Normandie*. In 1913–14 he became involved in an exchange of polemics with Alain, the philosopher of radicalism. Although not liable for the draft, in 1914 this nationalist enlisted in the army. In 1917 he married a descendant of one of Joan of Arc's brothers. During the thirties he broke with *Action française*. He came to literature belatedly. In 1926 he achieved a huge success with *Sous le soleil de Satan*. *La Joie* (1929) earned him the Prix Fémina. Then the polemicist took over. In 1935 he published *La Grande Peur des bien-pensants*, in which he launched a vituperative attack on Catholic conformism. The following year he returned to the novel with *Le Journal d'un curé de campagne*. The Spanish civil war inspired him to write *Les Grands Cimetières sous la lune* (1938). In it this former member of the Camelots du Roi became a spokesman for the war dead. In 1938 he left France for South America. During World War II his two sons joined the Free French. Bernanos was a divided man who remained faithful to the Christianity of his childhood, but who also saw himself as the defender of ideals of purity, honor, and love of country. Recalled by General de Gaulle, he returned to France in 1945 and published *Monsieur Ouine* (1946). *Dialogues des Carmélites* appeared in 1949.

Bertin, Célia. 1920–

One of the people responsible for the survival of the novel. Her *La Parade des impies* (1946) attracted much attention. *La Dernière Innocence* won the Prix Renaudot. Author of a dozen novels, Bertin also wrote essays: *Haute-couture, terre inconnue* (1956). She moved to the United States after 1968. Since then she has published *Je t'appellerai Amérique* (1972). She has been able to persevere on the path of the traditional novel, confronting fictional characters who have not turned their backs on the past with first the modern, and then the new world.

Billetdoux, François. 1927–

Although he has also been involved with radio and television, Billetdoux is above all a man of the theater. A graduate of the Institut des Hautes Etudes Cinématographiques and a malicious novelist (*L'Animal*, 1955; *Royal Garden Blues*, 1957; and *Brouillon d'un bourgeois*, 1961), he was a producer-director with the French Radio, director of cultural programming for the RTF in Martinique, and then program director for the Société de Radio-diffusion d'Outre-mer. It was in 1959 that he had his first real success in the theater, with *Tchin-tchin*, a comedy for which he received the Prix U and the Prix Lugné-Poë. His complete plays have been collected in two volumes: *Théâtre I—A la nuit, la nuit, Le comportement des époux Bred-burry, Va donc chez Torpe* (1961); *Théâtre II—Pour Finalie, Comment va le monde, Môssieu? Il tourne Môssieu!, Il faut passer par les nuages* (1964). His daughter, novelist Raphaële Billetdoux, won the 1976 Prix Interallié for her novel *Prends garde à la douceur des choses* (Le Seuil, 1976).

Blanchot, Maurice. 1907–

Blanchot began his career as a writer for *Le Journal des Débats, L'Insurgé,* and *Aux Ecoutes.* He led a quiet life during World War II, publishing the first version of *Thomas l'Obscur* (1941), and then a novel, *Aminadab* (1942). In 1945 he was asked to join the jury for the Prix des Critiques. He published a number of stories: *Le Dernier Mot* (1947); *L'Arrêt de mort* (1948); *Celui qui ne m'accompagnait pas* (1953); *Le Dernier Homme* (1957); *L'Attente, l'Oubli* (1962). Blanchot continually returns in his work to the problems of language and being. He is a seminal thinker who has also published numerous essays, among them: *Lautréamont et Sade* (1949); *L'Espace littéraire* (1955); and *Le Livre à venir* (1959). His work was slow to attract the attention of the critics, but in the sixties it began to appear obvious that Blanchot was the writer who, both as novelist and as critic, had gone farthest in conjecture on the very act of writing.

Blanzat, Jean. 1906–77

After a childhood spent on the banks of the Gartempe, Blanzat moved to Paris, where he worked on the review *Europe,* edited by Jean Guéhenno. He published his first story, *Enfance,* in 1930. During World War II he was active in the Resistance as a member of the Musée de l'Homme network, and in 1942 he won the Grand Prix du Roman de l'Académie Française for *Orage du matin.* He was a charter member of the Comité National des Ecrivains. After the war he joined Editions Grasset as literary director, and later became a member of the editorial committee at Gallimard. In 1964 he won the Prix Fémina for his novel *Le Faussaire.*

Blondin, Antoine. 1922–

Blondin, a finalist in the Concours Général, was preparing for his *licence* in philosophy when he was sent to Austria in 1943 as a member of the compulsory labor force (STO). In 1949 he obtained the Prix des Deux-Magots for his novel *L'Europe buissonière.* He went on to publish *Les Enfants du bon Dieu* (1952), and *L'Humeur vagabonde* (1955). In 1959 he won the Prix Interallié for *Un Singe en hiver.*

Bonnefoy, Yves. 1923–

Philosopher, scholar, art critic, Shakespearean critic, but above all poet, Yves Bonnefoy, after studying mathematics and philosophy, went to Paris where he joined the surrealist group. In 1953 he published his first work, *Du mouvement et de l'immobilité de Douve,* followed by *Hier régnant désert* (1958) and *Pierre écrite* (1965). In 1959 he won the Prix de la Nouvelle Vague for his essay *L'Improbable.* In 1967 he founded the review *L'Ephémère,* which was devoted to poetry, with Gaëtan Picon, André du Bouchet, and Louis-René des Forêts. Bonnefoy's work reveals a poet who is difficult, who is primarily heir to the Mallarmé tradition, and who ranks with the foremost poets of his generation.

Bosco, Henri. 1888–1976

Bosco's work was profoundly influenced by Provence. He had an *Agrégation* in Italian and taught until his retirement in 1945, the year he was awarded the Prix Renaudot for *Le Mas Théotime.* Particularly memorable among his works are *L'Ane culotte* (1937); *Malicroix* (1948), which won him the Prix des Ambassadeurs; and *Sites et Mirages* (1951), a book of impressions of Algeria. Little read today, Bosco's work is strongly stamped with the occult.

Bosquet, Alain, pseud. (Anatole Bisk). 1919–

"A man from everywhere and nowhere," Bosquet was born in Russia during the Revolution. He was raised in Belgium and fought for the Free French from 1941 to 1942. He then became editorial secretary of the periodical *La Voix de la France* in New York. There he met André Breton, Saint-John Perse, and Salvador Dali. In 1945 he published his first collection of poems, *La Vie est clandestine.* In 1952 he received the Prix Apollinaire for *Langue morte,* in 1957 the Prix Sainte-Beuve for *Premier Testament,* in 1960 the Prix Max Jacob for *Deuxième Testament,* in 1962 the Prix Fémina-Vacaresco for his essay *Verbe et Vertige,* in 1966 the Prix Interallié for his novel *La Confession mexicaine,* and in 1968 the Grand Prix de poésie de l'Académie Française. *Le Livre du doute et de la grâce* was published in 1976. He was influential as a translator, and as both a literary and an art critic. His role in relation to other poets was that of discoverer and intermediary.

Bouchet, André du. 1924–

After spending some time at Harvard, du Bouchet in 1951 published his first collection of poems, *Airs,* followed by *Sans couvercle* (1953); *Au deuxième étage* (1956); *Le Moteur blanc* (1956); *Dans la chaleur vacante* (1961), which won the Prix des Critiques; and *Où le soleil* (1968). Two other texts, *La Couleur* and *Hölderlin aujourd'hui (Le Collier de Buffle),* appeared in 1976. A difficult and inaccessible poet, du Bouchet is also a Joyce translator.

Bousquet, Joë. 1897–1950

Bousquet was wounded during World War I by a bullet that severed his spinal chord. The poet "whose life was paralyzed by a bullet" remained bedridden and in pain for the rest of his life. In 1924 he moved to the rue de Verdun in Carcassonne, where he lived in a "room with shuttered windows" that he was never again to leave. Literature was his salvation. He signed the surrealist Manifestos, became friends with Alibert the poet, and joined the editorial board of Les Cahiers du Sud. In 1930 he published an essay, *Voie libre;* in 1931 *Il ne fait pas assez noir* and, in collaboration with Suarès and Daumal, *La Comédie psychologique.* In 1936 he publised a novel, *La Tisane de sarments.* During World War II, Aragon, Elsa Triolet, and Julien Benda were living near him. In 1941 he published *Traduit du silence, pages de journal.* The poems published under the title *La Connaissance du soir* came out in 1945. He died in 1950 from an attack of uremia.

Brasillach, Robert. 1909–45

Son of an army officer, Brasillach entered the Ecole Normale Supérieure in 1928 and became friendly with Roger Vailland, Thierry Maulnier, and Maurice Bardèche—the latter subsequently becoming his brother-in-law. In 1932 he joined *L'Action française,* where he published his "Causeries littéraires" each week. His first novels were *Le Voleur d'étincelles* (1932); *L'Enfant de la nuit* (1934); *Le Marchand d'oiseaux* (1936); and *Comme le temps passe* (1937). In 1936 he joined *Je Suis Partout* as a member of Pierre Gaxotte's group. Two years later he attended the Nuremberg Congress. He was drafted in 1939, made a prisoner of war, and freed in 1941, after which he held a post on the film board, and accompanied Abel Bonnard to the German Writer's Congress at Weimar. He went to Russia with F. de Brinon in support of the Légion des Volontaires Français Contre le Bolchevisme. He went into hiding in Paris from 14 August to 14 September 1944, and then gave himself up to the authorities. His trial opened in 1945, and he was executed on 6 February. Besides his fiction, he also composed numerous essays, among them *Corneille* (1938), an *Anthologie de la poésie grecque* (posth. 1950), and miscellaneous pieces: *Histoire du cinéma,* with Maurice Bardèche (1935), and *Notre avant-guerre* (1941).

Breton, André. 1896–1966

Breton's life was inextricably mingled with the history of the surrealist movement he founded, and for which he served as theoretician and mainstay. He was drafted in 1914 and assigned to the neuropsychiatric corps, which led him to anticipate the importance of psychoanalysis. In 1919 he founded the review *Littérature,* with Aragon and Soupault. In 1924 the *Premier Manifeste du surréalisme* was published. In it, Breton and his friends extolled the power of dreams and the imagination over reason. In 1928 *Nadja* was published, and in 1929 the *Second Manifeste du surréalisme,* followed by the creation of the review *Le Surréalisme au service de la révolution.* Breton published *Les Vases communicants* in 1932, and *Position politique du surréalisme in 1935.* That year he broke with the Communist Party, with which he had been momentarily allied. In 1937 *L'Amour fou* came out. Breton was not favorably regarded by the Vichy government, and he left France for the United States during World War II (March 1941). In New York he organized an exhibition in collaboration with Marcel Duchamp, founded a review called *Triple V,* and published *Prolégomènes à un troisième manifeste du surréalisme ou non.* He returned to Paris and, in 1947, published *Ode à Charles Fourier* and *Arcane 17.* The surrealist group formed around him again, but few of the original members still remained. The movement was extremely active in all areas, in politics as well as in art and literature. But surrealism's greatest moments were the exhibitions staged as a kind of total spectacle (surrealist exhibitions were held in Paris in 1947, 1959, and 1965). Breton's poems are collected in *Clair de Terre* (1966) and *Signe Ascendant* (1968). A translation, *What is Surrealism?,* edited and introduced by Franklin Rosemont, was published in 1978.

Butor, Michel. 1926–

Butor was educated by the Jesuits and continued his studies in Khâgne at Louis-le-Grand. At the Sorbonne he obtained a *licence* in philosophy and went on to earn a *diplôme d'études supérieures* with a thesis entitled "Les mathématiques et l'idée de nécessité." He then taught in Minieh (Egypt), Manchester (England), and Salonica. He is now professor of French literature at Geneva. His *Passage de Milan* was published in 1954. When *L'Emploi du temps* appeared two years later, it won the Prix Fénélon. It was then that Butor was recognized as a pioneering member of the fifties generation attempting to develop the novel in new ways. In 1957 he received the Prix Renaudot for *La Modification. Répertoire I* (1960) received the Grand Prix de la Critique Littéraire. In the same year Butor published *Degrés,* and in 1961 *Histoire extraordinaire,* on Baudelaire. He wrote an opera, *Votre Faust* (1962), in collaboration with Henri Pousseur. Continuing his work as an essayist, he published *Répertoire I à IV* (1964–76) on the subject of literature, and *Illustrations I à IV* on the subject of art. He also wrote what he called *stéréoscopies,* works projected on different levels and requiring the active participation of the reader: *Mobile* (1962); *Réseau aérien* (1962); *6,810,000 litres d'eau par seconde* (1965). With Robbe-Grillet, he is considered one of the spokesmen of the *nouveau roman.* Following in the footsteps of great experimenters like Marcel Duchamp and Francis Picabia, Butor sought new ways to represent reality, such as his "book" *USA 76,* a case made out of blue altuglas, produced with the help of painter Jacques Monory, and containing a collection of objects, serigraphs, and texts designed to stimulate the activity of the "reader." In 1975 Butor undertook a course of "introspection" with *Matière de rêves,* followed by *Second soussol* (1976).

Cadou, René-Guy. 1920–51

Cadou was the son of a schoolmaster who loved nature and the simple life. His first poems were inspired by the death of his mother. He was seventeen years old in 1937 when his first collection, *Les Brancardiers de l'aube,* was published. During the war he joined the poets of the Ecole de Rochefort. Influenced by Max Jacob, he published *Bruits du coeur* and *Lilas du soir* (1942). After the war he took a post as a teacher near Nantes, and wrote a novel, *La Maison d'été,* which was published posthumously (1955), as were two collections of poems published under the title *Hélène ou le règne végétal* (vol. 1, 1952; vol. 2, 1953).

Camus, Albert. 1913–60

Camus always remained extremely attached to Algeria, where he was born. Unable to complete his degree in philosophy because of poor health, in 1937 he founded an amateur theatrical company, *L'Equipe,* and joined the newspaper *Alger républicain* as an editor. He published *L'Envers et l'endroit* (1937) and, one year later, *Noces* (1938). In 1942 he brought out *L'Etranger* and *Le Mythe de Sisyphe.* During World War II he participated in the Resistance movement with Pascal Pia in the *Combat* group, and after the Liberation he assumed the editorship of the newspaper *Combat* with him. In 1947 *La Peste* was hailed as the great postwar novel. When *L'Homme révolté* came out in 1951, he quarreled with Sartre, who accused him of exhibiting an attitude that was "idealist, moralizing, and anti-communist." The Algerian war caused him agonies of conscience, and the political positions he was forced to take alienated him from a segment of leftist intellectual opinion. In 1956 he published *La Chute,* followed by a collection of short stories, *L'Exil et le Royaume. Journaux des Voyages,* edited by Roget Quilliot, was published posthumously in 1978. Although controversial, Camus was indisputably one of the greatest French writers of the post–World War II period. In 1957 he received the Nobel Prize for Literature, three years before he died in an accident.

Cassou, Jean. 1897–

Poet, essayist, sociologist, moralist, polemicist, historian, and accomplished translator, Jean Cassou began his career as temporary administrative director of the *Mercure de France.* Shortly afterward he entered the ministry of public instruction, where one of his colleagues was Jean Paulhan. In 1936 he worked in Jean Zay's office, took over the editorship of the review *Europe,* and went to Spain to celebrate the victory of the Front Populaire. He was forced by the Vichy government into retirement from his official position in 1940 and joined the Resistance movement. To his arrest in 1941 we owe the *Trente-trois sonnets composés au secret,* published in 1944. Cassou was the author of a large number of novels—*Eloge de la folie* (1925); *Les Harmonies viennoises* (1926); *La Clef des songes* (1929); *Les*

Inconnus dans la cave (1933); and *Légion*—and after World War II continued his work as an essayist with *Parti pris* (1964), and as an art critic with *Situation de l'art moderne* (1950) and *Panorama des arts plastiques contemporains* (1960). Longtime curator of the Musée d'Art Moderne, in 1965 he joined the Ecole Pratique des Hautes Etudes, and in 1967 was elected to the Académie Royale de Belgique and received the Prix Prince Pierre de Monaco.

Cayrol, Jean. 1911–

Cayrol founded a literary review in 1926, *Abeilles et Pensées*. After his military service he published his first poems. He was arrested by the Germans in 1942 and sent to a deportation camp in Mathausen. Poet-witness of man's suffering, he wrote *Poèmes de la nuit et du brouillard* (1946). In 1947 he published *Je vivrai l'amour des autres* and *On vous parle*, which won the Prix Renaudot. While pursuing his work as a poet (*Les Mots sont aussi des demeures*, 1952), a novelist (*La Gaffe*, 1957; *Les Corps étrangers*, 1959; *Midi minuit*, 1966), an essayist (*Lazare parmi nous*, 1950), and literary editor for editions du Seuil, he became a member in 1950 of the Prix Victor Hugo jury and the Fondation Del Duca, and took up movie making: he collaborated with Resnais on the film *Nuit et Brouillard*, directed *Mureil*, and produced *Le Coup de grâce*. In 1968 he won the Prix Prince de Monaco for his work as a whole, which expanded continually (*Histoire d'une prairie*, 1970; *Histoire d'un désert*, 1972; *Histoire de la forêt*, 1975; *Histoire d'une maison*, 1976).

Céline, Louis-Fernand, pseud. (Louis Destouches). 1894–1961

Seriously wounded in November 1914, Céline was discharged from the army and traveled in Africa and the United States. After the Armistice, he continued to study for a degree in medicine. From 1925–28 he was a physician with the SDN in Geneva. *Voyage au bout de la nuit* was published in 1932. The impact of this first book was enormous. Céline's writing talent was confirmed by *Mort à crédit*, published in 1936. But he began to lose the sympathy of the leftists, particularly after publication of *Bagatelles pour un massacre* and *L'Ecole des cadavres* (1937), both clearly anti-Semitic. After his return from the USSR the same year, he brought out *Mea culpa;* from that point on, the divorce between Céline the born anarchist and the revolutionary Left was definite. He published *Les Beaux draps* in 1941 and *Guignol's Band* in 1944. At the end of World War II he fled through Germany to Denmark, where he was arrested and held for seventeen months in prison. In 1951, the year he returned to France, he settled in Meudon, where he practiced medicine. Continuing the transformation in his fiction style foreshadowed in *Voyage au bout de la nuit*, he published novels, stories, and essays: *Casse-pipe* (1952); *Féerie pour une autre fois I* (1952); *Féerie pour une autre fois II* (1954); Entretiens avec le professeur Y (1955); *D'un cha-*

teau l'autre (1957); *Ballet sans musique, sans personne, sans rien* (1959); *Nord* (1960). Published posthumously were *Le Pont de Londres* (1964) and *Rigodon* (1969). In the sixties, Céline's work emerged from obscurity and was confirmed as being among the most significant of the period.

Césaire, Aimé. 1913–

Césaire was born in Martinique. As a student in Paris, Césaire met Senghor and founded a newspaper in collaboration with him, *L'Etudiant noir*. After the conclusion of his studies at the Ecole Normale Supérieure on Rue d'Ulm, he returned to Martinique in 1940 and taught at the Fort-de-France lycée. At this time he published his first pieces in the review *Tropiques*. As a poet he published, immediately after World War II, *Les Armes miraculeuses* (1946), followed by *Soleil cou coupé* (1948); *Corps perdu* (1950); *Cahier d'un retour au pays natal* (1956); *Ferrements* (1959); and *Cadastre* (1961). His main dramatic works are *La Tragédie du roi Christophe* (1963) and *Une saison au Congo* (1967). In 1946 Césaire was elected as the deputy for Martinique. A poet of the black rebellion against white cultural supremacy, Césaire popularized the term "negritude" coined by Senghor.

Char, René. 1907–

Char published his first poems, *Les Cloches sur le cœur* in 1928, and then moved to Paris where—through the intermediary of Eluard—he met Aragon and Breton and collaborated on issue no. 12 of *La Révolution surréaliste*. In 1930 he published *Ralentir travaux* with Eluard and Breton. In 1934 he brought out *Le Marteau sans maître*. He then moved away from surrealism. Accused of being a communist during the war because of his activities with the surrealists, he joined the Free French underground. In 1944 he went to Algiers where he was assigned to the Allied Command Headquarters for North Africa. After the war he published *Feuillets d'Hypnos,* written when he was with the underground. The following titles cover most of his published work: *La Parole en archipel, Fureur et Mystère* (1962); *Les Matinaux, Commune présence* (1964); *Recherche de la base et du sommet, Retour amont* (1966). He received the 1966 Prix des Critiques for his work as a whole. Char is a difficult poet who succeeded in putting between himself and others the detachment that comes from rigor.

Chardonne, Jacques, pseud. (Jacques Boutelleau). 1884–1968

Rejecting both the Catholicism of his mother and the Protestantism of his father, Chardonne led the life of an upper-class agnostic. Discharged from the army in 1914, he spent the remainder of World War I in Switzerland, and it is there that he wrote the first part of *Epithalame,* a novel published in 1921 for which he obtained the Prix Fémina–Vie Heureuse. In 1932, after *Claire* was published, he won the Grand Prix du roman de l'Académie Française. The three volumes of his trilogy entitled *Les Destinées sentimen-*

tales came out between 1934 and 1936. During World War II he published *Les Chroniques* (1941) and *Attachements* (1942). His son was deported during the war, and he himself was arrested after the Liberation for having published under the German Occupation, but he was released immediately. In 1951 he named Editions Albin-Michel official publisher for his complete works.

Chedid, Andrée. 1920–

Born in Egypt into a family of Lebanese origin, Andrée Chedid completed her education at the American University of Cairo. After publishing an initial volume of poems in English entitled *On the Trails of my Fancy* (1943), she decided to write in French. In 1946 she settled in France (adopting French nationality in 1962), and published her poetic works in that country. They include: *Textes pour le vivant* (1953); *Double-Pays* (1965); *Contre-Chant* (1968); and *Visage premier* (1972). In 1972 she won the Aigle d'Or for poetry at the International Book Festival in Nice. A poet, but also a novelist (*Le Sixième jour*, 1960; *L'Etroite Peau*, 1965; *La Cité fertile*, 1972), Chedid has written for the theater as well (her play *Le Montreur* was staged at the East Berlin Festival).

Cioran, Emile-M. 1911–

The son of a Greek Orthodox priest, Cioran was born in Romania and studied philosophy in Bucarest. In 1937 he won a scholarship and settled in Paris. In 1947 this last of the moralists began to write in French. His first two books made him famous: *Précis de décomposition* (1949) and *Syllogismes de l'amertume* (1952), to which were added in the course of time *La Tentation d'exister* (1956); *Histoire et Utopie* (1960); *La Chute dans le temps* (1964); *Le Mauvais Démiurge* (1969); and *De l'inconvénient d'être né* (1975). An upholder of the "will to powerlessness," Cioran believed his ideas to be both a continuation and a negation of Nietzsche. Both anarchist and reactionary, he harked back to Joseph de Maistre, whose selected writings he presented with verve and dash in 1957.

Cixous, Hélène. 1937–

Cixous was already able, as a beginning writer, to construct a work of which she could later say, "I aim for a space and I fill it." A brilliant university student, she taught at Nanterre, took part in the 1968 *Révolution de mai*, defended a doctoral thesis on James Joyce, and, with Gérard Genette and Tzvetan Todorov, founded *Poétique*. Her first novel, *Dedans*, won the 1969 Prix Médicis. She then published *Le Troisième, Les Commencements* (1970); followed by *Neutre* (1972); *Tombe* (1973); and *Révolution pour plus d'un Faust* (1975). She made her début as a writer for the theater with *Le Portrait de Dora* (1973).

Cocteau, Jean. 1889–1963

Cocteau came from a wealthy middle-class family whose members were patrons of the arts. His protected childhood was clouded, however, by his father's suicide. Cocteau was undisciplined as a student, but showed obvious talent in drawing and gymnastics. He took to writing at an early age, under the influence of fashionable poets such as Catulle Mendès, the Comtesse de Noailles, and Laurent Tailhade. He was twenty years old when he published his first collection of poems, *La Lampe d'Aladin* (1909), followed by *Le Prince frivole* (1910), and *La Danse de Sophocle* (1912)—three *niaiseries,* he was later to declare. Intensely interested in theater, music, and ballet, he attended the Ballets Russes performances in Paris and met Diaghilev, who told him, "Surprise me!" He wrote a stage adaptation of Wilde's *Portrait of Dorian Gray,* and staged a one-act play at couturier Doucet's entitled *La Patience de Pénélope,* with music by his friends Reynaldo Hahn and André Paysan—with whom he composed another ballet (*Le Dieu bleu,* 1912), produced by the Ballets Russes and starring Nijinsky. The review *Schéhérazade,* which he founded in 1909 and which ran for six issues, was open to light, pleasant works contributed by Anna de Noailles, Fagus, Jean Pellerin, Maurice Rostand, Jean-Marc Bernard, Alain-Fournier, etc., and furnishes an example of Cocteau's interests at the time. His early contacts with Stravinsky, and the 1913 performance of the latter's *Sacre du Printemps,* led Cocteau to the view that the path of official art was not the one he wanted to follow; that a poet must seek his salvation off the beaten path. This realization formed the basis for his reflection on aesthetics entitled *Le Potomak* (1919). During World War I, Cocteau published a patriotic satirical newspaper called *Le Mot,* with Paul Iribe. He also worked as a trapeze artist with Roland Garros, an experience he rendered in *Le Cap de Bonne Espérance* (1918) in *vers brisés.* He drove an ambulance for the Red Cross on the Belgian front, and in 1916 he came back from the battlefield with a poem, *Discours du Grand Sommeil,* and a novel *Thomas l'Imposteur* (1923). In Paris, during the final years of the war, Cocteau met Picasso, Max Jacob, Apollinaire, Cendrars, Kisling, Modigliani, and Satie. With Satie and Picasso he produced the ballet *Parade,* staged by the Ballets Russes in 1917. In the same vein he composed *Le Bœuf sur le toit* (1920) with Darius Milhaud, and *Les Mariés de la tour Eiffel* (1921). In *Le Coq et l'Arlequin* (1918), "notes based on music," he made a case for the austere art of Satie, opposed to that of Wagner and Debussy. Entranced by anything avantgarde, he celebrated the machine and the airplane, and contributed to the review *Dada.* Although Cocteau did not belong to any specific group, following the publication of his collection *Poésies 1917–1920* (1920) he fell under the influence of the young Radiguet, who moved him in the direction of a new classicism of which *Le Secret professionnel* (1922) was an example. In 1922 he published *Thomas l'imposteur.* He continued his work as a poet:

Plain-Chant (1923); *Opéra, Oeuvres poétiques* (1927). He became depressed, suffered from nervous disorders, started smoking opium, and in 1925 underwent treatment to cure him of his addiction. He corresponded with Maritain, met Christian Bérard, was reconciled with Stravinsky, and broke with the surrealists. In 1926 his play *Orphée* was staged at the Théâtre des Arts. In 1929 he wrote *Les Enfants terribles.* In 1932 he produced his first film, *Le Sang d'un poète.* Two years later he produced *La Machine infernale* at the Comédie des Champs-Elysées. In 1936, on a bet, he went "around the world in eighty days." During World War II the Vichy government regarded him as a symbol of decadence, and his plays were banned. He made a film, *L'Eternel Retour* (1943). After the war, Cocteau proved the versatility of his gifts. As a film maker he produced *La Belle et la Bête* (1945), *L'Aigle à deux têtes* (1947); *Orphée* (1949); *Le Testament d'Orphée* (1959). As a poet he published *Le Chiffre sept* (1952); *Clair-obscur* (1954); and *Le Requiem* (1962). Two volumes of his plays came out in 1948: *Théâtre I (Antigone; Les Mariés de la tour Eiffel; Les Chevaliers de la table ronde; Les Parents terribles),* and *Théâtre II (Les Monstres sacrés; La Machine à écrire; Renaud et Armide; L'Aigle à deux têtes).* At the age of sixty-six Cocteau accepted a commission to do the frescoes for the town hall in Menton and for the Chapelle Saint-Pierre in Villefranche-sur-Mer. He was a member of the Académie Royale de Belgique and was named to the Académie Française in 1955.

Crevel, René. 1900–1935

Capping his university studies with a thesis on Diderot, Crevel then founded the review *Aventure* with Arland, Limbour, Morisse, and Vitrac. This was also when he met Aragon, Breton, Soupault, and Tzara. A born rebel, Crevel was a fervent supporter of surrealism. His first novel, *Détours,* came out in 1924. Afflicted with tuberculosis at an early age, Crevel spent time in the mountains. He also underwent psychoanalysis. After the *Second Manifeste du surréalisme,* he became one of the small number of surrealist faithful. He published several novels, *Mon corps et moi* (1925); *La Mort difficile* (1926); *Babylone* (1927); *Etes-vous fous?* (1929); and a virulent pamphlet, *Le Clavecin de Diderot* (1932). He published his last novel, *Les Pieds dans le plat,* in 1933. He was expelled from the Communist Party for signing the surrealist tract *La Mobilisation contre la guerre n'est pas la paix.* In 1934 he renewed his ties with the party and engaged actively in the preparations for the First International Writers' Congress in Defense of Culture. During the Congress Breton slapped Ehrenberg in public and the Russians demanded the expulsion of the surrealists from the proceedings. Crevel intervened in an attempt to act as mediator. That day, 18 June 1935, when he returned to his home, he took his own life.

Crommelynck, Fernand. 1885–1970

Crommelynck was born into a theatrical family and had his first plays produced before 1914. But it was in 1920 at the Théâtre de l'Oeuvre that Lugné-Poë produced, and performed in, *Le Cocu magnifique*, an enormously successful farce. Drawing on metaphor, Crommelynck was able, by using masquerade and lies as dramatic pivots, to give twentieth-century theater new dimensions and a new language. His complete plays were published by Gallimard. Volume 1 came out in 1967 *(Le Cocu magnifique; Les Amants puérils; Le Sculpteur de masques)*, and volume 2 in 1968 *(Tripes d'or; Carine ou la jeune fille folle de son âme; Chaud et froid ou l'Idée de Monsieur Dom)*, and volume 3 in 1969 *(Le Chevalier de la lune ou Sir John Falstaff; Une femme qu'a le cœur trop petit)*.

Curtis, Jean-Louis, pseud. (Louis Lafitte). 1917–

In 1946 Curtis won the Prix Cazes for *Les Jeunes Hommes* and in 1947, the Prix Goncourt for *Les Forêts de la nuit*. He held an *Agrégation* in English and traveled widely under the auspices of the Alliance Française, teaching in America. An informed critic and highly talented translator and adapter of English and American literature (Shakespeare, Henry James, etc.), Curtis over the years continued producing a body of fiction that bore witness to the times he lived in: *Les Justes causes* (1954); *Une âme d'élite* (1956); *Un Saint au néon* (1956); *La Quarantaine* (1966); and *Un jeune couple* (1967).

Dabit, Eugène. 1898–1936

A leftist, a man of the people, an artist "untouched by the bourgeoisie," Eugène Dabit was born in Montmartre to a family of workers (his father was a coachman-delivery man; his mother a garment worker). Apprenticed as an art metalworker, he became an electrician on the Nord-Sud subway line in Paris, eventually lost his job, and joined the artillery in 1916. His discovery of Charles-Louis Philippe and his dawning desire to write happened while he was at the front. He lived through years of great hardship, and then in 1927 met André Gide and Roger Martin du Gard. He then wrote the first version of *Hôtel du Nord*, which, when published in 1929, earned him the Prix Populiste. Next came *P'tit Louis* (1930); *Villa Oasis* (1932); *Un Mort tout neuf* (1934); *La Zone verte* (1935). He supported the leftist intellectuals, but refused to join any specific party. In 1936 he accompanied Gide to the USSR; he contracted typhus while there, and died of it.

Daumal, René. 1908–44

Daumal met Roger Gilbert-Lecomte, Roger Vailland, and Robert Meyrat at his lycée in Reims. At the age of seventeen he attempted various experiments of a psychic and sensory nature. "To find out what it's like," he took opium, hashish, and carbon tetrachloride. Intrigued by the poets of the diabolic and by occultism, he studied sacred Hindu texts and set out to learn Sanskrit. He continued his education at the lycée Henri IV, where one of his teachers was Alain. Shortly afterward he and his friends created the review *Le Grand Jeu* (1928). In 1930 he broke with Breton and surrealism and had his decisive meeting with Salzmann, a disciple of Gurdjieff's. A pilgrim of the Absolute, for a dozen years he followed the *way* of the initiates. In 1935 he obtained the Prix Jacques Doucet for his collection of poems *Le Contre-ciel*. He published a story, *La Grande Beuverie* (1938). Impoverished and tubercular, he belonged for a while to the editorial committee of the review *Fontaine*. He died in 1944. In 1952 his best-known novel, *Le Mont Analogue*, was published, followed by *Chaque fois que l'aube paraît* (1953) and *Poésie noire, poésie blanche* (1954).

Deguy, Michel. 1930–

A poet attentive to "Virgil's shade become Virgil's voice," Deguy, who held an *Agrégation* in philosophy, published *Meurtrières* (1959), followed by *Fragments du cadastre* (1960); *Poèmes de la presqu'île* (1961); *Biefs* (1963); *Actes* (1966); and *Ouï-dire* (1966). A contributor to *Critique* and the *NRF*, he founded the *Revue de poésie*, a journal devoted to reflections on poetry and great poets.

Deleuze, Gilles. 1925–

Professor of philosophy at the University of Vincennes, Deleuze today is one of the intellectual leaders for French students and the French avant-garde, particularly since publishing *L'Anti-Oedipe* (1972), written in collaboration with Félix Guattari. Deleuze attacks the Oedipal pattern, which he sees as one of the ways in which society exercises control over the individual. He and Guattari also attack psychoanalysis, which they consider to be an institution that "prohibits all production of desire." They also aim their attack at the signifying language by means of which the obsession is perpetuated. Deleuze has a considerable body of work to his credit: *Empirisme et subjectivité* (1953); *Nietzsche et la philosophie* (1962); *La Philosophie critique de Kant* (1963); *Marcel Proust et les signes* (1964); *Spinoza et le problème de l'expression* (1964); *Différence et Répétition* (1969).

Derrida, Jacques. 1930–

Derrida was born in Algiers. An outstanding philosopher of the younger generation, he declared war on logocentrism, fighting semiology with grammatology. A philosopher of the tragic because a philosopher of the "ultimate fate of representation," Derrida has exerted considerable influence on the direction taken by the *Tel Quel* group. Professor of history and philosophy at the Ecole Normale Supérieure, he has published numerous articles and essays, notably *L'Ecriture et la Différence* (1967) and *De la grammatologie* (1968). In 1972 he published *De la Dissémination* and *Marges de la philosophie*.

Des Forêts, Louis-René. 1918–
After a childhood spent in le Berry, Des Forêts went to Paris to study law. During the war he published his first work, *Les Mendiants* (1943). In 1946 he brought out *Le Bavard* and became literary consultant to the publisher Laffont. A taciturn man haunted by words, he retired to the country and then returned to Paris, where he took part in publication of the *Encyclopédie de la Pléiade* at Gallimard. In 1960 he won the Prix des Critiques for his collection of short stories, *La Chambre des enfants*.

Desnos, Robert. 1900–45
Born near the Bastille in Paris, Desnos started out as a delivery boy for a local general store before writing his first poems. Desnos's influence on surrealism was a major one from the beginning. Better than almost anyone else, perhaps, he was able to demonstrate the rich potential of automatic writing and of verbal delirium, particularly in his *Deuil pour deuil* (1924) and *Corps et biens* (1930). Without losing his sense of the humorous and the fantastic, with *Etat de veille* (1943) and *Contrée* (1944) Desnos rediscovered the path of a genuine humanism.

Devaux, Noël. 1905–
A graduate of the Ecole Supérieure d'Electricité, Devaux worked in hydraulic electric stations. Illness several times prevented him from pursuing his activities. In 1932 he met Boris de Schloezer who encouraged him to write and introduced him to the *NRF* circle. His first pieces were published in 1938, but it was after World War II that this writer, who was dedicated to the fantastic, published his most important works: *L'Auberge Parpillon* (1945); *Le Pressoir mystique* (1948); *Bal chez Alféoni* (1956); *La Dame de Murcie* (1961); and *Frontières* (1965).

Dhôtel, André. 1900–
A subtle novelist absorbed in the mysterious, the fantastic, and in explorations of the marvelous, Dhôtel is a son of the region where he was born, the Champagne region and the Ardennes. During his military service he met Arland, Vitrac, Limbour, and Desnos. This led to his participation in the review *Aventure*. He earned a *Licence* in philosophy and taught abroad, and then in France in various provincial secondary schools. In 1928 he published a first collection of poems, *Le Petit livre clair*, followed in 1930 by his first novel, *Campements*. His most memorable works of fiction are *David*, which won the 1948 Prix Sante-Beuve; *L'Homme de la scierie*, published in 1950; and *Le Pays où l'on n'arrive jamais* (Prix Fémina, 1955). He also wrote two works on Rimbaud, who was born in the same region: *L'Oeuvre logique de Rimbaud* (1933) and *Rimbaud et la révolte moderne* (1952).

Dib, Mohammed. 1920–
French-speaking Algerian Mohammed Dib started out as a schoolteacher
and then, in 1950, joined the newspaper *Alger-Républicain* as an editor-
reporter. He married a young Frenchwoman and in 1952 published *La
Grande Maison,* a novel that won the Prix Fénéon. In 1959 he settled in
France and the next year published *Un été africain.* In 1960 he wrote *Ombre
gardienne,* a collection of poems for which Aragon wrote a preface. In 1956
a collection of his short stories was published, *Le Talisman;* and of his plays,
Théâtre I (La Fiancée du printemps; Wassem; Une paix durable). Several
novels followed: *La Danse du roi* (1968); *Dieu en barbarie* (1970); and a
volume of poems, *Formulaires* (1970).

Drieu La Rochelle, Pierre. 1893–1945
Drieu La Rochelle seems very early in life to have been haunted by the
idea of death. When he left for the front in 1914, his feeling was one of
exhilaration. He was wounded repeatedly. After World War I he became a
contributor to the *NRF* and published *Mesure de la France.* With Aragon
and the surrealists he attacked Anatole France in a pamphlet entitled *Un
cadavre.* In 1928 he published *Blèche,* a novel, and an essay *Genève ou
Moscou.* Four years later he left for Argentina, where he conducted a
speaking tour on "the crisis of democracy in Europe." It was after 1934, the
year he published *La Comédie de Charleroi,* that Drieu began to veer toward fascism. Shortly thereafter he joined Doriot's Parti Populaire Français.
On the eve of World War II he published novels dealing with middle-class
decadence, such as *Rêveuse Bourgeoisie* (1937) and *Gilles* (1939). Dreaming of a France that would be both aristocratic and socialist, he collaborated
with the Germans during the Occupation, and started publishing the *NRF*
again. Threatened with arrest after the Liberation, he took his own life on
15 March 1945.

Duras, Marguerite, pseud. (Marguerite Donnadieu). 1914–
Duras was born in Indochina, spent her entire childhood in Asia, and then
came to France to complete her education. During World War II she joined
the Resistance and published her first books, *Les Impudents* (1943) and *La
Vie tranquille* (1944). After the Liberation she became active in politics and
joined the Communist Party (she was expelled in 1955). Her childhood in
Indochina was her inspiration in 1950 for *Barrage contre le Pacifique.* Next
she published *Le Marin de Gibraltar* (1952); *Les Petits Chevaux de Tar-
quinia;* and *Des Journées entières dans les arbres* (1953). She entered
wholeheartedly into the opposition to the Algerian war. While engaged in
her role as a political activist, Duras, for whom speech is primordial, also
wrote her first play, *Le Square,* produced in 1957 at the Théâtre des
Champs-Elysées. In 1959 she wrote her first film scenario, *Hiroshima mon
amour.* Between 1975 and 1977 she was responsible for several films, *India*

Song (1975); *Son nom de Venise dans Calcutta désert* (1976); *Baxter, Véra Baxter* (1976); and *Le Camion* (1977). *L'Eté 80* was published in 1980 and *Outside, Papiers d'un jour* in 1981. Novel, play, or film, Duras's work conforms to no genre except that of a muted conversation on the dual theme of love and death. She once said, "No love in the world can ever take the place of love."

Eluard, Paul, pseud. (Paul-Eugène Grindel). 1885–1952
Eluard in his own lifetime was one of the poets to have influenced French poetry the most decisively. A fervent surrealist, he was a contributor in the twenties to the review *Littérature,* founded by Breton and Aragon, but he nonetheless remained faithful to traditional poetry, something for which he was later taken to task by Breton. He was an early and active supporter of the communists and took part in the antifascist struggle. During World War II he joined the Resistance and after the Liberation became one of the literary glories of France. He used his poems to exalt not only love of liberty and political aspiration, but the simplest feelings as well. His first major book, *Capitale de la douleur,* dates from 1926. His first poems, written between 1913 and 1921 but not published until 1948, retained a unanimist quality. This was followed by Eluard's surrealist period (*Dessous d'une vie,* 1926; *La Rose publique,* 1934; *Les Yeux fertiles,* 1936), and then by a return to a poetry that was more direct (*Cours naturel,* 1938; *Chanson complète,* 1939; *Le livre ouvert,* 1942) and more political (*Poésie et Vérité,* 1942; *Une leçon de morale,* 1949).

Emmanuel, Pierre, pseud. (Noël Mathieu). 1916–
After a childhood in America, Emmanuel returned to France to complete his education. In 1938 he met Pierre Jean Jouve, a decisive contact in terms of his vocation as a poet, and he composed his first poem, *Christ au tombeau.* During World War II he was recognized as one of the major poets of the Resistance (*Cantos,* 1942; *Jour de colère,* 1942). After the war he continued his verbal experiments and renewed his links with the inspiration provided by the Bible and Christianity (*Babel,* 1952; *La Nouvelle Naissance,* 1963; *Ligne de faîte,* 1966; *Notre Père,* 1969; *Jacob,* 1970). Emmanuel also published essays, among them *Baudelaire* (1967), *Le Monde est intérieur* (1967), *La Vie terrestre* (1976).

Estang, Luc. 1911–
Estang's first article was written in 1933 for the newspaper *La Croix,* whose literary editor he later became. Shortly afterward he founded a review, *Le Beau Navire.* During World War II he fled to the Free Zone of France and joined the Resistance. By then he had already published several volumes of poetry: *Au-delà de moi-même* (1938); *Transhumances* (1939); *Puissance du matin* (1941); *Mystère apprivoisé* (1943). In 1944 he was

asked to be a member of the jury for the Prix Renaudot, and in 1949 he won the Grand Prix de la Société des Gens de Lettres for *Les Stigmates,* the first volume of a trilogy entitled *Charges d'âmes.* Continuing his work as a poet, novelist, and essayist, in 1955 he left *La Croix* and went to work for *Le Figaro* and the ORTF. In 1962 he received the Grand Prix de Littérature de l'Académie Française for his work as a whole. His 1968 novel *L'Apostat* describes his break with Christianity. Estang is one of the editors at Editions du Seuil.

Etiemble, René. 1909–

Etiemble studied at the Ecole Normale Supérieure and received his *Agrégation de grammaire* in 1932. He gave up a thesis on Chinese philosophy before it was completed and began his still unfinished work on the *Mythe de Rimbaud.* He has taught general and comparative literature at the Sorbonne since 1956. He is a novelist (*L'Enfant de chœur,* 1937; *Blason d'un corps,* 1961). The three initial volumes of *Peaux de couleuvre* (1948) await the addition of two others. Between 1952 and 1967 he produced the five-volume *Hygiène des Lettres.* Between 1956 and 1976 he published numerous works on the philosophy and politics of China and Europe: *Confucius* (4th ed. 1968); *Le Nouveau Singe pèlerin* (1958); *Connaissons-nous la Chine?* (1964); *Les Jésuites en Chine* (1966); *Quarante ans de mon maoïsme* (1976); and *L'Orient philosophique,* in a series of three installments that were photocopied (1957–59). An avowed cosmopolite (*Comparaison n'est pas raison,* 1963; *Essais de littérature (vraiment) générale,* 1974), Etiemble as nonetheless an enemy of *Le Babélien,* which he attacked in three volumes (1960–62), *Le Jargon des sciences* (1966), and *franglais,* a subject that earned him his success as a bestseller with the 1964 *Parlez-vous franglais?* He is "one of the freest spirits of the time" (F. Alquié).

Faye, Jean-Pierre. 1925–

Faye published his first poems in 1945. After earning his *Agrégation* in philosophy, he spent some time in the United States. In 1964 he obtained the Prix Renaudot for his novel *L'Ecluse.* He participated in the activities of the *Tel Quel* group but broke with it in 1967, at which time he formed the *Change* group. Basing his work on the principle that there has existed in history "an action-as-the-result-of-narration effect," he published two essays: *Langages totalitaires* in 1972, and *Migrations du récit sur le peuple juif* in 1974. In 1975, *Inferno* and *Versions* were published.

Féraoun, Mouloud. 1913–62

Born to impoverished parents, in Upper Kabylia, Féraoun obtained a scholarship to study at the Collège de Tizi-Ouzou. In 1950 he published *Le Fils du pauvre,* a novel that may have been autobiographical, which earned him the Grand Prix Littéraire de la Ville d'Alger. His correspondence with

Camus dates from this period. In 1953 he won the Prix Populiste for *La Terre et le Sang*. When war broke out in Algeria, Féraoun began to keep a diary. A political moderate and a supporter of Franco-Algerian rapprochement, he was a victim of the repression. On 15 March 1962 he was shot by an OAS squad.

Finas, Lucette. 1921–

Novelist Finas (*Les Chaînes éclatés*, 1955; *L'Echec*, 1958; *Le Meurtrion*, 1968; *Donne*, 1976), occupies a place in the avant-garde of the *nouvelle critique* because of her readings of Bataille, *La Crue* (1972), and of Derrida and Mallarmé, "Le coup de D. et Judas," *in Ecarts* (1973). She is the author of numerous critical articles (in *NRF; Lettres Nouvelles; La Quinzaine littéraire*).

Follain, Jean. 1903–71

A reserved poet absorbed in the past, Follain began his career as a lawyer in Paris. In the late twenties he was associated with the "Sagesse" group, and he published his first works in private reviews such as *Le Derner Carré* or *Feuilles inutiles*. In 1937 he published a collection of reminiscences, *L'Epicerie d'enfance*. In 1939 he received the Prix Mallarmé. After the war he served on the committee of the Pen Club. He published numerous works of poetry and poetic prose (*Canisy*, 1942; *Exister*, 1947; *Chef-Lieu*, 1950; *Territoires*, 1953; *Appareil de la terre,*1954). In 1970 he won the Grand Prix de Poésie de l'Académie Française.

Foucault, Michel. 1926–

Foucault served as professor of philosophy at the universities of Clermont-Ferrand, Tunis, and Vincennes, before being named to the Collège de France in 1970. Until 1968 he was one of the outstanding figures in the structuralist movement. As a politically committed philosopher he has for several years been active in the GIP (Groupe d'Information sur les Prisons) fighting for penal reform in France. In 1961 his *Histoire de la folie à l'âge classique* was published, followed by *Les Mots et les Choses* in 1966, *L'Archéologie du savoir* in 1969, and, finally, *Surveiller et Punir* in 1975. All of Foucault's works hinge on the same theme: How can the question of power be stated, and what is power? Basing his work on the idea that discourse is the manifestation of one kind of power, Foucault inevitably became the genealogist of "kinds of power." In late 1975 he published his first volume, *La Volonté de savoir,* of his *Histoire de la sexualité* ("Bibl. des Histoires," Gallimard).

Fouchet, Max-Pol. 1913–80

Poet and critic, of both art and literature, Max-Pol Fouchet was interested in every contemporary intellectual movement, but particularly in archaeology and in the civilization of the African, Indian, and North and South

American peoples. During World War II he founded and directed the review *Fontaine* in Algiers, a periodical that was one of the last refuges of freedom of thought. In 1953 he began to appear as a literary critic on French television. A media personality, he used the airwaves to initiate the public into the intellectual and artistic life of the period. The following among his many works deserve special mention: *Anthologie de la poésie française* (Seghers, 1955; 5th ed.), *Les Appels* (critical study and prefaces, 1967; *Un jour je m'en souviens (Mémoire parlée*, 1968, Mercure de France). In 1976 he published his first novel, *La Rencontre de Santa Cruz* (Grasset).

Frénaud, André. 1907–

Captured and imprisoned in 1939, Frénaud was released in 1942. With the help of Aragon, he published his first poems the same year in *Poésie 42*. *Les Rois Mages* came out in 1943. The main part of his poetic works is collected in two volumes: *Il n'y a pas de paradis* (1962) and *Sainte Face* (1968).

Gary, Romain. 1914–80

Born in Moscow into a family of actors, Gary started out speaking Russian, then Polish, and finally French. Although he was subsequently to write three novels directly in English, his cultural conditioning, as he himself has admitted, made him an essentially French writer. He completed his education at Nice. During World War II he joined the Free French Forces in England. His career as a writer began in 1945 with *Education européenne*, which earned him the Prix des Critiques. He became a career diplomat but continued to write, over the years publishing *Les Racines du ciel* (Prix Goncourt, 1956); *Lady L.* (1963); *Les Mangeurs d'étoiles* (1966); *La Danse de Genjis Cohn* (1967); and *La tête coupable* (1968).

Gascar, Pierre, pseud. (Pierre Fournier). 1916–

Fournier had an impoverished peasant childhood. He was captured and imprisoned during World War II and made an attempt to escape. He was recaptured and sent to the Rawa-Ruska concentration camp. In 1946, when he returned from captivity, he published his first writing in *Fontaine*. In 1953 he won the Prix des Critiques for his novel *Les Bêtes* and the Prix Goncourt for *Le Temps des morts*. He continued his work as a novelist and essayist with publication, among others, of *La Graine* (1955); *Le Fugitif* (1961); *Les Charmes* (1965); *Chine ouverte* (1955); *Histoire de la captivité du Français en Allemagne* (1967); *Vertiges du présent* (1962); and *La Chine et les Chinois* (1971). He won the Grand Prix de Littérature de l'Académie Française in 1969, and in 1976 published *Dans la forêt humaine*.

Gatti, Armand. 1924–

The son of immigrants, Gatti was fifteen years old when his father, a union member, was bludgeoned to death by the police during a strike.

Working to support himself Gatti continued his education. In 1942 he joined the Resistance. He was arrested and sent to a concentration camp in Germany, escaped, and got safely to England. After the war he was a journalist and won the Prix Albert Londres in 1954. His first play, *Le Poisson noir*, earned the 1957 Prix Fénéon. A witness of the times he lived in, Gatti's work was one of ideological commitment, and his plays were political: *L'Enfant-Rat* (1960); *La Vie imaginaire de l'éboueur Auguste G.* (1962); *La Deuxième Existence du camp de Talenberg* (1962); *Chant public devant deux chaises électriques* (1964); *V comme Viet-nam* (1967); *La Passion du Général Franco* (1968).

Genet, Jean. 1910–

Genet was a Public Assistance child, placed with a family of peasants in the Morvan region of France. When he was sixteen years old, he was sent to reform school. He was in the Prison de Fresnes when he wrote *Le Condamné à mort* in 1942. It was also during these years of obscurity that he wrote *Notre-Dame-des-Fleurs* and *Miracle de la rose*. In 1947 his play *Les Bonnes* had its first performance at the Athénée. In 1951 Sartre wrote a preface about him, *Saint Genet, comédien et martyr*, which became volume 1 of the complete works of Jean Genet; volume 2 (1951) covering *Notre-Dame-des-Fleurs*, *Miracle de la rose*, and *Condamné à mort;* volume 3 (1953) *Pompes funèbres*, *Querelle de Brest*, *Le Pêcheur du Suquet;* and volume 4 *L'Etrange mot D'. . .*, *Ce qui est resté d'un Rembrandt déchiré en petits carrés*, *Les Bonnes*, *Haute surveillance*, *Lettres à Roger Blin*, *Comment jouer Les Bonnes*, *Comment jouer le Balcon*. After deciding to give up literature, Genet nevertheless returned to the theater, writing *Le Balcon* in 1956, *Les Nègres* in 1959, and *Les Paravents* in 1965.

Genette, Gérard. 1930–

Genette holds the post of Directeur d'études de sémiotique littéraire at the Ecole des Hautes Etudes en Sciences Sociales in Paris and is codirector of the review and the series entitled *Poétique*, put out by Editions du Seuil. His main publications are: *Figures I* (1966); *Figures II* (1969); *Figures III* (1972); and *Mimologiques* (1976). Gérard Genette's writing and research have been concentrated on what in the classic tradition was called "poetics," i.e., both the general theory of literary form, and the analysis of individual works, in his case studied from a methodological perspective inspired by structural semiology. In the three *Figures*, the major areas of practical application were the problems of poetic discourse and of narrative in the works of Stendhal, Flaubert, and Proust, and in Baroque poetry. *Mimologiques* is a historical and theoretical analysis of the linguistic imagination from Plato to the present, based on the theme of the mimetic relation between words and objects. After 1976 Genette's research has dealt with examples of "transtextuality," i.e., the relation between different texts and between individual texts and different genres.

Genevoix, Maurice. 1890–1980

Genevoix was born on an island in the Loire, in the Nièvre region of France, and as a writer was profoundly rooted in the land. In 1912 he entered the Ecole Normale Supérieure. In 1914 he was drafted and seriously wounded, and he began to write his reminiscences of the war. *Sous Verdun* was published in 1916. After the war was over he devoted himself entirely to literature. His first novel, *Jeanne Robelin*, appeared in 1920. With *Raboliot*, published in 1925, he won the Prix Goncourt. A lover of animals and of mankind, Genevoix wrote more than thirty novels celebrating nature and the mysteries of life on the land: *La Dernière Harde* (1938); *La Loire, Agnès et les garçons* (1962); *Tendre bestiaire, bestiaire enchanté* (1969); *Bestiaire sans oubli* (1973); *Un homme et sa vie* (1974); and *Un jour* (1975). Elected to the Académie Française in 1946, he served as Secrétaire perpétuel from 1958 to 1973.

Ghelderode, Michel de, pseud. (Adolphe-Adhémar-Louis-Michel Martens). 1898–1962

Ghelderode was Flemish, but also a man who almost involuntarily remembered that Flanders had once been Spanish. All of his works evoke a world in which living creatures are torn between God and the devil, life and death, Flanders and Spain. He wrote stories, *Sortilèges* (1962), and nonfiction, *La Flandre est un songe* (1953), but his obsessive world was expressed primarily in plays. His first play, *La Mort regarde à la fenêtre*, was produced in Brussels in 1918. His works were published in Belgium, and most of his plays were produced in Brussels. It was not until after World War II that they began to be known in France. Gallimard published his complete plays: *Théâtre I (Hop Signor!; Escurial; Sire Halewyn; Magie rouge; Mademoiselle Jaïre; Fastes d'Enfer)*, 1952; *Théâtre II (Le Cavalier bizarre; La Ballade du Grand Macabre; Trois Acteurs; Un Drame; Christophe Colomb; Les Femmes au tombeau; La Farce des ténébreux)*, 1952; *Théâtre III (La Pie sur le gibet; Pantagleize; D'un diable qui prêche merveilles; Sortie de l'acteur; L'Ecole des bouffons)*, 1953; *Théâtre IV (Un soir de pitié; Don Juan; Le Club des menteurs; Les Vieillards; Marie la misérable; Masques ostendais)*, 1955; *Théâtre V (Le Soleil se couche; Les Aveugles; Le Ménage de Caroline; La mort du Docteur Faust; Adraif et Jusemina; Piet Bouteille)*, 1957.

Giono, Jean. 1895–1970

Grandson of a *carbonaro* (member of French revolutionary secret society with roots in Italy), Giono was obliged to interrupt his education when World War I broke out and he was drafted. He described the horror of his wartime experiences in *Refus d'obéissance* (1937). After the Armistice he devoted himself entirely to literature, settling in Manosque in the house he was to occupy until his death. Here he wrote *Colline* (1928); *Regain* (1930);

Le Grand Troupeau (1931); *Jean le Bleu* (1932); and, most importantly, *Le Chant du monde* (1934) and *Que ma joie demeure* (1935). These two works marked the beginning of Gionoism. Disciples gathered around him, and he clarified his ideas in *Les Vraies Richesses* (1936); *Le Poids du ciel* (1938); and *Vivre Libre I, Lettres aux paysans sur la pauvreté et la paix*, followed by *Vivre Libre II* (1938). In 1939 he was put in prison for tearing down posters announcing the mobilization. On the other hand, he was sympathetic to the Vichy regime, which caused him some trouble after the Liberation. He continued writing novels—*Mort d'un personnage* (1949); *Les Ames fortes* (1949); *Les Grands Chemins* (1951)—but it was with *Le Hussard sur le toit* (1951) that he once again occupied the center of the literary stage. The critics claimed to have discovered a new Giono in the author of *Moulin de Pologne* (1952); *Voyage en Italie* (1953); *Angelo* (1958); and *Les Désastre de Pavie* (1963). *Angélique* and *Oeuvres cinématographiques* were published posthumously in 1980. He was seen as a chronicler inspired by Stendhal, and yet he was also still celebrating the joys of a pagan humanism. In 1954 he was elected to the Académie Goncourt.

Giraudoux, Jean. 1882–1944

Graduated first in his class from the Ecole Normale Supérieure, Giraudoux spent a year in Munich and then took up a career as a diplomat. In 1918 he published *Simon le pathétique;* in 1920, *Suzanne et le Pacifique;* and, in 1922, *Siegfried et le Limousin*. His first experience with the theater was with *Siegfried*. Meeting Jouvet was a crucial event in his career. Almost every year until the outbreak of the war, that great actor produced or starred in a new play by Giraudoux: *Amphitryon 38* (1929); *Judith* (1931); *Intermezzo* (1933); *La Guerre de Troie n'aura pas lieu* (1935); *Electre* (1937); and *Ondine* (1939). At the beginning of World War II, Giraudoux was named Commissioner of Information, but events soon put an end to his job, and the author of *Bella* retired to Cusset. He died a few months before the Liberation. Jouvet produced *La Folle de Chaillot* in 1945. *Pour Lucrèce*, another posthumous play, was premiered in 1953.

Gracq, Julien, pseud. (Louis Poirier). 1910–

Graduate of the Ecole Normale Supérieure, holder of an *Agrégation* in history, with teaching experience in several lycées, Gracq was primarily interested in literature. An heir to the surrealists (André Breton was the subject of an autobiographical essay he wrote in 1948), this distant disciple of Chrétien de Troyes, and close relative of Barbey d'Aurevilly's maintained his detachment from all coteries. In 1951 he even went so far as to turn down the Prix Goncourt he had won for his novel *Le Rivage des Syrtes*. An enemy of commercialization in literature he himself produced works that were few in number but strong in impact. His other novels were: *Au Château d'Argol* (1938); *Un beau ténébreux* (1945); *Un balcon en forêt*

(1958); *Lettrines* (1967); *La Presqu'île* (1970); and an essay, *La Littérature à l'estomac* (1950).

Green, Julien. 1900–

Of Anglo-Saxon ancestry, his father from Georgia and his mother from Virginia, Green was raised in an atmosphere of Puritanism. After his mother's death he renounced Protestantism and in 1916 converted to Catholicism. This did not, however, stop him from publishing a *Pamphlet contre les catholiques de France* in 1924. His first novel, *Mont-Cinère*, came out in 1926, and his next, *Adrienne Mesurat*, in 1927, earning him the Prix Bookman and initiating a series of novels with an atmosphere heavily charged with anguish. Green returned to the United States frequently, and he settled there during World War II. In 1950 he published *Moïra*. The following year he received the Grand Prix Littéraire de Monaco. He then began his career in the theater with *Sud* (play produced in 1953), followed in quick succession by *L'Ennemi* (1954) and *L'Ombre* (1956). Green has also published childhood reminiscences and a large segment of his diary, in which are found the obsessions of a writer tormented by the problem of evil and of sexuality (the devil and sex being synonymous, for him). He was elected a member of the Académie Française in 1972.

Grenier, Roger. 1919–

Grenier was educated in Pau. Drafted in 1940, he returned to civilian life in 1942 and completed his *Licence* in letters. In 1944 he joined the staff of *Combat,* then *France-Soir.* He began publishing in 1949. His main novels are *La Voie romaine* (1960) and *Le Palais d'hiver* (1965). He has been literary consultant at Gallimard since 1964.

Grosjean, Jean. 1912–

Grosjean traveled in the Far East and then was ordained as a priest. Captured by the Germans in 1940, he spent two years in prisoner-of-war camps. In 1946 he published *Terre du temps,* which won the Prix de la Pléiade. He left religious orders in 1950. A biblical poet, a poet of the sacred and the beyond of language, he published, successively, *Hypotases* (1950); *Le Livre du juste* (1952); *Fils de l'homme* (1954); *Apocalypse* (1962); and *Elégies* (1967), which won the Prix des Critiques.

Guillevic, Eugène. 1907–

A Breton poet and a Marxist, Guillevic's first published work was *Terraqué,* 1942, entirely devoted to men, to things, and to the land. *Exécutoire* (1947) is a collection of poems written during the German Occupation. *Carnac* (1961) evokes a world with neither miracles nor gods. *Sphère* (1963) and *Avec* (1966) celebrate a certain vision of the world, along with insights into the poet and his encounter with others.

Guilloux, Louis. 1899–1980

A writer of the people and disciple of Vallès, Guilloux set most of his books in Sainte-Brieuc. He was the son of a militant socialist and very early in his life became involved in populist causes. He published his first novel, *La Maison du peuple*, in 1927. Although sympathetic with the aims of the Russian Revolution, he refused to become a member of the Communist Party. He did, however, agree to serve as secretary for the First International Congress of Antifascist Writers, held in 1935, the same year *Le Sang noir* was published. In 1942 he was awarded the Prix Populiste for *Le Pain des rêves;* in 1949 he won the Prix Renaudot for *Le Jeu de patience.*

Hériat, Philippe. 1898–1972

Son of a jurist, Hériat began his career as assistant director under Marcel Lherbier and Louis Delluc. He even took part in Bourdet's *Le Sexe faible* as an actor. In 1931 he won the Prix Renaudot for his novel *L'Innocent;* and in 1939 he was awarded the Prix Goncourt for *Les Enfants gâtés,* volume 1 of *Les Boussardel,* the fourth volume of which came out in 1968. Hériat won the Grand Prix du Roman de l'Académie Française in 1947 and became a member of the Académie Goncourt in 1949. A novelist in the traditional style, he wrote works illustrating the society of his period.

Hervé Bazin, Jean. 1911–

A great-nephew of René Bazin, Hervé Basin is a descendant, through the latter's family, of Urbain Grandier et de Ménage. He was raised by his grandmother; and it was only in 1920 that he renewed contact with his parents, who had been living in China; the impact was immediate and negative. A rebellious teenager, he did badly in school but was nevertheless first prize winner in the Concours Général. After trying his hand at jobs of various kinds, he began to publish his poetry. In 1934 he married and broke with his family. He met Paul Valéry around this time. The life he led was a hard one. In 1946 he founded a small poetry review, and the following year he received the Prix Apollinaire for his collection of poems entitled *Jour.* In 1948 he made his fiction début with *Vipère au poing,* which won the Prix des Lecteurs; the book deals with teenage rebellion, a theme he returned to in *La Tête contre les murs* (1949). Author of *La Mort du petit cheval* (1950) and *Lève-toi et marche* (1952), he won the Prix Prince Pierre de Monaco in 1957. He was made a member of the Académie Goncourt in 1958 and continued his career as a novelist with *Au nom du fils* (1960); *Le matrimoine* (1967); and *Les Bienheureux de la désolation* (1970).

Hougron, Jean. 1923–

After a stifling provincial childhood he was later to describe in *Histoire de Georges Guersant* (1964), Hougron earned his doctorate in law and went to Indochina, where he remained for five years. He worked at various jobs while there, criss-crossing Southeast Asia. In 1953 the Grand Prix du Roman de l'Académie Française was awarded Hougron's six-volume *La Nuit indochinoise*, which deals acutely and sensitively with the problem of colonialism.

Ikor, Roger. 1912–

Born of a Lithuanian father and a mother of Polish ancestry, Ikor attended the Ecole Normale Supérieure and earned an *Agrégation de Grammaire*. Drafted in 1939, he spent the duration as a prisoner of war in a Pomeranian *Oflag*. In 1955 he won the Prix Goncourt for *Les Eaux mêlées*, volume 1 of a cyclical work entitled *Les Fils d'Avron* and chronicling the life of a Jewish family. The final volume came out in 1966.

Ionesco, Eugène. 1912–

Born in Romania, Ionesco settled in France in 1938, where he prepared a doctoral thesis on "the themes of sin and death in French literature since Baudelaire." He led the life of a typical family man and breadwinner until the day when, if the story is to be believed, he decided to learn English and stumbled on the *Méthode Assimil*. From this discovery was born *La Cantatrice chauve*, staged in 1950 at the Théâtre des Noctambules. Ionesco immediately became a leading figure in the antitheater movement, along with Beckett and Adamov. Volume 1 of his plays was published in 1954 *(La Cantatrice chauve; La Leçon; Jacques ou la soumission; Les Chaises; Victimes du devoir; Amédée ou comment s'en débarrasser)*; volume 2 in 1958 *(L'Impromptu de l'Alma; Tueur sans gages; Le Nouveau Locataire; L'Avenir est dans les œufs; Le Maître; Le Jeune Fille à marier)*; volume 3 in 1963 *(Rhinocéros; Le Piéton de l'air; Délire à deux; Le Tableau; Scène à quatre; Les Salutations; La Colère)*; volume 4 in 1966 *(Le Roi se meurt; La Soif et la Faim; La Lacune; Le Salon de l'automobile; L'Oeuf dur; Pour préparer un œuf dur; Le Jeune Homme à marier; Apprendre à marcher)*. In 1970 Ionesco's career was crowned by the supreme honor of membership in the Académie Française. In addition to his plays, he also published *Journal en miettes* (1967) and a collection of thoughts on modern theater, *Notes et contre-notes* (1963).

Jaccottet, Philippe. 1925–

Poet, essayist, and translator Philippe Jaccottet, born in Switzerland, settled in Paris in 1946. He was a contributor to the *NRF*. His first poems, *L'Effraie et autres poèmes*, were published in 1954 and followed shortly by *La Promenade sous les arbres* (1957); *L'Ignorant* (1958); *Airs* (1967); and *Leçons* (1969). He wrote notebooks, *La Semaison* (1963); and an account of poetry writing, *L'Entretien des muses* (1968). He has translated Robert Musil, Ungaretti, Hölderlin, and Rilke.

Jouhandeau, Marcel. 1888–

Jouhandeau spent his childhood in Guéret, in the Creuse region. He was a studious youth, weaned on Christian writings, and he went to Paris to study for his licence ès-lettres. From 1912 until 1949 he taught in a private school. In 1924 he published *Les Pincengrain;* the book caused a scandal in Guéret. In 1929 he married the dancer "Caryathis," who also took up literature, under the name of Elise. Tireless and prolific, Jouhandeau produced a considerable body of work over the years. To name a few titles: *La Jeunesse de Théophile* (1921); *Monsieur Godeau intime* and *Monsieur Godeau marié* (1927 and 1933); *Chaminadour I, II,* and *III* (1934, 1936, 1941); to which we should add the six volumes of *Le Mémorial* and more than twenty for *Journaliers,* Jouhandeau's continuing autobiography.

Jouve, Pierre Jean. 1887–1976

It has been said of Jouve that he was the poet of the creative subconscious. At the age of sixteen he suffered a serious illness and experienced a grand passion for an officer's wife: the image of this woman can be seen in the character of Hélène. From 1906 to 1908 Jouve published a review of the symbolist persuasion, *Les Bandeaux d'or.* He published his first volume of poems, *Présences,* in 1912, following it with *Parler* (1913). In 1922 he married the psychoanalyst Blanche Reverchon. He wrote a series of strong and original novels, among them *Paulina 1880* (1925); *Le Monde désert* (1927); *Hécate* (1928); *Vagadu* (1931); *Histoires sanglantes* (1932); and *La Scène capitale* (1935). Jouve's gifts as a poet were confirmed with *Mystérieuses Noces,* followed by *Nouvelles Noces* (1926); *Noces* (1928); *Sueurs de sang* (1933); and *Hélène* (1946). Jouve published the Resistance poems *La Vierge de Paris* (1946) after World War II. In 1960 he received the Prix Dante, in 1962 the Grand Prix National des Lettres, and in 1966 the Grand Prix de Poésie de l'Académie Française.

Kessel, Joseph. 1898–

Born in Argentina of Russian parents, Kessel spent a part of his childhood in Orenberg at the foot of the Urals, and then in Nice. In 1914 he joined the *Journal des Débats* as an editor while continuing his studies in literature. He enlisted in 1916 and fought in the air corps; he discovered adventure and how to live dangerously. After World War I was over he went to Asia as a reporter. He began writing novels, and in 1927 he received the Grand Prix du Roman de l'Académie Française. In 1936 he was a war correspondent in Spain. He went to England during World War II and, with his nephew Druon, wrote *Chant du partisan.* After the Liberation he continued to write novels and to work as a reporter—a great one. Some of his novels are: *L'Equipage* (1923); *Les Cœurs purs* (1927); *Fortune carrée* (1930); *Le Lion* (1958); *Les Cavaliers* (1967). He was elected to the Académie Française in 1963.

Klossowski, Pierre. 1903–

Klossowski, who came from an old Polish family and whose brother was the painter Balthus, early became involved in artistic circles and with literary personalities (Bonnard, Rilke, and Gide). After completing his military service he became a friend of Paulhan, Groethuysen, and Jouve (he translated Hölderlin's *Poèmes de la folie* in collaboration with Jouve), but it was Bataille whose influence was decisive. In 1934 he experienced a crisis of mysticism and entered the Dominican order of monks. On his return to civilian life he published *Sade mon prochain* in 1947, following it with *La Vocation suspendue* in 1950, and *Les Lots de l'Hospitalité* and *Le Baphomet* (1965).

Kristeva, Julia. 1941–

Kristeva holds an *Agrégation de Lettres Modernes* from the Institut de Littérature de Sofia, Bulgaria, where she was born; when she came to France in 1966, she presented a *troisième cycle* doctoral thesis, and then a thesis for the *Doctorat d'Etat*. A tenured professor at the Université de Paris VII, in the Département des Sciences du Texte, she is secretary general of the International Association of Semiotics, associate editor of the review *Semiotica*, and a member of the editorial board of *Tel Quel*. She published *Séméiotikè* (research for a semanalysis) in 1969, and then *Révolution du langage poétique* (1974), *La Traversée des signes* (1975) and, in the same year, *Les Chinoises*. She has been a contributor to what is known as "the theory of the text"; she has also attempted to reinstate the feminist discourse into the domain of language.

Lacan, Jacques. 1901–81

Lacan is one of the most controversial figures in the field of sexual psychology. A misunderstood genius according to some, a mere trickster for others, he is nevertheless one of the most amazing reinterpreters of Freud.

A friend of the surrealists, in 1932 Lacan published his doctoral thesis, *De la psychose paranoïaque dans ses rapports à la personnalité*. In 1953 he founded the Société Française de Psychanalyse with Daniel Lagache and the same year led his first seminar at the Ecole Normale Supérieure. Basing his work on the writings of Freud and modern linguistic research, Lacan has stated the problematic of the relationship created between a person who is speaking and what he says. The theoretical positions Lacan adopted led him to create the Ecole Freudienne de Paris. In 1966 he published *Ecrits I* and *II*, and in 1968 and 1970 he was a contributor to the review *Scilicet*. *Livre XI: Les quatre concepts fondamentaux de la psychanalyse* and *Livre XX: Encore* came out in 1973 and 1975, respectively, inaugurating the publication of Lacan's oral work in its entirety; this enterprise was undertaken by Editions du Seuil on the basis of stenographic records taken during the courses given by Lacan at the Ecole Normale Supérieure and the Ecole Pratique des Hautes Etudes.

Lanza del Vasto. 1901–81

Lanza del Vasto's ancestry was Italian, but also Flemish and French. Part of his poetic work was written in Italian and never published. He was born in southern Italy, attended secondary school in Paris, earned his doctorate in philosophy at Pisa; in 1925 he was converted to Catholicism, the religion of his childhood. He became an errant adventurer of the Spirit, meeting Luc Dietrich, who helped him to become the commemorative novelist of *Le Bonheur des tristes,* and *L'Apprentissage de la ville,* and the poet of *L'Injuste Grandeur.* Lanza del Vasto abhorred totalitarianism of any kind and, having witnessed Mussolini's seizure of power in Rome and Hitler's in Berlin, he left for India in 1936, "to learn from Gandhi how to be a better Christian," and also to seek a cure for the ills of the West. Famous as a Zone Libre poet during the early years of World War II, his piece *Le Pèlerinage aux sources* (1943) earned him a fervent readership. He established the foundations for a nonviolent, direct action movement and, with his wife, musician Chanterelle, created the l'Arche community.

La Tour du Pin, Patrice de. 1911–75

This author's complete works are collected under a single title *Une Somme de Poésie,* three volumes published by Gallimard. Made famous with the publication of *La Quête de Joie* (1933), Patrice de La Tour du Pin is a poet of the present moment, the inner life, and of spiritual quest; he belongs to the line of Christian poets that includes Claudel, Péguy, and Milosz. His attempt to reconcile poetry and prayer led him on an itinerary starting in the sensual fogs of adolescence *(Enfants de Septembre)* and with a liturgical celebration of God's love. The first part of the *Somme* is bathed in a dreamlike light. *Le Second Jeu* (1959) is swept by the winds of solitude and asceticism; this leads to the third part, "Le Jeu de l'homme devant Dieu," dominated by a mystic illumination. Patrice de La Tour du Pin has almost completed a thorough revision of the *Somme;* this definitive version remains to be published.

Le Clec'h, Guy. 1917–

Son of a journalist, Le Clec'h was studying for admission to the Ecole Normale Supérieure when he left to fight in World War II, earning a *Licence* in history after his discharge. After the Liberation he joined the administration of Les Arts et Lettres, and was employed as a reader with the publisher Albin Michel. He published his first novel, *Le Témoin silencieux,* in 1949. He was awarded a Blumenthal fellowship after publication of *La Plaie et le Couteau* (1952). He traveled, contributed articles to *Le Figaro Littéraire,* and published, successively, *Le Défi* (1954); *Tout homme a sa chance* (1957); *Les Moissons de l'abîme* (1968).

Le Clézio, Jean-Marie. 1940–
   Le Clézio is from a family of Breton extraction that emigrated long ago to the île Maurice. He spent his childhood and completed his education in the South of France. In 1963 he published *Procès-verbal,* which won him the Prix Renaudot. He was famous at the age of twenty-three. He published two other novels, *Le Déluge* (1966) and *Terra amata* (1967), collections of short stories; and an essay, *L'Extase matérielle* (1967). These were followed by *Le Livre des fuites* (1969); *La Guerre* (1970); *Les Géants* (1973); *Voyages de l'autre côté* (1975); *Les Prophéties du Chilam Balam* (1976).

Leduc, Violette. 1907–71
   The child of a father who refused to recognize his paternity, Violette Leduc was raised by her grandmother. She worked in public relations for the publishing firm Plon and began her career as a journalist. In 1932 she met Maurice Sachs; a decisive meeting for her. She led an unsettled life, married, had an abortion, attempted suicide. In 1946 she published *L'Asphyxie.* Her writing talent was recognized by Camus, Genet, and Jouhandeau. She went on to publish *L'Affamée* (1948), *Ravages* (1955), *La Vieille Fille et le mort* (1958), and *Trésors à prendre* (1960), but it was not until the 1964 publication of *La Bâtarde,* with a preface by Simone de Beauvoir, that Leduc finally achieved success.

Leiris, Michel. 1901–
   Leiris, a friend of Max Jacob and André Masson, was a supporter of surrealism at the age of twenty-three. He was interested in the study of dreams and in experiments with language, both of which inspired him to write *Aurora,* written between 1927 and 1928 but not published until 1946. Leiris became an ethnologist, went to Africa in his official capacity, and published *L'Afrique fantôme,* a travel book and the beginnings of an autobiography. With *L'Age d'homme,* published in 1939, Leiris declared his intention to "create a book which would be an act." Pursuing his quest for self, which was also a quest for the good life and the responsible life, Leiris embarked on *La Règle du jeu,* published in four volumes (*Biffures,* 1948; *Fourbis,* 1955; *Fibrilles,* 1966; *Frêle Bruit,* 1976). In 1969 and in 1973 Gallimard published two collections of his poems, *Note sans mémoire* and *Haut-mal;* his articles are collected under the title *Brisées* (Mercure de France, 1969).

Lévi-Strauss, Claude. 1908–
   Lévi-Strauss's work as a social anthropologist had profoundly influenced the social sciences. By applying structural analysis to ethnology, he at-

tempted to develop a new analytical method, one borrowed from general linguistics. Directeur d'Etudes at the Ecole Pratique des Hautes Etudes, in 1955 Lévi-Strauss published *Tristes Tropiques*, a travel book that was also about the experience of traveling itself. In *Anthropologie structurale* (1958) he emphasized the differences that separate history from anthropology, the latter "organizing its information in relation to the subconscious conditions underlying social life." In his sixties he turned toward the science of myth and published what amounted to a summa: *Mythologies I, II,* and *III (Le Cru et le Cuit, Du miel et des cendres, L'Origine des manières de table);* and in 1975 *La Voie des masques.*

MacOrlan, Pierre, pseud. (Pierre Dumarchey). 1882–1970
    After an impoverished childhood, MacOrlan took to the roads, especially those of Northern Europe. He started publishing humorous tales in 1912. But the major part of his work was written between the two World Wars: *Le Chant de l'équipage* (1918); *A bord de l'Etoile Matutine* (1920); *Le Quai des brumes* (1927); and *La Bandera* (1931)—the last two of which inspired films that stand as masterpieces of the genre. Continuing to write, MacOrlan lived a secluded life at Saint-Cyr-sur-Morin, leaving home occasionally to fulfill assignments as a reporter. He was elected to the Académie Goncourt in 1950.

Mallet-Joris, Françoise, pseud. (Françoise Lilar). 1930–
    Daughter of a Belgian statesman and the writer Suzanne Lilar, Mallet-Joris published her first novel, *Le Rempart des béguines,* in 1951. The subject of the novel, a father and daughter sharing the favors of the same woman, caused a scandal. In 1956 she won the Prix des Libraires for *Les Mensonges* and in 1958 the Prix Fémina *L'Empire céleste.* In *Les Signes et les Prodiges* (1966) the author raises the question of whether or not a meeting between God and mankind is possible. She has written many essays, among them *Lettre à moi-même* (1963) and *La Maison de papier* (1970). Elected to the jury of the Prix Goncourt in November 1971, she subsequently published *Le Jeu du souterrain* (1973) and *Allegra* (1976).

Malraux, André, pseud. (Georges Malraux). 1901–76
    Malraux published his first books when he returned from a trip to the Far East: *La Tentation de l'Occident* (1926); *Les Conquérants* (1928); *La Voie royale* (1930); and *La Condition humaine,* which earned him the 1933 Prix Goncourt. He was a member of the International Antifascist Committee. His part in the Spanish civil war, which inspired *L'Espoir* (1937), is well known. Malraux was taken prisoner by the Germans in 1940, escaped, and joined the Resistance. He published *Les Noyers de l'Altenburg* in Switzerland. Named Minister of Information after the war, he subsequently followed de Gaulle when the latter removed himself from the center of power.

Malraux wrote several major essays on the history and philosophy of art: *Le Musée imaginaire* (1947); *La Création artistique* (1948); *La Monnaie de l'absolu* (1950); *Saturne, Essai sur Goya* (1949); *Les Voix du silence* (1951); *Le Musée imaginaire de la sculpture mondiale* (1952–55); *La Métamorphose des dieux* (1957). Named as Secretary of State for Cultural Affairs by de Gaulle in 1958, and then as Minister of State, he remained in the latter post until 1969. His *Antimémoires I* was published in 1967; *Les Chênes qu'on abat...* and *Oraisons funèbres* in 1971; *La Tête d'obsidienne, Lazare* in 1974; *Hôtes de passage* in 1975; and, finally, continuing what he had begun with *La Métamorphose des Dieux*, two major works of art history: *L'Irréel* (1975) and *L'Intemporel* (1976). His work entitled *L'homme précaire et la littérature* was published shortly after his death.

Marceau, Félicien, pseud. (Louis Carette). 1913–

Born in Belgium, Marceau was a journalist working for Belgian radio when his first novel, *Le Péché de complication*, was published in 1941. After World War II he settled in Paris, where he won the Prix Interallié for *Les Elans du cœur*. But it was in the theater that he made his reputation, with *L'Oeuf* (1956); *La Bonne Soupe, La Preuve par quatre*, and *Un Jour j'ai rencontré la vérité* (1958–67). He was elected to the Académie Française in 1975, much to the indignation of Pierre Emmanuel.

Martin du Gard, Roger. 1881–1958

Son of solidly middle-class parents, Roger Martin du Gard attended l'Ecole des Chartes. Having decided on a future in literature for himself, he wrote *Jean Barois* (the story of a generation affected by the Dreyfus Case). Welcomed by Gide and Schlumberger as a contributor to the *NRF*, he produced a play, *Le Testament du père Leleu*, staged in February 1914 at the Vieux-Colombier. After World War I he began editing his journal, and in 1922 he started publishing *Les Thibault*, the last volume of which, *Epilogue*, came out in 1940. Martin du Gard won the Nobel Prize for Literature in 1937.

Masson, Loys. 1915–69

Masson left his home in Ile Maurice for France in 1939. He had by then already discovered a world of injustice, the problem of race, and the differences of color. During World War II he was active in the Resistance, assisted Mounier in editing the review *Esprit*, and met Pierre Seghers. Although he was Catholic, in 1945 he joined the Communist Party and became secretary of the Comité National des Ecrivains, and then editor-in-chief of *Les Lettres Françaises*. He broke with the party in 1948. A poet and novelist, he published war poems, *Délivrez-nous du mal* (1942), and approximately fifteen novels, among them *Les Tortues* (1956); *Les Sexes foudroyés* (1958); and *Le Notaire de noirs*, which won the 1962 Prix des Deux Magots.

Mauriac, Claude. 1914–

The eldest son of François Mauriac, Claude Mauriac made his debut as a literary critic before World War II. He was General de Gaulle's private secretary from 1944 to 1949, and in 1947 joined *Le Figaro Littéraire* as film and later as literary critic. An essayist as well as a novelist, he received the 1949 Prix Sainte-Beuve for his book on André Breton and the 1959 Prix Médicis for *Le Dîner en ville,* volume 2 of a four-volume set entitled *Le Dialogue intérieur.* Mauriac has also published large portions of his personal journal: *Le Temps immobile* (1974); *Les Espaces imaginaires* (1975); and *Et comme l'espérance est violente* (1976).

Mauriac, François. 1885–1970

Born into an upper-middle-class family in Bordeaux, Mauriac's adolescence was provincial, bourgeois, and conditioned by a stint with the Marianists. At the beginning of his career he frequented the men connected with Le Sillon. He received much encouragement from Barrès. Mauriac's aspiration was to be "a Catholic who writes novels." Success came quickly and was brilliant. In 1925 he received the Grand Prix du Roman for *Le Désert de l'amour.* In 1933 he was elected to the Académie Française. An acerbic moralist, he became involved in politics early. He attacked fascism and joined the Resistance, but in 1945 he pleaded indulgence for others who had not been as clearsighted as he. This great novelist, author of *Génitrix* (1923), *Thérèse Desqueyroux* (1927), *Le Mystère Frontenac* (1933), and winner of the 1952 Nobel Prize for Literature was also a career journalist and polemicist: his columns in *Le Figaro, L'Express,* and *Le Figaro Littéraire* influenced the era of decolonization in France, and of de Gaulle's return to power.

Memmi, Albert. 1920–

A Tunisian Jew, Memmi both by birth and conditioning belonged to several different worlds, Africa and Europe, the world of the colonized and the world of the alien. His education was interrupted by World War II, and he was employed as forced labor. In 1958 he published *La Statue de sel* which won him the Prix Fénéon. In 1957 he wrote an essay entitled *Portrait du colonisé,* with a preface by Jean-Paul Sartre. He next addressed the question of Jewish identity, writing *Portrait du'un juif* (1962) and *La Libération du juif* (1966). In 1965 he edited an *Anthologie des écrivains maghrébiens d'expression française.* In 1968 and 1969 *L'Homme dominé* and *Le Scorpion ou la Confession imaginaire,* respectively, were published by Gallimard.

Métérié, Alphonse. 1887–1967

Métérié spent his youth in Angers. First a newspaper editor and then a teacher in Aix-en-Provence, he wrote harmonious verses that evoke the romance of the past, the charm of childhood, the glory of love and the memory of those who have died: *Carnets* (1910); *Le Livre des sœurs* (1922); *Le Cahier noir* (1923); *Nocturnes* (1928). In 1925 he left France for Morocco, where for seventeen years he occupied the post of Inspecteur des Beaux-Arts. In his poems the ironic refrain of human sorrow alternates with lyric nostalgia for a transfigured past: *Petit Maroc* (1929); *Petit Maroc II* (1934); *Cophetuesques* (1934). He returned to France and received the Prix Lasserre in 1942. The end of his life, which he spent in Savoie and Lausanne, was a time of withdrawal and resignation. His final volumes of poetry were *Les Cantiques du Frère Michel* (1944), *Vétiver* (1946), *Proella* (1951), and *Ephémères* (1957); they exhibited total opposition to the modern world and to modern poetry.

Michaux, Henri. 1899–

Michaux began medical school, but soon gave it up to travel in North and South America. Strongly influenced by his reading of Lautréamont, in 1925 he became friendly in Paris with Klee, Ernst, and Chirico. He traveled widely for many years, and also began to paint. In 1927, when he came back from a trip in the southern hemisphere, he published *Qui je fus,* followed by *Ecuador* (1929), and *Un barbare en Asie* (1933). With *Plume* (1938) and the preceding *Lointain intérieur,* Michaux entered a phase that led him to the discovery of another world. *Meisodems,* which he published in 1948, was accompanied by thirteen of the author's lithographs; his verbal poetry had acquired a graphic phantasmagoria to go with it. In 1956 Michaux started to experiment on himself with hallucinogenic drugs, primarily mescaline, an experience he described in *L'Infini turbulent* (1957); *Connaissance par les gouffres* (1961); and *Les Grandes Epreuves de l'esprit* (1966). In 1965 Michaux was awarded the Grand Prix National des Lettres, but he refused to accept it. *Une voie pour l'insubordination* was published in 1980, *Chemins cherchés; Chemins perdus; Transgressions* in 1981. The author of *Emergences-résurgences* (1972) had sought to deny the limitations of experience, and as poet and painter he did succeed in expanding the field of the *libido sciendi.*

Montherlant, Henry de. 1896–1972

Montherlant spent his school years at the Collège Sainte-Croix de Neuilly, and at the age of fifteen fought two bulls in the arenas of Burgos, Spain. During World War II, seven shell fragments lodged in his back. His next encounter with the camaraderie he had known in school and in the bull ring was in sports arenas (*La Relève du matin,* 1920; *Les Olympiques,* 1924). He left France for Spain and North Africa; there he wrote *Les Jeunes Filles* (1934) and began *La Rose de sable,* which was not published until 1968. His major novels were *Les Célibataires* (1934); *Le Chaos et la Nuit* (1963); *Les Garçons* (1969); and *Un assassin est mon maître* (1971). But his most spectacular works were the plays he wrote between 1942 and 1965: *La Reine morte* (1942); *Fils de personne* (1944); *Le Maître de Santiago* (1947); *Malatesta* (1948); *La Ville dont le prince est un enfant* (1951); *Port-Royal* (1954); *Le Cardinal d'Espagne* (1960); and *La Guerre civile* (1965). Montherlant was elected to the Académie Française in 1960. He was a writer who celebrated the individual, and who worked hard at perfecting his style. An heir to the wisdom of the ancients, he died by his own hand.

Morand, Paul. 1888–1976

Morand became familiar with artistic circles at an early age through his father, who was director of the Ecole des Arts Décoratifs. In 1913 he embarked on a diplomatic career. A friend of Proust's and Cocteau's, he began after World War I to write works imprinted with a cosmopolitanism that was divided between intelligence and imagination. A lucid and idiosyncratic reporter, he peopled his stage with characters from the postwar generation in books such as *Ouvert la nuit* (1922) and *Fermé la nuit* (1923). After his marriage into a wealthy family he began to travel extensively and published a large number of novels, collections of short stories, and essays. During World War II he was France's ambassador to Bucharest. He was recalled in 1944 and took up residence in Switzerland. And, finally, in 1968 he was elected to the Académie Française. Morand was a man who loved speed, and also space. Notable among the countless works he published were: *Lewis et Irène* (1924); *Bouddha vivant* (1927); *Magie Noire* (1928); *L'Homme pressé* (1941); *Hécate et ses chiens* (1954).

Nizan, Paul. 1905–40

A graduate of the Ecole Normale Supérieure, where he knew Jean-Paul Sartre, Nizan left France in 1925 for Aden; while there he served as a tutor in an English family. When he returned to France, he was active in the Communist Party, founded the *Revue Marxiste,* received his *Agrégation* in philosophy and responded to the lure of politics (he ran for legislative office in 1931). He served as secretary of the Association des Ecrivains Révolutionnaires and wrote for *l'Humanité* and *Ce Soir.* In 1932 he published *Les Chiens de garde;* when the German-Soviet pact was signed in 1939, he left the Communist Party. He has described his own personal rebellion in *Aden Arabie* (1932) and in *La Conspiration* (1933). A convinced communist but also an anarchist and an atheist, he was in favor of World War II and died at the front on 23 May 1940.

Noël, Marie, pseud. (Marie Rouget). 1883–1967

Noël, a woman who never left Auxerre and the shadow of its cathedral, wrote her first poem at the age of twenty-five. In her own words, her work is "not so much a body of work as the song of a life." She achieved fame after

World War II. In 1947, *Chants et Psaumes d'automne* was published, and in 1966 she received the Grand Prix Littéraire de la Ville de Paris for her writing, a body of work distinguished by religious inspiration, love of nature and heartfelt enthusiasms.

Obaldia, René de. 1918–

Born in Hong Kong, the son of a French mother and a Panamanian father, René de Obaldia started his writing career with a series of whimsical novels: *Tamerlan des coeurs* (1954), *Fuge à Waterloo* (1956), and *Le Centenaire* (1959). But his main contribution to literature was as the tender but impertinent author of short plays: *Le Sacrifice du bourreau; Edouard et Aggrippine; L'Air du large.* This poet of the absurd wrote his first great theatrical work, *Génousie*, in 1960. With *Du Vent dans les branches de sassafras* he took on, and not without success, one of the most popular myths of our time: the Western.

Ollier, Claude. 1923–

An emulator of the nouveau roman, Claude Ollier was a novelistic technician who took Robbe-Grillet's methods and pushed them to their limits. Faced with the inability of language to express the emptiness of the void, Ollier created characters who ultimately lose their way in their own search for themselves. He published numerous novels: *La Mise en scène* (1958); *Le Maintien de l'ordre* (1961); *L'Eté indien* (1963); *L'Echec de Nolan* (1967); *La Vie sur Epsilon* (1972); *Enigma* (1973); *Our, ou vingt-cinq ans après* (1974).

Oster, Pierre. 1933–

"Poet of living unity," Pierre Oster used language to examine being, to examine the All. The world is not contained in the word; but through words, the world can be understood. Pierre Oster's first poems appeared in 1954 in *Mercure de France* and the *Nouvelle revue française.* His major works are: *Le Champ de mai* (1955); *Solitude de la lumière* (1957); *Un nom toujours nouveau* (1960); and *La Grande Année* (1964).

Pagnol, Marcel. 1895–1974

Pagnol was a talented dramatist who achieved popularity with a broad public. He created characters from life who spoke in the accents of everyday language. Drawing on the vitality of Marseille's inhabitants for his inspiration, he added satire and a touch of poetry. His success began with the production of *Topaze* (1928) and *Marius* (1929). Aided by the collaboration of some of France's greatest actors (Raimu, Jouvet, Fresnay) Pagnol was one of the first serious writers to transfer his plays successfully to the screen: *Marius* was filmed in 1931, *Fanny* in 1932, *Topaze* in 1932, and *César* in 1933. Elected to the Académie Française in 1946, he subsequently published several volumes of reminiscences, all bearing the mark of the love he always bore his native Provence: *La Gloire de mon père* (1957); *Le Château de ma mère* (1957); and *Le Temps des secrets* (1960).

Paulhan, Jean. 1884–1968

After studying at the Sorbonne, Paulhan left France in 1907 for Madagascar, where he engaged in various activities, among them digging for gold. He learned the language of the country and became interested in Madagascan poetry: "I had taken to be words what the Madagascans understood as things." On his return to France, Paulhan fought in World War I as a sergeant in the ninth regiment of Zouaves, and it was then that he wrote his first story, *Le Guerrier appliqué* (1917). He served as Jacques Rivière's assistant, and in 1925 succeeded him as Director of the *Nouvelle revue française,* a post he was to fill for almost half a century. He discovered and offered encouragement to writers like Jouhandeau, Giono, Ponge, Artaud, and Michaux, and gained early recognition as a foremost critic. In 1941 he joined the Resistance and in conjunction with Jacques Decour founded *Les lettres françaises,* but this did not prevent him from rising up at the time of the Liberation to attack the excesses of the political purge. In 1941 he also wrote *Les Fleurs de Tarbes,* considered a major work of modern criticism. In the course of his investigations into language and expression, he published, among other things, *Un Rhétoriqueur à l'état sauvage* (1928–45); *Le Clerc malgré lui* (1948); *La Preuve par l'étymologie* (1953); *Les Douleurs imaginaires* (1956); *Le Clair et l'Obscur* (1958); *Le Don des langues* (1967). Always alert to innovation, he was keenly interested in painting, but his major concern was the construction of a new rhetoric; throughout his work he asked the question: "What are we thinking when we aren't thinking about anything?"

Perret, Jacques. 1901–

Two books were responsible for Perret's literary success, *Le Corporal épinglé* (1947), and *Bande à part* (1951), which won the Prix Interallié. Perret was captured during World War II, escaped, and joined the Resistance. He wrote for *Aspects de la France* and was an active supporter of French Algeria. His son was condemned to a heavy sentence for his participation in the ranks of the OAS. Perret wrote in celebration of manly comradeship, the games of childhood, and the warrior spirit. Nostalgic for the immemorial past, Perret waged his fight against the bourgeois world in the name of childhood reveries haunted by heroism. He is one of France's best storytellers.

Peyrefitte, Roger. 1907–

A career diplomat, Peyrefitte published *Les Amitiés particulières*, for which he received the Prix Renaudot, in 1944. This book appeared to mark the birth of a great writer. However, with the exception of *Mort d'une mère* (1950) and possibly *Du Vésuve à l'Etna* (1952), Peyrefitte's subsequent works fall under the categories of scandal sheet gossip, police blotter incidents, or personal vindictiveness (*Les Clés de Saint-Pierre, Manouche,* 1972; *Tableaux de chasse,* 1976). By writing sensational novels, Peyrefitte gained mass popularity.

Pichette, Henri. 1924–

With Paul Eluard's support, Pichette published his first *Apoème* in 1945. He then met Artaud and Gérard Philipe. His *Apoèmes* collection was published in 1947. That same year Gérard Philipe produced *Epiphanies* at the Théâtre des Noctambules. In 1952 *Nucléa* was produced at the TNP. *Revendications* was published in 1957. Pichette, a chaotically lyric poet of revolt, was able to envision going beyond surrealism to "cosmism," without turning his back completely on tradition. His work celebrates God, but also revolution. He believed that "to be fundamentally political is to be a poet."

Pieyre de Mandiargues, André. 1909–

With its origins in Nîmes, the Pieyre de Mandiargues family counted among its members a member of the National Convention, several historians, and a celebrated collector of impressionist paintings, Paul Bérard. André Pieyre de Mandiargues's writing career began in 1943 with *Hedrera, ou la persistance de l'amour pendant une rêverie,* and publication of his first volume of poems, *Dans les années sordides.* He belonged to the surrealist tradition, and his works are a mixture of the marvelous and the fantastic aimed at expressing pure sensation in an atmosphere of obsessional eroticism common to the novels, the stories, and the poems. His major works are *Le Musée noir* (1946); *Soleil des loups* (Prix des Critiques, 1951); *Le Lis de la mer* (1956); *La Motocyclette* (1963); and *La Marge* (Prix Goncourt, 1967).

Pingaud, Bernard. 1923–

A graduate of the Ecole Normale Supérieure, Pingaud went on to the post of parliamentary correspondent at the Assemblée Nationale. In 1960 he was forced to resign when he signed the *Manifeste des 121.* Essayist and novelist, Pingaud published *Madame Lafayette par elle-même* (1959) and a collection of pieces on the contemporary novel, *Inventaire* (1965), as well as several novels of his own, among them *L'Amour triste* (1950); *Le Prisonnier* (1959); and *La Scène primitive* (1965).

Pinget, Robert. 1919–

Pinget published his first collection of short stories, *Entre Fantoine et Agapa* in 1951. For him, "anything that isn't writing is death." A novelist who was atuned to the Spoken, Pinget elaborated a body of work—*Graal*

Flibuste (1956); *Baga* (1958); *Le Fiston* (1959); *L'Inquisitoire* (Prix des Critiques, 1962); *Quelqu'un* (Prix Fémina, 1965); and *Le Libera* (1968)—of which he could say, "it would be wrong to think of me as belonging to the school of observation. When it comes to being objective, the ear has its own tyrannical demands to make." In 1969 he published *Passacaille*, in 1971 *Fable*, and in 1975 *Cette Voix*, while also producing plays for the theater: *Identité, Abel et Bella* (1971), *Pour alchimie, Nuit* (1973).

Plisnier, Charles. 1896–1952

A Belgian writing in French, Plisnier composed his first poems in about 1912. He was profoundly affected by the Russian Revolution of 1917. He was one of the first Belgians to join the Third International, from which he was later banned when he elected to follow Trotsky. With the 1936 publication of his novel *Mariages*, he was greeted as another Balzac. The following year he was awarded the Prix Goncourt for *Mariages* and a collection of short stories entitled *Faux Passeports ou les Mémoires d'un agitateur.* Throughout his work as novelist and poet, Plisnier followed the path leading from revolutionary mysticism to spirituality; he was a man seeking "the sainthood for which God has no name."

Ponge, Francis. 1899–

Ponge first appeared before the reading public in 1942 with publication of *Le Parti pris des choses.* Sartre noted the revolutionary character of the work, and Ponge later provided an explanation (in *Le Grand Recueil,* 3 vols., Gallimard, 1961) of what he was trying to do: "My inclination is toward description-definitions that account for the actual content of ideas." Ponge gave priority to "the object," and man only intervenes in his poems in terms of a disembodied observer. Ponge believed that man is superfluous in nature and must "recognize the superior, indefeasible right of the object in opposition to the poem." Ponge applied this discipline in *Pour un Malherbe* (1965) as well as in *Le Savon* (1967) and *Le Nouveau Recueil* (1967).

Poulaille, Henry. 1896–1980

Orphaned at an early age, Poulaille was employed as a pharmacist's assistant, and then went on to try various trades. While working to earn a living, he also wrote novels, mainly *Le Pain quotidien* (1932), *Les Damnés de la terre* (1935), *Pain de soldat* (1937), and *Les Rescapés* (1938). He was quickly confirmed as one of the first proletarian writers. He continued to write, embarked on an intense journalistic career, and edited reviews whose contributors were men like Trotsky, Joyhaux, Gorki, and Barbusse. He engaged in lengthy polemics against the populist government, attacked Gide and Ghéhenno, supported Ramuz and Giono. He established the "Musée du soir," a cultural center for workers. Late in life he took up literary criticism, producing notably *Tartuffe de Pierre Corneille* and *Corneille sous le masque de Molière*. Less well known than they deserve, Poulaille's work and his role have clearly marked the path for a genuine proletariat literature to take.

Poulet, Georges. 1902–

Poulet belongs to what has been called the "Ecole de Genève," along with Jean Rousset, Starobinski, and Marcel Raymond. A thinker in the Bachelard mode, he chose to explore certain fundamental intellectual categories such as time and space. His major works: *Etudes sur le temps humain* (starting in 1950); *Les Métamorphoses du cercle* (1961); *L'Espace proustien* (1964); and *Trois essais de mythologie romantique* (1966).

Pourrat, Henri. 1887–1959

Pourrat's ambition was to be an agricultural engineer. For health reasons, he was forced to live a quiet life. From this was born the literary vocation of a poet and storyteller who has been called a regional writer, but who, as such, became the epic bard of his native Auvergne. He was one of the first postwar writers who attempted to recreate "rustic" literature. As one of his own characters says, "I take the sap in the trees and I make something of it." In 1941 he received the Prix Goncourt for his book *Vent de mars*. But it was with *Gaspard des montagnes*, adapted in 1966 for television, that he reached a mass public. The thirteen-volume *Trésor des contes*, which began to appear in 1948, constitutes a compendium of Auvergne folklore.

Prévert, Jacques. 1900–1977.

Prévert was a poet unlike any other. With *Paroles* (1945), *Histoires* (1948), and *Spectacles* (1951), he immediately gained the attention of a mass audience. His poems have been set to music and sung in the streets. Active for a time in the surrealist movement, he was able to detach himself from it without turning his back on it. In 1932 he became a member of the Groupe Octobre, a group of people interested in the *Théâtre de choc;* this is where he first forged the tools of his craft and wrote his first dialogues. In collaboration with Marcel Carné, he wrote a number of film scenarios between 1936 and 1946. All the films he worked on have since become famous: *Jenny; Les Visiteurs du soir; Les Enfants du Paradis; Drôle de drame; Le Jour se lève; Les Portes de la nuit.*

Prévost, Jean. 1901–44

The son of a schoolteacher and a graduate of the Ecole Normale Supérieure, Prévost published stories, including *Les Frères Bouquinquant* (1930); literary essays such as *La Création chez Stendhal* (published in 1951) and *Baudelaire* (1953); pieces on sports, dance, architecture, and French history. A writer who was also an athlete, Prévost sought to master his mind as well as his body. At the age of forty-three he died a hero's death in the Vercors, shot by the Germans.

Queffélec, Henri. 1910–

A graduate of the Ecole Normale Supérieure and holding an *Agrégation* from the university, Queffélec gave up teaching as a profession in 1942. In 1944 he published three novels in rapid succession: *La Fin d'un manoir; Journal d'un salaud; Un recteur de l'Ile de Sein*. Succumbing to the influence of existentialism, he described the lower depths and the descent into abjection, but also showed himself haunted by the possibilities for salvation. Opening before this former student of Mounier's was the path toward grace. In *Celui qui cherchait le soleil* (1953) he followed the pathway to spiritualism. In 1958 he was awarded the Grand Prix du Roman de l'Académie Française for *Un royaume sous la mer*. During the sixties he found inspiration in a return to his native Brittany. From then on he wrote stories of the sea, stories of sea voyages, and hymns to the ocean.

Queneau, Raymond. 1903–76

"My mother was a small shopkeeper, and so was my father," said Queneau of his parents. After taking part in the surrealist adventure, he broke with Breton in 1929. His first novel-poem, *Le Chiendent*, won the 1933 Prix des Deux-Magots. Early in his career he declared war on literary language as opposed to the language as spoken. After three autobiographical novels, *Les Derniers Jours* (1936), *Odile* (1937), and *Les Enfants du limon* (1938), Queneau devoted himself entirely to writing. He continued his work as a novelist-poet, producing writing that was marked by whimsy but not devoid of emotion (*Pierrot mon ami*, 1942) or even anguish (*Saint-Glinglin*, 1948), experimenting boldly with the language in a way that was halfway between mathematics and music (*Exercices de style*, 1947; *Cent mille milliards de poèmes*, 1961). Presiding over the efforts of the *OU.LI.PO. (Ouvroir de littérature potentielle)*, he simultaneously served as director at Gallimard for the *Encyclopédie de la Pléiade*. A rhetorician, a humorist, but also a poet touched by existential anguish, Queneau wrote: "Here is where the problem of language becomes a problem of style, and the problem of writing a human problem."

Radiguet, Raymond. 1903–23

Radiguet was a unique phenomenon in French literature. A mediocre student, he was barely fifteen years old when he met Cocteau, who introduced him to avant-garde literary circles. He left his parent's house immediately after World War I and wrote *Le Diable au corps*, which was launched to the accompaniment of a loud publicity campaign by Grasset in 1923. This novel burst like "a final cannon shot into the sky of the Armistice." That same year, Radiguet died of typhoid fever. *Le Bal du comte d'Orgel* (1924) was published after his death, a book which according to Edmond Jaloux was "absolutely classic." It was followed by a posthumous volume of poetry, *Les Joues en feu* (1925).

Rebatet, Lucien. 1903–72

Film critic for *L'Action française*, under the pseudonym François Vinneuil, Rebatet was a contributor to *Je suis partout* from its inception. Allowing himself to be seduced by fascism, he became a mainstay of the new order inaugurated by the Vichy regime. In 1924 he published a vehement pamphlet entitled *Les Décombres*. Condemned to death at the time of the Liberation, he escaped execution and in 1952 published a fine novel, *Les Deux Etendards*. His great talent as a writer did not, however, save him from scorn. A new, partial edition of *Décombres* was published by Pauvert in 1976, and *Une Histoire de la musique* by Laffont in 1969.

Renard, Jean-Claude. 1922–

A poet of the sacred, Jean-Claude Renard officiated as a poet of the world's metamorphosis, a human witness before God. He believed that writing poetry is an attempt to "vanquish time and death, to come to know in some way the fundamental present of beings and things." In 1957 he received the Grand Prix Catholique de Littérature and in 1966 the Prix Sainte-Beuve for his collection *La Terre du sacré*. With *La Braise et la Rivière* (1969) Renard went further still in his exploration and questioning of the cosmic mystery.

Richard, Jean-Pierre. 1922–

Currently professor at the University of Paris IV, Richard is the author of an impressive body of work dealing with thematic criticism. In *Littérature et Sensation* (1954), in his thesis on *L'Univers imaginaire de Mallarmé* (1962), and in *Onze Etudes sur la poésie moderne* (1964) he has concentrated more specifically on the intial contact of a writer with the world; and in *Paysage de Chateaubriand* (1967) and *Etudes sur le romantisme* (1971) he has attempted to restore for the reader the "imaginary universe" that presides over the act of creation. In 1974 he published a major essay on Proust: *Proust et le monde sensible*.

Robbe-Grillet, Alain. 1922–

An agricultural engineer, Robbe-Grillet published the first of his antinovels, *Les Gommes,* in 1953. Breaking with the psychological novel, he inaugurated the era of the object novel. His theory was that the writer should thoroughly cover the phenomenology of the object, appealing to the reader to make the act of reading part of the total creative process. Illustrating this theory is a body of work that spanned twenty years: *Le Voyeur* (1955); *La Jalousie* (1957); and *Dans le labyrinthe* (1959). Robbe-Grillet transferred his passion for minute description to the screen with *L'Année dernière à Marienbad; L'Immortelle; Trans Europe Express; L'Homme qui ment; L'Eden et après*. The observer of objects transformed himself into a demonstrator of images. In 1970 he published *Project pour une révolution à New York.* In a return to the novel, in 1976 he published *Topologie d'une cité fantôme.*

Roblès, Emmanuel. 1914–
Born in Algeria, Roblès was a friend of Feraoun and Camus. He published his first novel, *L'Action,* in Algiers in 1938. After World War II he received the Prix Populaire for *Travail d'homme* (1945). Like Camus, in whose footsteps he followed, he translated the lyricism of sun and sea onto the written page, and in *Les Hauteurs de la ville* (Prix Fémina, 1948) he gave expression to a humiliated Algeria struggling to regain its dignity. Robles's work (*La Mort en face,* 1951, reprint 1973; *Cela s'appelle l'Aurore,* 1952; *Plaidoyer pour un rebelle,* etc.) celebrates brotherhood, honor, sensuality, political activism, and freedom.

Roche, Denis. 1937–
A member of the *Tel Quel* group, Denis Roche writes "functional" poetry, meaning poetry written not to be spoken or looked at but to be read; and to be read not as an exploration of what lies within but as if the very meaning of the poem comes from without. A poet determined to destroy the "poetic," Roche has published *Récits complets* (1963); *Les Idées centésimales de miss Elanize* (1964); and *Eros énergumène* (1968).

Rochefort, Christiane. 1917–
In her novel *Le Repos du guerrier,* Rochefort was one of the first women to treat female eroticism with a facility formerly reserved to men. Her success was the result of the scandal caused by her first book, though the book itself was not so much scandalous as it was an attempt to come up with a truer morality. In her other novels, *Les Petits Enfants du siècle* (1961), *Les Stances à Sophie* (1963), and *Printemps au parking* (1969), Rochefort attempted to depict a society in transition, a society of highrise public housing and consumerism. She has been active in the women's liberation movement. In 1975 and 1976 she published two books on children's rights: *Encore heureux qu'on va vers l'été* and *Les Enfants d'abord.*

Romains, Jules. 1885–1972
A graduate of the Ecole Normale Supérieure with an *Agrégation* in philosophy, Jules Romains had a vision one night in 1903 that revealed to him that we are not *archipelagos of solitude.* Thus was unanimism born. And thus, on the basis of this belief in human solidarity and socialistic brotherhood, was born the work of Jules Romains. Although he hesitated between drama, poetry, and the novel, Romains's magnum opus was *Les Hommes de bonne volonté,* a twenty-seven-volume publishing venture spanning the years 1932–46.

Roy, Claude, pseud. (Claude Orland). 1915–

A politically committed writer, Claude Roy was captured by the Germans in 1940; escaped; joined the Resistance; and became friends with fellow members Aragon, Eluard, and Vailland. He was a poet (*Le Poète mineur,* 1949), but also a novelist (*A Tort ou à raison,* 1955; *Léone et les siens,* 1963); an essayist (the six-volume *Descriptions critiques,* published from 1949 to 1965); art critic, and journalist; and a longtime activist in the Communist Party, from which he was expelled in 1956. He has published three volumes of autobiography: *Moi, je* (1969); *Nous* (1972); *Somme toute* (1976).

Roy, Jules. 1907–

The son of a colonial family settled in Algeria, Roy joined the RAF in World War II. This expedition without Crusade is recounted in *La Vallée heureuse* (Prix Renaudot, 1946), *Retour de l'Enfer* (1951), and *Le Navigateur* (1954). Roy subsequently fought in Indochina, traveled, and did some journalism. In 1960 his book *La Guerre d'Algérie* provoked some controversy. In *Les Chevaux du soleil* (1967), *Une Femme au nom d'étoile* (1968), and *Les Cerises d'Icherridène* (1969), he retraced the entire history of Algeria in fictionalized form, from the original Fench conquest to decolonization.

Sagan, Françoise, pseud. (Françoise Quoirez). 1935–

Sagan was barely twenty when her novel *Bonjour Tristesse* was published in 1954. Its success was phenomenal. A certain disillusion expressed with great economy of means seemed to reflect the attitudes of "disenchanted" youth for whom "life is just a process of demolition." While continuing to add to a body of fiction in which Maurice Nadeau saw "a neoclassic reaction," Sagan made her debut as a playwright in 1960 with *Château en Suède.* Her production has remained steady ever since. With a private life providing constant food for the popular press, a Sagan legend was born that rebounded on Sagan's books.

Saint-Exupéry, Antoine de. 1900–(?)1944

Saint-Exupéry rode in the Védrines airplane when he was twelve years old. When he failed his entrance examination for the Ecole Navale, he did his military service in the air force. In 1926 he became a commercial pilot, later squadron commander for the Toulouse-Casablanca line. In 1930 he published *Courrier Sud. Vol de nuit* came out one year later and won the Prix Fémina. He continued his career as a pilot, flew in the Paris-Saigon rally, did some journalism. In *Terre des hommes* (1939) he celebrated a sense of human solidarity. During World War II he managed to get to New York, where he published *Le Petit Prince* in 1943. He began flying again, and on 31 July 1944 he disappeared over the Mediterranean while returning from a mission. *Citadelle,* which in some ways constitutes his moral and spiritual testament, was published in 1948.

Saint-John Perse, pseud. (Marie-René Alexis Saint-Léger). 1887–1975

Perse, who was born in Guadeloupe, began his career as a poet at the age of seventeen with the extraordinary *Images à Crusoé* (1904), followed by *Eloges* (1912). Having participated successfully in the competitive French diplomatic corps examinations, he was sent to Peking, where he served as secretary in the embassy from 1916 to 1920. He published *Anabase* (1924) and was put in charge of Briand's diplomatic office. He was soon named to an ambassadorial post and then as Secretary General of the Quai d'Orsay, but in 1940 his career was smashed and he went into exile in the United States. He published *Exil* between 1941 and 1944 (followed by *Poèmes à l'Etrangère; Pluies; Neiges*) and *Vents* in 1945. With *Amers* (1957), Perse's poetry took a new turn: his epics found a center, the image of a man reconciled with his desires. The poet of great, elemental forces became more human, and his poems, without losing any of their beauty or breadth, gained in unity. In 1959 Saint-John Perse received the Grand Prix National des Lettres, and in 1960 he was awarded the Nobel Prize for Literature. His grandiose, highly distinctive works, created outside the visible currents marking his era, made him one of the greatest of the great poets.

Salacrou, Armand. 1899–

Salacrou, who was momentarily attracted by communism, spent a great deal of his time with the surrealists. He then became interested in business. But his true vocation was the theater. His *L'Inconnue d'Arras,* produced in 1935 by Lugné-Poë at the Comédie des Champs-Elysées, was a great hit. Obsessed with death and in search of an unattainable God, Salacrou sought a metaphysical theater. After World War II he produced plays in the vein of social satire: *L'Archipel Lenoir* (1947) and *Une femme trop honnête* (1961).

Sarraute, Nathalie. 1902–

Born in Russia but having settled in France at an early age, Sarraute became a lawyer. After 1939, however, she devoted herself entirely to literature. Primarily a novelist but also a playwright, her first book, *Tropismes* (1938) was not discovered until after World War II. A theoretician of the antinovel, Nathalie Sarraute's goal was to make literature "objective." In her essay, *L'Ere du soupçon* (1956), she traced the progressive degeneration of the novel since the nineteenth century. In her own work she has concentrated on stripping bare the linguistic mechanisms of people who are, or who aspire to be, members of the cultivated middle class. Her novels are: *Portrait d'un inconnu* (1948); *Martereau* (1953); *Le Planétarium* (1959); *Les Fruits d'or* (1963); *Entre la vie et la mort* (1968); *Vous les entendez?* (1975); *Disent les imbéciles* (1976). A pioneer of the nouveau roman,

Nathalie Sarraute may have wanted, as Sartre once put it, to "write a novel about an unwritten novel." She has also written for the theater: *Le Silence* (1964); *Le Mensonge* (1967); and *Isma* (1970).

Sarrazin, Albertine, pseud. (Albertine Damien). 1937–67

An orphan on public assistance, Albertine Sarrazin was adopted by an older couple and raised at the Bon Pasteur convent in Marseille. She ran away, spent time in jail, and, while there, wrote *L'Astragale* (1965), "a short love novel for Julien"—Julien being the man she married after he finished serving time in prison himself. Her two other novels, *La Cavale* (1965) and *La Traversière* (1966), confirmed a writing talent that had come to maturity in the shadow of the prison walls.

Sartre, Jean-Paul. 1905–80

Born into a bourgeois family, Sartre "ended up by rebelling only because he had pushed submission to the limit." A graduate of the Ecole Normale Supérieure with an *Agrégation* in philosophy, he was named to a post at the Institut Français in Berlin, where he discovered Husserl's phenomenology in 1933. Captured by the Germans during World War II, he was liberated in 1941 and published *L'Etre et le Néant* in 1943. Novels: *La Nausée,* 1938; *Le Mur,* (1939); *Les Chemins de la Liberté,* 1945–50. Plays: *Huis clos,* 1944; *Les Mains sales,* 1948; *Les Séquestrés d'Altona,* 1959. Sartre's plays can be defined as situational, with "options being selected in given situations." Consideration must also be given to his works of literary criticism, to the ten-volume *Situations;* to his *Baudelaire;* his *Saint Genet, comédien et martyr;* and to *L'Idiot de la famille* (in which, referring to Flaubert, Sartre asks, What can anyone know about a man of today?). Philosopher, novelist, and essayist, Sartre was also a political activist. Several times in his life he was drawn toward, and then away from, the Communist Party. In the years following 1968 he sponsored several militant leftist organizations, *L'Idiot international,* and *Libération.*

Schéhadé, Georges. 1910–

A French-speaking Lebanese poet, born in Egypt, Schéhadé was discovered by Saint-John Perse and remained for many years under the influence of the surrealists. However, he wrote poems that were limpid and spare (*Les Poésies,* 1952). Schéhadé is also a playwright, and his *Monsieur Bob'le* was produced in 1951, *Histoire de Vasco* in 1957.

Senghor, Léopold Sédar. 1906–

A graduate of the Ecole Normale Supérieure with an *Agrégation* in grammar, Senghor became president of the Republic of Senegal, the land of his birth, in 1960. Although his poems celebrate the African struggle against

Europe, he has also practiced "cultural cross-breeding." His poems (*Chants d'ombre*, 1945; *Hosties noires*, 1948; *Ethiopiques*, 1958; *Nocturnes*, 1961) were inspired by Claudel and Saint-John Perse but also by the lyric magic of oral African poetry. With Césaire and Léon Damas, Senghor founded the review *Etudiant noir* in 1934, launching the theme of "Negritude."

Simenon, Georges. 1903–

Considered by Gide to be a great novelist, Simenon, who wrote a colossal number of books, can with justice be regarded as a phenomenon. A French-speaking Belgian, Simenon began his career by writing hundreds of popular novels under various pseudonyms. In 1930 he created the character of Maigret, a police inspector and the hero of countless murder mysteries. In 1934 Simenon began writing what he called *hard novels*, in which, with the art of both a clinician and a moralist, he painted cruel, unsparing pictures of how people behave. Sometimes compared with Balzac, Simenon often quoted this passage from *La Comédie humaine:* "A character in a novel can be any man in the street, but must be one who lives right up to his own limit." Between 1970 and 1977 Simenon published several autobiographical works: *Quand j'étais vieux* (1970); *Lettres à ma mère* (1970); and *De la cave au grenier* (1977).

Simon, Claude. 1913–

After writing several books marked by classicism, in *Le Vent* (1957) Claude Simon employed a technique and a selection of themes that revealed him as one of the mainstays of the *nouveau roman*. History serves as the backdrop for most of his novels (*L'Herbe*, 1958; *La Route des Flandres*, 1960; *Le Palace*, 1962; *Histoire* and *La Bataille de Pharsale*, 1969; *Les Georgiques*, 1981) because time is one of his major themes, even if he believes that "not only is man incapable of making history, he is incapable of making his own history."

Sollers, Philippe. 1936–

Winning a warm response early in his career from Mauriac and Aragon with the publication of *Une curieuse solitude*, a novel structured along traditional lines, Sollers turned a sharp corner in 1963: he assumed the editorship of the review *Tel Quel* (founded in 1960). The novelist was transformed into a theoretician of language, and the theories put into practice in *Drame* (1965). Sollers was the leader of the *Tel Quel* group and a contemporary of *la nouvelle critique* (Roland Barthes), the philosophy of Foucault and Derrida, psychoanalytic theories of Lacan, and the Marxism of Althusser. Under his leadership the *Tel Quel* group elaborated a theory of writing which they then applied to the history of mankind considered as a text to which a revolutionary meaning could be attributed.

Starobinski, Jean. 1920–

Holder of doctorates in medicine and literature, Starobinski served as an intern in various hospitals, mainly in psychiatric wards, but he also taught French literature in the United States before becoming Professor of the History of Ideas at the Faculté des Lettres of the University of Geneva. Drawing his inspiration from both psychoanalysis and phenomenology, he has published an important work *Jean-Jacques Rousseau, la transparence et l'obstacle* (1958); *L'Oeil vivant* (1961); and *L'Oeil vivant II: la relation critique* (1971).

Tardieu, Jean. 1903–

A poet of contained lyricism, Tardieu sought to elucidate the problem of existence. His early works were published in the *NRF* in 1927. A collection of poems written between 1924 and 1960, *Le Fleuve caché*, was published by Gallimard in 1968. But in his job with the RTF he served as a discoverer of young talent, while at the same time pursuing his own experiments in dramatic expression. He was himself the author of several plays, and his stylistic exercises are not unreminiscent of Ionesco: *Théâtre de chambre* (1955) and *Poèmes à jouer* (1960).

Thibaudeau, Jean. 1935–

Thibaudeau, who joined the *Tel Quel* group in 1960, embarked on experiments with a mode of expression which for him "involved continually extracting from the repetition of elements or the organization of cases a single tiny difference, a slender generality." In *Une Cérémonie royale* (1960), the detailed description gives rise to various possibilities. But with *Ouverture* (1966) and especially with *Imaginez la Nuit* (1968), the subject engaged in writing the book is even freer of traditional constraints; he produces the text, and the text engenders the subject.

Thomas, Henri. 1912–

Thomas published his first works as a poet, *Travaux d'aveugle*, in 1941. He subsequently developed a keen interest in foreign literature and translated the works of Junger, among others. As a novelist, he won the 1960 Prix Médicis for *John Perkins* and the Prix Fémina in the following year for *Le Promontoire*. In his work he becomes the defender of an extremely personal metaphysic revolving around a particular conception of death, of death seen as one way of being.

Tortel, Jean. 1904–

Tortel joined the editorial board of *Les Cahiers du Sud* in 1938, and himself published numerous scholarly studies in its pages. But Tortel the poet soon came to the fore with the publication of a volume of poems, *De mon vivant*, in 1942. Continuing in the line of Saint-John Perse and Segalen, Tortel also followed the path marked out by Francis Ponge, experimenting with "free expression," in a continuation of postsurrealist poetry. Collections such as *Naissance de l'objet* (1955), *Les Villes découvertes* (1965), and *Relations* (1968) showed him to be an avant-garde poet concerned with the relation between being and expression.

Triolet, Elsa. 1896–1970

Elsa Triolet was born and educated in Russia. She was momentarily attracted by architecture and the plastic arts, but soon concentrated on literature, publishing her first novels in Moscow. It was thanks to her relationship with the poet Mayakovski that in 1928 she met Louis Aragon, who later became her husband and the "celebrator of Elsa." Determined to become a writer, she published her first work in French in 1938: *Bonsoir Thérèse*. During World War II she was active in the Resistance movement and published several more works, among them *Le Cheval blanc* (1943). In 1945 she won the Prix Goncourt for *Le Premier Accroc coûte deux cents francs*. She also published a cycle of romances, *L'Age du nylon* (*Roses à crédit*, 1959; *Luna-Park*, 1959; *L'Ame*, 1963) and numerous translations from the Russian, notably Chekhov's plays. Joint publication of the works of Elsa Triolet and Aragon was undertaken in 1964 by Laffont.

Troyat, Henri, pseud. (Lev Tarassov). 1911–

Troyat, born in Moscow, emmigrated to France as a youth, began to publish in 1935, and in 1938 won the Prix Goncourt for his novel *L'Araigne*. Troyat belongs to the last of the naturalist writers and built his popularity on the publication of his great novel cycles: *Tant que la terre durera* (1947–50); *Les Semailles et les Moissons* (1953–58); *La Lumière des Justes* (1959–62); *Les Eygletières* (1965–67); and *Les Héritiers de l'avenir* (1968–70). Troyat, a prolix writer, has been reproached for his facility. He is also known for his voluminous biographies of Dostoevski, Lermontov, Pushkin, Tolstoy, and Gogol.

Vailland, Roger. 1907–65

During his years in secondary school, Vailland became friendly with René Daumal. Together they participated in founding the review *Le Grand Jeu* (1928). Vailland then became a journalist. During World War II he joined the Resistance and became a communist fellow traveler. He represented a conjunction of the apostle of solidarity and the libertine obsessed by the aristocratic ideal. All of his works revolve around the dual themes of happiness and pleasure. His major works were published after the War (*Drôle de jeu*, Prix Interallié, 1945; *Les Mauvais Coups*, 1948; *Bon pied, bon oeil*, 1950; *Un jeune homme seul*, 1951; *Beau Masque*, 1954; *325,000 francs*,

1955; *La Loi,* Prix Goncourt, 1957). *Le Regard froid,* published in 1963, includes a certain number of pieces essential for an understanding of the man and his works, as does *Ecrits intimes,* published in 1966.

Vercors, pseud. (Jean-Marcel Bruller). 1902–

Originally a printer and engraver, Bruller assumed the name Vercors in the Underground during World War II. In 1941 he founded Les Editions de Minuit with Pierre de Lescure, and at the beginning they published authors writing in the Underground. In 1942 Vercors himself published *Le Silence de la mer.* After the war, while still continuing his literary activity, he traveled worldwide, gave lectures, and attempted to define a humanism that could reconcile men belonging to opposing ideologies (*Les Animaux dénaturés,* 1952). He broke with the Communist Party and published *P.P.C. Pour prendre congé* in 1957. *Les Chemins de l'être* (with P. Mistraki) was published in 1965.

Vian, Boris. 1920–59

Vian was the incarnation of one segment of post-World War II Parisian youth. "King" of Saint-Germain-des-Prés, he was in turn novelist, poet, jazz musician, and singer. A precursor of the *nouveau théâtre,* he wrote an explosive farce in 1947, *L'Equarrissage pour tous.* With the possible exception of the famous *J'irai cracher sur vos tombes* (1946), his novels attracted almost no attention when first published, but interest in them is increasing today (*Vercoquin et le Plancton,* 1946; *L'Ecume des jours,* 1947; *L'Arrache-coeur,* 1953). A one-man band of the fifties, Vian wrote poems, some of which also became songs; the best poems are collected in the volume *Je voudrais crever* (1959). His plays, for example *Les Bâtisseurs d'Empire,* are often revived by young theater troupes.

Vilmorin, Louise de. 1902–70

Louise de Vilmorin came from an old family of corn chandlers. Married several times, she once even lived in a castle in Hungary and then, almost as if on a dare, she started to write novels and poems in which she gave free reign to her genius for language. Hidden beneath an apparent casualness is a perfect knowledge of her milieu; and breaking through it, the subtle play of a mind that is a past master in the art of the feint and the pirouette. Everything, whether in *Madame de* . . . (1951), *La Lettre dans un taxi* (1958), or *L'Heure Maliciôse* (1967), serves as a pretext for the exercise of wit, for sophisticated banter, and for abandonment to the pleasure of making light of oneself and of others.

Weingarten, Romain. 1926–

A disciple of Jarry, Vitrac, and Artaud, Weingarten was a precursor and, in his early plays, an instigator of what was to be the theater of today. He produced his first play, *Akara*, in 1948, but he achieved his first success with *L'Eté*, premiered in Germany in 1965, and staged in Paris the following year. A collection of his plays was published in 1967 *(L'Eté; Akara; Les Nourrices)*.

Wiesel, Elie. 1928–

Wiesel was born in Transylvania. Deported with his entire family to Birkenau, he was present when his father died in Buchenwald. His mother and sisters died at Auschwitz. He himself was taken in charge by the charitable organization Secours aux Enfants and raised in France, where he completed his education at the Sorbonne. His first work, *La Nuit* (1958) placed him among the great writers. Throughout his other stories and novels—*La Ville de la chance* (1962); *Le Mendiant de Jérusalem* (1968), which earned the 1968 Prix Médicis; and his play, *Zalmen ou la Folie de Dieu* (1968)—he has stood as an example of the Hassidic tradition from which he sprang, and he has dealt with the question of persecution and, as a corollary, the death of God, the problem being: What does it mean to be a Jew? For Elie Wiesel it has often meant "waiting for someone who never comes and, when necessary, becoming that someone."

Yacine, Kateb. 1929–

An Algerian who wrote in French, Yacine got to know the inside of prison at an early age. He was arrested at the age of sixteen for taking part in the 1945 demonstrations in Sétif. After that he became a writer celebrating Algeria and the Algerian nation. His first novel, *Nedjma* (1956), published at the outbreak of the Algerian war, revealed him to be one of the most vigorous authors of North African literature. Persecuted in France, he lived for many years in exile. Little known in his own country, he developed, far from his own people, a body of work drawing on the source of the Arab soul. Primarily a poet and novelist, Yacine also published a series of plays, *Le Cercle des Représailles* (1959).

Yourcenar, Marguerite, pseud. (Marguerite de Crayencour). 1903–

Yourcenar received a conventional education. At the age of twenty-six she began leading a nomadic life that led her to the United States, where she settled permanently. Her best-known works are her historical-philosophical novels: *Les Mémoires d'Hadrian* (1951), an apocryphal autobiography of the second century Roman emperor; and *L'Oeuvre au noir* (1968), the imaginary biography of a sixteenth-century hero attracted by hermeticism and the new sciences. Other works that should be mentioned include *Alexis, ou le Traité du vain combat* (1929); her play, *Electre ou la Chute des masques* (1954); her essay *Sous bénéfice d'inventaire* (1962). In 1963 she published a revised edition of *Nouvelles orientales* (originally published 1938), and, in 1974, of *Feux* (originally published 1935). *Souvenirs pieux* appeared in 1974. With great erudition and great psychological insight, Marguerite Yourcenar constructed a body of work that is a meditation on the destiny of mankind. She was elected to the Académie Française in 1981, the first woman ever to be so honored.

French Journals and Reviews Published between 1920 and 1970

Weeklies

Candide. 1924–43. Editors: Jacques Bainville, Pierre Gaxotte, Pierre Dominique, André Chaumeix. (Maurrasian.)

Gringoire. 1928–44. Editors: Horace de Carbuccia, Georges Suarez, Joseph Kessel, Henri Béraud, Philippe Henriot. (Rightist.)

Je suis partout. 1930–39, 1941–44. Editors: Robert Brasillach, Lucien Rebatet, Pierre Gaxotte, Charles Lesca, Alain Laubreaux. (Classic and royalist.)

Marianne. 1933–40. Editors: Emmanuel Berl, André Cornu. (Moderate leftist.)

Regards. 1934–40 [1932–34], 1945–. Monthly. Editor: Léon Moussinac. (Communist.)

Vendredi. 1935–38. Editors: André Chamson, Jean Guéhenno, Andrée Viollis. (Leftist.)

Action. 1944–52. Editor: Pierre Courtade. (Resistance and labor movement.)

Established Literary Reviews

Review des deux mondes. 1831–1944, 1944–71, 1972–. Editors: René Doumic, André Chaumeix. (Conservative.)

Mercure de France. 1890–1965. Editors: Alfred Valette, Remy de Gourmont, Georges Duhamel, S. Silvestre de Sacy, Gaëtan Picon. (Critical.)

Revue hebdomadaire. 1892–1939. Editor: Fernand Laudet. (Conservative.)

Revue de Paris. 1894–1970. Editors: André Chaumeix, Marcel Thiébaut. (Bourgeois, conservative.)

Nouvelle revue française (NRF); Nouvelle nouvelle revue française (NNRF); later, *Nouvelle revue française* again.

1908–43, 1953–. Editors: André Gide, Jacques Rivière, Drieu La Rochelle, Jean Paulhan, Marcel Arland and Dominique Aury. (Literary, apolitical—except during World War II.)

Les Cahiers du Sud. 1914–66. Editors: Jean Ballard, Léon-Gabriel Gros. (Poetry; serious criticism.)

Les Nouvelles littéraires. 1920–. Editors: Maurice Martin du Gard, Ferdinand Lefevre, Philippe Tesson, J.-François Kahl. (Literary, artistic, scientific.)

Rightist Cultural Reviews

L'Action française. 1899–1944. Editors: Maurice Pujo, Henri Vaugeois, Charles Maurras, Léon Daudet. (Rightist; a daily with a major literary column.)

Etudes. 1896–1940, 1945–. Editor: Society of Jesus. (Catholic; cultural.)

La Revue française. 1903–33. Editors: J.-P. Maxence, Robert Brasillach, Thierry Maulnier, Maurice Bardèche. (Nationalist right.)

La Vie catholique. 1908–38. Editor: Abbé Dabry. (Democratic and Christian.)

Revue universelle. 1920–39. Editors: Jacques Bainville, Henri Massis. (Nationalist right.)

L'Ordre nouveau. 1933–37. Editors: Arnaud Dandieu, Robert Aron, Alexandre Marc, Philippe Lamour, Robert Loustau. (Young reformers; various tendencies.)

Leftist Cultural Reviews

Clarté, Bulletin français de l'Internationale de la pensée. 1919–28. Then became *La Lutte des classes, Revue théorique mensuelle de l'opposition communiste.* 1928–33 [1935]. Editor: Henri Barbusse. ("Social action" to "free mankind.")

Europe. 1923–39, 1947–. Editors: René Arcos, Jean Guéhenno, Jean Cassou, Pierre Abraham. ("Genuinely international review of free thought"; socialist, Rollandist, antifascist, activist.)

Philosophie. 1924–25. Editors: Henri Lefebvre, Georges Politzer. (Philosophical idealism.)

L'Esprit. 1926–27. (Marxism.)

La Revue marxiste. 1929. (Marxism.)

Esprit. 1932–41, 1944–. Editors: Emmanuel Mounier, Jean-Marie Domenach. (Leftist Christian.)

Literary Reviews with a European Bias

Ecrits nouveaux. (Paris). 1917–22. Editor: André Germain. (Modernist.)

La Revue de Genève. 1920–24. Joined *Bibliothèque universelle et revue*

suisse. 1924–30. Editors: Robert de Traz, Jacques Chennevière. (Cultural exchange.)
Le Disque vert (Signaux; Ecrits du Nord, Brussels). 1921–41. Editors: Franz Hellens, Melot du Dy. (Avant-garde.)
La Revue européenne (Paris). 1925–31. Editor: Edmond Jaloux. (Cosmopolitan.)
Botteghe Oscure. 1948–60. Editor: Marguerite Caetani. (International.)

Avant-garde Reviews

Littérature. 1919–22 [1924?]. Editors: Louis Aragon, André Breton, Philippe Soupault. (Dadaist, then surrealist.)
La Revolution surréaliste. 1924–29. Editor: André Breton. (Surrealist.)
Le Surréalisme au service de la révolution. 1930–33. Editor: André Breton. (Surrealist.)
Le Grand Jeu. 1928–30. Editors: René Daumal, Roger Vailland, Roger Gilbert-Lecomte. (Dissident surrealist; esoteric.)
Bifur. 1929–31. Editor: Michel Leiris. (Neosurrealist and eclectic.)
Documents. 1929–30. Editor: Georges Bataille. (Anthropology; art.)
Minutes. 1930–34. Editor: Guy-Lévis Mano. (Surrealist poetry.)

Recent Literary Reviews

Les Lettres nouvelles. 1953–. Editor: Maurice Nadeau. (Traditional.)
Nouveau Commerce. 1963–. Editor: André Dalmas.
Le Magazine littéraire. 1965–. Editor: Jean-Claude Fasquelle. (General public.)
La Quinzaine litteraire. 1966–. Editor: Maurice Nadeau.
L'Ephémère. 1967–69. Editors: Gaëtan Picon, Jacques Dupin. (Poets; rare texts; narrow audience.)
Création. 1971–. Editor: Marie-Jeanne Dury. (Unpublished poetry; research.)

Major Critical Reviews Founded after 1945

Critique. 1946–. Editors: Georges Bataille, Jean Piel. (Sociological, thematic, and structural research.)
La Revue des lettres modernes. 1954–. Editor: Michel Minard. (History of ideas and literature.)
L'Arc. 1958–. Editor: Stéphane Cordier. (Essays and research; major literary figures and history of ideas.)
Tel Quel. 1960–. Editor: Philippe Sollers. (Literary and linguistic theory.)
L'Herne. 1961–. Editors: Dominique de Roux, Henri Kellerbach. (Critical essays and articles on major literary figures.)

Change. 1968–. Editors: Jean-Pierre Faye, Jacques Roubaud. (Collective; Marxist literary creation.)
Poétique. 1970–. Editors: Hélène Cizoux, Gérard Genette, Tzvetan Todorov. (Literary analysis and theory.)

Luxury Reviews

Commerce. 1924–32. Editors: Léon-Paul Fargue, Paul Valéry, Valery Larbaud. (Publication of new literary works.)
Minotaure. 1933–39. Editor: E. Tériade. (Neosurrealist; artistic and cultural.)

Noncollaborationist Reviews Founded during the German Occupation

Fontaine (originally *Mithra,* 1939). 1939–47. Algiers, monthly. Editor: Max-Pol Fouchet. (Noncollaborationist writers and nonfascist foreign literature.)
Confluences. 1941–47. Lyon, 34 issues. Editors: Jacques Auberque, René Tavernier. (Defense of intellectual freedom.)
Lettres françaises. 1941–44. Buenos Aires, 3 issues per year. Editor: Roger Caillois. (Supplement to Victoria Ocampo's review *Sur.* Resistance, exiled, and nonfascist writers; welcomed poetry.)
Les Lettres françaises. 1942–72 (underground: 1942–44, 1944–45). Editors: Jacques Decour and Jean Paulhan. (Publication of the Comité National des Ecrivains Résistants.) 1946–53, 1953–72. Editors: Claude Morgan, Louis Aragon. (Communist.)
L'Arche. 1944–49. Algiers, monthly, 29 issues. Editors: Jean Amrouche, Jacques Lassaigne (with support from André Gide). (French literature and foreign literature in translation.)
La Nef. 1944–51. Algiers, monthly, 77–78 issues. Editors: Robert Aron, Lucie Faure. (French literature and foreign literature in translation.)

Bibliography

Includes English-language books listed in the original edition of this work, *Le XXe Siècle II: 1920–1970* (Paris: Arthaud, 1978), together with some more recent publications. For a fuller listing, the reader is referred to the French.

Bibliographies and Reference Works

Annual Bibliography. New York: Modern Language Association of America, 1922–.

Bibliography of Comparative Literature. Edited by Fernand Baldensperger and Werner P. Friederich. Chapel Hill: University of North Carolina Press, 1950.

Columbia Dictionary of Modern European Literature. Edited by Jean-Albert Bedé and William Edgerton. 2d ed. New York: Columbia University Press, 1980.

A Critical Bibliography of French Literature. Vol. 6: *The Twentieth Century*. Part 1, "General Subjects and Principally the Novel before 1940"; part 2, "Principally Poetry, Theater, and Criticism before 1940, and Essay"; part 3, "All Genres since 1940; Index." Edited by Douglas W. Alden and Richard A. Brooks. Syracuse, N.Y.: Syracuse University Press, 1980. (Comprises 17,939 items, each accompanied by brief descriptive and critical notes. An indispensable reference work for researchers.)

Dictionnaire de la littérature française contemporaine. Edited by Claude Bonnefoy, with the assistance of Tony Cartaro and Daniel Oster. Paris: Delarge, 1977.

Encyclopedia of World Literature in the Twentieth Century. Edited by Leonard S. Klein. 2d ed. New York: Ungar, 1981–. (Two volumes published to date. Contains survey articles on French African literature; Algerian, French, and American literatures; as well as separate entries on separate figures and movements.)

French VII Bibliography: Critical and Bibliographical References for the Study of Contemporary French Literature. New York: Modern Language Association of America, 1949–.

Yearbook of Comparative and General Literature. Chapel Hill: University of North Carolina Press, 1922–. (Annual; includes annotated bibliography.)

The Year's Work in Modern Language Studies. London: Oxford University Press, 1929–. (Annual.)

Background: Historical and Political

Amouroux, Henri. *La Grande Histoire des Français sous l'occupation, 1939–1945.* 5 vols. Paris: Laffont, 1976–81.

Andrews, William G., and Stanley Hoffman. *The Impact of the Fifth Republic on France.* Albany: State University of New York Press, 1981.

Benson, Frederick R. *Writers in Arms: The Literary Impact of the Spanish Civil War.* New York: New York University Press, 1967.

Cairns, John C. *Contemporary France: Illusion, Conflict, and Regeneration.* New York: New Viewpoints, 1978.

Ehrlich, Blake. *Resistance: France 1940–1941.* Boston: Little, Brown, 1965.

Gordon, David C. *The Passing of French Algeria.* New York: Oxford University Press, 1966.

Graubard, Stephen R., ed. *A New Europe?* Boston: Houghton Mifflin, 1964.

Kelly, George A. *Lost Soldiers: The French Army and Empire in Crisis, 1947–62.* Cambridge, Mass.: MIT Press, 1965.

Lusignan, Guy de. *French-speaking Africa since Independence.* New York: Praeger, 1961.

MacRae, Duncan. *Parliament, Parties, and Society in France, 1946–1958.* New York: St. Martin's Press, 1967.

Michaud, Charles. *The French Right and Nazi Germany, 1933–1939: A Study of Public Opinion.* 2d ed. New York: Octagon Books, 1964.

Mortimer, Edward. *France and the Africans, 1944–1960: A Political History.* London: Faber, 1969.

Novick, Peter. *The Resistance versus Vichy: The Purge of Collaborators in Liberated France.* London: Chatto & Windus, 1968.

Shirer, William. *The Collapse of the Third Republic: An Inquiry into the Fall of France in 1940.* New York: Simon & Schuster, 1969. (A magisterial study.)

Weber, Eugen. *Action Française: Royalism and Reaction in Twentieth-Century France.* Stanford: Stanford University Press, 1962.

Zeldin, Theo. *France, 1848–1945.* 4 vols. Oxford: Clarendon Press, 1973–77.

The Social Climate

Ardagh, John. *The New French Revolution: A Social and Economic Study of France, 1945–1967.* London: Secker & Warburg, 1968.

Beauvoir, Simone de. *The Second Sex.* Trans. H. M. Parshley. New York: Knopf, 1953.

Bosworth, William. *Catholicism and Crisis in Modern France: French Catholic Groups at the Threshold of the Fifth Republic.* Princeton: Princeton University Press, 1962. (Includes an excellent bibliography.)

Domenach, Jean Marie, and Robert de Montvalon. *The Catholic Avant-garde: French Catholicism since World War II.* New York: Holt, Rinehart & Winston, 1967.

Fraser, W. R. *Education and Society in Modern France.* London: Routledge & Kegan Paul, 1963. (A study of the thirties and the postwar period.)

———. *Reforms and Restraints in Modern French Education.* London: Routledge & Kegan Paul, 1967. (Covers the period since 1945.)

Glicksberg, Charles. *Literature and Society.* The Hague: Nijhoff, 1972.

Hamilton, Richard F. *Affluence and the French Worker in the Fourth Republic.* Princeton: Princeton University Press, 1967.

Hughes, H. S. *The Obstructed Path: French Social Thought in the Years of Desperation, 1930–1960.* New York: Harper & Row, 1968.

Marks, Elaine, and Esabelle de Courtivon, eds. *New French Feminisms: An Anthology.* Amherst: University of Massachusetts Press, 1980. (Includes a brief selected bibliography.)

Ouston, Philip. *France in the Twentieth Century.* London: Macmillan, 1972.

Pétrement, Simone. *Simone Weil: A Life.* Trans. Raymond Rosenthal. New York: Pantheon, 1976.

Talbot, J. E. *The Politics of Educational Reform in France, 1918–1940.* Princeton: Princeton University Press, 1969.

Thompson, Ian. *Modern France: A Social and Economic Geography.* London: Butterworth, 1970.

Wright, Gordon. *Rural Revolution in France: The Peasantry in the Twentieth Century.* Stanford: Stanford University Press, 1964.

Wylie, Lawrence. *Village in the Vaucluse: An Account of Life in a French Village.* Rev. ed. New York: Harper & Row.

Literary Life

Brenner, Jacques. *Tableau de la vie littéraire en France.* Paris: Juneau, 1982.

Brombert, Victor. *The Intellectual Hero, 1880–1955.* Philadelphia: Lippincott, 1961. Reissued 1964 by the University of Chicago Press.

Clapp, Jane. *International Dictionary of Literary Awards.* New York: Scarecrow Press, 1963.

O'Brien, Justin. *The French Literary Horizon*. New Brunswick: Rutgers University Press, 1967.

Intellectual Trends

Duplessis, Samuel. *The Compatibility of Science and Philosophy in France, 1840–1940*. Cape Town: Balkema, 1972.
Gilpin, Robert G. *France in the Age of the Scientific State*. Princeton: Princeton University Press, 1968.
Hirsch, Arthur. *The French New Left: An Intellectual History from Sartre to Gorz*. Boston: South End Press, 1981.
Stambolian, George, and Elaine Marks, eds. *Homosexualities and French Literature: Cultural Contexts/Critical Texts*. Ithaca: Cornell University Press, 1979.

Existentialism

Aron, Raymond. *History and the Dialectic of Violence: An Analysis of Sartre's "Critique de la raison dialectique."* Trans. Barry Cooper. Oxford: Blackwell, 1975.
Barnes, Hazel. *An Existential Ethics*. New York: Knopf, 1967.
Brée, Germaine. *Camus and Sartre: Crisis and Commitment*. New York: Delacorte Press, 1972.
Kaelin, Eugène F. *An Existentialist Aesthetic: The Theories of Sartre and Merleau-Ponty*. Madison: University of Wisconsin Press, 1962.
Kern, Edith. *Existential Thought and Fictional Technique: Kierkegaard, Sartre, Beckett*. New Haven: Yale University Press, 1970.
Poster, M. *Existential Marxism in Postwar France: From Sartre to Althusser*. Princeton: Princeton University Press, 1975.

Structuralism and Deconstruction

Culler, Jonathan. *Structuralist Poetics, Structuralism, Linguistics and the Study of Literature*. Ithaca: Cornell University Press, 1975. (Includes good bibliography.)
———. *The Pursuit of Signs: Semiotics, Literature, Deconstruction*. Ithaca: Cornell University Press, 1981.
Ehrmann, Jacques, and others. *Structuralism*. Garden City, N.Y.: Anchor Books, 1970.
Gardner, Howard. *The Quest for Mind: Piaget, Lévi-Strauss, and the Structuralist Movement*. New York: Knopf, 1973.
George, Richard T. de, and M. Fernando, eds. *The Structuralists from Marx to Lévi-Strauss*. Garden City, N.Y.: Anchor Books, 1972. (A survey and

anthology, introducing Marx, Freud, de Saussure, Tyniaov, Jakobson, Lévi-Strauss, Barthes, Althusser, Foucault, Lacan.)

Jameson, Fredric. *The Prison-House of Language: A Critical Account of Structuralism and Russian Formalism*. Princeton: Princeton University Press, 1972.

Macksey, Richard, and Eugenio Donato, eds. *The Language of Criticism and the Sciences of Man: The Structuralist Controversy*. Baltimore: Johns Hopkins University Press, 1970. (Includes contributions by Lacan, Barthes, Derrida, Goldmann, and others.)

Rossi, Ino, ed. *The Unconscious in Culture: The Structuralism of Cla:·de Lévi-Strauss in Perspective*. New York: Dutton, 1974.

Sturrock, John, ed. *Structuralism and Since: From Lévi-Strauss to Derrida*. Oxford University Press, 1979.

Influences from Abroad

Beach, Sylvia. *Shakespeare and Company*. New York: Harcourt, Brace, 1959. (Reminiscences of the famous bookseller.)

Falb, Lewis W. *American Drama in Paris, 1945–1970: A Study of Its Critical Reception*. Chapel Hill: University of North Carolina Press, 1973.

France and World Literature. Special issue of *Yale French Studies*, 1950, no. 6.

Smith, Thelma, and Ward Miner. *Transatlantic Migration: The Contemporary American Novel in France*. Durham: Duke University Press, 1955.

Francophone Literature

Garret, Naomi. *The Renaissance of Haitian Poetry*. Présence Africaine, 1963.

Jahn, Janheinz, and C. Dressler. *Bibliography of Creative African Writing*. Nendeln: Kraus-Thomas, 1971. (Black African writers, both French- and English-speaking.)

Literary Criticism

Doubrovsky, Serge. *The New Criticism in France*. Trans. Derek Coltman. Introduction by Edward Wasiolek. Chicago: University of Chicago Press, 1973.

Fowlie, Wallace. *The French Critic, 1894–1967*. Carbondale: Southern Illinois University Press, 1968.

Lawall, Sarah N. *Critics of Consciousness: The Existentialist Structures of Literature*. Cambridge: Harvard University Press, 1968. (Excellent study, covering Raymond, Poulet, Richard, Starobinski, Rousset, Blanchot.)

Simon, John K., ed. *Modern French Criticism: From Proust and Valéry to Structuralism.* Chicago: University of Chicago Press, 1972.

Wellek, René. *History of Modern Criticism.* Vol. 5, *The Twentieth Century.* New Haven: Yale University Press, 1965. (Magisterial work, covering European and American criticism.)

Music and Ballet

Davies, Laurence. *The Gallic Muse.* London: Dent, 1967. (Biographies and critical essays on six composers from Fauré to Poulenc.)

Grigoriew, S. *The Diaghilev Ballet, 1909–1929.* London: Constable, 1953.

Harding, James. *The Ox on the Roof: Scenes from Musical Life in Paris in the Twenties.* London: Macdonald, 1972.

Myers, Rollo. *Modern French Music: Its Evolution and Cultural Background from 1900 to the Present Day.* Oxford: Blackwell, 1971.

The Literary Space

Barnes, Hazel. *The Literature of Possibilities: A Study in Humanistic Existentialism.* Lincoln: University of Nebraska Press, 1959.

Bowie, Malcolm. *Henri Michaux: A Study of His Literary Works.* Oxford: Clarendon Press, 1973.

Denat, Francis. *Francis Ponge and the New Problem of the Epos.* Brisbane: University of Queensland, 1963.

Lemaître, Georges. *From Cubism to Surrealism in French Literature.* 2d ed. Cambridge: Harvard University Press, 1947.

Mehlman, Jeffrey. *A Structural Study of Autobiography: Proust, Leiris, Sartre, Lévi-Strauss.* Ithaca: Cornell University Press, 1974.

Tint, Herbert. *France since 1918.* London: Batsford, 1970.

Weightman, John G. *The Concept of the Avant-garde: Explorations in Modernism.* London: Alcove Press, 1973.

Poetry

Balakian, Anna. *Literary Origins of Surrealism: A New Mysticism in French Poetry.* New York: King's Crown Press, 1947.

Caws, Mary Ann. *The Poetry of Dada and Surrealism: Aragon, Breton, Tzara, Eluard, and Desnos.* Princeton: Princeton University Press, 1970.

Fiction

Bersani, Leo. *Balzac to Beckett: Center and Circumference in French Fiction.* New York: Oxford University Press, 1970.

Brée, Germaine, and Margaret Guiton. *An Age of Fiction: The French Novel from Gide to Camus.* New Brunswick: Rutgers University Press, 1957.

Heath, Stephen. *Le Nouveau Roman: A Study in the Practice of Writing.* Philadelphia: Temple University Press, 1972.

Matthews, John H. *Surrealism and the Novel.* Ann Arbor: University of Michigan Press, 1966.

Mercier, Vivian. *The New Novel from Queneau to Pinget.* New York: Farrar, Straus & Giroux, 1971.

Peyre, Henri. *The Contemporary French Novel.* New York: Oxford University Press, 1955.

Roudiez, Leon. *French Fiction Today: A New Direction.* New Brunswick: Rutgers University Press, 1972.

Sturrock, John. *The French New Novel.* New York: Oxford University Press, 1969. (Covers Simon, Butor, Robbe-Grillet.)

Theater

Fowlie, Wallace. *Dionysus in Paris: A Guide to Contemporary French Theater.* New York: Meridian, 1960. (From Giraudoux to Beckett.)

Grossvogel, David I. *The Self-conscious Stage in Modern French Drama.* New York: Columbia University Press, 1958. (From Jarry to Beckett.)

Guicharnaud, Jacques, and June Beckelman. *Modern French Theatre from Giraudoux to Genet.* Rev. ed. New Haven: Yale University Press, 1969.

Knowles, Dorothy. *French Drama of the Inter-war Years, 1918–39.* London: Harrap, 1967.

Lee, Vera G. *Quest for a Public French Popular Theater since 1945.* Cambridge: Schenkman, 1970.

Pronko, Leonard. *Avant-garde: The Experimental Theater in France.* Berkeley: University of California Press, 1962.

Literary Figures

Simone de Beauvoir

Cottrell, Robert D. *Simone de Beauvoir.* New York: Ungar, 1975.

Leighton, J. *Simone de Beauvoir on Women.* Rutherford: Farleigh Dickinson University Press, 1974.

Marks, Elaine. *Simone de Beauvoir: Encounter with Death.* New Brunswick: Rutgers University Press, 1972.

André Breton

Balakian, Anna Elizabeth. *André Breton: Magus of Surrealism.* New York: Oxford University Press, 1971.
Browder, Clifford. *André Breton: Arbiter of Surrealism.* Geneva: Droz, 1967.
Sheringham, Michael. *André Breton: A Bibliography.* London: Grant & Cutler, 1972.

Albert Camus

Braun, Lev. *Witness of Decline: Albert Camus—Moralist of the Absurd.* Rutherford: Farleigh Dickinson University Press, 1973.
Brée, Germaine. *Camus.* 4th ed. New Brunswick: Rutgers University Press, 1972.
Cruickshank, John. *Albert Camus and the Literature of Revolt.* London: Oxford University Press, 1959.
Freeman, Edward. *The Theatre of Albert Camus.* London: Methuen, 1971.
Lazere, Donald. *The Unique Creation of Albert Camus.* New Haven: Yale University Press, 1973.
Lotman, Herbert R. *Albert Camus: A Biography.* Garden City, N.Y.: Doubleday, 1979.
Parker, Emmett. *Albert Camus: The Artist in the Arena.* Madison: University of Wisconsin Press, 1965. (Study of Camus as a journalist.)
Roeming, Robert. *Camus: A Bibliography.* Madison: University of Wisconsin Press, 1968.
Thody, Philip. *Albert Camus: A Study of His Works.* London: Hamish Hamilton, 1957.

Louis-Ferdinand Céline

Gibault, François. *Céline.* Mercure de France, 1977.
Knapp, Bettina L. *Céline: Man of Hate.* University of Alabama Press, 1974.
McCarthy, Patrick. *Céline.* New York: Viking, 1976.
Ostrovsky, Erika. *Céline and His Vision.* New York: New York University Press, 1967.
Thiher, Allen. *Céline: The Novel as Delirium.* New Brunswick: Rutgers University Press, 1972.

Jean Cocteau

Brown, Frederick. *An Impersonation of Angels: A Biography of Jean Cocteau.* New York: Viking, 1968.

Oxenhandler, Neal. *Scandal and Parade: The Theater of Jean Cocteau.* New Brunswick, Rutgers University Press, 1957.
Steegmuller, Francis. *Cocteau: A Biography.* Boston: Little, Brown, 1970.

Marguerite Duras

Cismaru, Alfred. *Marguerite Duras.* New York: Twayne, 1971.

André Malraux

Blumenthal, Gerda. *André Malraux: The Conquest of Dread.* Baltimore: Johns Hopkins University Press, 1960.
Boak, Denis. *André Malraux.* Oxford: Clarendon Press, 1968. (Useful but sometimes hostile.)
Frohock, Wilbur M. *André Malraux and the Tragic Imagination.* Stanford: Stanford University Press, 1952.
Goldberger, Avriel. *Visions of a New Hero.* Lettres Modernes, 1965.
Hartman, Geoffrey H. *Malraux.* New York: Hillary House, 1960.
Kline, Thomas Jefferson. *André Malraux and the Metamorphosis of Death.* New York: Columbia University Press, 1973.
Madsen, Alex. *Malraux.* New York: Morrow, 1976.
Payne, Robert. *A Portrait of André Malraux.* Englewood Cliffs, N.J.: Prentice-Hall, 1970.
Richter, William. *The Rhetorical Hero: An Essay on the Aesthetics of André Malraux.* New York: Chilmark Press, 1964.
Savage, Catharine H. *Malraux, Sartre and Aragon as Political Novelists.* Gainesville: University of Florida Press, 1964.
Wilkinson, David. *Malraux: An Essay in Political Criticism.* Cambridge: Harvard University Press, 1967.

Jean-Paul Sartre

Barnes, Hazel E. *Sartre.* Philadelphia: Lippincott.
————. *Sartre and Flaubert.* Chicago: University of Chicago Press, 1981.
Bauer, George M. *Sartre and the Artist.* Chicago: University of Chicago Press, 1969.
Catalano, J. S. *A Commentary on Sartre's "Being and Nothingness."* New York: Harper & Row, 1974.
Caws, Peter. *Sartre.* London: Routledge & Kegan Paul, 1979.
Collins, Douglas. *Sartre as Biographer.* Cambridge: Harvard University Press, 1980.
Contat, Michel, and Michel Rybalka, eds. *The Writings of Jean-Paul Sartre.* Trans. Richard C. McCleary. Evanston: Northwestern University Press, 1974.

Fell, Joseph P., IV. *Emotion in the Thought of Sartre*. New York: Columbia University Press, 1965.

Greene, Marjorie. *Sartre*. New York: New Viewpoints, 1973. (Philosophical work; examines *Etre et le néant* and *Critique de la raison dialectique*.)

Jameson, Fredric. *Sartre: The Origins of Style*. New Haven: Yale University Press, 1961.

Kaelin, Eugene F. *An Existentialist Aesthetic*. Madison: University of Wisconsin Press, 1962.

Laing, R. D., and David Cooper. *Reason and Violence*. New York: Pantheon, 1971.

Lapointe, E., and C. Lapointe. *Jean-Paul Sartre and His Critics: An International Bibliography, 1938–1975*. Bowling Green State University, Ohio, 1975. (Indispensable; includes 5,148 titles.)

McCall, Dorothy. *The Theatre of Jean-Paul Sartre*. New York: Columbia University Press, 1969.

McMahon, Joseph. *Humans Being: The World of Jean-Paul Sartre*. Chicago: University of Chicago Press, 1971. (Includes useful bibliography.)

Manser, Anthony R. *Sartre: A Philosophic Study*. London: Athlone Press, 1966.

Ranwez, Alain D. *Jean-Paul Sartre's "Les Temps modernes": A Literary History, 1945–1952*. Troy, N.Y.: Whitston, 1981.

Thody, Philip. *Jean-Paul Sartre: A Literary and Political Study*. London: Hamish Hamilton, 1960.

Wilcocks, R. *Jean-Paul Sartre: A Bibliography of International Criticism*. University of Alberta Press, 1975.

Claude Simon

Loubère, J. A. E. *The Novels of Claude Simon*. Ithaca: Cornell University Press, 1975.

Index

References to the Dictionary of Authors are printed in boldface type.